**World Congress
on Land Policy,
1980**

Books from
The Lincoln Institute of Land Policy

The Lincoln Institute of Land Policy is a school that offers intensive courses of instruction in the field of land economics and property taxation. The Institute provides a stimulating learning environment for students, policy-makers, and administrators with challenging opportunities for research and publication. The goal of the Institute is to improve theory and practice in those fundamental areas of land policy that have significant impact on the lives and livelihood of all people.

Constitutions, Taxation, and Land Policy
  Michael M. Bernard

Constitutions, Taxation, and Land Policy—Volume II
  Michael M. Bernard

Federal Tax Aspects of Open-Space Preservation
  Kingsbury Browne

Taxation of Nonrenewable Resources
  Albert M. Church

Taxation of Mineral Resources
  Robert F. Conrad and R. Bryce Hool

World Congress on Land Policy, 1980
  Edited by Matthew Cullen and Sharon Woolery

Incentive Zoning
  Jerold S. Kayden

Building for Women
  Edited by Suzanne Keller

State Land-Use Planning and Regulation
  Thomas G. Pelham

Land-Office Business
  Gary Sands

The Art of Valuation
  Edited by Arlo Woolery

World Congress on Land Policy, 1980

Proceedings

Edited by
Matthew Cullen
Sharon Woolery
Lincoln Institute of Land Policy

LexingtonBooks
D.C. Heath and Company
Lexington, Massachusetts
Toronto

Library of Congress Cataloging in Publication Data

World Congress on Land Policy (1st: 1980: Harvard Law School)
Proceedings.

    1. Land tenure—Congresses. 2. Land reform—Congresses. 3. Land use—
Government policy—Congresses. 4. Land value taxation—Congresses.
I. Cullen, Matthew. II. Woolery, Sharon. III. Title.
HD1245.W67 1980   333.73   81-47762
ISBN 0-669-04836-4   AACR2

56,861

Contents

Contents

**Part I
First Session**

Introductory Remarks

Matthew Cullen, Arlo Woolery,
and *Nathaniel Lichfield*

Cullen: The background for this conference and the role of the two cosponsoring organizations, the International Centre for Land Policy studies and the Lincoln Institute of Land Policy, will be explained by the executive directors of those two organizations. I would like to examine now not the background but our intention, our expectations, and our hopes and aspirations for the outcome of this meeting.

It was our intention, in coming together, to examine not only the major issues in land policy around the world but to look at those successful and unsuccessful examples of tools and instruments that have been used to implement land policy so that we might learn from them. We know that many things are going on in other countries of which even the most expert of us are not aware, and we know that we can learn from these experiences. So we thought we would bring people here in a common sharing, and we anticipate that one of the outcomes will be the beginning of a network around the world of people with common interests who will have a continuing opportunity to exchange information, to exchange experience, to compare the situations in which successes and failures have resulted, and to attempt to understand the reasons and the social, cultural, and political conditions within which successes can occur.

Woolery: This meeting really began, as many other big projects do, with some notes written on the back of an envelope. At a meeting in Hamburg about two years ago, we were discussing the future of the International Centre for Land Policy Studies, and I suggested it was time we did something significant by bringing together the world's outstanding scholars in the field of land policy and include in that gathering the practitioners. Our goal was to bring together the people who are responsible for developing theory and those who are responsible for getting theory applied. And as a result, we are doing it.

The Lincoln Institute of Land Policy is a school. It is small but, I think, still significant. Its field of interest is land economics and the property tax. We are anxious to explore the relationship between tax policy and land policy. It is our feeling that how we tax our land resource determines in large measure how we use that land resource and also how we allocate the benefits of the use and ownership of that land resource. We like to bring together people and ideas with the hope of improving both, and we like to

3

get sound theory applied. There can be no good practice unless it is based upon good theory. So I would hope that we will develop a sound theoretical underpinning that will support sound practice as far as the relationship between people and land is concerned.

The thing that strikes me in land policy is the apparent division between social goals and economic goals. I have difficulty rationalizing this division between these two worthy goals. I would hope that as we proceed we will ask ourselves, "Is it possible to achieve social goals without economic sacrifice, and is it possible to achieve economic goals without social sacrifice?" Are we only looking at what we call a zero-sum game—that one person's losses become another person's benefits but the benefits never exceed the losses so you have a positive total? It seems to me that we should be trying to invent a new land policy game, one in which the gainers or the winners are going to be greater than the losers and that the losers have enough compensation so they are not going to be impeding the game out of frustration over what they have lost.

Also I think that we need to look at countries not only from our own individual viewpoints but with the idea of developing national land policy goals and national land policy programs that have global dimensions. I don't think any one country can afford to go its own way, oblivious of the needs of other countries as far as the benefits of use and ownership of our lands are concerned. It seems to me the global dimension on a national land policy will be the wave of the future. We should be thinking about land policy as a way in which we can feed, clothe, and shelter the people of the world in a manner better than we are doing today. So I hope as we go through this conference we will be asking ourselves what the strategies are and how we can implement these strategies, for better feeding, better clothing, and better housing our world's people.

We are inclined to be guided by past experience in most of our reactions to present problems. But if you look at where we are today, we are someplace we have never been before; and having never been here before, we don't have the experience to guide our future course. We may be in the position of having to invent experience, also. So I would hope that we could invent some land policy experiences that will result in the attainment of the larger goal of greater good for greater numbers.

We should also be asking ourselves, To what extent do the rights in landownership carry the obligations of responsible stewardship for that land because we are, indeed, temporary stewards of the land that we occupy. But how seldom do we really ask ourselves what the responsibilities are that attend the rights that we have in this land that we occupy? We exhibit a multifaceted degree of ambivalence when we do our thinking about land policy. In fact, if you analyze how we have organized our workshops, we are somewhat ambivalent and perhaps a bit confused in our thinking about land policy.

In workshop 1 we are talking about private-ownership mechanisms necessary for taxation and development. The banks find it difficult, if not impossible, to lend money if landownership is not well defined, if it is not defined well enough to allow the land to serve as collateral for loans. So in workshop 1, we have dedicated ourselves to exploring the private control of the land resource.

In workshop 2 we have moved to a polar position. We have moved away from the concepts that we have here in the United States and are considering in workshop 1, and are exploring public landownership in which the benefits of landownership are reserved for society as a whole. Government, here, is placed in a custodial position, which determines the uses of the land, and in addition controls and allocates the financial rewards arising from those particular uses.

Then in workshop 3 we attempt to bring these polar positions together; we are attempting to harmonize the public and the private interests in our land. We talk about bringing private and public ownership into middle ground, a partnership that may reflect stern realities. In countries largely with private landownership, we may have to move from that polar position toward a more-central, public partnership. And I think that in countries in which there is full public ownership or control of land, there is a trend toward the center. Very likely we will find ourselves people in motion, as far as policies are concerned, and we are going to be moving toward each other. So no matter which pole you occupy at the present time, I would hope by the end of this conference that you occupy a position somewhat closer to the pole of the person whose viewpoint you are not able to encompass this morning.

The fact that we need nine different workshops to explore what we see as the issues in the field of land policy should serve as a caution. And it should remind us that our Congress must end not with necessarily firm conclusions but rather with the resolve to make a start on solving the difficult problems that we identify and to take some steps toward better understanding our relationship to land, a puzzle that dates back to the dawn of humanity.

Lichfield: We have two purposes this week. One is to enjoy the Congress and the other is to begin to consider how we can shape the International Centre, which is now about six years old, toward the future.

I want to say something about the origins for those of you who are not familiar. Our involvement with the land goes back to the time when humanity started. As far as the International Centre is concerned, we were very late in arriving. The reasons for the lateness were the very reasons for the importance of the International Centre. Land is common the world around. The farmer of Tibet and the farmer of Saskatchewan can talk to each other, if they could understand each other's languages. When you come to land policy, which is simply the policies of governments and laws and constitutions relating to the utilization, the ownership, the possession, the disposition of land in a private and a public sense—private in the sense of land-ownership and possession, public in the sense of government influence, control, and interest in such land—the real problem has been that it is difficult for people to communicate across boundaries because different countries treat land—emotionally, religiously, constitutionally, legally—differently. This was why there are no journals in the literature of the world exchange on the land.

It was this simple idea that was born in the mind of the late Haim Darin-Drabkin, my friend and collaborator, when we were working together on our book: why don't we have an international exchange? And he found in me an enthusiastic collaborator. His death last November prevented him from being here and seeing the realization of his great idea. Therefore I would like to feel that I'm associating with myself the thoughts and the wishes and the intentions of Haim Darin-Drabkin as if he were here. He and I were invited to Vancouver Habitat as observers and experts on land, and that was our tremendous stimulus because we found, under the brilliant direction of Enrique Peñalosa, this great international move in human settlements and development. And we found, soon after we started thinking in 1975, that the governments of the world with the guidance of their international civil servants were really taking land seriously. We felt that we were right in wanting to think about international exchange as Vancouver Habitat talked about it and of international action they have seen. Arlo Woolery has said how the Lincoln Institute sees that. They have seen it: the utilization of land policy as instruments for the betterment and improvement of human settlements. That is the way I think that Haim Darin-Drabkin and I saw it. We've had a continuing stimulus in the Centre for Human Settlements in Vancouver with Peter Oberlander carrying on this work.

The International Centre has been a success in the sense that we had the right idea at the right time and I think the right motivations. We would have been far more successful, I think, if we'd had far more financial resources acting in endowments. Having launched ourselves, we now feel we need to move in a new dimension that needs resources and new membership. And this leads us to the questions for the future: Where are we going? How can we use the opportunities of this Congress to help us to get there?

Where are we going? How do we advance the international exchange that Arlo Woolery has rightfully said is the foundation of this Centre? How do we ensure that people around the world are in meaningful contact with each other on this very difficult, important, and pressing subject? Thinking about the Centre, we started out with certain aims. Are they the right aims?

We started out with certain activities, most of which we have begun to cover to a larger or smaller degree. Are they the right activities? What sort of priorities should we be thinking of? The third question is, How should we make sure that we are addressing the real, the critical, and the important problems relating to land and land policy around the world? How do we choose our strategy? How can we use the impetus of this Congress to launch us into this new future? We certainly do not wish to continue doing just what we were doing before; that would be fatal. We must find a new dimension.

What can the Centre do for those of you who wish to join us and work with us, and equally well, what can you do for the Centre? How can the Centre, with its wide-world linkage and network of knowledge and information, help particular countries to arouse the national interest in land policies that are so necessary in those countries?

Why should we organize? Is the present arrangement the right kind of organization for us to be pursuing, or should we change? Finally, and critically, how can we fund our activities? We have been working on a shoestring, a pitiful shoestring, and in that way there's no question about the measure of our success for the money we have had available. But we cannot continue working with people who simply put in time and enthusiasm and devotion. We need proper financing. We must think in terms of how we can earn income, attract financing, attract funding, attract contributions, attract research contracts by which we can begin to finance our work.

1 Opening Address: Land in Historical Perspective

Lewis Mumford

I begin with a commonplace item that my wife picked up from a Boston radio station a few weeks ago. She is good at picking up interesting and rewarding items when I don't happen to be around and then she is kind enough to share these items with me. This is a fairly accurate report, I think, of what the announcer, Robert J. Lurtsema, said. He was pleased to be able to say something positive at last after so many disastrous items that he has to report. This shows that he is an intelligent man because so many items that have been coming out in the news not merely for the last year but for the past thirty-five or forty years have been disastrous items. We smile when we read the newspaper, but it is a bitter smile indeed since we read again and again about signs of a breakdown of what we think is the most advanced civilization in the world. And those of you who come from the so-called Third World—and many of you have been educated in the European or the American world—you must beware of some of the learning you have acquired. Maybe the culture that you represent is that of an enormous population but with nothing like the physical standard of living of the upper 10 percent in our civilization wherever it is; perhaps you have more to offer the world than you realize. It must not lead you to say we learned this in Europe and we learned this in America—you must beware of that. That is my personal word to you. Well, the announcer had good news to report. In a survey conducted by qualified teams in California and the Midwest using five categories to determine results they had come up with from seventy-five different countries, the United States was first. But I must caution those of you who are Americans to think twice before you shout hurray. The researchers had chosen their categories very carefully and very scientifically, but they had found no way in which to judge spiritual values, and so they left these values out of their study. That is a very funny conclusion for a scientific statement: they left out half of the activities of the human race. That's all on the basis of the analysis and, as my wife remembered, the headings were economic, health and education, employment, feeling of attachment to and security with their nation, and a few others. But the remarkable thing is that in the feeling of attachment to and security with their nation, we must ask, What kind of objective thing is that? That is purely qualitative analysis of something that plays a part in every individual life. So in the very act of saying we cannot deal with subjective matters, a

9

purely subjective thing keeps entering into the program that was being carried out.

I can only point to the significance of the things that they left out. The greatest achievements of the human race are not in technology. Don't forget that technology begins in the animal world. A basic technology based on the mechanization of responses is the most primitive of all organic resources. In many of these responses, not even a brain is required. More than 60 million years ago, ants had the brain capacity needed to create a highly organized society in which everything worked promptly and well. Not only that, they could make paths, they could build fabrics, they had agriculture, they had servants—perhaps the aphids that created food for them—little plants were being nurtured for their benefit. It was an organized, technological, and automated society in every respect except that it was not a human society.

But the basic technology that underlies human society was in place more than 60 million years ago. We have somewhat improved upon it during the last three centuries, but the basic technology that works automatically without the brain was already in existence 60 million years ago. A human brain and a human mind cannot be separated, they are so closely bound together. When you say *brain* you must say *mind*, and when you say *mind* you must say *brain*. This is the most complex of all the artifacts. And it is not the result of the computer; it is not the result of all the great inventions of our time. It existed in the human organism and slowly developed. The marvel of life is that out of the primitive hominoids, the use of language, the ultimate achievement of people, developed. This took 1.5 million years at least and perhaps 2 million or 3 million years before people had a brain that made them capable of doing things in the world that no other creatures could do.

The technology was in the human body. It was a complete technology; it involved every part of the body. The least important part were tools. The best of our anthropologists and archeologists keep looking for bones, looking for evidence that people appeared before there were any visible bones or stones for us to inspect. But there is one early mark of man's emergence, and I am almost tempted to close on this because it is worth a great deal of silent thinking. What is the one characteristic, technologically, that distinguishes humans from all other creatures apart from language? What is the one great technological fact that has changed the whole face of the world for us and has changed our own life at every point? People are the only creatures that dare to play with fire, and in the caves of Peking we see the remains of the ashes of that fire and the beginning of the hearth and since we know the history of the hearth, we know that this is a female trait. We had a technology that was capable of using the female as effectively as it ever used the male as hunters. This is not the puzzle but rather the solution to many problems that we cannot solve otherwise. We have to deal with the fact that the brain is the most important thing that people possess. It is not just a physical brain or its physical size, but it is the fact that the brain and the mind have found a way of using every physical fact of the past, every aspect of human experience.

I came across this fundamental truth early in my career. While a young man, I wrote two articles, almost the very first articles that I ever wrote. One appeared in *Scientific Monthly*; it was called "The Marriage of Museums." On the basis of my experiences as a child wandering around the city with my grandfather, visiting the art museum and the Museum of Natural History, it occurred to me that there was a great deal of art in the Museum of Natural History and there was a great deal of technology and science in the art museum. These two things cannot be separated. They are fundamental parts of people represented finally and fixed slightly, but not forever, in the right and left lobes of the brain. The brain had sufficient time to develop so there was sufficient specialization, and yet that specialization is never absolute because a whole area of the brain can be destroyed and another area, another lobe, will take up some of the work—not quite as well as if it were all present, but nevertheless it is a marvelous example of technology that is capable of being renewed and replacing itself and continually enlarging the scope of our real world, but not the world as imagination.

After writing "The Marriage of Museums" in 1918, in 1922 I wrote another article, which I regard as equally decisive; it was called "The Collapse of Tomorrow." In 1922, young men were still very much aware of the great world war, that is, World War I. It was fought basically in Europe, but we still called it the Great World War, and in that article, I said the reason the young feel so disappointed and so cynical is that tomorrow has collapsed for them. They are not certain that there will be any tomorrow, and yet real life consists of a past that extends to the bounds of antiquity, far into the origins of humans and all other creatures. And always, the future is present. The future, though, is exactly what we see now. If we think three-dimensionally, we realize that past, present, and future are already existing and are already having an influence.

I tried to express this later in one of my bigger books by giving a biological and cultural interpretation of this. I divided human culture into four phases. First came the dominants—that which is visible in society, just as the machine is visible in society, and all the mechano-centric ideas and proposals—and then the recessives—those attributes that don't have the same strengths as the dominants but are still there and play a part. The conservative institutions of society are recessive. And then the most difficult to detect, to recognize in time, are the mutations. Mutations have already come into existence, but to be aware of them and to put one's fingers on them is a work of genius. We have had great geniuses, not necessarily scientists. One of the greatest historians is Jacob Burckhardt who saw the coming collapse of our civilization. Nobody wants to believe him, so he's never been regarded as a genius. Nobody wanted to pay any attention to Henry Adams when he predicted, in light of the way things were going, that our ordinary environment and life would disappear, and by 1918, he said, we would live in a world that is now unthinkable today. That was the year that the first intimation came that there were new factors in existence in science and the human mind that would greatly transform all the possibilities of life, not merely all technology, but systematic knowledge would have reached a point where it would transform the life that was immediately in prospect. Henry Adams was laughed at by the great historians, but he had an intuition that even his contemporaries in science refused to recognize as a possibility that the seemingly stable scientific world of the nineteenth century would disappear, and that quite another world, much more unstable, would come into existence, greatly moved by fantasies that are outside of the realm of science.

The fourth category consists of the survivors. These original artifacts and discoveries are the most durable things that we have, more durable than any building. Buildings can be destroyed, and whole civilizations can be wiped out. We are living in a civilization that lives under that threat and wants to call it progress. This is the threat of extermination, one of the realities of our life.

I would like to open up a subject that is very easy to ignore. That is, by taking the immediately visible institutions and practices and inventions as if they were perfect, as if they weren't more fragile than some of the artifacts of the early Stone Age, and the faith that life will go on anyway, is an item that no one will discuss. The last scientific congress I attended, I had the duty of giving the final report, and I had to point out that although there had been a lot of very interesting discussion, nobody had dealt with the very real threat that impends. Nobody had even considered as a hypothesis the fact that we may all be wiped out by accident, not even by an intention. And this could be done by the misreading of a computer or a failure in the apparatus itself, which could send the visible world of the United States and Europe on its way to total destruction. People don't like to discuss these unpleasant facts. But what's the point of pretending to be scientific, of looking objective realities squarely in the face, if you say that objective realities are really subjective? We must learn that nothing is unthinkable, and for a good reason. In the midst of the marvelous achievements of the human brain, with its endless command of important values, projects, and inventions, we also are the victims of an irrationality that counterbalances that. That irrationality is written into the very structure of civilization. From the time that we have any visible records, we are conscious of the fact that war, slavery, and extermination were patterns that developed, for no rational reason. Even the great conquerors, such as Alexander the Great, when he had conquered the city, what did he do? He wiped it out and built another city on the same site. That is not the work of a rational mind; that was the work of somebody who wanted to say in one word that his power was more important than anything else. Nature had another answer to that; Alexander the Great died at a very early age through drunkenness and dissipation, which illustrates the fact that he was not a perfect organism and was not able to recognize the dangers inherent in his course of conduct and to correct his mistakes.

Perhaps we should leave things here. You have many more very important things to discuss. Don't think for a moment that I despise dealing with the recognizable facts of our culture of today. I respect the work that you are doing, but only if you remember things that you have left out or if you will take account of those things which have been omitted. You cannot wipe out the subjective life without wiping out man's highest achievements—his higher culture, the operations of the brain. What do we really know about the universe? We only know as much as the human mind has revealed to us. Wipe out the human mind, and we have not even the power to conjecture about whether other planets have similar or better cultures than ours because there would be nobody here to record them. Our errors in that sense will be self-canceling. If we wipe everything out, there will be nobody to record the fact that we did make a slight mistake.

2

Current Land Policy Issues in a Changing World

Enrique Peñalosa

Land is an important issue anywhere in the world and at any time in history, but it acquires an even keener relevance in today's developing world context. At this very moment, the way humanity has organized itself on earth is undergoing one of the most profound transformations in history. The population on earth, which throughout history had been overwhelmingly rural, will be by a large majority urban by the year 2000.

The beginning of the process of urbanization can be traced to the origins of capitalism and the rise of the Italian city-states. Since about 1950, the process has been gaining momentum and has reached unprecedented magnitudes. By the year 2010 it will reach its peak, and by the year 2080 it will be essentially completed.

At the end of the nineteenth century, out of a world population of 1,650 million, only 250 million was urban. By 1960, the urban population passed the 1,000 million mark, out of a total population of 3,000 million. By the year 2000, out of 7,000 million humans on earth, 4,000 million will live in cities. In the next twenty years, the cities of the world will have to accommodate an increase of nearly 2,000 million inhabitants. Over the next fifty years, we are going to build two and one half times the equivalent of all cities today in existence.

At a planetary scale the ciphers are impressive. Yet as one focuses the problem closer to home, to the developing countries and to Latin America particularly in my case, the challenge takes on large proportions. The surge of urban migration and extremely high birthrates prevailing in today's developing world have historical parallels in today's developed countries. They are qualitative parallels because the scale of today's phenomenon is manyfold larger than it was for the industrializing countries of the eighteenth and nineteenth centuries.

In 1950, the Latin American population was 165 million, of whom 68 million lived in cities. By the year 2000 the population of Latin America will have increased to 620 million, 470 million of whom will be urban dwellers. That represents an increase of 700 percent for the urban population in fifty years. During the next twenty years, the Latin American cities will have to englobe adjacent lands totaling more than 10,000 square kilometers (assuming an average density of 15,000 inhabitants per square

15

kilometer, which is higher than the density found today in most Latin American cities). During the next twenty to thirty years, most of Latin America's large cities will double and on occasion treble their populations. People pass; cities remain. We are now creating the framework in which many generations' lives are going to take place, to bloom creatively or to wilt, stultified by an environment out of tune with the nature of human needs.

It is now that we are deciding, by decision or omission, whether we will have chaotic squatter settlements where it will be impossible to provide adequate services for hundreds of years to come because of the original layout of the construction. It is now that we must implement the measures and regulations that will allow the millions who will come to our cities to house themselves adequately. It is now that the physical distribution of industrial, agricultural, recreational, and residential areas is to be fixed, for every day that passes without such physical planning is a day too late to do it. It is now that decisions to distribute a country's population over the national territory must be expressed in concrete policy actions. It is now that transportation, educational, health, and recreational facilities must be planned in harmony, integrated with all other aspects of the human settlements.

Each time that we consider a factor that we must control in order to improve the quality of the human settlements, we come to an unescapable fact. When we talk about human settlements, the solution to every issue is dependent, totally or partially, upon the land question. We must orientate cities' growth; we must meet the housing, transportation, recreational, and other needs of the society. Yet how can we talk of solving societal needs if the very base on which any societal solution is to be founded is managed with interests that are contradictory in practically every respect with those of society as a whole?

In the period between 1840 and 1870, land prices in the expanding London suburbs increased between ten and twenty times. In Japan's twenty post-World War II years, land prices increased 4,000 percent within the Tokaido conurbation. In the 1950s and 1960s, the rates of land-price increases in Paris and Madrid often surpassed 25 percent yearly. The real prices of land in Bogotá have been increasing by more than 30 percent yearly in the last few years despite a relative abundance of outlying areas that could be urbanized.

The benefits of the capitalist market are dubious when it deals with a resource whose supply cannot be augmented, as is the case with urban lands. On the other hand, the obstacles that the private ownership of land poses to the rational and human development of a human settlement are immense. The patterns of growth of too many cities have been and are being dictated not by rationally planned considerations but simply by speculation. To solve the housing problem, particularly that of the poor who have migrated to the city, becomes an impossible task for the government of a poor country when the land prices are constantly rising. As a result chaotic squatter settlements arise that lack all services, recreational areas, and other amenities. But when such settlements have become a fact, even the best government intentions and funds can do little to turn them into adequate living environments. In Bogotá, 140 hectares are taken up every year by illegal home building. In 1979, nearly 30 percent of Bogotá's population lived in such illegal neighborhoods.

Land held by speculators may remain unused for many years, even after it has been covered by all city services. Once land is trapped in the net of private land speculation, society has little hope of providing itself with an adequate amount of recreational land.

The private ownership of urban land causes these and other problems. Sometimes the society has the tools to overcome the impediments represented by private land ownership. Where private land is in the way of infrastructure projects such as roads, governments usually have relatively adequate mechanisms to appropriate the land. However, when the societal need is less materially or economically measurable in terms of cost-benefit analysis, governments are impotent. This is the case for housing and recreational lands. Therefore governments must develop the institutional means to dispose of all urban and suburban lands as they see fit. Just as mechanisms exist for acquiring the land necessary for infrastructure building, the means to appropriate land for other societal needs, such as housing, must be available to government.

To say this in a land experts' conference is to repeat a truism. It is now accepted on a theoretical level that society, through its government, must rationally control its cities' growth; use all natural resources such as land, water, and air for the benefit of the society as a whole; and receive all increases in land value due to zoning changes or, more generally, to the normal growth of the city. But these conclusions do not go very far in the real world if the technical and political means necessary to act upon them do not exist. First, we have to face the fact that unless social revolutions of the most drastic sort take place, urban land will not come under direct government control in the near future. Alternatively, there is a plethora of recommendations for governments to effect an indirect control over the use of land by such means as taxing all of the profits derived from land speculation. Unfortunately all of the idealistic recommendations and schemes suggested at urban-planning or land-policy congresses and seminars are rarely implemented, and when they are, they function much more poorly than expected.

What is the explanation for such a failure? In my opinion, and this is so for a great majority of the developing countries, the paramount obstacle to a rationalization of the use of land is that no effective mechanisms for monitoring land prices have been devised. In the absence of reliable and constantly updated land prices, the fiscal and other tools that market economies use for their planning are nullified.

I am not a land expert, but throughout my life, different circumstances have linked me very directly to the issue of land. More than twenty years ago, I was elected twice to the Bogotá City Council, which I even headed for a period. At that time Bogotá was a city with barely 1.5 million inhabitants. We, the members of the council at the time, never imagined that only twenty years later Bogotá would have more than 5 million inhabitants. Yet at that time we were already facing the challenges represented by the planning of the city—that of taxing property, for example. At that time I espoused and defended before Congress the institution of a presumptive income tax based on patrimony and the setting up of an automatic valuation system for land and real estate.

After the city council, I headed a newly established regional development authority for the surrounding region of Bogotá. At that time I became conscious of the intense interdependence between the city and the surrounding countryside. The city depends on the area around it for land to expand, for recreational purposes, and for food products, among others. Protection of the landscape from desecration by billboards, quarrys, etc.; protection of streams and rivers; safeguarding of the best agricultural lands, directing the cities growth: in all these instances, it is the city that menaces, ironically, its own welfare. In the case of Bogotá, too much of what should have been avoided has not been.

Upon leaving the regional development authority I became the first director of the Colombian Land Reform Institute, which focused until recently on rural land reform. Because large parcels of rural land were not being used, they were an obstacle to economic development and the main source of social inequality and exploitation. Latifundia had regional labor monopsonies, which they abused; they charged very high rent for land use; and they blocked land sales to potential buyers of small parcels.

The shift of populations from rural to urban areas has redirected our attention to the latter. Urban land reform should become a fundamental issue for developing countries in the years to come. Urban land reform is justified economically by problems such as that of fully serviced lots that are left idle. Socially, the justification lies in the need for governments to control fully the development of the city, ensuring the provision of necessary services, such as housing, recreational areas, and transportation.

The newly urban populations need land for their housing, recreational, and other needs. In fact the housing problem is the land problem, especially in the developing countries, where the large majority of housing is self-built.

In the mid-1970s I became the director of Habitat. There I advocated the inclusion of the most revolutionary clauses on the issue of land ever to be promoted by the United Nations. Such clauses, part of the resultant Vancouver Declaration, were finally voted for by more than a hundred countries' representatives. They include the following:

> Land is one of the fundamental elements in human settlements. Every state has the right to take the necessary steps to maintain under public control the use, possession, disposal and reservation of land.[1]

> Human settlement policies can be powerful tools for the more equitable distribution of income and opportunities.[2]

> Land, because of its unique nature and the crucial role it plays in human settlements, cannot be treated as an ordinary asset, controlled by individuals and subject to the pressures and inefficiencies of the market. Private land ownership is also a principal instrument of accumulation and concentration of wealth and therefore contributes to social injustice; if unchecked, it may become a major obstacle in the planning and implementation of development schemes. Social justice, urban renewal and development, the provision of decent dwellings and healthy conditions for the people can only be achieved if land is used in the interests of society as a whole.

> Instead, the pattern of land use should be determined by the long-term interests of the community, especially since decisions on location of activities and therefore of specific land uses have a long-lasting effect on the pattern and structure of human settlements. Land is also a primary element of the natural and man-made environment and a crucial link in an often delicate balance. *Public control of land use is therefore indispensable* to its protection as an asset and the achievement of the long-term objectives of human settlement policies and strategies.[3]

> Land is a scarce resource whose management should be subject to public surveillance or control in the interest of the nation.[4]

> Taxation should not be seen only as a source of revenue for the community but also as a powerful tool to encourage development of desirable locations, to exercise a controlling effect on the land market and to redistribute to the public at large the benefits of the unearned increase in land values.[5]

> The unearned increment resulting from the rise in land values resulting from change in the use of land, from public investment or decision or due to the general growth of the community must be subject to appropriate recapture by public bodies [the community], unless the situation calls for other additional measures such as new patterns of ownership, the general acquisition of land by public bodies.[6]

> Public ownership, transitional or permanent, should be used, whenever appropriate, to secure and control areas of urban expansion and protection; and to implement urban and rural land reform processes, and supply serviced land at price levels which can secure socially acceptable patterns of development.[7]

One hundred twenty ministers from all over the world attended Habitat. Joining them were 12,000 more people, many of them high government officials or leaders in the academic or other fields. And yet few countries today evince even a minimum degree of consciousness about the topic the Habitat recommendations dealt with.

My frustration is great. After twenty-five years of interest in land problems, of working toward possible solutions, toward the enactment of legislation at the municipal, national, and even international levels, I have seen little actually happen. Even when legislation is enacted, its rulings often are circumvented because we lack the most fundamental ingredient for real land control: an efficient cadastral system. Colombia now has a municipal tax amounting to 1 percent of the land's value; a national tax amounting to 2 percent of the land's value; an established presumption that land must yield at least 8 percent of its value, and that 8 percent can be taxed up to 50 percent; and a capital gains tax of up to 50 percent on land sales. This is one of the stiffest tax systems in the world theoretically, but it does not work because there are no reliable land-price estimates. Land is registered at 20 percent or so of its real value.

To a large degree, the welfare of the earth's inhabitants is dependent upon the good use of land. It is difficult for me to accept the fact that modern technology is incapable of solving the cadastral problem. Of course, the problem is largely political, but the experts have a share of responsibility too. The experts have not been able to offer an efficient, workable solution. Either they seem not to make use of all the technical resources available to them, or else they devise schemes that are inapplicable on a large scale. The politicians, responding no doubt to certain interests, argue that nothing can be done until more-technical methods of keeping the cadastral control are devised. Ironically the politicians call for more technical means but reject some imperfect but practical formulas that are proposed.

One of those imperfect formulas is that of automatic valuations, or self-valuations. Under this system, each property owner periodically reports what he or she estimates is the value of his or her land or real estate. This he or she does under the caution that the government can buy the property at any time for a price 20 percent above that last quoted.

There are many formulas, and despite their defects, we must advocate their application until we develop better ones. The great message emanating from this forum should be that it is feasible to put into effect very important land policies if the political decisions to do it are taken.

A great question, still unanswered, is whether market economies will be able to control and orientate the use of land in such a way that it will benefit society as a whole and not simply the privileged few. I believe this is possible, and I hope it is so because drastic social revolutions permitting the socialization of land are relatively unlikely. To insist absolutely upon government ownership of land is to take the easy way out.

Our efforts should be directed to practicalities. This conference cannot end with simply another set of philosophical recommendations. It is imperative that we find solutions quickly. Every day that passes without operative means of community land control produces costs that will be endured by many generations to come. It is now that cities are being built—faster and on a scale that dwarfs all earlier urbanization processes. Fifty years from now the urbanization process will be essentially finished. It is not easy to change the structure of a city once it has been built. Whatever cities there will be fifty years from now will fundamentally determine the evolution of those cities for hundreds of years to come.

Today's land policies largely determine whether two hundred and more years from now there will be humanely designed urban communities, an adequate supply of recreational lands, a harmonious equilibrium between the city and its surrounding agricultural lands, appropriate transportation systems, and correctly safeguarded historical and environmental patrimonies.

We cannot shy away from the enormous responsibility we have today, arguing cynically about our historical irrelevance. I hope that you will take up the challenge that our historical moment offers. It implies a heavy responsibility but also a marvelous opportunity to participate, to create, to realize our human potential to the fullest.

Notes

1. *Report of Habitat: United Nations Conference on Human Settlements,* Vancouver, Canada, May 31–June 11, 1976; Declaration of Principles, sect. II, item 10.

2. Ibid., recommendation A.4.

3. Ibid., preamble to section D.

4. Ibid., recommendation D.1(b).

5. Ibid., recommendation D.3(a).

6. Ibid., recommendation D.3(b).

7. Ibid., recommendation D.4(b).

3

Comments on Peñalosa's Paper

Isaac Ofori,
William S.W. Lim,
Pierre Laconte,
Guillermo Geisse,
Mona Serageldin, and
Charles Haar

Africa

Isaac Ofori: Dr. Peñalosa has drawn our attention to the tasks ahead and has listed about five of them: prevention of squatter settlements; supply of housing for our ever-burgeoning populations; sensible physical planning to accommodate the many uses for our nation's land resources, including agricultural, industrial, recreational, and residential; a rational distribution and redistribution of the nation's population over the national territory; and sensible planning of our urban settlements to accommodate transportation, educational, health, and recreational facilities without which urban life becomes a dreadful misery rather than a joy.

Dr. Peñalosa rightly focused attention on the factor that is the primary disposing factor in all our planning: land. This factor enters into every capital structure and combination of capital for urbanization. He then invited us to find solutions to the problems of land use, landownership, and land speculation. He was correct in asking how we can talk about solving societal needs if the very base on which any societal solution is to be founded is managed with interests that are contrary in practically every respect to those of society as a whole.

I would like to add a dimension of my own to all that he has told us, a dimension that is often overlooked or disregarded by land experts and other land policy makers, especially those from the developed countries, but which is of particular significance to the land planners and land policy makers from the Third World countries. This is the factor of costs of urbanization. It is perhaps this dimension of urbanization and the human settlement equation that must worry most acutely the Third World countries, especially those of Africa, in which discussions of human settlements are raised in forums such as this. The Third World countries of sub-Sahara Africa are justifiably worried: they are poor countries. As one authority has stated, in developing countries, which must amass capital for industrial breakthroughs, planners are faced with competing claims on scarce resources for industrial development on the one hand and social overhead costs on the other hand. In examining the land factor and the land market, we are irresistibly drawn to the conclusion that the benefits of the capitalist market are dubious. When that market deals with a resource, the supply of which cannot be augmented, as is the case with urban land, what shall we do? In thinking about policies for the 1980s, Dr. Peñalosa has given us one of the theoretical prescriptions when he said that society, through its government, must rationally control its cities' growth; use all the natural resources such as the land, the water, and the air for the benefit of society as a whole; and receive all increases in land values due to zoning changes or, more generally, to the normal growth of the city. He forcefully reminds us of the many powerful resolutions that more than a hundred countries' representatives finally voted for at Habitat '76 in Vancouver, Canada. All of the resolutions touch on landownership, land use, land taxation, land management, and the legislative and social powers that the governments of the world must exercise over the one essential commodity in planning the human settlement: the commodity land.

How does all of this apply to sub-Sahara Africa? In relation to the Peñalosa paper, and indeed to the recommendations of Habitat '76, in analyzing the situation in sub-Sahara Africa, I would suggest that we do as Alice in Wonderland in Lewis Carroll's amusing and interesting book. In that little book, Alice asks, "Where shall I begin, Your Majesty?" And the king replies, "Begin at the beginning, and go on until you come to the end, and stop." We may not have time at this conference to reach the end, but I believe we must sharpen our understanding of the problem within the African context and begin by looking at the problems of landownership and land tenure in that region south of the Sahara, excluding South Africa.

The fundamental principle upon which ownership of land in many of the countries of the African region is based is that land is owned by the community or a group. The community or the group is represented by either a *stool* or a symbol, as the acknowledged identity of the group. When no symbol or identity is so acknowledged, the ownership is vested in the family or the tribe, but still as an entity. Therefore title to land in the African context is always traced to a particular group. Hence there is a cardinal axiom of land in these African states, which is very often forgotten. Although there may be much unused and vacant land, there is no land in the African context without an owner. The fundamental title in land in such societies is the absolute, or paramount, title. There are families who are subjects of a *stool* or members of a fundamental group, and these families have an inherent right to occupancy of portions of the land. What families own together is coextensive over the lands owned by the *stool* or the authority. The acquisition of paramount titles in land was acquired in ancient times, either by conquest or original occupancy or discovery, or purchase, or gift.

It is necessary to remember that an individual acquires land in the African context by purchase, gift, or inheritance. Under traditional practices or usage, the individual has the inherent right to occupy any portion of the land not already in the occupation of some other person. He cannot be deprived of it without his consent, not even by the owner of the paramount title. A stranger, on the other hand, can acquire land only by some form of grant, be it a license or a contract, and this is irrespective of the use that is involved. A subject of a family or a *stool* has to obtain a formal grant only when development of a permanent nature is concerned, such as the building of housing. The only exception is the compulsory acquisition of land by governments in the interest of, or for, the public purpose. The title that governments acquire using either the compulsory acquisition or the principle of eminent domain is the absolute, or paramount, title.

Sub-Sahara Africa is also experiencing the trauma of urbanization and human settlements. We have slums. We have insufficient and unplanned housing. We have environmental pollution. We have land speculation, insufficient infrastructure, and all the rest. Yet there is very little evidence that the recommendations of the Habitat '76 have ever been followed or even examined in detail in the countries of Africa, with the exception of Nigeria, where a land-use decree was passed by the military two or three years ago. And with the further exception of Tanzania and its peculiar brand of socialism called *ujama*, African countries have largely ignored the recommendations of Habitat '76.

It is my belief that if the policy recommendations of this Congress and any future ones are not to be ignored by sub-Saharan African countries, then it is necessary to look at the land policy problems of these African countries somewhat differently from the context of your own expertise, political development, economic development, and goals. If we are to reach the Third World developing countries of sub-Sahara Africa in conferences like this, perhaps our advice to them on the necessity of land-use planning and their national policies for economic development for the remainder of this century should contain a few of the following. First, they should identify those parts of their territory that are best suited for a particular use—be that use agricultural, mineral, forestry, industry, defense, recreation, tourism, or human settlement. Second, let us suggest to them an examination of the extent to which their present land-use patterns reflect the potentialities of the given areas. Third, we should try to convince them to adopt measures that will ensure that each piece of land is put to the best use. Fourth, where multiple uses are possible, they should try to adopt measures designed to prevent the present misuse of land and the better use of land by future generations. Finally, given the rapid growth of population that is occurring in Africa and the pattern of economic development in those countries, perhaps it would be in their interests and in the interest of those governments to devise steps that will ensure that the requirements of the major land users will be met by the end of this century within the context of a national land-use plan.

Asia

William Lim: As I see it, the first issue that Dr. Peñalosa identified is the magnitude of the urban land problem. It is very important for us to focus on urban land now; the rural land issue has already been the center of attention in many countries. Now urban land must occupy the attention of both government and the academic sector. The second issue is the urgency for action. It is not enough to acknowledge the magnitude of the problem; we must take effective action immediately. There is no time to be wasted because the problem gets bigger every day. The third issue is to understand that rapid land-price increase has become a major obstacle to any effective and rational development in urban centers. Though this may be an obvious problem to many, it has seldom been put across so forcefully.

Dr. Peñalosa has identified the cause of land-price escalation: the imperfection of the free-market system in allocating land resources. Under this system, the benefit of landownership has been reserved mainly for the urban elite and not for society as a whole. More often than not, the benefit is at the expense of the urban poor. Dr. Peñalosa also identified the close relationship of politicians, urban elite, and experts. At times, their close collaboration resembles a conspiracy. The experts have provided the necessary tools to support the urban elite, often at the expense of the urban poor. Thus, we are often faced with situations where the proposed legislation is very complicated and too difficult to implement. This must create obvious loopholes, and the legislation becomes ineffective.

Several points that Dr. Peñalosa raised are relevant to the part of the world I come from, which includes the developing countries in East and Southeast Asia. One of the interesting characteristics of this region is the high population density coupled with high economic growth rates. The development strategy is nearly always urban oriented. This has often accentuated problems relating to rapid urban growth and disparities of income between urban and rural areas. Very often, we call in experts. In many instances, the results have not been successful. The question we have to ask is why. To a certain extent the answer has been provided by Dr. Peñalosa. He has indicated that the lack of meaningful urban land reform is not necessarily a technical problem brought about by lack of expertise. The main stumbling block is the lack of political will. It is very difficult to bring about effective changes to correct the income imbalances. I submit that urban land reform cannot be looked at in isolation from other equally important issues, such as a more-equitable income distribution, social justice, and job opportunities.

We do not know the extent of restructuring priority necessary in order to bring about new policy directions. In many countries, the alignment of decision makers and the urban elite is strong. Grass-roots pressure with direct participation by the people is necessary to bring about some kind of balance in the power structure. Experts should change their approach and be prepared to adopt alternative urban strategies. They should look at energy conservation seriously and its relationship to the development of land resources in the Third World urban centers. A low-resource input does not necessarily mean lower quality. We should be realistic in assessing the human, financial, and technical resources available. Policies must be implemented within the resource constraints imposed. This often leads to important and extensive changes in the present patterns of development.

In conclusion, I would like to refer to Lewis Mumford's message that when we examine problems, we must examine them from the humanistic point of view. We should not focus only on the technical aspects of problems and overlook the human elements. When we take an action, we should test the action against the yardstick of who is going the pay the price and who is going to benefit from the action. We should always ask whether the action we are taking serves to decrease inequities, to increase social justice, and to improve the quality of human life for the majority of the people, and in particular the urban poor. Without these important considerations, many of the proposals for action flowing from congresses such as this become purely academic exercises with no long-term consequences.

Western Europe

Pierre Laconte: If we echo the remarks by Enrique Peñalosa—that in the next twenty years cities will double or triple in dimension and in population—we must say that the answers for Europe are very different. The urban trends in Europe have recently been analyzed by two different groups of scholars. One group was headed by Roy Drewett from the London School of Economics, and the other one was headed by Peter Hall of the University of Reading. These two scholars indicate that from one country to another, the urban trends are almost totally different. If one could state their findings in a simplified way, one could say that the deconcentration has been most extreme in the United Kingdom, while in France the concentration has kept its pace. Lying between these two extremes are a large number of other countries with specific patterns of urban growth, particularly in central Europe. Everywhere in Europe we are observing an intense migration between or among districts within metropolitan areas.

The affluence of the 1960s has encouraged a preference for space and a desire for mobility, which has been encouraged by large highway investments. People have become used to spending different portions of their daily time in places relatively far apart from each other. One could call it a dislocation of time.

But now we are in a period of change in this respect. The context of the 1980s for urbanization and for land policy will be very different from the context of the 1960s and the early 1970s. The recession will probably bring, in Europe as well as on other continents, deep readjustments of the role of national governments in financing local-level activities, including land policies. Probably the burden of expenses related to urbanization will be shifted increasingly to the local level. This phenomenon is already quite evident in some countries in Europe. Also, some of the effects of inflation will be felt at the level of urbanization and land policies. Inflation is something that Europeans have learned to live with for many years. America is discovering the problems raised by inflation combined with high rates of interest for the housing market. Also, the energy issue will have a deep effect upon urbanization and migration. Because it affects the cost of transportation and therefore the transportation system itself, it will probably reduce mobility in some way and give an advantage to existing clusters. As for the role of communication forms other than transportation and the substitution of telecommunication for actual physical transportation, its future is difficult to predict, but it is bound to have an effect on the movement of people and their location decisions within the national and regional context.

The European experience has generated land policy tools that are not well known around the world. Therefore, we should intensify exchanges of ideas and experiences. The most extreme European land policy is found in Sweden where the acquisition of land by government has become so easy in legal and economic terms that land banking makes almost no sense anymore. It is much easier for the government to let private individuals and corporations keep the land until it needs it and at that point acquire it at a cost that is often lower than the market cost. Land policies in other countries, particularly in the southern part of Europe, are closer to the U.S. experience.

A new legal development that emerged in France in the 1970s is the Galley Law of 1975, by which all new construction built at a density above a floor-area ratio of 1.5 in Paris and 1 in other cities is subject to a heavy tax. The consequences of that law are far-reaching, but they have not been analyzed in depth or from a comparative perspective. It might be interesting to compare the effects of taxation on built densities in Paris, London, and New York City to see the evaluation of these densities according to their institutional context.

One of the emerging issues of the 1980s is whether we will be able to provide a large portion of our population access to individual ownership of their homes and apartments. What kind of imaginative formulas can we develop to encourage such individual ownership?

As to the balance between public and private influences in shaping the urban land use of the future, one should not forget the role of organized or unorganized movements of citizens at the neighborhoods level or at the level of larger areas. Citizen groups tend to exert pressure on governments in order to achieve certain urban-policy goals. These movements have a tremendous influence on land values and the actual extent of the traditional rights of landownership.

Finally, one may ask, what will be the relationship between land planning and land policies in the 1980s? I believe that in the quest for livable cities and livable settlements, the experience of 3,000 years of urbanization centered around the Mediterranean region tells us many things about what we can do in the future. The top of the pyramid in the urban system of Europe has shifted from the south to the north. At one time it was in Venice and Genoa, the cities that were the springboard for the discovery of America. Later it went to Bruges and Antwerp, and from there to Amsterdam, and finally to London, but always there has been a very closely knit system of cities. I believe the study of this urban system can help us understand the problems of our urban world and solve some of them. The feeling of security, the feeling of attachment of people to their city possibly has much more to teach us than a few decades of functional or monofunctional zoning that did so much to affect urban land use. I believe we should continue to divide urban land into small plots in which individuals have the right to the security of ownership. The policies to divide land are as important as the policies to acquire and divest oneself of land. In this respect, Italian cities today are showing a number of interesting and imaginative solutions to our problems. These cities might provide a rich field for comparative studies.

More generally, a better understanding of the urban and rural problems of each of the fifty-one countries represented at this Congress has much to teach to the others. We in Europe have much to gain from the knowledge of those who come from other parts of the world. This exchange of information will be essential to the finding of the solutions needed during the difficult decades ahead.

Moderator

Arlo Woolery: I think that Pierre opened another land policy door and that is the creation of a new set of property rights that lie outside the traditional ownership sector. In many of our communities where we have government interventions such as rent control, we have created a new property right for the occupant of the property that lies entirely outside of the traditional sphere of legal ownership or fee title. And we have many neighborhood groups or associations whose actions abridge the traditional ownership rights to the extent that these associations have created for themselves a new property right without the traditional legal trappings of co-ownership.

Latin America

Guillermo Geisse: Dr. Peñalosa has made a claim for the democratization of land in developing countries, a claim that I fully endorse in the general form that he presented. He mentioned that the access to land now for all the population implies social and political transformations that are beyond the scope of land itself. He envisions the urbanization process in Latin America as one of a kind and pace that will seriously restrict the options that will be open in the future for more-efficient and equitable uses of space. Undoubtedly cities will continue to grow and proliferate, as Dr. Peñalosa anticipates. However, when anticipating the consequences of these processes there is a difference between the concepts of spatial and physical structures of cities that has to be considered.

Spatial structures are not necessarily static, as physical structures and layouts seem to suggest. Spatial structures of cities can be radically changed—with little or no change in their physical structures—as future political and social transformations of society demand different social uses of urban land. For example, I do not think that the golf courses used by Somoza and others in Managua for their private entertainment will need to be destroyed or destined to other private uses by the new government of Nicaragua. They would probably be open to the green-space-starved segment of the urban population as one of the ways of democratizing land in that country. Probably a new spatial structure is emerging in Nicaragua, and I don't think that the existing physical structure will be a major restraint to it. In this respect, I am inclined to be less pessimistic than Dr. Peñalosa and to place more emphasis on the political precondition of the needed land reforms.

Let me raise the following questions regarding this issue. To what extent do the urbanization processes as projected toward the future by Dr. Peñalosa contribute to the social and political transformations that may lead to more-equitable and efficient uses of space than the ones existing today? Who are the social agents most likely to emerge as leaders of such transformations? And how do land aspirations of the rural and urban poor link to the broader social movements in the pursuit of this change?

My emphasis on the political aspect of land development is not arbitrary and in no way means to underestimate the technical aspects. It is my belief that technical recommendations for democratization of land such as those made at Habitat '76 in Vancouver have not been adopted for reasons to be found in the power structure both internal and external to Latin American countries. On the other hand, change in the existing power structure is not likely to occur as a result of appeals to the conscience of the wealthy and the powerful classes or to the intellect of the local technical bureaucracy. It will depend also to a great extent upon the progress made in the organization of the majority of poor people who suffer most from the consequences of the prevailing development styles within Latin America.

If by democratization of land Dr. Peñalosa means that the access of peasants to agricultural land in Latin America is a necessary condition for feeding all its population now and to preserve natural resources for future generations and that access to urban land adequately serviced should be granted to all as a basic right regardless of income, then I agree with him. Such a statement may be considered general philosophy, and he is right when he says that general philosophies are not enough to include in our recommendations. But I would also consider insufficient his emphasis on practicalities if he is referring only to the technical aspects of land development. We know that merely technical recommendations calling for equity in land development will be widely endorsed even by representatives of political regimes with little respect for human rights that are more critical than the alleged rights on land. We also know that the endorsements of those resolutions have very little meaning. Therefore, we must also explore political practicalities for land development.

What I have in mind are recommendations that could contribute to the organization of the popular sector of the city and of the countryside for becoming a social force with an impact on the power structure. I am not calling for subversion. I am assuming that even within the most-repressive regimes there is a possibility for such an effort without a revolution. This is particularly true concerning land, which is seen by the popular classes as important to their survival as it is seen by Dr. Peñalosa for the society as a whole. After all, power is very rarely exercised in an absolute manner by the privileged classes. I am inclined to see the rapid pace of the urbanization in Latin America and its trends toward the concentration of population in large cities with less pessimism than does Dr. Peñalosa. In the large cities, the growing claim for adequately serviced land by the majority of the poor will sooner or later strengthen the pressures from below for a more-equitable distribution of political power.

Middle East and North Africa

Mona Serageldin: Mr. Peñalosa addressed the land policy issues confronting us with an insight derived from a long involvement with land-related problems. My presentation will seek only to highlight certain legal and institutional aspects with which planners in the Middle East and North Africa are struggling today.

During the past decade, this region has experienced dramatic urbanization as a result of population growth, constraints on agricultural expansion, ambitious industrialization programs, and a massive infusion of capital resources. Sustained flows of rural migrants and, in many cases, large numbers of expatriate laborers are pouring into the larger cities. Speculation and the intense activities of large- and small-scale investors and developers have sent land prices skyrocketing, with values doubling every three years. In many countries, uncontrolled urban expansion is encroaching on valuable agricultural land.

The inability of governments to control urban development seems paradoxical in light of the wide latitude granted to the state by Islamic jurisprudence and its subordination of private interests to the public interest. Under Islamic law, private ownership of land is a conditional right subject to the right of the state at all times to enforce any action deemed necessary to ensure the public welfare. However, three major legal issues impede rational development of urban land.

The first issue derives from a historical legacy. Traditionally the state has maintained tight control over agricultural land, the principal source of wealth and the reliable tax base of the nation. Urban land, however, was another matter altogether. Real property in villages and towns has always been in private ownership and, until colonial times, neither land nor structures were ever taxed. This accounts to a large extent for the great reluctance encountered regarding government interference in the ownership and transfer of urban land. Traditionally only rent income can be taxed. Hence, despite wide taxation powers and in some instances heavy tax burdens, there has been a great reluctance to tax vacant land or unearned increment in value except when this appreciation results from some government action and is collected as a betterment tax.

The second issue derives from the Islamic law of inheritance, which mandates the distribution of real estate among heirs and has led to both fragmentation of property and joint ownership of property rights. Land assembly, transfer, and registration of titles present such problems that government authorities find eminent-domain procedures difficult, time-consuming, and expensive.

The third issue relates to the *waqf* or *habus* system, a kind of charitable endowment unique to Islamic countries. It is a form of trust where capital, which includes land, can never be repossessed, alienated, or subdivided among heirs. The social justification of the system was to finance through private donations public services such as water supply, education, and health. Today these services are considered basic needs and are provided by the government. Yet throughout history and despite flagrant abuses, *waqf* authorities have resisted all attempts at interference in their affairs. Today a significant amount of prime land in all of the urban centers and particularly in the capital cities is held by *waqf* authorities, and despite widespread deterioration among the older properties, the land cannot be expropriated by the state except for public-utility projects. Consequently because of the location of its properties, *waqf* can be a major obstacle to redevelopment and upgrading of older areas.

While the wide latitude given to the state in the administration of land eventually could overcome most legal impediments, the capability of government to implement new approaches is seriously hampered by basic deficiencies in the institutional framework for urban planning. National development plans deal almost exclusively with economic strategies, and the consideration of physical aspects is notable by its absence. This omission obscures the importance of land in the overall development process. It is all the more regrettable at a time when national resources are being committed to physical infrastructure on an unprecedented scale for large-scale development, construction of new towns, and the opening up of undeveloped regions. Land is viewed as an issue of local concern, and land problems are delegated to municipal authorities ill equipped to deal with them. This situation is attributable to two major factors.

The first is the intrinsic weakness of municipal institutions. Historically cities were not considered distinct corporate entitites in the Islamic state. Municipal institutions copied from Western models were established in the twentieth century. Irrespective of the degree of centralization or decentralization prevailing in local administration systems today, municipal authorities struggling with urban land problems are attempting to control the physical manifestations of demographic, economic, and social processes over which they have very little influence.

The second factor is that municipalities are working with mechanisms modeled on conventional Western land policy instruments. These instruments are ill suited to the sociocultural character of the region and have proved inefficient in situations of rapid urban expansion. Furthermore, development controls regulating the utilization of land are considered administrative controls issued by the executive authorities. They are subject to frequent reviews and amendments in an effort to adjust to rapidly changing conditions. Legally they are much weaker than the tenure system established by Islamic law and embodied in modern civil codes. It is not surprising, then, that they have invariably broken down in the face of mounting pressures for development while basic tenure systems have endured practically unchanged.

The scarcity of urban land serviced by basic infrastructure and utilities has led to unabated violations and the proliferation of uncontrolled settlements despite stringent laws and wide municipal powers to remove all violations and impose sanctions on violators. Disregarding the impressive body of legislations threatening their activities, settlers are patiently awaiting the regularization of their status and the extension of utilities to their settlements, deriving security from their right to shelter as guaranteed by Islamic law.

Thus our most-pressing land problems are deeply rooted in our historical and cultural legacy. Consequently solutions cannot successfully be transplanted from outside. Our search for solutions has to evolve from inside in order to achieve a balance between valued customs and traditions and the imperatives of economic development. In the 1980s, strengthened organizational structures and more-efficient regulatory measures will have to be devised to upgrade the urban environment and ensure orderly development. In initiating immediate action, we must accept the fact that in a highly dynamic situation, only partial control can be exercised. We must be willing to adopt pragmatic approaches and work with practical tools to achieve incremental improvements. However, we must never lose sight of our broader goals if our responses to pressing problems are to be curative rather than merely palliative.

North America

Charles Haar: I think the major points of Dr. Peñalosa's paper on which most of us would agree are that (1) land is central to the quality of life; (2) increasing populations place a heavy burden on already-overcrowded cities, especially in the developing nations, and this problem will require action now or in the immediate future; (3) government should control the use of land for the benefit of society as a whole; (4) private ownership of land, and this I would suggest is unique to that form of land tenure, poses many obstacles to proper and wise planning; but (5) restructuring the private property system is not now politically feasible. Those seem to me to be five points that at times clash, and it is our duty during the next few days to put them together into a harmonious and coherent pattern.

In the United States, these same issues have had to be addressed. Briefly, the U.S. experience since World War II is that our urban regions have experienced different pressures of population growth between regions and within regions. Although the migration is nowhere near as dramatic as in Asia and Africa, we have had a strong shift that has been somewhat imperceptible until the census told us otherwise. The 1980 census figures show the shift to the sunbelt and the slowing of suburban growth in the other parts of the country. Now the growth is primarily in the migration push toward the South and the Southwest portions of this country.

This migration of jobs and of people has brought about the increase in land prices that Dr. Peñalosa referred to. Soaring land prices affect housing for the poor and, increasingly now, for the middle classes. There is increasing pressure on urban planners to allow for the highest but not always the best use of urban land. Site-acquisition costs have made redevelopment in rundown and blighted areas of our older cities extremely expensive. They have made less and less land available for the nonbiddable uses by the market so that the issues of pollution of air and water that affect the quality of land use are becoming more pressing. And finally, the high land prices have contributed along with other factors—land is never to be seen in isolation but is always seen in relationship to these other public factors—to jobs being moved to rural and suburban areas, raising unemployment among the central-city poor.

The first major effort in terms of land comes not through a land program but through other societal pressures and programs. In our country, soaring land prices have most greatly affected minorities because our urban poor are for the most part either black or Hispanic. So we have a two-sided problem for public policy to cope with. We are dealing with the social injustices created by the inequalities in our private system of landownership, and we are also dealing with attitudes of people toward those of different racial origins. Thus the mirror which reflected our land policies through the 1960s and 1970s was often the struggle for civil rights. In the 1960s, major legislative steps were taken to guarantee equal opportunity for housing, employment, and education to all citizens regardless of race. One such piece of legislation was the Civil Rights Act. And the various Fair Housing Acts brought land use into context against the issues of these broader social problems. The most recent fair-housing law gives the Department of Housing and Urban Development the power to bring action where there is discrimination. And it is interesting to note that a program that started in the early 1960s is taking another major step in 1980.

While we are all impatient and anxious for speed, this is the pace we have established, a pace that we must accelerate. Government programs and policies were begun to provide opportunities to minorities. Not only in terms of affirmative action in employment and housing but in the Model Cities Program that dealt with the marshaling of resources and the choice of cities in which to concentrate, these programs again dealt with the problems of the poor and the minorities. As we are all aware and as has been pointed out already, it is not only a problem for the executive and the legislature representing the popular will and the desire of citizens, but all branches of government have been involved, at least in the United States and in Canada.

The courts had been involved to ensure that laws dealing with land and housing and dealing with their being made accessible to all groups and free of discrimination and prejudice have been part of the judicial mandate. We have had a series of equal-services cases, primarily in *Hawkins* v *Shaw* where the Fifth Circuit and the other courts held that there is an obligation to provide equal infrastructure to all parts of a city; that is, roads, sewers, lights, and paving must be the same for all portions of the city so that there is no discrimination against certain groups or sectors. We have had the *Mount Laurel Township* kind of local land cases, and again the courts have come in and held that the local communities must take their fair share of responsibility for housing all income groups. And finally, a third trend is that of the public use—that is, the compulsory acquisition of land. Despite the long-standing institution of private property, the courts have redefined, as every generation must, what private property means. They have so broadly redefined public use that private land may be compulsorily acquired with just compensation to the owner. And public purpose has been so broadly defined that land can be taken for any public use that can be rationally conceived by the highest reaches of the mind to be a public use, so that city planning, urban planning in and of itself, has become a public use.

This is a remarkable transformation of the bounds and restraints that private property might otherwise interpose to public activities. My major point about this development and this response to migration and to urban land prices is that these efforts can be said to have been inspired by a belief that government could solve the land problem by itself. One of the major lessons that has to be utilized now in the United States and in other countries is that while government and public ownership can have very vital and catalytic effects, in dealing with attitudes toward property and toward race, government alone cannot solve all of the problems. It is not that once we move to a public system, the problem will be solved. It is not that simple. It is a problem of attitudes, of education, and economic power; no conference fiat or edict can waive these things away. I think we are moving in a healthy direction—somewhat less in the direction of government and its ability to solve all of these problems and more toward a joint-venture relationship, a public-private partnership that we are seeing develop in many areas and most prominently in the fields of housing and land use.

What does all this start from? We were left with two alternatives: (1) we can propose a utopian solution based upon notions of collective ownership of land because we feel that the private market economy can never be directed to serve the interest of society as a whole or (2) we can leave everything to the private market system, subject to a few nuisance controls. Or perhaps there is a third alternative, and there are some devices and incentives that government can provide to the private sector to benefit the larger societal interest. The manner and order in which I presented these alternatives must make clear my opinion about the directions in which things are moving. I guess there is a powerful myth that we are attempting to find because there are tremendous human problems of shelter and of living. We have to deal creatively with the realities of the private market economy.

Although the question is still unanswered, I think that some of the attempts in the United States are worthy of description here such as the joint venture—that is, the public-private partnership. Because we seem to be becoming more involved in that process without being fully aware of everything involved, we are attempting to work with and in conjunction with enterprise capital rather than against it. Here are a few examples of that. We have that phenomenon that arose from the Great Depression of the 1930s with government being able to insure risky mortgages and guarantee other risky loans and thereby induce private capital to flow into housing and land uses. We have moved into other programs in which government subsidizes interest rates on privately loaned money, which is the foundation of our housing program today. The combination of the government, the taxes, the resources is not adequate alone, but by providing these incentives, it creates a leverage point at which private enterprise capital can be attracted. Sometimes we have government lending directly at interest rates below the market or taking an extremely long-term position. Above all, we also have tax policy. We have the J-51 property tax abatement system in New York City; we have our own Internal Revenue Code, which provides tax incentives to the private sector in order to get that sector to do what we think is a more appropriate use of land and of housing.

How are the goals and the benefits of this type of joint venture different from the private-public confrontation in which this debate is usually cast? First, we have leveraging. You use a small amount of government money to encourage large amounts of private capital, both in a specific project and then for an entire area or neighborhood. This is where a new kind of master plan becomes essential. The second factor to be emphasized is that of targeting. Government resources can be placed in areas of greatest distress in order to use scarce funds more effectively. Third, there are the control aspects. Governments can see that their programs mesh with other governmental programs and governmental policy in accordance with a comprehensive plan. And fourth, the energy crisis is redirecting the international flows of capital and posing a new series of problems for urban land development.

We should examine some of the costs and potential dangers of this new joint venture of government working with private enterprise because everything has costs and benefits, as the dreary economists like to remind us. What are the costs of working with private enterprise? First of all, private business has to be watched closely. Executives watch their own businesses very closely, and in turn I think this is one of the major issues. Public officials dealing in housing and in land uses must have a knowledge of the institutions of finance and of law just to avoid being ripped off. This is something that we see on occasion when the lion and the lamb lie down together. We also need a new kind of training and education for our public officials that will enable them to deal with the graduates of our law and business schools. We have a problem with favoritism and bribery in government, and we need to institute review mechanisms, whether they be judicial review or a high ministerial form of review. We must always be aware of the different cash discounts over time that the public and private sector place on certain investments. And above all, there is a need for flexibility and a method of dealing with the unanticipated consequences of any act, whether it be private or public.

In conclusion, I would like to say a few words about this joint venture in local land-use controls. We are dealing with financing, but most of the land problem—that is, the decision where roads are going to go, the kind of housing we are going to build, the kind of infrastructure we are going to install—are matters in which the decision-making authority is granted from the national government back to the local authority. And here we have examples of accommodating the needs of private developers and lenders while gaining valuable concessions to suit the municipality's needs. We have incentive zoning as a growing device whereby greater density and bulk controls are given to private developers in return for their providing public amenities—perhaps a theater, a park, an open space—or perhaps low-income housing in return for this incentive zoning. We have transfer of development rights whereby the government works closely with the private sector by granting greater or intensive use of private property in exchange for acceptance of certain controls or restrictions on growth. We have seen in the past few years the use of planned unit developments where we have examples of the success of planning a large site to accommodate many different land uses, and thereby we have been able to make more housing sites available and have been able to generate a mix of economic and social classes within the development. So I think we are beginning to see this public-private partnership approach working on the local land level as well as on the fiscal federalism level.

Finally, I should address what Mr. Peñalosa has raised as a puzzling question: why have the Habitat recommendations with all these antecedent commitments and publicity of governments not been put into practice? We must ask ourselves why they have been so largely ignored. I was one of the U.S. delegates to that conference, and I know that we worked very hard to make a system of recommendations that would be feasible. The question comes back to how land can be used best or, as Dr. Peñalosa asks, whether the private market economy can be marshalled to control land for the benefit of society as a whole. We must be cognizant of the differences, variations, and conditions among various countries and even different regions within the same countries and different cities within the same regions. The answers are not in yet on the joint-venture approach because we are just beginning to observe the impacts of the application of this approach. With proper direction and incentives from the public sector, the answer is shaping as a highly tentative yes.

The hopes and goals of this conference can be boiled down into five smaller points. First, we have to accept the reality of the private-market concept concerning land in many countries and the very special attachment of individuals to land. In a way, private property at times is a form of civil right. Your land and your house is an insulation against the arbitrary acts of a big government. It is this attitude that is exemplified by our civil-rights movement. This points up the need to make land a civil right. Access to land and housing is part of the civil-rights movement. This may be a unique contribution of our country's experience. Second, we have to develop ways and performance standards that require the government to set out what it is trying to achieve in its plans for land. Then we should let the ingenuity of the citizens and the private sector come up with different forms of responses because we have no final answers. We do not know the kind of land patterns, tenure systems, and arrangements that individuals might devise. In this way we can direct the power and the energy of individuals to socially desirable ends. Third, we must learn by example and mistake. Fourth, we must direct our efforts toward practicalities. To plan is human; to implement is divine. To the making of congressional manifestos, there is no end. And our problem is somehow to devise the master plan for land use so that it pivots about institutional, legal, and financial constraints and resources as it does about the physical. And finally, Dr. Peñalosa and others have raised for us the issue of quality of life on earth, of which we are custodian and stewards. And as Mr. Mumford told us, how we develop the land, our housing, our cities, and our settlements is really an artifact of culture. It is the clearest physical manifestation and expression of institutions and an articulation of our values. I think it is our values for the individual and his use of land toward which the shaping of land policies has to be directed.

Moderator

Arlo Woolery: Implicit in Professor Haar's comments is the conclusion that if there were no private land markets, we would have to invent them in order to get the benefit of the land-resource-allocation information that the action of the market provides. We are seeing in the United States a movement toward the center by both private landowners and government. Partnerships are being formed between the private and the public sector, and those partnerships are beginning to yield benefits for society as a whole.

The picture may be somewhat less bleak than Dr. Peñalosa may have painted. Possibly Dr. Peñalosa is catching that North American disease of impatience, which is uncharacteristic of the Latin Americans. Could it be that together, taking the best of each of our cultures, we can begin to put together a formula that will have the ingredients required to develop a series of national land policies within our individual countries that will have a truly global perspective?

4 Land Policy as a Tool of Social and Economic Development

Robert C.T. Lee

The land problem has a long history. People live upon food grown on the land, but because land is limited and population tends to keep increasing, land distribution and use are problems meriting serious attention. Maladjustments in institutions controlling land use and unfair distribution of wealth arising from land have led to cries for redress.

In Chinese history, many statesmen have addressed the land problem, but few met with success. Since 1949, however, the province of Taiwan has logged a good record in successfully implementing a land reform program that has played an important role in promoting economic development and social justice in Taiwan.

Land Policy of the Republic of China

The land policy of the Republic of China is based primarily on the teachings of Dr. Sun Yat-sen, the founding father of the republic. His Principle of Livelihood envisaged a plan of equalizing land rights as the best method to solve China's land problem. This ideal, incorporated into the republic's Constitution adopted in 1948, serves as the basic component of the Republic of China's land policy.

The overall objective of the Principle of Livelihood is to equalize the wealth of society by equalizing land rights and the regulation of private capital.[1] Why equalizing land rights? Dr. Sun considered land as a free gift from nature. It was there before mankind; it is not a product of human labor. Since land is limited in area, its value is bound to increase as population expands. Owning as much land as possible has become a fast way of getting rich and a cause of social injustice.

Although there were not many big landlords in China at the time when Dr. Sun publicized his idea of equalizing land rights, he thought that precautions should be taken against future difficulties. According to Dr. Sun's teachings, the equalization of land rights can check landowners' unjust income from land, equalize social wealth, and prevent land speculation.[2] Dr. Sun first focused his attention on the urban land problem, but his emphasis later shifted to farmland.

Land-rights equalization does not mean outright redistribution of land. Instead it proposes to levy taxes on land-value increments that result not from the ownership per se but from the progress of society. Since increments in land value are a product of society, tax revenues from this source should be enjoyed by the public. In the Republic of China, taxation of this kind has been made into law to guard against any administrative distortion.[3]

To implement the program, Dr. Sun suggests in his Principle of Livelihood four steps: report land values to authorities, collect the land-value tax, collect the land-value increment tax, and purchase land at the reported value.[4]

To illustrate the importance of Dr. Sun's idea of equalization of land rights and its impact on China's land policy, I would like to quote some articles of the Constitution regarding land policy. On the equalization of land rights and the sharing of benefits arising from land among the people, article 142 stipulates, "National economy shall be based upon the Principle of People's Livelihood and shall seek to effect equalization of land ownership," and article 143 specifies, "Privately owned land shall be liable to taxation according to its value, and the government may buy such land according to its value. . . . If the value of a piece of land has increased not through the exertion of labor or the employment of capital, the State shall levy thereon an increment tax, the proceeds of which shall be enjoyed by the people in common." In regard to land and the tiller, the same article states, "In the distribution and readjustment of land, the State shall, in principle, assist the self-farming landowners and persons who make use of the land by themselves." In order to make the most of land, article 146 provides, "The State shall, by the use of scientific techniques, develop water conservancy, increase the productivity of land, improve agricultural conditions, plan for the utilization of land, develop agricultural resources, and hasten the industrialization of agriculture."[5]

In sum, Dr. Sun Yat-sen's teachings combine with specific provisions in the Constitution to serve as the supreme guiding principle of China's land policy. This policy calls for equal distribution of land rights, but it also pays attention to efficient land use and the integrity of private ownership. To carry out the land policy, the government of the Republic of China has enacted the Land Law, the Farm Rent Reduction Act, the Land-to-the-Tiller Act, the Regional Planning Law, the Urban Planning Law, the Equalization of Land Rights Act, the Land Tax Act, the Agricultural Development Statute, Measures for Land Consolidation, and various other statutes and regulations designed to promote land use and distribution. All of the laws and regulations but the Land Law were enacted after the Chinese government moved to Taiwan in 1949.

Farmland Reform

The major interest of this Congress is urban land policy, but farmland reform is an important part of Dr. Sun's Principle of People's Livelihood and of China's land policy. It was the first land reform program in Taiwan and the result was very successful. The program was undertaken in three phases: reduce rental rates of tenanted land, sell public land to cultivators and tenants, and carry out the land-to-the-tiller program.[6]

Rent Reduction

Beginning in 1949, farm rents were reduced to a maximum of 37.5 percent of the annual yield of the major crops. This new rent level was substantially lower than the previously prevailing one, which often amounted to approximately 50 percent of the annual output. To assess the annual output, all farmland was classified into twenty-six grades according to productivity. After that, an estimated standard yield was assigned to each plot of land, and on the basis of this standard the reduced amount of rent was fixed. In addition, new farm-lease contracts were signed between landlord and tenant to replace the old ones, and the tenure of lease for tenant farmers was lengthened to six years. This program was enforced on all the 260,000 hectares of private tenanted holdings (29 percent of the total); some 300,000 tenant families (42 percent of the total farm households) benefited. As a result, tenants' income increased, their tenure security was ensured, and landlords could not evict tenants and dispose of the lands farmed by them with impunity. All of this led to a drop in the market value of tenanted land and the position of the landlords. The low land prices enabled tenant farmers to purchase land with their own savings. From 1949 to 1973, 70,000 hectares of tenanted land in total was purchased by 135,000 tenants.

Sale of Public Land

Encouraged by the success of the rent-reduction program, the Chinese government proceeded in 1951 to the second phase. After World War II, the Chinese government acquired from Japanese nationals and corporations some 180,000 hectares of lands. To set an example for private landlords, the government started selling these lands to their current cultivators. The amount of public land that could be purchased by one farm family was limited to between 0.5 and 2 *chia* of paddy land and between 1 and 4 *chia* of dry land, depending on its quality. (One *chia* is equal to 0.9699 hectare.) Some 130,000 hectares were sold to 177,000 tenant families from 1950 to

1973. The price was set at 2.5 times the annual crop yield and was to be paid in twenty installments over ten years.

Land-to-the-Tiller

Following the sale of the public land, the government embarked in 1953 upon the redistribution of excess landlord holdings. As a first step, the government surveyed and grouped all landholdings in Taiwan and then enacted the Land-to-the-Tiller Act in order to translate the program into action. Under this program, a landlord was allowed to retain a maximum of 3 *chia* (2.9 hectares) of medium-grade paddy field or its equivalent for himself. All tenanted lands in excess of this maximum limit were compulsorily purchased by the government and resold to the incumbent tenants. The purchase price was 2.5 times the crop yield. It was paid for by the government with 70 percent in commodity bonds and 30 percent in stocks of four government corporations. The government collects two installments of the resale price in kind from the farmer-purchasers each year. Under this program, 140,000 hectares (18 percent of the total) of excess land were purchased from 106,000 landlords and resold to 195,000 tenant families (25 percent of the total farm households).

One result of the land reform is that more farmers own land. Before 1949 when the reform was effected, 39 percent of all farmers in Taiwan were tenant farmers, 36 percent were owner farmers, and 25 percent were part-owner farmers. By 1953 the land-to-the-tiller program had reduced tenant farmers to 21 percent and increased owner farmers to 55 percent. At present, owner-operated farms accounted for 79 percent of all farms, part-owner farms 11 percent, and tenant farms 10 percent. The increase in the number of owner farmers in Taiwan resulted in the expansion of owner-cultivated land. Before the land reform, out of a total of 681,154 hectares in privately cultivated land in Taiwan, 61.4 percent was cultivated by owners; now this percentage is 91 percent.

The reform also effected changes in individual landholdings. Before the program, 25 percent of the farm holdings were below 1 hectare, 33 percent between 1 and 3 hectares, 26 percent between 3 and 10 hectares, and 16 percent over 10 hectares. After the completion of the program, farm holdings below 3 hectares increased from 58 percent to 77 percent, and those over 3 hectares decreased from 42 to 23 percent. Despite changes in the tenure structure, the land reform did not split up individual farms or fragment land plots. What it did split up was the size of landownership.

The land reform program in Taiwan reorganized the agrarian structure into a true family farm system essential to the development of a productive and progressive agricultural system. According to a study made by T.H. Lee, the land reform has brought about changes in production, consumption, investment, and the transfer of income from landlords to tenant farmers.[7] Between 1950 and 1955, farm expenditure increased considerably, signifying a great improvement in farmers' standard of living. Higher consumption, on the other hand, reduced savings in the same period, but more was invested in farm implements, land improvement, farm houses, and other facilities. More cash crops and livestock were produced, probably because tenant farmers were no longer obliged to produce rice for rental payment. Resource productivity also rose. Land productivity grew faster than the productivity of labor, indicating that technological improvements after the reform largely centered on intensive land use with more labor inputs.

As to the effect on income distribution, Samuel P.S. Ho analyzed how the land reform affected equity.[8] The reform substantially cut down the wealth of landlords because the price basis of 2.5 times the annual yield of the major crop was far below the market level.

In the period of the land reform, at least toward the end of it, there was a substantial capital outflow from agriculture to other economic sectors, which amounted to about 22 percent of the total value of agricultural production.[9] It would thus appear that even in the early period of development, the agricultural sector performed the crucial function of supplying the rest of the economy with capital resources.

Following ownership and tenure changes, attention shifted to the improvement of land use. A follow-up consolidation program was therefore introduced. Land consolidation is an effective measure to optimize land use and raise per-unit yield by reshaping farmland plots and providing public facilities serving them. After a few years of experimentation, land consolidation was officially launched in 1962. Fragmented plots were combined into a rectangular-sized plot of 0.25 hectare, and public facilities were greatly improved by making irrigation, drainage, and transportation directly accessible to all plots. Thus far, 270,000 hectares of farmland have been consolidated. Surveys indicate that consolidation has increased the per-hectare yield and decreased production costs.[10]

Urban Land Reform

As population and the economy continue to expand, Taiwan's urban land problem has become as serious as that in the rural areas about thirty years ago. In 1952 Taiwan had a population of 8,128,000, of which 47.6 percent (3,869,000 persons) lived in urban areas and in the same year there were twelve cities with a population of over 50,000. By the end of the 1960s, the population had soared to 11,149,000, of which 50.2 percent were urbanites, and the number of cities with over 50,000 people rose to thirty. In 1977, the urban population jumped to 66.9 percent of the total, and sixty-six cities had a population of more than 50,000. Increases in the two metropolitan areas of Taipei and Kaohsiung have been particularly fast. The city of Taipei currently has a population of over 2 million; in 1945 it had only 300,000. During the same period, the population of Kaohsiung City has risen ten times—from 100,000 to over 1 million. This urban population explosion has resulted in housing shortages, inadequate public facilities, and serious traffic congestion, all of which have caused living conditions to deteriorate. Furthermore, fast urbanization and encroachments upon nonurban land have given rise to other problems. Urban planning has failed to keep pace with the speed of urban expansion, resulting in numerous cases of improper land use. It is difficult to secure land for the construction of public facilities because of prohibitively high land prices, which have resulted from rapid urbanization. Moreover the fragmented condition of lands prevents their economical and sound utilization.

These problems had become serious in some areas as early as the mid-1950s. To prevent them from becoming even worse, the Chinese government took reform action, enacting the Equalization of Urban Land Rights Act in 1954 and its bylaws in 1956. Since then, land-value increments have been taxed in many cities in Taiwan. The act was revised as the Equalization of Land Rights Act in February 1977, extending its authority over rural areas as well. Land taxation is the principal tool for carrying out the policy of equalization of land rights.

Land-Tax System

A practical land-tax system rests on sound land registration and classification. Of Taiwan's total area of 3,598,900 hectares, 48 percent has been officially surveyed and registered. The rest consists of roads, dikes, rivers, and remote forests, which are largely owned by the government. Land in Taiwan is classified into four types and twenty-one categories. Of the twenty-one categories, eleven are taxable.[11] Three types of land taxes are directly involved in the land-rights equalization program.

Farmland Tax: This is a tax with a long history. By nature, it is a tax on a presumptive basis. During the period of Japanese occupation, it was slightly modified and made a presumptive net-produce tax. In order to determine the productivity of land, periodical surveys were conducted and the cadastre revised accordingly. For farmland, productivity was assessed by surveying crop output at harvesttime. For nonagricultural land, the annual rental value was taken as the basis for the assessment. Finally, different sets of rates were applied to the net standard values of each grade, and then each grade of each category was taxed progressively in accordance with standard tax units.[12] After Taiwan was returned to the Republic of China, this land-tax assessment system was retained, except that collection in kind was introduced. Since then the standard tax units for different grades have been used for the computation of land tax.

Land-value Tax and Land-value Increment Tax: These two taxes are essential to the implementation of urban land reform. Under the equalization of urban land-rights program, all lands covered by it are subject to the land tax. If land is currently used for agricultural purposes, the farmland tax will apply, but in case of transfer, all lands are subject to the land-value increment tax.

Tax on Rural Property Transfer: Before the nationwide implementation of the equalization of land rights and in areas where land value has not been assessed, the transfer or exchange of land ownership is subject to a deed tax, which ranges from 2.5 to 7.5 percent. For land already subject to the land-value increment tax, however, the deed tax is not applicable.

Procedure for Equalization of Land Rights

The procedure for equalizing land rights, mainly as outlined by Dr. Sun Yat-sen, includes the assessment of land value, collection of the land-value tax, purchase of land at declared value, and collection of the land-value increment tax.

Land-value Assessment. Land-value assessment as an essential part of the land-rights equalization program is prerequisite to the collection of both the land-value tax and the land-value increment tax. According to the Equalization of Land Rights Act, land value shall be assessed either by the comparative-market approach or by the income-capitalization approach, and it shall be reassessed once every three years after its initial assessment. In practice, the comparative-market approach has been used primarily, particularly for urban land. The assessments are submitted to the Land Evaluation Committee for consideration. After approval, the results are made public to serve as a reference for the landowners to declare the value of their land. Declaration within 80 to 120 percent of the government-announced value is considered to be appropriate. In other words, landowners are free to make an assessment between 80 and 120 percent of the value announced by the government.

The practice of asking landowners to assess the value of their land is based on the belief that they will not report the value too low or too high under the equalization program. If they make a low assessment, they run the risk of having their land purchased by the government at that value and suffering a loss. On the other hand, if they make too high an assessment, they will have to pay a proportionately high tax. Therefore, they are likely to strike a mean and report a median value.

Since the implementation of the Equalization of Land Rights Act, the self-assessment of land value has been satisfactory. Over 90 percent of the landowners declared their land value according to government-announced prices. They want to avoid a heavy increment tax that may occur in view of rapid rises in land prices.

Collection of Land-value Tax: The land-value tax is a progressive tax on the value of land, collected according to the self-assessed land value. In case the land value declared by the landowner is higher than 120 percent of the announced value, the upper limit shall be used as the tax base. But if the land value declared is lower than 80 percent of the announced value, two things could happen. First, the government could buy the land at the reported value; second, the lower limit of 80 percent of the announced land value shall be adopted as the tax base. If the landowner fails to declare the value of his land before the deadline, the announced value of the land shall be deemed final.

The land tax is levied on the value of land minus improvements.[13] It is meant not just to raise government revenue but also to promote land use. To serve the two purposes at the same time, the tax rate must be carefully considered. According to the Equalization of Land Rights Act, the basic rate is 1.5 percent, and it will progress whenever the land value is 500 percent in excess of the progressive starting value (PSV).

The PSV is a figure at which the progressive tax rate starts. It is the average of the land values of 7 ares of land, excluding land for industrial and agricultural uses, as well as land exempted from tax in the respective county or municipality. The PSV varies with regions. At present, there are twenty-one PSVs in the province of Taiwan, one for each county or city. In the second half of 1977, for instance, the PSVs ranged from NT$145,000 in Taitung County to NT$1,076 million in Keelung City. For Taipei City it was NT$1 million in the same period. The tax rates are as follows:

On aggregate land value not in excess of PSV, 1.5 percent.

On the part of first 500 percent in excess of PSV, 2.0 percent.

On the part of second 500 percent in excess of PSV, 3.0 percent.

On the part of third 500 percent in excess of PSV, 4.0 percent.

On the part of fourth 500 percent in excess of PSV, 5.0 percent.

On the part of fifth 500 percent in excess of PSV, 6.0 percent.

On the part thereafter, 7.0 percent.

There are also preferential rates for self-used residential land, land within industrial zones, and land reserved for public facilities. For lands that have not been put to use before the deadline set by the government, the punitive tax rates, two to five times higher than the regular ones, apply.

Purchase at Declared Value: Purchase at declared value is designed to prevent landowners from intentionally holding down their land values. Dr. Sun advocated the declaration of land value by landowners themselves. According to the Equalization of Land Rights Act, land whose declared value is lower than the announced value of over 20 percent is subject to government purchase. The government is also entitled to purchase the land that has been zoned off for building-construction purposes but has not been used within the period assigned. Thus purchase at declared value has the positive effect of fostering land use. It also enables the government to obtain land for public facilities, defense construction, and other purposes.

Since 1956 the government has purchased 1,135 lots of undervalued land in Taiwan Province with a total area of 37 hectares. In Taipei City lands thus purchased have totaled 23 hectares.

Collection of Land-value Increment Tax: Land-value increments result from social and economic development. Since they come not as a result of the owner's labor, they should be shared with the public.

By and large, land-value increments are in the nature of capital gains. According to Dr. Sun, the increments should be collected by the government and spent for the public. This idea was incorporated in the Equalization of Urban Land Rights Act when it was first enacted in 1954. The tax rate was as high as 100 percent, but it was later lowered to 40 to 60 percent of the total increment. The rate varies:

Forty percent on the increment not exceeding by 100 percent the originally declared value or the value of the last transfer.

Fifty percent on the part of increment that exceeds by 100 percent to 200 percent the originally declared value.

Sixty percent on the part that exceeds by over 200 percent the originally declared value.

Some tax exemptions and preferential rates are applicable in certain situations:

1. Public lands sold by the government shall be exempted from the land-value increment tax.
2. When lands are transferred because of inheritance, the land-value increment tax is not levied.

3. For self-used residential land within 3 ares in urban areas or 7 ares in
    nonurban areas, the rate is 10 percent of the increment, but if the area is
    larger than allowed, the regular tax will be levied on the excess.
4. The tax will be reduced by 40 percent to 70 percent in the case of a com-
    pulsory purchase by the government.
5. The tax will be reduced by 20 percent on the first transfer after land
    consolidation.
6. The tax will be reduced by 20 percent if the formerly idle land has been
    improved for use.
7. If a self-used residential lot, a self-managed industrial lot, or a self-
    cultivated farm is sold and in the meantime another piece of similar
    land is purchased, the increment tax previously paid may be refunded
    upon request.

The land-value increment tax is collected when land is transferred. The
increment generally refers to the positive difference between the value at
transfer and the value declared. In case there is a transfer after the first
value declaration, the tax becomes the difference between the value
transferred and the value of the preceding transfer. Usually the tax is paid
by the seller. In case of a gift it is paid by the donee.

The Taipei Experience

Taipei was the first city to carry out the Equalization of Urban Land Rights
Act.[14] Under this act and the later Equalization of Land Rights Act, the
Taipei city government has undertaken a number of reforms. In addition to
land-value assessment and land-tax collection, measures like zone expropriation, land consolidation, and housing projects have also been carried out.

Ownership concentrations are the root cause of the land problem.
Taipei has accomplished much in breaking up such concentrations. In 1974
Taipei had 273,083 households that owned land; by the end of 1978 the
figure had increased to 334,277. In this period the area of private lands rose
by 9.8 percent while the number of landowners jumped by 26 percent. The
result is smaller landholdings.

Equalizing land rights has enriched the treasury of Taipei City. In fiscal
1974, land taxes (including the farmland tax, land-value tax, and land-value
increment tax) totaled NT$1,392 million (US$38 million), accounting for 8
percent of the total tax revenue of that year. Four years later land taxes
made up about 15 percent of the city tax revenue; they reached NT$5,844
million (US$162 million). The expansion of the land-value increment tax
was especially remarkable: from NT$714 million in 1974 to NT$3,893
million in 1978. The increment tax has greatly enhanced the city govern-

ment's ability to finance projects for the public welfare, including low-income housing and education.

To develop new communities and to accelerate urban renewal, the Taipei municipal government has initiated two zone-expropriation projects and several consolidation projects. The areas involved totaled 68 hectares for the expropriation projects and 195 hectares for the consolidation projects. Under projects of the first category, the landowner has a right to buy back 3 ares of the expropriated land. Under a consolidation project, the landowner can usually retain 60 percent of his land.

Urban Land Consolidation:
A Case Study of Kaohsiung City

An industrial city in southern Taiwan, Kaohsiung is the second-largest city in Taiwan.[15] It has an area of 155 square kilometers, accounting for 0.4 percent of the total area of Taiwan.

Along with prosperous commerce and industry, the city's population has increased markedly, almost doubling from 515,153 in 1962 to 1,019,417 in 1978. The fast population increase and booming economic activity have exerted heavy pressure on the city's housing, transportation, and public facilities.

To solve or at least to alleviate uncontrolled urbanization, huge amounts of money and personnel are required. To improve the situation drastically and without imposing a heavy financial burden upon the government, an urban land consolidation program was undertaken.

Farmland consolidation boosts agricultural production; urban land consolidation improves land use in cities. In accordance with city-development trends, urban land consolidation aims to rearrange, through exchange or merger, all irregular-shaped, ill-demarcated, and fragmented lands in areas covered by city plans or lying on the outskirts of urban centers. This rearrangement, coupled with planning for public facilities, produces standard land plots of convenient sizes and promotes economical and proper land utilization. More specifically, urban land consolidation ensures overall planning to optimize land use. It will hasten the day when landowners may realize the hope of having their land reasonably urbanized and will also accelerate land appreciation. Land consolidation provides land for public facilities without imposing a heavy financial burden upon the government, eases land expropriation, and protects the interests of those landowners whose lands may otherwise be expropriated. Finally it promotes community development, environmental beautification, and social harmony. Cadastral administration will also benefit.

Procedure of Consolidation

Because urban land consolidation involves city government, public welfare, and the interests of individual landowners, it must be handled with considerable care. In Kaohsiung City the procedure goes like this:

1. Select areas eligible for consolidation.
2. Seek consent from landowners.
3. Formulate consolidation projects and gain approval from the superior agency.
4. Survey area to be consolidated.
5. Start planning.
6. Assess land value.
7. Exchange or merge land plots.
8. Promulgate consolidation plans.
9. Begin construction work.
10. Redistribute land and allocate compensation.
11. Rearrange cadastral and landownership data.
12. Prepare report.

Selecting an area for consolidation must be made in accordance with one or more of the following principles: the need and planning of urban construction and development; the size and distribution of population; or the demand for effective use of scattered lands, for removing illegally constructed structures, for renewing slum districts, for building low-income housing, for building new communities, or for industrial districts.

Funding Land Consolidation

In principle, landowners should bear all the consolidation expenses in proportion to the benefits they will receive. The expenses shall be paid by the landowners with proceeds from the sale of part of the consolidated land. According to the regulations on urban land consolidation, the expenses to be borne by the landowners are:

1. Consolidation expense, including compensation for buildings dismantled and part of the administrative costs.
2. Payment for land used for public purposes, including roads, ditches, community parks, and market sites.
3. Construction costs of public facilities.
4. Interest on loans required as advances to cover consolidation and construction costs.

In most cases, payments were made in kind rather than in cash. In other words, landowners paid their share of consolidation expenses with consolidated land. Generally landowners lost about 40 percent of their land as a result of land consolidation. The lands contributed by the owners were then sold by the municipal government to generate funds for consolidation expenses.

Although the landowners bore the consolidation expenses, they did not suffer any loss because land consolidation has greatly increased the land value. In the case of Kaohsiung City, land prices after consolidation increased by 500 to 1,000 percent. So even though the landowners retained on average about 60 percent of their land, financially they made considerable gains.

Since the introduction of land consolidation in 1958, sixteen consolidation projects have been carried out, and the areas consolidated have totaled 1,177 hectares. But land consolidation must be combined with other measures—zone expropriation, expropriation of land for public facilities, urban renewal, and land-use zoning and control.

Evaluation and Conclusion

Taiwan has carried out a series of land reforms based on the principle of equalizing land rights. Its farmland reform, turning most tenant farmers into owner cultivators, was very successful. Giving the tenants ownership of land provided a strong incentive for them to accelerate agricultural development, which in turn made possible the expansion of the economy as a whole.

Economic prosperity and population increase have greatly raised land values, especially in urban areas and suburbs. To prevent concentrations of unearned increment and to promote optimum land use, an effort was first made in 1956 to equalize land rights in some urban areas. Since then, all land covered by city plans and whose land value has been officially determined has been subject to the land-value tax, and when urban land is transferred, it has been subject to the land-value increment tax.

Under the policy of equalization of urban land rights, land speculation was subdued to some extent, but land value continued to soar on the outskirts of city-planning areas and in rural areas where new highways had been planned or were under construction. Thus, the government decided in 1969 to extend the policy to all lands. In 1977 the Equalization of Land Rights Act was enacted. By the end of 1979 all land values had been officially determined, but for practical reasons, most lands that are now subject to the farmland tax will still be thus taxed, but the land-value increment tax will be levied on lands, urban or rural, when their ownership is transferred.

Revenues from the three land taxes (the land-value tax, farmland tax, and land-value increment tax) in fiscal 1978 (July 1, 1977–June 30, 1978) amounted to NT$15,732 million (US$437 million), which represented an increase of about 18 percent over 1967. More significant probably is the percentage increase of the land taxes in the total tax revenue. In fiscal 1967, land taxes accounted for 5.8 percent of the total revenue; in fiscal 1978 they rose to 9.3 percent. Among the three land taxes, the increment tax grew fastest: from 0.4 percent to 5.5 percent of the total tax revenue during the same period.[16] The increase, though not very impressive, is a meaningful first step in carrying out the equalization-of-land-rights policy.

The second objective of the policy is to arrest speculation in land, thereby eliminating unearned income. In this regard, the result has not been very satisfactory; land value has continued increasing, and land speculation has occurred. One of the reasons is that the law has some loopholes. For example, the maximum tax rate for land-value increment is 60 percent, which means 40 percent of the increment can be retained by the landowner. This is not likely to prevent people from investing in land. Second, the world economy since 1974 has been plagued by inflation, and land, like gold, has been considered a hedge against inflation.

The effect of the land policy on the distribution of wealth is difficult to measure, but Taiwan is one of the few places in the world that has achieved both substantial economic growth and improved income distribution. Together with other income-policy measures, Dr. Sun's land policy has played a positive role. This is particularly true for the farmland reform in the early years.

The policy to equalize land rights is basically sound in principle. During the course of implementation, however, many technical problems have been encountered, and the experience gained over the years indicates that there is still room for improvement. Land-value assessment, tax rates, and other taxation matters should be improved. It is believed that with the experience of the past years and the determination of the government, many of these problems will be solved in the near future.

Notes

1. Sun Yat-sen, *The Principle of Livelihood* (Taipei: Chinese Culture Service, 1953).
2. Ibid., p. 29.
3. The Equalization of Land Right Act, article 51.
4. Sun, *Principle,* pp. 39-40.
5. Constitution of the Republic of China.

6. Good references for land reform process in Taiwan are Hui-sun Tang, *Land Reform in Free China* (Taipei: Joint Commission on Rural Reconstruction, 1954), and Chen Cheng, *Land Reform in Taiwan* (Taipei: China Publishing Company, 1961).

7. T.H. Lee, "The Impact of Land Reform on Taiwan's Farm Economy," mimeographed paper, Joint Commission on Rural Reconstruction (JCRR), 1972.

8. Samuel P.S. Ho, *Economic Development in Taiwan 1860-1970* (New Haven: Yale University Press, 1978).

9. T.H. Lee, "Strategies for Transferring Agricultural Surplus under Different Agricultural Situations in Taipei," mimeographed paper, Joint Commission on Rural Reconstruction (JCRR), 1971.

10. Robert C.T. Lee, "Land Consolidation in Taiwan" (paper presented to the Land Consolidation Seminar, Land Reform Institute, Taoyuan, Taiwan, June 1979).

11. The taxable-land categories are paddy field, twenty-six grades; dry land, twenty-six grades; fish pond, nineteen grades; forest land, eight grades; water reservoir, eleven grades; salt field, eighteen grades; mines, fifteen grades; pasture, one grade; wild land, thirty-two grades; construction land, ninety-two grades; miscellaneous land, ninety-two grades.

12. Wei-shin King, "Land Taxes of the Republic of China" (lecture notes, Land Reform Training Institute, Taoyuan, Taiwan, 1976).

13. That is, the land value at the time of reporting. It is sometimes referred to as the value of bare land.

14. Statistical information presented in this section was provided by the Department of Land Administration, Taipei Municipal Government.

15. Information presented in this section was largely obtained from "The Experience of Urban Land Consolidation in Kaohsiung City" (mimeographed pamphlet, Department of Land Administration, Kaohsiung Municipal Government, May 1979).

16. *Yearbook of Tax Statistics, Republic of China* (1978).

Moderator

Arlo Woolery: A study conducted about four years ago commented on the tremendous progress in rural land reform areas where the productivity of the land had increased 227 percent after the land was turned over to the tillers. With 17 million people on a very limited land area, the Chinese in Taiwan have been able to feed their people at a daily caloric consumption of 2,700 calories per capita and still have had food for export. The former landlords were compensated in a manner that was so interesting that it bears retelling.

The landlords were compensated in part for their land in land bonds that were redeemable not in money but in the inflation-proof commodities of the land: rice and sweet potatoes. The payment of the land bonds called for so many tons of rice and so many kilos of sweet potatoes per hectare. As a result, any inflation that might have taken place in the price structure would be indemnified simply through the increment in pricing of the basic commodities. The other part of the landlord compensation came about from shares of stock in the basic industries of Taiwan, which had been owned up to that time by the government. The result was a new generation of capitalists: the landlords who had turned land over to the tenants who now became the new generation of landowners and produced this startling gain in productivity.

Some aspects of the land-value increment tax are worthy of comment. The land-value increment tax has a marginal rate now of 60 percent of the gain over the base year. It previously had brackets running from 20 to 80 percent. These brackets were changed recently to 40 to 60 percent, depending upon the amount of gain over the base year. So what you have here is a realized capital gains tax in which government recaptures up to 60 percent of the gain in price on land. The interesting thing to me was that in the cities that were examined in a recent study in Taiwan, there were budget surpluses (a record our American cities would envy); and the land-value increment tax is generating more revenue to municipalities in Taiwan than is the land-value tax. The land-value tax has an upper rate of 7 percent, depending upon the gains value over the base year.

The land consolidation program in both the rural and the urban areas has been very exciting. In some of the urban areas the landownership was so fragmented there could be up to two hundred different owners of a 1-hectare parcel; this gives you postage-stamp-sized individual ownerships. When these were combined and developed and the original owners were allocated a portion of the developed land and the buildings based upon the value of their initial contribution, there were substantial gains for the individual owners. The municipalities that were able to take compensatory lands for public services were able to recover, with no municipal investment, substantial land for streets, for parks, and for all of the public services. If they had been required to pay market price for these public lands that were acquired, in just the city of Kaohsiung where over 5,000 hectares have been converted under consolidation, the cost to the city would have been about $2 billion.

Also, there has been a provision in the tax structure of Taiwan to tax the unrealized capital gains with the land-value tax, which is an annual capital-value tax with a progressive rate structure of 1.5 to 7 percent. The rate structure is based upon the conformity of use with the land policy guidelines issued by the municipalities and the increment in value over the base year's value. So even though there is no transaction, there is a recovery to government of a portion of the increased value on an annual basis.

5 Major Differences between Developed and Developing Countries in Application of Land Policy Instruments

William S.W. Lim

The task of studying urban land policy instruments in Third World countries is difficult because literature on the subject is scarce and difficult to obtain. Furthermore, there are often wide discrepancies between the laws and legislation and their effective application. I am further restricted by my limited language ability and my not working in academic or research institutions. However, as an architect, urban planner, and development consultant in private practice, I am able to make firsthand contact with developers and many government authorities. This experience has given me invaluable insights into the divergence between declared government intentions and their actual implementation.

For many years, I have been observing and analyzing the dynamics of urban development in the Third World, particularly in the five Asean countries: Indonesia, Malaysia, Philippines, Singapore, and Thailand. (See table 5-1.) It is possible that some of my observations of these countries can have general relevance to other Third World countries.

Table 5-1
Asean Statistics

Country	Area (kilometers)	Population (millions)		Population Growth Rate		Per-Capita GNP (US$)	
Indonesia	1,904,569	138.3	(1970)	2.0	(1979)	130	(1974)
Malaysia	329,749	12.7	(1977)	2.6	(1977)	660	(1975)
Philippines	300,440	46.3	(1976)	2.3	(1976)	332	(1974)
Singapore	616	2.3	(1978)	1.2	(1978)	2,540	(1975)
Thailand	542,373	45.2	(1978)	2.4	(1979)	330	(1974)

Sources: *Asia 1980 Yearbook;* respective embassies; and *Singapore Year Book.*

Existing Urban Land Policy Instruments

Urban land policy instruments cannot operate in a vacuum. Different models based on conditions in developed countries can have only limited applicability even in urban centers of the economically advanced countries.[1] Existing planning theories cannot cope with the changing economic and social conditions. On the other hand, much progress has been made in recent years in analyzing and identifying appropriate laws and legislation, as well as various forms of urban taxation. However, the application of these legal and taxation instruments has rarely taken into consideration their effects on the overall physical urban environment.

With the energy crisis and growing resource limitations, the era of continuous economic growth in developed countries is about to come to a halt, so it is necessary to reexamine the priorities upon which development has been based since the industrial revolution. Consumerism as a way of life must be challenged so that the quality of life of individuals can be improved without escalating the consumption of the limited available resources.

The failure of Western planning theories to provide a satisfactory physical environment, to improve the quality of life, and to increase the mobility of people has now been recognized. Short-term solutions, such as the construction of more highways and the conversion of land for further suburbanization, have only accelerated the environmental deterioration of urban centers. The adaptation of these outdated Western physical planning theories in the urban centers of Third World countries have led to disastrous results. Examples of this can be seen in Manila and Mexico City. It is not feasible to apply existing land policy instruments to the rapidly expanding Third World urban centers, until their conditions can be better understood and alternative planning strategy can be developed.

The issues are clear. Urban land policy instruments can be effective only when the different aspects of the problems can be more fully understood and the obvious contradictions resolved. Sufficient time must be allowed for land policy instruments to be introduced and implemented before results can be seen. Generally results from legal and taxation instruments can be realized in a much shorter time than planning instruments affecting physical planning and building construction. When the urban authorities lack continuity, policy coordination is seriously jeopardized. Singapore's case clearly illustrates that a committed and intelligent political leadership, which has been in power for over two decades, can effectively implement a whole package of policies, especially when these policies are introduced in a pragmatic manner independent of any overall physical-development strategy.[2]

Conditions in Third World Countries

Underdevelopment in Third World countries means far more than just a low average per-capita income. It also means economic dependency on and exploitation by the metropolitan powers, income disparity within the urban centers, and widespread poverty in the rural areas.

The process of urbanization in Third World countries is fundamentally different from the historical experiences of developed countries. Third World countries need an urban strategy that is responsive to their political, economic, social, and cultural conditions. The legitimate demand for a more-balanced development, better income distribution, and basic human needs must be satisfied.[3]

Much effort has been made to identify basic problems relating to rural development. One of the most basic and important land policy instruments is land reform. Land for the tillers is now theoretically acceptable to most governments, and it is no longer a subversive slogan. In some Third World countries, such as China, India, and Formosa, rural land reform has been successfully implemented in varying degrees. Unfortunately, policymakers view urban land very differently. Ownership of and profiteering from the rapid price increases of urban land have become a vital and integral pursuit of the new urban elite in Third World countries.

The improvement of the living and working conditions of the urban poor cannot be achieved without major structural changes and improvement in the rural sector.[4] However, urban bias in Third World countries continues.[5] The poverty in the rural sector accentuates the real and imaginary benefit to be derived from migrating to the urban centers. With this internal migration, unemployment and underemployment become even more serious. The importance of the informal sector in providing millions of jobs must be recognized. However, the informal sector's ability to provide even low-wage employment opportunities has often been extended to its limits.

Inappropriate urban strategies have resulted in gross misuse of limited funds and serious misallocation of available resources. At present, even well-meaning policymakers have to depend on outdated proposals often recommended by foreign consultants and international agencies. Implementation of these proposals has sometimes led to disastrous consequences adversely affecting the urban poor; examples are large-scale clearance of slums and squatter areas and indiscriminate displacement of hawkers and street vendors without providing viable alternatives.

The physical development in the Third World has often attempted to imitate the images provided in the developed countries. This is particularly evident in the major cities where financial, human, and technical resources are concentrated. Road-network and physical infrastructure facilities have been greatly improved. Tall commercial buildings, luxurious residential accommodation, air-conditioned shopping centers, international hotels, and sophisticated cultural and entertainment facilities have been provided. Roads are crowded with private vehicles. Superficially, great progress has been made, and yet the number of slums and squatter dwellers are rapidly increasing. Living conditions of the urban poor are often appalling. Public transportation and personal mobility of the majority have deteriorated. The magnitude of urban problems is often in direct proportion to the economic growth rate, population density, and rural poverty. The environmental crises of many major urban centers in Third World countries are now self-evident.[6]

In Third World countries that have a market economy, the main benefactors of rapid urban growth and infrastructure development are the urban elite, irrespective of the size of the urban centers or the stage of economic development. Furthermore, the benefits are usually obtained at the expense of the majority, particularly the urban poor, as well as the quality of the total urban environment.

Application of Land Policy Instruments

The effectiveness in the application of land policy instruments differs greatly among countries, with the differences generally reflecting the stage of economic development, the extent of urbanization, the political system of government, and the social and cultural values of the society. The possibilities of and constraints in their application are influenced substantially by the financial, human, and technical resources available, the magnitude of the urban problems, the existing physical infrastructure and services, and the quality and commitments of key decision makers, as well as the checking mechanism of opposition parties, the mass media, and citizen pressure groups. It is therefore obvious that there must be considerable differences in applying land policy instruments not only between the development countries and Third World countries but also among the various Third World countries.

In order to successfully develop an overall strategy of urban land policy instruments, it is necessary to integrate ideas from four different disciplines: physical planning, architecture and environment, laws and legislation, and land taxation. To understand the complex nature of urban land policy instruments, we need interaction of these various disciplines. Similarly, their effective implementation calls for coordinated effort from several departments of government.

In developed countries, there is usually effective grass-roots pressure to ensure that the application of urban land policies is initiated for the benefit of the community and for the improvement of the environment and quality of urban life. The effectiveness and failure in the application are well documented, so I will illustrate here some of the major differences where these same policies are applied to Third World countries.

Physical Planning

The first master plan was sponsored and implemented in the 1930s. Since then, most urban centers in developed countries have commissioned master plans. With the assistance of foreign consultants and international agencies, many master plans have also been initiated in Third World countries to regulate traffic and land use, as well as density and intensity of development. In some instances, these master plans have been legally adopted for implementation. Unfortunately, the phenomenal population growth in Third World countries often requires that master plans be changed and modified, often beyond recognition. Furthermore, the outdated assumptions of these master plans inevitably have produced a tremendous drain on the financial, technical, and human resources available. Their selected implementation has provided only cosmetic improvement, often at the expense of the majority of the population.

Another land policy instrument is land-use zoning, which provides for single usage in specified areas. This instrument has greatly disrupted the existing patterns of land use. It has no advantage besides satisfying the clinical approach of Western-trained planners. Traditionally, mixed-land usage has been able to respond more effectively to market demand and to provide accommodation and work opportunities for the urban poor. This multiuse, low-rise, high-density environment is especially conducive to generating employment in the informal sector, such as hawkers and street vendors. These activities are threatened by rapid urban growth, which exerts tremendous pressure to increase the development intensity and to change the usage of land.

Many planning regulations adopted by Third World countries are usually outdated and difficult to implement. The problem is compounded by the acute shortage of competent and committed professionals. Some urban centers have introduced sophisticated Western planning regulations, which gives considerable discretionary powers of implementation to meet different development conditions. Unfortunately this exercise is often counterproductive because it also provides new avenues for bureaucratic obstruction and corruption. Planning regulations should be reexamined from first principles. They must be related to the technical competence available and the social, economic, and cultural environment for effective implementation.

The relationship between land values and planning regulations governing permissible usage and development intensity is now clearly recognized.[7] High-intensity commercial development in central areas has enriched landlords at the expense of displacing millions of urban poor and destroying the bustling life of the traditional central areas. We see examples of this in Singapore, Manila, and Hong Kong. In many urban centers, improvements are made in the road systems and infrastructure facilities, while the public transportation systems continue to deteriorate, adversely affecting the mobility of the majority. The improved infrastructure facilities are usually located in the modern commercial sector and high-income residential areas. The urban poor are fortunate if they can just obtain water supplies and get their sewerage waste and garbage collected.

Architecture and Environment

After World War I, Europe was in a state of shock and despair. A new god, technology, was canonized. It was an act of faith, filled with hope and confidence. Technology and machine aesthetic became its masters. Modern architecture was born, and the visual images of a new world were quickly created. The old environment was destroyed; coexistence was considered impossible.

The idealism of the modern architectural movement of the 1930s has not been realized. The introduction of tall buildings, the acceptance of high-intensity development, and the construction of major road networks have seriously disrupted and even destroyed the traditional character of many central areas of urban centers. Commercialization of modern architecture in the postwar period has substantially contributed to the environmental disaster, particularly in the major urban centers of the developed countries. A bureaucratic-and-establishment international style of architecture soon became entrenched. Eclectic, stylistic, and decorative design approaches were adopted, notwithstanding the growing awareness of the need for multidisciplinary solutions to the increasingly complex urban problems.

Modern architecture is dehumanizing. It only rarely can be understood by or communicate with the majority of people whom it is supposed to serve. This realization has yet to penetrate through to the upper levels of decision makers in both the public and private sectors. Many younger architects, particularly the exponents in the postmodern and postmetabolist movements, have now challenged the visual and environmental contribution of modern architecture, but no viable alternative has yet been developed.[8]

Architects have now lost their pivotal role in shaping the physical environment of urban centers. Often their contributions are restricted to designing buildings within well-defined slots regulated by two-dimensional conceptional guidelines. Opportunities for innovative work is straight-jacketed.

In Third World countries, the architect's ability to influence major policies effecting the urban environment is inadequate. This situation is further constrained by the consulting services provided through various international organizations. Planning reports presented to Third World countries—for example, regarding the planning and implementation of self-help housing, site and service projects, and slum- and squatter-improvement schemes—seldom acknowledge the role of architects and their close relationship with and contribution to the urban environment. This is unfortunate because architecture is the only academic discipline in the planning team that gives major emphasis to three-dimensional visual forms and the aesthetic quality of the built environment.

In urban centers of Third World countries, historical buildings and existing environmental areas are neglected or destroyed; this has happened in Singapore. Canals are sometimes filled up for road improvement; this has happened in Bangkok. Rivers are often polluted. Industries are indiscriminately located. Tall buildings are often constructed as prestige symbols and are believed to be the only means to achieve high-density development. This myth has serious consequences, particularly in low-income housing in Third World countries. If the environmental crisis in urban centers is to be averted, architects must once again be given their appropriate role.

Laws and Legislation

One of the most effective land policy instruments is land-acquisition laws. But such laws can be effective only if the authorities exercising them have adequate power and sufficient financial resources to acquire land for public purposes. There are considerable differences among Third World countries in the powers given to implement land acquisition. The basis of compensation also varies greatly.

Some Third World countries have introduced comprehensive legislation to acquire land. In some instances, fragmented land from the private sector has also been acquired to permit more-comprehensive development by the public sector or reassignment to the private sector under specific conditions. In Singapore, this exercise has been in operation for over a decade. Prime urban land is auctioned for private-sector development, with specific usages, size, and completion time schedule specified.[9] It has been very successful in stimulating building-investment activities and in reducing the rising land prices in a rapidly expanding economy. Land sales for private development can be a major means to raise revenue; for example, the projected revenue in 1980 from land sales in Hong Kong is about US$1 billion.[10]

Compensation at market value is often a major deterrent for authorities to acquire land even for essential public usage. Tougher measures are needed in Third World countries because financial resources are limited. It is arguable whether landlords should receive compensation based on market value because rapid urban growth and improvement to infrastructure facilities have inevitably resulted in phenomenal rises of land cost in Third World countries. In the 1960s and 1970s in Singapore, the value of prime commercial land increased about fourteen times and prime residential land about eight times (based on converted value of U.S. curency).

Investment and speculation in urban land is profitable. These activities are permitted even in countries that have implemented meaningful rural land reform. The close relationship between landlords and key decision makers has usually prevented the adoption of tough land legislation. Land conversion, particularly from agriculture to urban usage, is often granted to those closely connected with key policymakers. There is a conversion tax in some countries, although the surcharge may be nominal or bargainable. Considerable profit can be made especially from the conversion of agriculture land to urban usage. Ample opportunities are created for corrupt practices, especially when checking mechanisms are ineffective and public opinion is strictly controlled.

Escalation of land prices and the inability to acquire land for public purposes are major deterrents to effective implementation and improvement of the urban environment. Unless land is socialized or at least placed under much stricter control, landowners will continue to make enormous profits at the expense of the community as a whole. In many Third World countries, reactionary governments may even adopt apparently socially progressive legislation, realizing the inability of the civil service to implement them effectively.

The concern for health and safety in the substandard accommodation of slums and squatters is understandable and commendable. However, when these improved standards are implemented in Third World countries, they lead to the demolition of these premises without first providing viable alternative accommodation. This inexcusable remedy has been widely applied in many countries. Even as a temporary measure, we need to introduce appropriate legislation to protect the occupational rights of the urban poor living in slums and in squatter areas.[11] Otherwise efforts to improve the physical facilities and environment of the urban poor are meaningless.

The historical central areas of many urban centers in Third World countries have suffered severe destruction as a result of rapid economic growth and population explosion. The importance of historical conservation is only beginning to be realized. Effective legislation has seldom been introduced or implemented. Conservation of historical buildings and environment is often considered to be sentimental and obstructive to national development objectives.

Land Taxation

There are great differences in the rates and methods of property tax on land and buildings in urban centers of Third World countries. In most instances, the rates are unrealistically low. There is usually no regular reassessment because of administrative incompetence and the acute shortage of valuers. Furthermore, corrupt practices have often resulted in gross undervaluation. This situation has seriously eroded collectable revenue.

Increase of density and plot ratio, as well as change of use, can generate substantial revenue for the users, especially in the fast-expanding major urban centers. Recently Singapore has imposed a tough surcharge rate of 70 percent on the increased land value arising from change of use. (See tables 5-2 through 5-4). However, this is an exception. In most Third World coun-

Table 5-2
Commercial Land Values in Singapore
(Singapore dollars per square foot)

Year	Robinson Road	North Bridge Road	Orchard Road	Shenton Way	Raffles Place
1962	25	125	7	15	100
1963	35	150	30	25	150
1964	50	200	40	30	250
1965	50	150	25	25	200
1966	50	150	30	25	200
1967	75	150	30	30	250
1968	100	175	40	75	300
1969	150	200	25	100	350
1970	250	250	150	150	400
1971	350	300	200	200	500
1972	500	350	250	300	600
1973	700	400	400	500	800
1974	690	390	390	490	790
1975	650	370	370	460	750
1976	615	352	352	442	714
1977	588	338	338	427	684
1978	688	385	385	485	785
1979	805	455	455	570	920

Source: Philip Motha, Department of Building and Estate Management, University of Singapore.

Note: The currency conversion of Singapore dollars to U.S. dollars is difficult because of the devaluation of the U.S. dollar. Between 1967 and 1971, US $1 = S$3.30 (approximately); in 1973, US $1 = S$2.50; in June 1975, US $1 = S$2.25; and in May 1980, US $1 = S$2.16.

Table 5-3
Residential Land Values in Singapore
(Singapore dollars per square foot)

Year	Katong	Stevens	Holland	Pasir Panjang Road	Geylang Road
1962	4	3	2	2	4
1963	6	4	4	3	6
1964	8	6	8	5	10
1965	5	5	6	4	6
1966	6	5	6	4	6
1967	7	5	7	4	7
1968	7	5	8	5	8
1969	10	8	10	8	10
1970	12	10	12	9	12
1971	15	15	15	10	15
1972	20	25	25	12	20
1973	25	35	30	20	25
1974	23	33	28	19	24
1975	21	31	27	18	22
1976	20	29	26	17	21
1977	19	27	25	16	20
1978	18	26	24	15	19
1979	25	35	30	20	25

Source: Ibid.

tries, the surcharge imposed is insignificant. Furthermore, the legislation is often ambiguous and the surcharge is likely to be bargainable.

Few countries have effective capital gains tax legislation on land and buildings. Profits derived from land and buildings are taxable only in the usual course of business under income-tax laws. This has provided many opportunities for tax avoidance in the investment and speculation of land. Property-development companies and individual landowners are able to avoid tax by separating the legal identity of each transaction and using other, even-more-dubious devices. In short, the absence of capital gains tax has added to the windfall profits arising from rapid land-price escalation.

In Third World countries, the opportunity to use tax devices to obtain substantial revenue for financing urban development is usually not fully exploited. The ineffectiveness of the collection of land and property taxes reflects the character and orientation of the political power structure. The political will to extract this source of revenue is lacking because of the high concentration of political and economic power, the dominance of a powerful urban and military elite, a lack of grass-roots pressure and participation, and a strict control of the mass media and the underprivileged.

Table 5-4
Industrial Land Values in Singapore
(Singapore dollars per square foot)

Year	Bukit Timah Road	Macpherson	Alexandra
1962	3	3	3
1963	5	4	5
1964	7	6	7
1965	5	5	5
1966	5	5	5
1967	5	5	5
1968	7	7	8
1969	10	10	11
1970	12	12	13
1971	15	15	17
1972	20	20	22
1973	30	30	35
1974	30	30	33
1975	29	29	32
1976	28	28	31
1977	27	27	30
1978	28	28	29
1979	32	32	34

Source: Ibid.

Conclusion

Land policy instruments are powerful tools for the achievement of a wide range of political, economic, and social objectives. There are major differences in their application between developed and Third World countries. With proper land-use planning, government can regulate land usage and intensity of development within the overall planning strategy. With committed and competent architects in key positions, the quality of the urban environment can be greatly improved. With implementable laws and legislation, corruption can be minimized. With effective land taxation, government can recoup a substantial share of the benefits from increased value of land and property. However, irresponsible politicians are usually able to manipulate these same tools to benefit themselves and their influential supporters at the expense of the community at large, particularly the urban poor. It is therefore necessary to identify the real development objectives of policymakers before assessing the effectiveness of the land policy instruments adopted.

The limitation of financial, human, and technical resources may restrict development options, but many effective actions can still be taken to resolve urgent existing problems. However, the influence and self-interest of the urban elite, including in many instances the military elite, cannot be easily discounted. Corruption is directly related to the payoff system of the political structure. When corruption escalates beyond certain limits, it nullifies many of the efforts to improve conditions for the majority, especially the underprivileged.

The close interrelationship of physical planning, architecture and environment, laws and legislation, and land taxation must be recognized. Urban land policy instruments cannot be effectively introduced without an overall alternative strategy for urban development. This is particularly true for Third World countries. An alternative development strategy for low-resource urban centers must be adopted.[12] Efforts by professionals and academics are urgently needed. However, no solution can be achieved without a major restructuring and the introduction of socially committed priorities in order to obtain for the millions of urban poor in the Third World a fair share of benefits from the painful process of economic development and rapid social change.

Notes

1. Haim Darin-Drabkin, *Land Policy and Urban Growth* (New York: Pergamon Press, 1977); World Bank, *Urban Land Policy Issues and Opportunities*, World Bank Staff Working Paper 283 (Washington, D.C.: World Bank, 1978), vols. 1-2.

2. William S.W. Lim and Philip Motha, "Land Policy in Singapore," in *An Alternative Urban Strategy* (Singapore: DP Architects (Pte)., 1980), pp. 159-168.

3. T. Mulya Lubis and Fauzi Abdullah, eds., *Annual Report on Fundamental Human Rights in Indonesia 1979* (Jakarta, Indonesia: Lembaga Bantuan Hukum, 1979); Soedjatmoko, "National Policy Implications of the Basic Needs Model," Seminar on "Implications of the Basic Needs Model." (The Hague, February 24, 1978).

4. Gelia T. Castillo, *Beyond Manila: Philippine Rural Problems in Perspective* (Ottawa: International Development Research Centre, 1979).

5. Michael Lipton, *Why Poor People Stay Poor: A Study of Urban Bias in World Development* (London: Temple Smith, 1977).

6. William S.W. Lim, "The Impending Urban Crisis—with Special Reference to Developing Countries," in *Equity and Urban Environment in the Third World* (Singapore: DP Consultant Service Pte. Ltd., 1975), pp. 163-185.

7. Nathaniel Lichfield, "Land Values and Planning: A Common Interest of Land Policy and Land Taxation," *Urban Law and Policy* 2 (June 1979):111-131.

8. Charles A. Jencks, *The Language of Post-Modern Architecture*, rev. and enlarged ed. (London: Academy Editions, 1978); Michael Franklin Ross et al., *Beyond Metabolism: The New Japanese Architecture* (New York: McGraw-Hill, 1978).

9. Singapore, Urban Redevelopment Authority, *Annual Report 1978/79* (Singapore, 1979); Singapore, Housing and Development Board, *Annual Report 1978/79* (Singapore, 1979).

10. "Land Sales to Swell Coffers by Massive $5b," *South China Morning Post* (Hong Kong), February 28, 1980.

11. Amendment to Planning Act, chap. 279 of the revised edition, Acts Supplement No. 2, February 1, 1980, Planning (Development Charges) Rules, 1980, S29/80, pp. 91-100 (Singapore: Singapore National Printers).

12. William S.W. Lim, "An Alternative Development Strategy for Urban Centres in the Third World," in *An Alternative Urban Strategy*, pp. 3-20.

Urbanization and Counterurbanization: The Future of World Metropolitan Areas in the 1980s

Brian J.L. Berry

Coming hard on the heels of Mr. Lim's condemnation of conventional wisdom in the international planning community, I am at a loss as to whether to begin by countering his equally conventional uses of dependency theory. Certainly we should all be quite careful about rushing to substitute for the problems of efficiency-led growth the equally debilitating problems of a walled-off autonomy that ensures only the equality of common poverty. Nor should we be too ready to substitute for sophisticated Western concepts the second best, or worse, simply because an existing cadre of bureaucrats finds them to be more easily implemented. Quality results demand hard work, imagination, and both the flexibility and willingness to change.

If current policies are so bankrupt, one should ask what the alternatives are. It is to the emergence of creative alternatives that I turn. In listening to what I have to say, be aware of my underlying premise: that urban form simply mirrors the human and natural forces that both drive and constrain societies and economies.

It should be with the greatest humility that anyone talks about urban futures, for what was conventional wisdom less than a decade ago has been found wanting in developed and developing countries alike. Those of us from the United States should recall that it was only a decade ago, in 1970, that we applauded a Housing and Urban Development Act, which said in its preamble that

> the rapid growth of urban population and uneven expansion of urban development in the United States, together with a decline in farm population, slower growth in rural areas, and migration to the cities, has created an imbalance between the Nation's needs and resources and seriously threatens our physical environment. . . . The Congress . . . declares that the national urban growth policy should—favor patterns of urbanization and economic development and stabilization which offer a range of alternative locations . . . help reverse trends of migration and physical growth . . . treat comprehensively the problems of poverty and employment . . . associated with disorderly urbanization and rural decline.[1]

Yet less than ten years later a new president's White House staff prepared an urban policy stating that

> three major patterns of population change can be traced in the Nation today: migration from the northeastern and north central regions of the country to the south and west; the slower growth of metropolitan areas and the movement from them to small towns and rural areas; and movement from central cities to suburbs. . . . Today's widespread population loss in the Nation's central cities is unprecedented . . . the thinning out process has left many people and places with severe economic and social problems, and without the resources to deal with them. . . . Our policies must reflect a balanced concern for people and places . . . to achieve several broad goals: [to] preserve the heritage and values of our older cities; maintain the investment in our older cities and their neighborhoods; assist newer cities in confronting the challenges of growth and pockets of poverty . . . and provide improved housing, job opportunities and community services to the urban poor, minorities, and women. . . . If the Administration is to help cities revitalize neighborhoods, eliminate sprawl, support the return of the middle class to central cities, and improve the housing conditions of the urban poor it must increase the production of new housing and rehabilitation of existing housing for middle class groups in cities. . . . We should favor proposals supporting: (1) compact community development over scattered, fragmented development; and (2) revitalization over new development.[2]

Fewer among us may be aware that in 1974, 1976, and again in 1979 United Nations statistical analysts significantly reduced their expectations as to Third World urban growth. Thus, investigators using U.N. estimates of 1974 and earlier generally concurred with Renaud's conclusion that

> the rate of urbanization of developing countries is much faster then what has been experienced historically by the developed countries. . . . This very rapid rate of urbanization applies to populations that are still growing extremely rapidly at rates that are often two or three times the rates experienced by the advanced economies.[3]

On the other hand, those experimenting with the 1979 U.N. materials conclude otherwise:

> The empirical evidence thus seems to indicate that . . . the process of urbanization has been slower than the historical pattern of today's more developed nations, and that the association between it and economic growth seems to have been running counter to the one posited by the "overurbanization" theorists.[4]

Old theories and not-so-old forecasts clearly have been found wanting. Throughout the world, the city appears to be approaching a climacteric in its history, but there is little agreement as to what is about to happen. Some see in the West a withering away of the city, to be followed by its total obsolescence by the early twenty-first century. Others predict the emergence of new settlement patterns that will constitute the full flowering of five millennia of urban evolution. Meanwhile, in the developing countries the most common prediction is of the emergence of metropolitan areas at a scale not yet experienced. But whatever the interpretation, it is clear that the nature and tempo of urbanization changed dramatically throughout the world during the 1970s, running counter to most of the forecasts made at the beginning of the decade.

Counterurbanization Defined: The U.S. Case

"Urbanization," wrote Hope Tisdale, "is a process of population concentration. It proceeds in two ways: the multiplication of the points of concentration and the increase in size of individual concentrations. . . . It implies a movement from a state of less concentration to a state of more concentration."[5] The process is far from smooth; there have been and are today great variations in the tempo.

A useful indicator of the tempo of urbanization is the difference between the average annual growth rates of the urban and the total population, $R(u) - R(t)$.[6] This measure separates the changing ratio of urban to total population (urbanization) from mere increase in numbers (urban growth), and it displays both characteristic long-term changes and cyclical variations.

In the United States, for example, the long-term trend was one of acceleration to a mid-nineteenth-century peak of some 6 percent annually as the country was settled and an active process of town formation unfolded. This has been followed by a steady decline as the urban proportion has increased.[7] (See figure 6-1.) Superimposed on the long-term trend are the marked consequences of cyclical perturbations that reduced the tempo to zero in the decades 1810-1820 and 1930-1940 and halved it in the period 1870-1880. Today, however, it is the long-term trend that has reduced the tempo to zero.

Precursors of this new situation have been with us for some time. The nation's rural population has stabilized. Population gains in exurban counties and more-distant areas are now outpacing gains in metropolitan counties (not just, as heretofore, in the centers of cities). More people now live in the suburban rings surrounding metropolitan areas than in either the centers of cities or in nonmetropolitan areas. The most-active new growth is occurring in remote regions beyond the orbit of any metropolitan area. The great metropolises are turning themselves inside out, and to the extent that urban areas are growing, they are smaller places in nonmetropolitan America. (See figure 6-2.) Many investigators now argue that the demographic shifts since 1970 have been profound enough to represent a clean

Note: *Tempo* is defined as the difference between the average annual growth rate of the urban population, *R(u)*, and the average annual growth rate of the total population, *R(t)*.

Figure 6-1. Tempo of U.S. Urbanization

break with the past.[8] To highlight the difference, I coined the term *counterurbanization* for what has been happening, defining it in the style of Tisdale as "a process of population deconcentration; a movement from a state of more concentration to a state of less concentration."[9]

More than mere demographics are involved, however, and if we can understand the additional factors involved, we can gain insight into the emerging settlement patterns. Most importantly, the traditional core-periphery organization of the national economy has been eliminated by a combination of developments in transportation, communications, and industrial technologies and related shifts in individual preferences for locations and life-styles. The classic regional organization of the national economy was one of a core region, the northeastern industrial belt, linked to a constellation of resource-dependent hinterland regions by rail and water-transportation routes radiating from gateway cities and growing as a

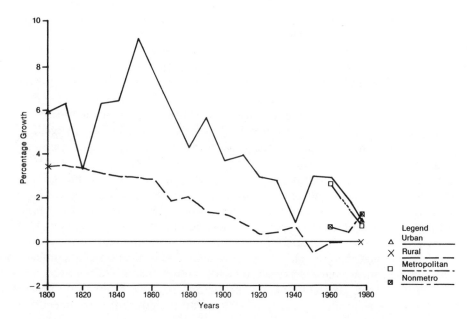

Figure 6-2. Long-term Changes in the Rates of Urban- and Rural-
Population Growth in the United States

result of a process of circular and cumulative causation. Clustering of
activities in the heartland's industrial cities promoted increasing returns, a
result of the internal and external economies present in centers of
agglomeration, and resulted in regional income and opportunity differences
that so swamped the cheaper factor prices of the periphery that they produced continuously disequilibrating flows of labor and capital from the
poor hinterland regions to the rich and growing heartlands. Greater supplies
of high-quality labor, entrepreneurial skills, and capital in their turn maintained the great cities of the manufacturing belt as the centers of innovation
and growth. Peripheral regions could grow only at the demand of the
heartland, as its requirements for their raw materials and foodstuffs expanded, or if standardized industries were filtered to cheap labor supplies
elsewhere.

Today this classic regionalization no longer exists. The glue of centrality
that restricted innovative new developments to the core cities of the industrial heartland has been dissolved. Regions throughout the nation are
sharing in the newer forms of employment growth. Transportation
improvements and new forms of communication have virtually eliminated
the classic localizing effects of transportation inputs and the significance of
proximity in speedy transmission of new ideas and practices. The nation's

rapid-growth industries are dispersed throughout the former exurban, nonmetropolitan, and sunbelt peripheries, and they are being followed by the postindustrial management and control functions of the private sector. From the mid-1960s to mid-1970s, these latter functions, together with finance, insurance, real estate, and the like, supported a downtown office boom in the nation's twenty or so international trading centers and regional capitals, but even for these activities the exurbs and/or medium-sized sunbelt metropolitan areas now provide the greater pull. What has emerged, in effect, is a national space economy that transcends the regional organization that emerged in the early industrial revolution. Indeed, in the new order of locational choice, decisions increasingly are being made not simply on a national map but by multifirm, multiproduct, multinational conglomerates whose view of the relative merits of alternative locations is played out in global frameworks in which traditional location factors are compared with new arrays of variables, including environmental attributes and the dictates of international finance. The scale of decisions has changed, and the radii of interdependence have increased, together with the relative importance in locational choice of traditional access factors, negative externalities perceived to be concentrated in high-density central cities, and new amenity variables.

To illustrate the last point at a different level, let us consider the forces working upon the mobility, migration, and locational choice of individual Americans. In all urban-industrial countries, a certain minimum amount of geographical mobility is a structured part of the life cycle, with the greatest rates occurring at the stage when young adults leave the parental home and establish an independent household soon after formal schooling is completed. Continuing occupational mobility produces further shifts as individuals follow their career trajectories, while life-cycle changes such as marriage, child rearing, and retirement produce home-related relocations. During the years that the baby-boom cohort moved into its most-mobile period, the growing numbers employed by national and multinational corporations found themselves confronted by the formalization of career trajectories in corporate-job-dictated transfers and the accompanying suggestion to relocatees of the appropriateness of particular residential areas. To meet the needs of these relocatees, nationwide real estate companies developed, specializing in the art of moving families from one region to another without disturbing their life-styles, or changing it only to the extent warranted by the transfer-related promotions. Several results emerged. There now are growing groups of *national* citizens whose ties are to peer groups that share common job experiences and life-styles located in particular kinds of communities within every region of the nation. Interests are shared in common across these communities, and, linked by the interchange of migration, such life-style communities are closer to each other in perception and attitudes than they are to geographically contiguous neighborhoods offering alternative life-styles to different population subgroups, especiallly blue-collar "locals" who are far more place bound. Each region in the nation now offers a common and increasing array of life-style communities so that on the one hand interregional differentiation has diminished while on the other intraregional segmentation has increased. In short, there is now a national system of settlement that mirrors the divisions in the national society.

The increase in the array of life-styles comes from opposing but inter-related trends. National interdependence, increasingly tightly woven by more-potent forms of communication, has brought with it countervailing tendencies for particular subgroups to assert their independent identities or for new subcultures to try to invent one. The lesson that the new communications media could be instrumental in the process of social activation was first learned in civil rights and has been used most effectively by the environmentalists. The result is that there is now increasing pluralism based upon various forms of subcultural intensification: racial, ethnic, life cycle (swingles, gentrifiers, the elderly "snow-birds" and so on), and based upon a range of other types of preferences, such as hippie, or homosexual. This intensification has been possible because of the exposure afforded by nationwide communications. Each group can exist because it can establish its separate identity not only by an internal process of self-definition but also through comparative perceptions created by the communications media. Because of the potency of the media, there is now a nationwide im-agery that transcends locality and a speed and commonality of subgroup response that negates older leads and lags of metropolis-centered dependency. No longer does a new idea, fashion, or fad appear in the big city and play itself out twenty years later in the rural periphery. Time-space convergence has produced a differentiated but highly interconnected national society and economy. Growth of peripheries and decline of traditional cores—counterurbanization—is but a reflection of an essential accompaniment of this convergence, a national settlement system.

Looking backward in 1899, Adna Weber concluded that "the most remarkable social phenomenon of the [nineteenth] century is the concentration of population in cities. . . . The tendency toward concentration or agglomeration is all but universal in the Western World."[10] Looking forward in 1902 H.G. Wells believed he could sense something quite different about to unfold, however:

> These giant cities will reach their maximum in the [twentieth] century. In all probability they are destined to such a process of dissection and diffusion as to amount almost to obliteration within a measurable further space of years. These coming cities will not be, in the old sense, cities at all; they will present a new and entirely different phase of human distribution. . . . The

> city will diffuse itself until it has taken up considerable areas and many of the characteristics of what is now country. . . . The country will take itself many of the qualities of the city. The old antithesis will cease, the boundary lines will altogether disappear.[11]

It has taken a full three-quarters of a century for Wells's predictions to come true, but they are now a reality. Counterurbanization has replaced urbanization as the dominant process shaping U.S. settlement patterns, and a new and different tempo of change has emerged.

Other Developed Countries

Similar tendencies have been noted by other investigators in many other developed countries.[12] The overall rate of urban growth is slowing down as natural increase slackens and rural-to-urban migration decreases or even reverses. Older central cities and larger core metropolitan regions are seeing the onset of absolute decline, and growth is concentrated in small towns in rural peripheries.[13] To quote Vining and his associates, "The century-long migration towards the high density core regions is over."[14]

Examining internal migration statistics for twenty countries, covering the period 1950-1978, these same investigators concluded that three distinct categories of countries can be distinguished: those whose core regions have experienced a decline in net migration over the entire period and are now experiencing net out-migration and commensurate inner-city and older-metropolitan area decline (Belgium, Denmark, France, the Netherlands, and West Germany); those in which there was an increase in net migration toward the core regions during the 1950s and the 1960s, followed by a sharp decline in the 1970s, though not to the point where a sustained flow of population away from the core region has been observed even though particular metropolitan areas and many central cities may be declining (Canada, Finland, Iceland, Italy, Japan, Norway, Spain, Sweden, and the United Kingdom); and those where migration toward the core regions has yet to show a systematic decline—largely the socialist states of Eastern Europe and newly industrializing countries in Asia (Czechoslovakia, East Germany, Hungary, Poland, South Korea, and Taiwan).

The distinguishing feature of the countries in the first category, according to Vining, is that their less-urbanized, peripheral regions offer sites for urban and industrial development that are competitive with those of the core regions. Population losses from these peripheral regions in the past were due to the agglomeration advantages of the more densely populated core regions, advantages that appear now to be much weaker or absent altogether. In contrast to the countries of category 1, the peripheral regions of the countries of the second category, according to the tentative thesis put forward by Vining, offer fewer competitive sites for industrial and urban development because of fundamental deficiencies in their peripheries.[15] Thus, despite the disappearance of the agglomeration advantages of the core regions, a sustained flow of population away from these regions has yet to be observed. Finally, the countries of the third category, according to our hypothesis, are those in which diseconomies of further agglomeration in the core regions have yet to appear due to a lower level of economic development; these are countries in which industrialization and urbanization are taking place.

Developing World Expectations

What emerges from these observations is a strong hypothesis that goes beyond the traditional view of the interrelatedness of urbanization and economic development that is summarized in figure 6-3, derived from the World Bank's Urbanization Sector working paper of June 1972.[16] In that document, the bank's staff concluded that the relationship is essentially logistic, with low-level preindustrial urbanization levels of 10 percent or less followed by acceleration of urban growth during takeoff, a gradual leveling off of the urbanization rate as the economy matures, and establishment of a new equilibrium at levels in excess of 75 percent.[17] But from the developed world's recent experience, we learn that traditional centers of agglomeration do not stabilize at the higher level. Many major metropolitan regions are now losing population, and in several cases (Canada and the United Kingdom) the urbanization ratio has actually declined since 1970.

What, then, of the developing countries? Recall the U.N. estimates dating from the early 1970s (table 6-1). From these estimates, investigators at the World Bank have confidently argued that:

By the year 2000 over half the world's population is likely to be living in urban areas.

The features of contemporary urbanization in developing countries differ markedly from those of historical experience. Whereas urbanization in the industrialized countries took many decades, permitting a gradual emergence of economic, social, and political institutions to deal with the problems of transformation, the process in developing countries is occurring far more rapidly against a background of higher population growth, lower incomes, and fewer opportunities for international migration.

Between 1950 and 1975, the urban areas of developing countries absorbed some 400 million people; between 1975 and 2000, the increase will be close to 1 billion people.

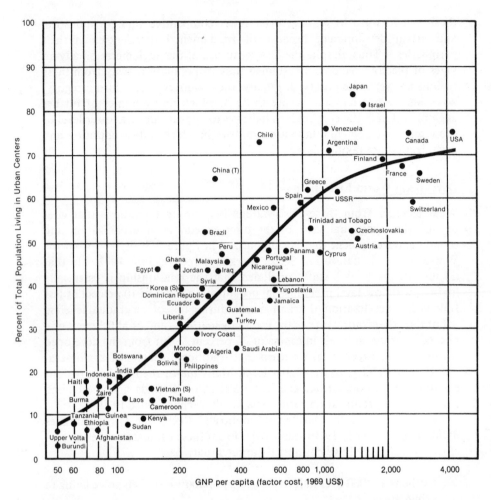

Sources:
1. GNP per capita—World Bank Atlas, 1971.
2. Urban Area Population—Kingsley Davis. World Urbanization 1950-1970, Vol. 1, University of California, Berkeley, 1969. Definition of "urban" is based on differing national standards.

Source: World Bank, *Sector Working Paper: Urbanization* (Washington, D.C.: The World Bank, 1972), p. 73. Reprinted with permission.

Note: Curve fitted to type $y = \dfrac{a}{1 + be^{(\log GNP)}}$

Figure 6-3. Degree of Urbanization Compared with GNP per Capita

The rate of urban population growth is expected to remain three to four times as high as the urban growth rates of the industrialized countries in this period.

Table 6-1
Urbanization Rates and Urban Population Growth, 1950-2000

	Urban Population as Percentage of Total Population			Average Annual Percentage Growth of Urban Population		
	1950	1975	2000	1950-1960	1970-1980	1990-2000
Developing countries	20.6	31.1	45.8	4.0	4.0	3.5
Industrialized countries	62.4	74.4	83.6	2.0	1.2	0.8
Capital surplus oil exporters	16.9	55.5	77.9	7.9	7.1	3.1
Centrally planned economies	20.7	34.4	49.2	5.2	2.7	2.4
World	29.0	39.3	51.5	3.5	2.8	2.6

Source: Data from United Nations estimates.

The number of very large cities in the developing world is expanding rapidly. In 1950, only one city in these countries (greater Buenos Aires) had a population of over 5 million, while five cities in the industrialized countries had reached or exceeded that size. By the year 2000, the developing world will have about forty cities of or above this size, compared with only twelve in the industrialized countries. Eighteen cities in developing countries are expected to have more than 10 million inhabitants, and one at least—Mexico City—may well have triple this number.

These assertions should be qualified on many grounds. First, the decline in rates of natural increase has been more rapid than most observers predicted only a few years ago. Second, many of the accompaniments of urbanization in the West appear not to be occurring in today's developing countries.[18] For example, extended kin groups appear not to be disintegrating into age-segregated nuclear families to the same degree. Moreover, migration appears to be attenuating as the phenomenon of circulation increases. Circulation takes place within kin groups that maintain multiple bases of residency and occupation, both rural and urban, traditional and modern, and it involves the cycling of family members between town and country, not their movement from one to the other. Indeed if counterurbanization in the West is eliminating the dichotomy between city and country that emerged during the process of industrialization there, creative coping by family groups and by others in the developing countries may lead to new forms of spatial organization that render valueless the forecasts of the doomsayers with their semilogarithmic graph papers and straight-edged rulers. There is no reason, for example, to expect that the massive scale of the largest cities that has been forecasted will in fact unfold. If we want to learn from the most recent Western experience, size

Six

and concentration do appear to have their limits, and at these limits new forces emerge that fashion new settlement systems reflecting new orders of national interdependence, new economics of location, and new modes of sociospatial organization.

Notes

1. Housing and Urban Development Act of 1970, Public Law 91-609, 84 Stat. 1791; 42 U.S.C. 4501, title VII, sec. 702.

2. Urban and Regional Policy Group, *A New Partnership to Conserve America's Communities. A National Urban Policy* (March 1978).

3. Bertrand M. Renaud, *National Urbanization Policies in Developing Countries*, World Bank Staff Working Paper No. 347 (Washington, D.C.: The World Bank, 1979), pp. 3-4. Reprinted with permission.

4. Jacques Ledent and Andrei Rogers, *Migration and Urbanization in the Asian Pacific*, IIASA Working Paper WP-79-51 (Laxenburg, Austria: International Institute for Applied Systems Analysis, 1979), p. 28. Reprinted with permission.

5. Hope Tisdale, "The Process of Urbanization," *Social Forces* 20 (1942):311-316.

6. E. Arriaga, "Selected Measures of Urbanization," in S. Goldstein and D. Sly, eds., *The Measurement of Urbanization and Projection of Urban Population* (Liege, Belgium: International Union for the Scientific Study of Population (IUSSP), 1975).

7. The percentage of U.S. population living in urban areas was 5.14 percent in 1790, 15.28 percent in 1850, 39.62 percent in 1900, 63.09 percent in 1950, and 73.44 percent in 1970. The tempo is, by definition, zero when the urban percentage is 100.0.

8. D.R. Vining, Jr., and A. Strauss, "A Demonstration That the Current Deconcentration of Population in the United States Is a Clean Break with the Past," *Environment and Planning A* 9 (1977):751-758; Andrew J. Sofranko, "Motivations Underlying the 'Rural Renaissance' in the Midwest," *Planning and Public Policy* 6 (1980):1-4.

9. Brian J.L. Berry, *Urbanization and Counter-Urbanization* (Beverly Hills, Calif.: Sage Publications, 1976), p. 17.

10. Adna Weber, *The Growth of Cities in the Nineteenth Century* (New York: Macmillan, 1899).

11. H.G. Wells, *Anticipations: The Reaction of Mechanical and Scientific Progress on Human Life and Thought* (London: Harper and Row, 1902). For an extended discussion of Weber and Wells, see Brian J.L. Berry, *The Human Consequences of Urbanization* (London: Macmillan, 1973).

12. See, for example, the papers in Berry, *Urbanization*.

13. Ira M. Robinson, *Canadian Urban Growth Trends: Implications for a National Settlement Policy* (Vancouver, B.C.: Centre for Human Settlements, University of British Columbia, 1980).

14. Daniel R. Vining, Jr., Robert L. Pallane, and Chung Hsin Yang, "Population Dispersal from Core Regions: A Description and Tentative Explanation of the Patterns in 20 Countries," Working Paper in Regional Science and Transportation (University of Pennsylvania, 1980). See also Vining and T. Contruly, "Population Dispersal from Major Metropolitan Regions: An International Comparison," *International Regional Science Review* 3 (1978):49-73. For addenda and corrections, see *IRSR* 3 (1978): 182, and ibid., 4 (1979):181-182.

15. But see Peter Hall and Dennis Hay, *Growth Centers in the European Urban System* (Berkeley: University of California Press, 1980).

16. World Bank, *Sector Working Paper: Urbanization* (Washington, D.C.: The World Bank, June 1972), p. 73.

17. Fitting a somewhat different logistic curve to the World Bank data, Ledent and Rogers, *Migration*, give an upper equilibrium level of 85 percent.

18. For a discussion of these consequences, see Brian J.L. Berry, *The Human Consequences of Urbanization* (Basingstoke, U.K.: Macmillan, 1973).

7 Introduction to Workshops

Arlo Woolery,
Ramon Casanova,
Neal Roberts,
Pierre Laconte,
Oliver Oldman,
Fran Hosken,
Darshan Johal,
Harold Dunkerley,
Ann Louise Strong,
and *John Montgomery*

Arlo Woolery: Some of the remarks that Professor Berry just made remind me of a turn-of-the-century American humorist who said, "It isn't so much what we don't know that hurts us; it's all the things we know that ain't so." I think that what Dr. Berry has pointed out is that there is a certain danger in a straight linear extrapolation, and there comes a time when the asymptote becomes an inflection point.

Workshop 1: Achieving Effective Systems of Land Cadastres, Evaluation, and Title Registration

We have nine workshop chairmen, each of whom will give a brief summary of what the workshops will cover.

Ramon Casanova: I am the director of the Bureau of Lands in the Philippines. I am not necessarily a geodesic engineer or a cartographer; I am a lawyer by profession. So I cannot claim expertise in the field of geodesy or cartography. Nevertheless, maybe I can share with you some of my experiences in my work as director of the Bureau of Lands, especially insofar as this concerns surveying and cartography.

This is not the first time that problems and issues about land cadastres, land evaluation, and land-title registration will be discussed in an international forum. The United Nations Conference on Human Settlements that was held in Vancouver, Canada, in 1976 called attention to survey plans, charts, and maps as one of the most effective means of communication among citizen groups, government authorities, and multidisciplinary groups at all stages in the creation and development of human settlements. Therefore it was urged that governments at all levels—national, regional, provincial, city, municipal—accelerate the exploration, investigation, charting, and mapping of land resources in order to gather, organize, and make available to planners all kinds of land information. This group also urged governments to modernize land-related information systems through computerized land-data banks and automated cartographic land information-retrieval systems.

Before that a conference was held in Bogotá, Colombia, among Pan-American countries on the subject of integrated surveys and the development of countries. During this conference it was generally accepted that lack of modern and effective cadastral systems is the cause of many serious economic and social evils. This problem has also surfaced in several U.N. regional conferences on cartography and remote sensing. Now here we are again, discussing the same problem.

Dr. Peñalosa has urged that governments act immediately, but perhaps many have not been able to act immediately because certain basic issues regarding the concept and application of land cadastre, land evaluation, and land registration remain unresolved. Our workshop, therefore, will try to focus its attention on these basic problems and issues regarding land cadastre, land evaluation, and land-title registration.

As chairpersons of these workshops, we have been asked to identify at least five issues that are related to these subjects. The first one that immediately occurred to me is that of concept. I know that *cadastral survey* means different things in different-countries. In some countries the concept of cadastral survey is limited to what we call legal or juridical cadastre, which means that it is a means of surveying or mapping land for land-titling purposes only. To some other countries, it has fiscal implications—to be used as a means of improving the fiscal-management capability of the government. In other countries, it is used as a method for gathering all other kinds of information related to land. Thus I think that the first issue that the workshop should discuss is the concept of cadastral surveys. Maybe this would be a good occasion for representatives from different countries to come forward with their own concepts of cadastral survey and then try to arrive at certain common denominators or common elements from these definitions.

Dr. Peñalosa expressed his frustration stemming from the fact that although the United Nations has repeatedly urged countries and governments to introduce new measures to improve land policies, it seems that only very few countries have responded positively. We should discuss why these countries have that lukewarm attitude toward the adoption of modern methods of cadastral survey.

Workshop 2: Public-Land Ownership

Neal Roberts: I think I probably was chosen to head this workshop because I had something to do with a conference on public land ownership a few years ago. Enrique Peñalosa, Anne Strong, and Bill Doebele, and a number of other people came. We spent three days, and I had the task of doing the book afterward. We discovered we had no idea what the subject meant. It could mean all sorts of things. It could mean an American-style exaction where you give part of the land to a park and take it away from the private owners; it could mean merely public ownership of national parks; it could mean owning all of the development land; it could mean a taxation scheme of taxing away the betterments; it could mean private-property tax, a site-value tax system.

Let me tell you about some of the questions that I will bring up in my workshop. When you are talking about public ownership, some of the questions you might ask are such things as "What?" For example, what are the assumptions underlying Enrique Peñalosa's comments on why we need public ownership? Does that eliminate the delays of the private market; does it control price? Does it reduce inequities among landowners? Is it merely enhancing the ability of the government to do what it could do through a control system? What is it supposed to be doing? The second question follows from the first: If you do need some ownership (meaning you take the fee away), are you taking the fee or are you just taking bits? Are you only taking leasehold away or development rights? Are you taking all the land by the city or all the land for schools or all the land within a mile of the edge of the city? What sort of intervention? Why do you distrust the private market so much? If you figure that out, you can see the extent of the public intervention.

Once you've decided that, do you take traditional public ownership or just bits and pieces: high tax, betterment levies, and so on? Then you might ask yourself an ideological question: Is this merely a way to make sure that those unscrupulous owners of land whom we all fear called speculators aren't somehow benefiting? If that's the reason we want public ownership, maybe we should just consider taxing them in some way and leave the ownership to them. Is it merely a way of bolstering a physical control system? Is it that the planners can't get what they want through regulatory schemes? Are planners any better at doing what they do merely because they have the fee in their ownership? Then a question that comes out is, How do you measure the costs of this public ownership? It's not merely the benefit of selling off a leasehold, say, but it also includes a lot of other costs for society to deal with: costs of running the planning system that now has turned into an owning system, costs of delay, costs of information.

Finally, leading from that, if you have control imposed that is very strict (a leasehold covenant or a fee-simple covenant), then you have a very fundamental question: How well do those work? If you told a person not to build some horrible edifice on his land, that you had given it to him only, say, in a lease, just to live there, is that sort of control going to work any better than merely an old-fashioned American-style zone? Maybe we hope it will, but it's certainly a question we have to deal with.

Workshop 3: Public-Private Codevelopment

Pierre Laconte: In my workshop we are going to speak first of the case of France. The law on the legal ceiling of density has been considered by many scholars as a very dramatic novelty in public-private interrelations. And something more will be said about it in the framework of the whole French planning system.

One of the issues of the 1980s is how it will be possible for a large percentage of the population still to have access to home or apartment ownership. In order to get that under present financial conditions, there will probably be a need for a certain number of imaginative formulas of cooperation between the public and the private sectors. Charles Haar has given such a good description of the different types of techniques that I need not repeat what he said.

Then Professor Seele, an expert on land policy and urban planning in Germany, will explain how the system works for developing mainly suburban developments in Germany. It's the same kind of technique where a certain property transfer takes place with the help and arbitration of the state.

We'll also hear from B.J. Pearce, who may say something about England along the same line. And if there is time I may say a few words about the experiment I am conducting in Belgium where the University of Louvain has bought 2,000 acres and is developing it entirely on the basis of long-term leases. It sells only development rights and no property and now has 15,000 inhabitants.

Workshop 4: Property Taxation Measures

Oliver Oldman: We will be considering both general and special property tax measures and examining some of the economic, legal, administrative, and political questions that are involved whenever one thinks about property tax measures as a way of having an impact on land policy. It might be helpful for all of us to take a look at some of these from that different point of view. We will look at such familiar and related problems as liquidity, inflation, lock-in, and the land, as practical aspects that must be considered when proposing theoretical measures. We also must look at constitutions and statutes to see what limitations exist in the way of proposed measures.

Inevitably, in a subject as broad as this, some topics will be left out. Such important topics as the role of valuation and the role of uniformity laws in land policy will not be covered specifically by papers but will, no doubt, come up during the discussion. We hope that, as a result of the overall presentations, people who have not previously looked into the property tax aspects of land policy will get a comprehensive introduction, both generally and specifically, to the issues.

In conclusion, I want to note that the role of property taxes in land policy is neither as important as to be regarded as the only tool for implementing different kinds of land policy (as some people would like to have taxation fee) nor is it unimportant enough to be ignored. There is a great world of the in-between, which is the real world of property taxes, and they must be taken into account in the formulation of land policies, just as land policies must be taken into account in the design and operation of property taxes.

Workshop 5: Women, Land Use, and Urbanization

Fran Hosken: This panel is not for women only; on the contrary. In case you were frightened off by the title, the whole objective is to invite men to come to this panel and participate in defining the legal rights of women vis-à-vis property. Our discussions will be concerned with the constraints that face women in gaining access to land use and property rights in both rural and urban areas and with the effects of worldwide urbanization on women's lives in the families, as well as how women influence and contribute to urban and city life.

The panel is divided into three main areas of concern. First is a world view of women's legal and customary rights to land, resources, and employment and the discriminatory constraints that women face in developing countries, especially rural areas where the majority of women live. Next, we are concerned with urbanization and its effects on women's lives of urban integration, as well as how women influence and contribute to new urban community development and modernization. Finally we examine the influence of women in shaping the historic development of land policies in U.S. cities as the basis for modern community development, the recent rapid growth of households headed by women, and the effect on housing and urban communities with comparison to similar developments in other parts of the world.

We heard this morning from Mr. Mumford, who talked about the sins of omission. The most striking omission of all is the fact that women are missing from all deliberations concerning land use, both rural and urban. We heard Mr. Peñalosa talk about the revolution of urbanization, which affects most of the developing world. I suggest that a much more far-reaching social revolution is taking place in developing countries, as well as in the industrial world: the empowerment of women, women whose consciousness is being raised about their own human rights, worldwide. Equal access to property, rural and urban, is a basic need of social justice anywhere. Equality for women has been set as a goal by all the states participating at the United Nations.

This panel is breaking new ground, and we hope to propose new initiatives in research and policies. We need to define property rights and legal access to land by women. We need to set examples, outline an approach, and, first of all, develop the research and tools on which new policies of equality must be based that guarantee social and human development. Women are the poorest of the poor in all countries everywhere in the world and in all societies, though they are almost everywhere responsible for their children and are the de facto heads of households, economically speaking. We must provide equal access to land, housing, and rural and urban property and do away with the damaging discrimination of women that prevails in legal instruments all over the world and which has so far been totally ignored. This is a vital new idea and a new issue.

Here is a book called *Law and the Status of Women*, which was produced by the *Columbia Human Rights Law Review*, with the participation of the Center of Social Development in Humanitarian Affairs. It came out two years ago, and it tells very broadly about the rights of women in fifteen countries around the world taken from the industrialized regions in Asia, the Pacific, Latin America, the Caribbean, Africa and the Middle East. Such an investigation is long overdue as far as women's property rights are concerned. Unfortunately, this book which is fascinating reading—it deals with the legal status of women in all these countries—almost wholly excludes property rights, and that is an omission that must be remedied. I hope to have all of the innovative people at this meeting help us define the property rights of women and make suggestions as to how the basic research will have to be done. We are not in a very sophisticated area as yet, but we have to define basics. And if you speak of discrimination or social justice or about development, without the participation of half the population of the world—women—I don't think you are going to make it.

Workshop 6: Physical Planning Measures
to Control the Land Market

Darshan Johal: I would like my workshop to concentrate on three or four areas or subjects. First of all, I think we should look at the seven recommendations of the Habitat conference. I don't think the world has seen that much in the last four years; after all, 132 countries assembled in Vancouver and agreed on certain recommendations relating to land, and perhaps in this atmosphere we will be able to get some new inspiration. We would, of course, not rehash those seven recommendations, but it would be worthwhile to refer to them. Second, we should examine the context of physical planning in land policy because a great deal of concern has been expressed that not many countries have been able to make significant progress in the implementation of those recommendations. There must be some good reasons. And I believe that we have the opportunity, in an audience and participation of this type, to bring together the experience of various countries and various regions of what type of difficulties the governments have faced in trying to implement some of these recommendations.

The real core of our discussion is the issues. First of all, we should examine the physical planning framework for a network or system of human settlements in the context of national development. This is important in view of the many rapid changes that have been mentioned today: new life-styles, new development priorities, new energy constraints. What is an optimum pattern of human settlement? We must get away from examining land-use policies on an individual settlement basis. So many factors are beyond the boundaries of individual settlements or regions that I think the subjects need to be examined in the total territorial context of the nation. That, of course, would have tremendous implications on the availability of land, and pricing as well. Let me take one example. One African nation has projected that the growth of population over the next twenty years will be around 20 million. Obviously a number of alternatives are available. You could put all this new growth into one metropolitan area; you could have twenty cities of 1 million each; or you could have 10 million in one metropolitan area and the rest in rural settlements. How does the government decide which of an almost infinite number of combinations or options to follow? What are the physical-planning land policy questions? How would they go about determining them?

The second issue that I suggest we examine is the integration of physical planning with other types of planning: economic and social planning, rural development planning, health planning, agricultural, industrial, energy, and transportation planning. The third one is that the reality of life today is that much of the growth in the next ten or twenty years will take place in or around the existing system of human settlements. That's something that has to be faced. Therefore we must address ourselves to the possibilities of potential problems of restructuring, to the extent possible, the existing patterns of settlements, the existing land-use patterns, the connection between the living places and the work places, the whole area of urban structures, urban land-use patterns that affect zoning, subdivision, and various other practices of physical planning that we have followed, particularly in the last forty or fifty years.

The fourth main issue I would like to examine is the development of appropriate physical planning standards. I think we are generally agreed that many developing countries particularly have been tempted simply to adopt the standards and regulations of other countries. Is there a possibility (under what conditions or situations, and how, using the experience of other countries) for a country to develop and evolve its own standards that would be appropriate for its own particular physical, social, and economic situation? Finally, the fifth issue is the development and implementation of special physical planning measures to address the living conditions of the poorer segments of the population living in the slum and squatter areas and in the rural settlements.

These are the five issues that this workshop would like to examine. Then we would like to be able to suggest various types of international programs that could be undertaken, together with activities of the nongovernmental organizations and intergovernmental organizations in the U.N. system to assist countries in implementing various types of measures and recommendations. For example, we could examine the role of direct technical assistance. Is it useful? How it could be changed? How it could be reoriented? What are the individual things that could be mentioned and examined?

We could examine the role of research and development activities of the international agencies and other institutes like this one. What are the key issues and areas on which research should be focused to have real relevance in the implementation of land policies in physical planning measures? What is the place of training? And finally, what is the role of information exchange, particularly among the countries that have similar problems or similar situations?

Workshop 7: Financial and Credit Interventions Other Than Taxation

Harold Dunkerley: In a sense, the title "Financial and Credit Interventions" is very appropriate because the workshop covers primarily and straightforwardly the nitty-gritty of the problems as seen and as experienced in the developing countries. And the developing countries are short of financial resources at the same time as they have had the highest rates of increase in the urban areas and hence a need for more resources and for innovation. The cases that we will look at are very much related to this.

Korea will have two speakers, and it is a very interesting case, because for a long time its residential and urban development was neglected. Korea is now introducing a number of innovations in the process of catching up, which I think will be of great interest to all developing countries. Songman Lee will talk about his institution, the Korea Land Development Corporation, and Bill Doebele will return to one of his favorite subjects: land readjustment schemes in Korea and their applicability over a wider number of countries.

Mexico is a case of very great interest. We have all heard a lot about Mexico City and how it will have 30 million inhabitants by the end of the century. But we have heard very little about what is being done to stimulate growth in other centers, including, in the state of Mexico, a city that has been planned for over 1.5 million people and already, after eight years, is over 300,000 and where the call upon public finances has been relatively low because techniques have been developed for stimulating the financial resource mobilization, from private sources in particular.

We will also hear from Egypt of some of the consequences of myopia, which is prevalent in a number of countries in official policy and how in ignoring problems you may, in fact, ignore the institutional needs for credit and for other ways of mobilizing financial credit that are essential in the solution of the problems. Finally, we will have a contribution on Cuba, where rural urbanization has been one of the main points of policy in the urban field and where various techniques have been developed for obtaining the resources for this policy.

In this workshop I hope we will be able to keep away from the straw men, which all too often are put up to be knocked down in the discussion of urban policy. I don't think any of us think in terms of 100 percent capture of surface values or of overall public ownership as a practical method for allocating all types of urban land for all purposes. What we want to see is how far we can go in practice and what is needed to achieve that degree of progress in the various fields that we consider—rather than to say this or that is impossible—or we need to have more statements of the ultimate objectives.

As for the kinds of issues on which we might dwell, I have a few preliminary thoughts. The division of costs in land development has received very little attention between various levels of government and the public-private side. In many projects, very heavy initial costs are involved that have to be financed over a period of time before they can be of aid to recovery. Who is to do the financing and how? What should the scale of development be? How much should be attempted at any one time? Should one be trying for incremental purchase or for much larger urban-extension schemes? Do we need subsidies as financial incentives for the private sector for them to cooperate? If so, under what conditions and in what form? In fact, because land development is such a source of wealth, why should it not be at least self-financing and not require subsidies? What is the cause? Why is there this shortage while it is such a source of wealth? And we may look at some of the financing institutions—and the case studies may point the way—including such areas as urban development banks.

**Workshop 8: Institution Factors: Problems of Land-Use
Legislation, Jurisdictional Boundaries, Standards
for Housing and Subdivisions, etc.**

Ann Louise Strong: Mr. Peñalosa's statement that private property in most
of our systems is a major obstacle to implementation of planning is certainly
a starting point for consideration of institutional issues. My personal bias is
a concern for a greater distribution of equity in any country's system and an
acceptance that this has to be achieved through a private enterprise system
in which the public sector has a strong role. I am concerned primarily with
the exploration of tools—legal tools, political tools, administrative
tools—that will increase equity and with an exploration of possible rate of
change in increase of equity within the system.

I hope that people will come to the workshop with success stories in mind
because, as Mr. Peñalosa said, I have spent many, many years advocating
change in land-use controls and have seen far too few results. An example
of the sort of problems I work on is the New Jersey pinelands case, where
there is a major federal concern with the preservation of a unique natural
resource and local and private opposition because the long-term federal interest violates local and private home-builder and farmer interests in land
development. The federal and state levels are interested in resource protection and preservation, in contrast to the local and private interest in short-
term profit from private development.

The workshop title has various subheadings. Under legislation, we
might talk about whether national legislation states land-use policies for
population distribution, dispersion, size of metropolitan areas, and densities; land-use priorities as between resource preservation, resource consumption, and allocation of land for development; to what extent these
policies conflict with one another or with other policies of the country; to
what extent social objectives—efficiency, equity, continuity of culture—are
advanced by land-use policies; whether the implementing legislation for carrying out the policies is adequate, which in most cases it certainly is not.
Control of land use, fiscal feasibility, administrative accountability, and
market response are some of the questions there.

Under the heading of boundaries, certainly anyone from the United
States is very familiar with the problems of court jurisdiction, federal versus
state roles, the assumption of major responsibility over land use by local
government, and the resistance to raising land-use control powers to a
higher level. Intergovernmental conflict occurs between various agencies at
the same level of government and between levels of government. Another
issue is the adequacy of any authorization or financing for metropolitan
and regional-scale planning and plan implementation.

Under the heading of standards, are the standards in land-use laws and regulations reasonable and appropriate for the country or the urban area that is adopting them? Are they too costly? Are they wasteful of resources? Are they exclusionary? Are they unsuited to the particular culture or setting? Does the system have the capacity to enforce the standards even if they are reasonable? With particular reference to housing, will enforcement of the standards limit the supply?

Dan Mandelker will talk about the land-use control system in Australia, Hawaii, and Russia. Milton Kaplan will discuss enabling laws for land-use control in Karachi. Professor Berry will examine standards for infrastructure in Indonesia and their possible inappropriateness. Dr. Angel will talk about land tenure for the poor in ten cities of Southeast Asia. And Ms. Flores will discuss family patterns of landownership in Mérida, Venezuela, from 1549 to 1980 and the politics of control by a certain number of families. We also are expecting a paper from Max Falque from France on preservation of agricultural land in France.

Workshop 9: Rural Workshop: Agricultural Land Policies; Legislation and Implementation Issues

John Montgomery: There are seven papers in this workshop, each dealing with very different contexts in which governments have adopted policies with the intent of changing land use in the rural areas. These seven countries or situations are Taiwan, Bangladesh, India, the Philippines, and Thailand, and we have two regional papers—one on Africa and one on Latin America.

If you look for a moment at the problems of agricultural productivity and the other problems that are affected by land policy to the rural area, you will immediately come up against some of the most important problems facing the developing world. First is the problem of food productivity. To what extent and in what ways do land policies affect the capacity of the rural population to produce food? The second question concerns the problem of rural employment. In what ways does the manner in which farms are organized and land is held affect the capacity of farms to create employment for our rapidly growing rural populations? The third problem that these papers consider is that of social equity. It is probably true that land distribution, inequitable as it is, is not as seriously distorted as is the distribution of other important aspects such as stocks or urban lands, but it is an important social-equity problem in countries where the vast majority of the population is living in the rural areas.

Three social responses to these problems are of special interest to the people participating in this conference: land development and resettlement, land reform (the redistribution of land), and urban migration. All three of these social responses to the problems of rural land will be examined in the context of these seven papers.

These papers have in common certain issues that are addressed in very different ways. One is the question of how a government can summon the political will to deal with these problems of rural land-tenure arrangements. Another is the problem of how small farms can become more productive than large mechanized farms. A third is what technology governments can introduce that will increase the capacity of farms to make productive use of the populations living on them. The last question that I think we will talk about is an administrative question: does land reform gain more when it is carried out abruptly, or is there a greater advantage to carrying it out gradually over a long period of time? What are the trade-offs? These are the problems, responses, and issues that seem to me to be the most interesting and important.

**Part II
Second Session**

Introduction to
Second Session

William Doebele

Our subject is urban land markets and methodologies for their analysis. I think possibly the most succinct comment on land markets ever made was by the American humorist, Will Rogers, who advised, "Buy land, young man, buy land. God isn't making any more." Actually we are gathered here today because of the existence of a paradox. Land is the one commodity that touches the lives of every human being. It has more powerful psychological associations than almost any other material thing. Economically, it constitutes one of the most valuable and most actively traded products in the world. Yet in spite of this overwhelming psychological and economic importance, actual studies of land markets and how they operate are amazingly scarce. A man named Hans Dieter Evans made a survey in 1975 and was able to find only a scattered handful of actual empirical field studies of the way land markets operated in very small, fragmentary situations around the world. We know more about the market in, say, tomatoes, than we do about land. This condition is particularly true with respect to the most valuable land of all: the land in cities. One of the main purposes of this Congress, in fact, and especially this particular session, is to bring together for the first time summaries of the most interesting research going on, much of it in the last few years, around the world in the field of land markets, not only in terms of what those results have been, but some of the methodologies that some of you might want to use to understand the land markets in your own countries—a subject that is becoming more and more politically sensitive and acute in almost every country in the world, including the United States.

We will begin this session with a broad overview by Dr. Gregory Ingram of a number of research findings. For the last two years Dr. Ingram has been the director of a study of the economics of Bogotá, one of the most extensive studies of the economy of a single city in a developing country that has ever been undertaken. We will then hear a report on what may be the most extensive and, in my opinion, the most innovative research projects on urban land markets that have ever been attempted, dealing with some seven metropolitan areas and extending over a period of three years. This will be the report presented by Professors James Brown and Neal Roberts. Next will be a fascinating account of some recent developments in land markets in Latin American cities. Professor Guillermo Geisse will describe a major, and what is to me a very ominous or threatening, change in the institutions that control land assembly, land development, and land marketing in Latin

America. Following that, Professor Miodrag Janic of Belgrade, Yugoslavia, will present research on the behavior of land markets under socialism. He has some fascinating material on how land markets work in that kind of a socialist system. We will then have a report on land markets in Japan, including the expensive Japanese system of continual evaluation of land prices in the entire country, a system that is not perfect but comes about as close as any other system that I know of, to the recommendation that was made by Dr. Peñalosa yesterday morning, of the first step in any land policy, of understanding how the price system actually works on a nationwide basis.

Emilio Haddad will report on the methods that have been developed to study one of the most-active and most-complex urban land markets—that of São Paulo. Next will be a presentation by Rakesh Mohan on the results of urban land-markets studies that have just been completed for Bogotá and Cali by the World Bank. This will be followed by a stimulating and possibly quite controversial paper by Professor Marcial Echenique, which will argue that the best way to affect the land market is by instruments that are not directed toward the buyers and sellers of land. He will argue that actions in quite a different economic sector will have a more-profound impact on land prices than the kind of mechanisms that are aimed directly at the land market itself. Next James Hoben will present some of the land-market research now being proposed and undertaken in the United States, where we have become very much concerned about this issue. And finally, I will make a few proposals for future directions for research in this field.

There is one thread running through all the presentations. It is a very simple but highly important point. All of us—researchers, policymakers, teachers—have been guilty of the same sin. For several decades now, we have held in our minds a very oversimplified stereotype of how urban land markets work. We have thought basically that there are two actors—buyers and sellers—and we have generally assumed that the sellers of land, particularly in developing countries, have been unjustly enriched and that the buyers of land have been unjustly overcharged. Consequently we have devised and discussed a whole set of policies to try to correct this injustice.

In fact urban land markets are far more complex than that very simple stereotype—both in the numbers of the actors involved in the process and in the complexity of their motivations. They are much more complex than any of us have imagined. And if we have been disappointed, disappointed about Vancouver, disappointed that our national and municipal policies about land have not succeeded, it may be because we have not really understood who the important actors are or what really motivates their behavior. Until we can understand the actors and their motivations, we cannot design effective policies.

8

Land in Perspective: Its Role in the Structure of Cities

Gregory K. Ingram

Given the importance of land in both urban and nonurban activities, this paper attempts to draw inferences about the role of land as a productive resource at the national level; examines aggregate land values at the level of cities or aggregated urban areas to determine how urban land values may change with levels of output, city size, or city growth rates; reports the results of the few available studies that describe the structure of land prices within cities and compares those results with other analyses of the distribution of population within cities; and deals with questions of market structure and ownership concentration of land as well as insights about the determinants of land values in cities from the literature on resource economics.

Although I attempt to provide empirical examples, this has proven to be difficult to do in a rigorous way. The data used are mainly from the United States, Korea, and Colombia; other data sets or case studies may exist, but I do not know of them. The available data have been manipulated using relatively simple techniques to develop or to investigate a number of conjectures about the role of land in urban areas. Because of data limitations, the paper deals more with conjectures than it does with conclusions.

Use and Value of Land at the National Level

The data in table 8-1 summarize information on land use and land values for Korea and the United States. These countries differ greatly in size, topography, average population density, and income levels, but the data in the table suggest one significant similarity: in both countries urbanized land is a relatively small fraction of total land area but a relatively large fraction of aggregate land values. In the United States, for example, only 14 percent of the land area was included in standard metropolitan statistical areas (SMSAs) in 1970, and it is doubtful that more than 3 percent of the total U.S. land area is urbanized. In Korea about 4 percent of land area is denoted urban, and over 80 percent of this urban area is devoted to agriculture and forests. The 4 percent of land denoted urban in Korea accounts for 45 percent of the total land value, and the half percent of land that is both urban and residential accounts for 38 percent of Korea's total land value.[1] Precisely comparable figures are not available for the United

Table 8-1
Land Area and Value by Use in the United States and Korea

	Private Farm	Private Nonfarm	Public	Total
		Land Use		
United States (1970)				
Land area				
10^6 acres	1,102	265	897	2,264
Percent	48.7	11.7	39.6	100
Land value				
10^9 dollars	171.3	404.6	182.1	758.0
Percent	22.6	53.4	24.0	100.0

	Arable	Residential	Forest	Total
		Land Use		
Korea (1975)				
Land area				
10^6 acres	5.45	0.41	16.04	21.91
Percent	24.9	1.9	73.2	100.0
Land value				
10^9 won	8,305	7,437	1,035	16,778
Percent	49.5	44.3	6.2	100.0

Sources: U.S. Department of Commerce, Bureau of the Census, *Statistical Abstract of the United States, 1978* (Washington, D.C.: Government Printing Office, 1979), pp. 235, 686; J.W. Kendrick, K.S. Lee, and J. Lomask, *National Wealth of the United States* (New York: Conference Board, 1976); E.S. Mills and B.H. Song, *Korea's Urbanization and Urban Problems, 1945-1975*, Korea Development Institute Working Paper 7701 (Seoul: Korea Development Institute, 1977), p. 167.

States, but urbanized land's share of total land value in the United States is probably similar to that in Korea.

These percentages help to place in perspective a commonly voiced concern about urban development encroaching on land suitable for other purposes such as agriculture. Such encroachment certainly does occur, but most nations are far from paving over the countryside. However, the high values placed on urban land reflected in the Korean and U.S. data also suggest that strong market forces underlie the transformation of land from rural to urban uses.

Although the percentages of total land value by category of use can be compared, it is difficult to make direct comparisons of land values across countries. Since land is a factor of production that is paid for with a share of the output produced in a country, it is possible to compare land values across countries in terms of their ratio to the national product. The ratio of total land value to gross national product for the United States and Korea, shown in table 8-2, reveals that land values are a much larger multiple of GNP in Korea than in the United States. These ratios must be interpreted with care, however, for they are the ratio of the value of a stock (the existing land) to the value of a flow (one year's production).

Table 8-2
Value of Land and Product by Sector in the United States and Korea

Item	United States (1970)	Korea (1975)
Land value in relation to GNP	0.77	1.85
Persons per square kilometer	23.0	388.0
Percentage of GDP from agriculture	3.2	22.0
Agricultural land value in relation to agricultural product value	5.4	4.2
Nonagricultural land value in relation to nonagricultural product value	0.62	1.2
Agricultural labor force (10^6)	3.46	5.0
Agricultural acres per agricultural worker	318.0	1.1

Sources: U.S. Department of Commerce (1978), pp. 407, 445, 899-900; Mills and Song (1977), pp. 37, 64.

It would be preferable to compare the value of one year's worth of land services—the land rent—to the value of GNP since expectations about the growth in land rent may differ across countries. Current land values represent the discounted value of future rents. If these rents are expected to rise more in country A than in country B, current land values may be higher as a proportion of GNP in country A than in country B even when land rents are the same proportion of GNP in the two countries. The present value, V, of an annual payment, a, discounted at rate r is $\Sigma\ a/(1 + r)^n$. When n is large, this sum converges to a/r. If a grows at an annual rate of g (when g is less than r), a approximately equals $\Sigma\ a/(1 + r - g)^n$ and converges to $a/(r - g)$ when n is large. Hence, expectations about the rate of growth of land rents affect the relationship between rents and values. Of course, discount rates may also differ between countries.

Analyses of land rents as a proportion of GNP over a one-hundred-year period in the United States show that land rents have been nearly constant as a proportion of GNP.[2] Hence, we hypothesize that land rents grow in proportion to total output. Korea's GNP has been growing at nearly 10 percent per year from 1960 to 1977, while U.S. GNP has been growing in the same period at roughly 3 percent per year. If these growth rates were expected to persist, land values in Korea would be a larger multiple of GNP in Korea than in the United States even if land rent was the same proportion of GNP in Korea as in the United States. Unfortunately, the information available does not indicate whether land rent as a fraction of GNP in Korea is higher or lower than in the United States.

Comparing the percentage of output paid to factors of production in a single country over time or across countries that have different factor endowments can tell us a great deal about the ease of substituting one factor of production for another. If factor-payment shares are relatively constant when factor proportions in production differ, it is relatively easy to substitute one factor for another; but if the factor payment rises as a proportion of output when the factor is scarcer, substitution is difficult.[3] In the aggregate table 8-2 shows that land is much more scarce in Korea than in the United States relative to population. Korea's gross population density is roughly sixteen times higher than that of the United States. Hence, higher factor-payment shares in Korea would imply that in the aggregate, it is difficult to substitute labor (and other inputs) for land. If this is true, it suggests that high-density countries would have higher land rents in proportion to GNP than low-density countries.

Given the lack of land-rent data, it is difficult to test for this directly; however, with the data on land values in table 8-1 and information on the sectoral composition of GNP, it is possible to estimate the ratio of the value of land to the value of annual production for two sectors: agriculture and nonagriculture. These estimates are based on the assumption that the value of all agricultural output stems from private farmland in the United States and from arable land in Korea; nonagricultural output stems from all other land in both cases. For agriculture, the ratios of land value to product in table 8-2 are fairly similar between the two countries, and the U.S. ratio exceeds the Korean ratio. Differences in relative growth rates between the countries are less relevant as a determinant of these ratios because agriculture is Korea's slowest-growing sector. Given the huge differences of three hundred to one in factor proportions of land to labor between the two countries, the similar land-value ratios suggest that labor and other inputs are quite substitutable for land in agriculture.

In the nonagricultural sector, however, the ratios of land value to product differ by a factor of two between the two countries, and the Korean ratio exceeds in the U.S. ratio. Because the relative growth rates in the nonagricultural sectors differ greatly between the two countries, it is impossible to conclude whether the ratios differ because of the growth rates or because of low substitutability between land and other inputs in the production of nonagricultural goods.

One problem with the data in table 8-2 and this analysis is that they have concentrated on land and labor and the substitution between them and ignored capital as a factor of production. This problem is particularly severe since we are accustomed to speak of the substitution of capital for land in urban areas while generally ignoring any substitution of labor for land. Available evidence does indicate that in urban areas land and capital are quite substitutable. Table 8-2 does not present data on urban capital because virtually none exist. Based on the available data and other studies, my conjecture would be that with a three-factor model including land, labor, and capital in the agricultural sector, we would find substitutability between land and labor and complementarity between land and capital, while in the urban sector we would find substitutability between land and capital and complementarity between land and labor.[4]

Aggregate Value of Land in Urban Areas

Several factors are likely to influence the total value of land in a city. First, there is evidence at the national level that land values are a relatively constant proportion of GNP, which implies that land values grow at the same rate as the value of output over time. This may also hold for cities. Second, the factor-share data imply that increases in urban population density will produce increases in land values. Since larger cities often have higher densities than small cities, city size may be positively associated with land values. Third, any difficulty in substituting labor for land in urban production implies that land values may grow in proportion to population but at relatively constant densities. That is, land values per capita may be constant in real terms. This section investigates each of these hypotheses using data from Korea and Colombia.

Evidence from Korea

The Korean government publishes statistics on urban land values in several forms. Table 8-3 displays six observations from an index of land values aggregated across twelve major Korean cities. This index has been decomposed into an annual growth rate for each time interval shown. For example, between 1965 and 1970 the land-value index increased at a compound annual growth rate of 43.4 percent. To test the hypothesis that urban land values grow in proportion to urban output, I have constructed an index of the value of the nonagricultural component of GNP as a proxy for urban out-

Table 8-3
Growth of Urban Land Values and Nonagricultural Product in Korea

Year	Land-Value Index in Twelve Largest Cities	Annual Growth Rate	Index of Nonagricultural GNP	Annual Growth Rate	Land Growth Divided by Nonagricultural Growth
1963	100		100		
1965	203	42.5	166	28.8	1.48
1970	1,233	43.4	636	30.8	1.41
1972	2,056	29.1	985	24.4	1.19
1974	2,582	12.1	1,798	35.1	0.34
1977	6,403	35.4	4,362	34.4	13.0

Source: Mills and Song (1977), pp. 64, 66, 67, 171.

put and calculated annual growth rates of this index for each time interval. The last column is the ratio of the land-value growth rate to the nonagricultural growth rate for each time interval. This ratio is an average elasticity of land values with respect to output values.

If urban land values grew strictly in proportion to output values, the two indexes would have similar values at each point in time, similar growth rates for each time interval, and the ratios in the last column would all have a value of unity. In fact, over the entire period 1963 to 1974, land values in the twelve major cities grew more rapidly than did the value of nonagricultural output. However, the comparison of index growth rates for each time interval shows that the growth rate of land values slowed relative to the growth rate of output; in the 1972-1974 period, land values grew much less rapidly than did output value. The reduction in the rate of growth of land values may reflect changes in expectations about future rents and/or output levels in a situation where land rents are proportional to output values. The results are ambiguous as a test of the hypothesis that urban land rents are a constant proportion of the value of urban output.

Table 8-4 shows the value of the land price indexes in 1974 (1963 = 100) for each of the twelve Korean cities included in the aggregate twelve-city land-value index. In addition, the table shows the annual compound growth rate implicit in each city's land-value index, each city's compound annual population growth rate from 1960 to 1973, and each city's population in 1973. To test for a relation between the growth rate of land values, population growth, and city size, a regression was run with the average land-value

Table 8-4
Land Value and Population Growth in Twelve Korean Cities

City	1963-1974 Land Value Index	Eleven-Year Average Annual Growth Index (%)	1960-1973 Population Growth Rate	1973 City Population (thousands)
		Y	X_1	X_2
Seoul	2,610	34.5	7.54	6,290
Busan	2,321	33.1	4.54	2,072
Daegu	2,668	34.8	4.51	1,200
Gwangju	1,605	28.7	4.43	552
Daejon	2,291	32.9	5.6	463
Incheon	2,235	32.6	4.53	714
Chuncheon	1,100	24.4	3.87	135
Jeonju	3,554	38.3	3.26	286
Suwon	3,020	36.3	5.92	192
Cheongju	4,303	40.8	4.69	167
Masan	2,967	36.1	5.16	304
Jeju	2,315	33.1	4.29	118

Source: Mills and Song (1977), pp. 38, 188.

growth rate (labeled Y in table 8-4) as the dependent variable, and the population growth rate and 1973 population in thousands (labeled X_1 and X_2, respectively) as independent variables. The results are

$$Y = 28.7 + 1.14 \cdot X_1 - 0.00045 \cdot X_2 \qquad R^2 = 0.04$$
$$(3\ 5)\ (0.6) \qquad\qquad (0.4)$$

where the numbers in parentheses are t ratios. The population growth and population level explain only 4 percent of the variation in land-value growth across the twelve observations. The coefficient of X_1 is close to 1.0, the value we would expect if land values grew at the same rate as population. However, given the poor performance of the equation, virtually nothing can be made of these parameter values in a positive sense. The equation does indicate, however, that there is no support for the hypothesis that land values grow more rapidly in large cities than in small ones.

Evidence from Colombia

Because of differences in available data, tests of hypotheses about the determinants of aggregate urban land values in Colombian cities differ from those used in Korean cities. The top of table 8-5 shows estimates of Bogotá's aggregate land values, the values of the city's gross regional product, and the ratios of land value to product value for three different years. In contrast to the results for Korean cities, where land values generally grew faster than product value, the ratios of land value to product value in Bogotá have been fairly stable, indicating similar growth of land value and output. The bottom half of table 8-5 shows population, density, and land value per capita in Bogotá and Cali. The per-capita land values have been relatively constant in Bogotá over the period shown, which supports the hypothesis that land values grow in proportion to population. This constancy is not evident in Cali. It is notable, however, that Cali's per-captia land values grew during this period to be equivalent to those in Bogotá in 1978. This suggests, as in Korea, that city size is not an important determinant of land-value growth and that land values in small cities may grow more rapidly than those in large cities. Table 8-5 also indicates that in neither Bogotá nor Cali does one find a strong relation between per-capita land values and population densities.

The data used in this section are not really equal to the tasks they have been asked to perform. However, the city-level data have not lent support to the hypothesis that land values in large cities grow more rapidly than do those in small cities. In fact, they have indicated that land values in large cities grow less rapidly than do those in small cities. The data have offered

Table 8-5
Land Value, Product, and Population in Bogotá and Cali

| Year | Bogotá | | | Population (thousands) | | Density (persons/km²) | | Land Value per Capita (1978 pesos) | |
	Aggregate Land Value (10⁶ 1978 pesos)	Regional Product (10⁶ 1978 pesos)	Land Value Product	Bogotá	Cali	Bogotá	Cali	Bogotá	Cali
1970	252,000	100,568	2.5	2,395	818	7,870	9,030	10,520	—
1975	280,000	141,079	2.0	3,098	1,007	10,180	11,110	9,040	6,040
1978	362,000	168,000	2.2	3,500	1,100	11,500	12,140	10,340	10,900

Source: Villamizar (1980); Velasco and Mier (1980).

weak support for the hypothesis that land values grow in proportion to output and in proportion to population.

Distribution of Land Values
within Cities

Our attention now turns to the description of urban land values within cities and the relation between those values and the distribution of activity within cities. The description of land values or activity intensities within cities can be very cumbersome because there are no simple ways of describing irregular distributions in two dimensions. A common simplification used in the description of urban phenomena is to assume that the distributions to be described are not irregular but rather are radially symmetric about the center of the city. The assumption of radial symmetry allows us to summarize the relevant two-dimensional distributions in terms of a distribution in one dimension—along a radial line from the city center. Experiments with a number of functional forms of the distribution of urban activity suggest that the exponential function is a simple and effective specification. This specification takes the form

$$V = V_o \, e^{-bx}$$

where V is the measure of the activity level found at distance x from the center, V_o is the activity level at the center, and b is a parameter often termed the gradient. The gradient value is the proportional change in V given a one-unit change in x. This functional form has been widely used to describe the spatial distribution of population density in cities. It will be used here to describe the spatial distribution of land prices in cities.

The exponential functional form for population density can be derived from rather simple models of residential location in cities. Moreover, in an equilibrium setting it is possible to demonstrate theoretically that there is a specific relationship between the shape of the land-price function within a city and the shape of the population-density function. It can be shown that the population-density function will be a transformation of the land-price function of the form,

$$D(x) = [R(x)]^{1-B},$$

where $D(x)$ is the population density function, $R(x)$ is the land-price function, x is distance from the city center, and B is a parameter. The parameter B is defined as $B = a(1 + E)$ where a is the share of land in the production of housing and E is the price elasticity of demand for housing.[5] This theoretical relationship is potentially very powerful for there are many empirical studies of urban population densities and relatively few empirical studies of the distribution of land values in urban areas. If the link between land prices and population densities can be confirmed, broader generalizations about urban land-value distributions can be made than would otherwise be possible.

The estimation of population-density gradients is more ubiquitous than the estimation of land-price gradients in urban areas because population data are more readily available than land-price data. In a few cities, however, both functions have been estimated, and the magnitude of the gradient parameter, b, is shown in table 8-6 for at least two points of time in six cities. The table reveals several consistencies. First, the gradient values of both population density and land values become absolutely smaller over time, indicating a flattening of both functions. Population is decentralizing over time and differences in land values between the city center and the periphery are declining. Second, the land-value gradients are consistently less steep than the population-density gradients. Within the simple theoretical model presented here, this pattern implies that the price elasticity of the demand for housing is absolutely larger than -1.[6] Third, there is a tendency in table 8-6 for small cities to have steeper population-density and land-value gradients than large cities.

Perhaps the most important characteristic of the land-value gradients is that they have been decreasing over time. This means that the ratio of land prices at the periphery to land prices at the center has tended to increase over time. Hence, if land prices in the city center have been rising, prices 10 kilometers from the center have been rising even faster in percentage terms. For example, if land prices have been increasing in Korean cities at an annual average rate of 30 percent, they have been increasing at peripheral locations at an even faster rate and at the center at a slower rate. This pattern of rapid rises in land prices at peripheral locations lies at the core of many of the current policy concerns with urban land. The rise in price at the periphery makes land less affordable to low-income households who seek it for housing, and it simultaneously enriches landowners who reap large gains with little or no effort. In many cases it is tempting to blame landowners for the price rise and to charge them with price manipulation or monopolistic practices. This temptation may be particularly great with respect to landowners at the periphery, for their gains will tend to be the largest.

Table 8-6 contains observations on only six cities, but the relation among the density and land-value gradients is quite consistent. Although few price gradients exist, density gradients have been estimated for many cities throughout the world. The decline in the gradient of population density over time has proven to be very consistent over long periods of time and

Table 8-6
Population-Density and Land-Value Gradients in Various Cities

Year	Population-Density Gradient (1/km.)	Land-Value Gradient (1/km)	City Population (thousands)
Bogotá			
1964	−0.25	−0.10	1,693
1972	−0.17	−0.07	2,538
1973	−0.15	−0.08	2,848
1978	−0.11	−0.03	3,500
Cali			
1973	−0.40	−0.26	939
1978	−0.27	−0.21	1,100
Seoul			
1965	−0.33	—	3,471
1970	−0.22	−0.20	5,536
1973	−0.19	−0.16	6,290
Busan			
1970	−0.13	−0.11	1,881
1973	−0.11	−0.09	2,072
Daegu			
1970	−0.74	−0.51	1,083
1973	−0.67 (1972)	−0.35	1,164
Suwon			
1970	−0.98	−0.83 (1968)	171
1973	−0.95	−0.68	192

Source: Villamizar (1980); Velasco and Mier (1980); Mills and Song (1977), p. 178.

across cities in both developed and less-developed countries. Given the similarity of population-density gradients and land-value gradients in table 8-6, I hypothesize that land-value gradients have also decreased in most cities of the world.

Resource Economics, Market Structure, and Land Values

A great deal of analysis has been done recently on the economics of natural resources, and many of the results of that work should be transferable to the analysis of land conversion to urban uses. Vacant land at the urban fringe can be viewed as a raw material that is transformed to a specific urban use when development occurs. Land dedicated to a specific urban use can then be transformed or recycled to an alternative use by "scrapping" its former configuration and recycling it. In this respect land is a durable resource that can be recycled like, for example, copper. One difference is that in recycling urban land from one use to another, the recovery rate is 100 percent. A number of general findings from the resource-economics literature may be transferable to the case of land and its development for urban uses, but only two will be mentioned here. The first is the result that a resource will be exploited (developed) only when its increase in value from period to period is equal to the interest rate. Owners of a nonproductive resource, such as vacant land, must be compensated for not developing their land in the present period. That compensation takes the form of capital gains. It can be shown that resource owners will exploit their resources so that their "royalty" (Ricardian rent in the case of land) will increase at the interest rate.[7] This result provides a link between the rate of return on holding land as an asset and the rate of return on holding other assets of similar riskiness.

A second result from the resource literature is that in a case where one is exploiting a resource that varies in quality (the resource content of the ore, for example), the high-quality deposits will be exploited before the low-quality deposits. In terms of urbanization, one can use distance from the city center as a proxy for resource quality. This result suggests, therefore, that vacant land close to the center will be developed before vacant land further from the center and that cities will expand through a process of peripheral growth. Simple measures of the location of new construction in cities support this. For example, the distance from the center of the city to the average location of new construction increases regularly over time. Between 1950 and 1970, the average distance of new residential units from the central business district increased from 9.0 to 11.2 miles in Pittsburgh and from 17.3 to 19.3 miles in Chicago.[8] Between 1971 and 1978 this distance increased from 8.8 to 9.7 kilometers for new single-family units in Bogotá.[9] The magnitudes of these distances and their growth over time are quite consistent with a process of peripheral expansion.

One last determinant of urban land values and urban land use that is thought to have great importance is the exercise of monopoly power by landowners. This is often hypothesized in both developed and developing countries. Thus, a recent study of land markets in Toronto devotes considerable space to examining whether landowners in Toronto exercise monopolistic power.[10] That study relies on traditional measures of concentration, such as the percentage of development activity or landholdings accounted for by the four largest firms, as a measure of monopolistic power. In the industrial-organization field, concentrations of less than 70 percent of the market in the top four firms are usually thought to preclude the exercise of significant market power. The concentration shares for Toronto, shown in table 8-7 for developers and landowners, led Markusen and Scheffman to conclude that the exercise of monopoly power by landowners

Table 8-7
Concentration of Landownership and Construction Activity

| | Percentage of all Development Approvals, by Largest Developers | | Percentage of all Land to Be Developed in next Ten Years, by Largest Owners | | |
	10 Largest	24 Largest	4 Largest	10 Largest	24 Largest
Toronto	59	75.5	17.5	27.7	40

| | Year | Percentage of Total Area Licensed Construction Built, by Largest Firms | |
		4 Largest	10 Largest
Bogotá	1974	12	20
	1975	16	25
	1977	24	37
	1978	19	28
Cali	1974	22	42
	1975	18	31
	1977	22	32

Sources: Toronto: Markusen and Scheffman (1977), ch. 5. Bogotá and Cali: Borrero (1978).

and developers was not a significant determinant of the rapid increases in land prices observed in Toronto in the early 1970s. Table 8-7 also displays concentration ratios for developers in Bogotá and Cali. Although Bogotá and Cali certainly have large developers, the concentration ratios suggest that monopoly power is unlikely to be exerted by developers in the two cities. One must not conclude from these numbers that developers or landowners will never wield market power in urban areas. The point is that it is possible to develop measures that will help to indicate whether monopolistic practices are likely to be a factor in particular urban areas. This is important because policy instruments may be developed to combat monopolistic practices where none exist and thus have no effect on controlling rapid increases in land prices that stem from other causes.

Conclusion

The data available on the distribution land values within urban areas provide strong support for the hypothesis that land values are closely related to the distribution of urban population as measured by population density. This empirical finding indicates that urban economic models of the spatial structure of cities can provide useful insights about the role of land in urban development. Moreover, this result is not limited to cities in developed countries, for the empirical relation seems to hold in Third World cities as well.

Land values within cities tend to decline as distance from the center of the city increases. This land-value gradient is steeper in small cities than in large ones, but in all sizes of cities, the gradient has become less steep over time. The relative flattening of the urban land-value gradients has accompanied the decentralization of urban population. Many analysts attribute the decentralization of population and the flattening of land-value gradients in cities to increases in household income and decreases in the costs of urban passenger transportation. A logical consequence of the flattening of the land-value gradient is that the rate of increase of land prices at the periphery of urban areas will exceed the rate of increase of land prices at the center of urban areas. There is much concern among policymakers in less-developed countries about "excessive" land-price increases at the periphery of cities because low-income households typically reside at peripheral locations. It is important to realize that higher-than-average rates of land-price increase at the urban periphery are an inevitable consequence of urban growth. This is due to both the flattening of land-value gradients over time and to the fact that large cities have flatter land-value gradients than do small cities.

In addition to examining the distribution of land values within cities, this paper also formulated and attempted to test several hypotheses about the determinants of aggregate land values and their growth in cities. Virtually no empirical support was found at the city level for the hypotheses that average population density or city size was associated with increases in urban land values. There was weak support, however, for the hypotheses that urban land values grow in proportion to the value of urban output and in proportion to the urban population. These relationships should help provide some guidance in determining when increases in urban land values may be large and reflect speculative pressures or monopolistic practices rather than efficient market outcomes. In the context of determining when a price increase is excessive, it is necessary to have a sound basis for what would constitute a normal price increase.

Finally, the literature on natural resources provides an additional insight about land-value increases: the total rate of return on land should be similar to that of other assets of similar risk. This total rate of return will have at least two components: annual rent income and capital gains. The return on developed land will be largely in terms of annual rents, while the return on underdeveloped land near the urban periphery will be largely capital gains. This systematic change in income components with distance from the city center illustrates one source of the declining land-value gradient and also provides another reference point for what constitutes a normal return in the land market.

Acknowledgments

I have benefited from discussions on various aspects of this paper with Eugene Kroch, Rakesh Mohan, Rodrigo Villamizar, and other members of the City Study; and I thank Sungyong Kang for research assistance. The views expressed are my own and should not be attributed to the World Bank.

Notes

1. These figures are derived from a detailed description of land use and value in Korea. See Mills and Song (1977), p. 167.
2. Cited by Mills (1972), p. 49. Land rents ranged from 7.7 percent of national income in 1850 to 6.4 percent in 1956.
3. For a technical exposition of this characteristic, measured by the elasticity of substitution, see Nicholson (1972), p. 346.
4. For an introduction to the notions of substitutability and complementarity in production functions with multiple inputs, see Berndt and Wood (1979).
5. For a derivation, see Mills (1972), pp. 79-84.
6. Direct estimates of housing-price elasticities in these countries have produced values between 0 and − 1. Population gradients may be steeper than price gradients because of adjustment lags.
7. See Herfindahl (1967) for an exposition of this point.
8. Ingram, Leonard, and Schafer (1976), p. 178.
9. Calculated from Bogotá sample data.
10. Markusen and Scheffman (1977).

References

Berndt, E.R., and Wood, D.O. 1979. "Engineering and Econometric Interpretations of Energy-Capital Complementarity." *American Economic Review*. 69 (June):342-354.

Borrero, Oscar. 1978. "Actividad Edificadora segun Firmas Constructoras en Bogotá y Cali 1974-1978." Paper CEN-41-78. Bogotá: Centro Nacional de Estudios de la Construccion.

Herfindahl, Orris C. 1967. "Depletion and Economic Theory." In Mason Gaffney, ed., *Extractive Resources and Taxation*. Madison: University of Wisconsin Press.

Ingram, Gregory K.; Leonard, Herman B.; Schafer, Robert. 1976. "Simulation of the Market Effects of Housing Allowances—Vol. 3: Development of the Supply Side of the NBER Urban Simulation Model." Report from the National Bureau of Economic Research to HUD. Contract H-1843.

Kendrick, J.W.; Lee, K.S.; and Lomask, J. 1976. *National Wealth of the United States*. New York: Conference Board.

Markusen, J.R., and Scheffman, D.T. 1977. *Urban Land Development: Speculation and Market Structure* (Toronto: University of Toronto Press).

Mills, Edwin S. 1972. *Urban Economics*. Glenview, Ill.: Scott-Foresman.

Mills, Edwin S., and Song, Byung Nak. 1977. *Korea's Urbanization and Urban Problems 1945-1975*. Working Paper 7701. Korea Development Institute.

Nicholson, Walter. 1972. *Microeconomic Theory*. Hinsdale, Ill.: Dryden Press.

Velasco, Julian, and Mier, Gilbert. 1980. "Valores y Caracteristicas de la Tierra en Cali." Planeacion Municipal de Cali, Cali, Colombia.

Villamizar, Rodrigo. 1980. "Land Prices in Bogotá between 1955 and 1978: A Descriptive Analysis." Urban and Regional Report No. 80-2. Washington, D.C.: Development Economics Department, World Bank.

9

Landownership and Market Dynamics at the Urban Periphery: Implications for Land Policy Design and Implementation

H. James Brown,
Robyn Swaim Phillips, and
Neal A. Roberts

Government policy toward land at the urban periphery has created a great many regulatory and tax laws and some of the most colorful anagrams. The PUDs and TDRs and development freezes and agricultural assessment districts have kept lawyers, legislators, and planners in business from the local town hall to the state house. Governments at the local, state, and federal level have churned out a vast array of mechanisms to regulate, tax, buy, and service fringe land. Often the government policies that are most crucial to the land market participant—such as the capital gains provision of federal income tax statutes or preferential treatment under local property tax laws—are spawned without regard for their impact on the built form.

Decision makers at the various levels of government and those who advise them are continually being asked to formulate and evaluate policies directed at problems associated with urban expansion. To evaluate the ability of land policies to accomplish their stated objectives and their equity implications, policymakers must first have some sort of an idea of the land market they are seeking to manipulate. To formulate policies, decision makers must either fall back on some intuitive or folk understanding of that market or use the conceptual pictures painted by various professionals.

Up to now there has been very little systematic research on land markets at the urban periphery. There is neither a well-developed theory that accounts for the large-scale shift of resources as rural land is developed for urban use nor a well-documented account of the personalized decision making of individual landowners. As Clawson pointed out in 1971, "Of all groups involved in the process of suburban growth, least is known about the landowners, speculators and dealers—and, considering how little we know about some other groups, that is a strong statement."[1] As public attention has focused on this land market, the lack of an empirical basis for policy formulation has become more noticeable. Sargent recently pointed out that because we do not understand the process, "existing land use controls such as planning and zoning decisions are typically built upon an inadequate conceptual and legal foundation and inevitably prove less than adequate in execution.''[2]

To address this need, a large-scale study of the land market at the urban periphery was initiated with the support of the Lincoln Institute of Land Policy. Over a two-year period, interviews were conducted with nearly seven hundred owners of undeveloped land at the periphery of six metropolitan areas in North America.[3] The survey focused on determining the characteristics of owners of urban fringe land and on the factors affecting their landholding behavior. The characteristics of individual owners and land parcels were subsequently aggregated to provide insight into the market dynamics that precede the conversion of rural fringe land to urban use. The survey was particularly directed at understanding the implications of these individual owner characteristics and of the aggregate pattern of transition for public-policy efforts directed at affecting the timing, location, or the form of urban expansion at the metropolitan periphery.

The findings from this research effort provide important new insight concerning the nature of the land market at the urban fringe. For example, the study identifies several distinct types of owners of fringe land with sharply differing ownership characteristics and motivations for holding rural land. These include rural users, investor speculators, and land developers. Further, the study shows that because of the opportunity for speculative profits, changes in the ownership and the character and use of land itself begin fifteen or more years before the land is actually converted for urban use. This means that the character of rural land and landownership has already changed in important ways in anticipation of future development long before public-policy efforts directed at influencing that development take form. Also, the fringe land market is considerably more active than has been previously thought, with a significant fraction of the land changing hands over a relatively short period. At the same time, another large segment of the market is characterized by stability and very long-term ownership, even on the part of investors.

These and other characteristics of landowners and the land market reveal that many of the policies and programs directed at public purposes are based on faulty conceptual models. Consequently they often are not very effective at achieving their intended purpose and may provide unintended subsidies for the wrong groups. In some cases, programs may actually promote other undesirable outcomes.

Landownership at the Urban Periphery

Owners of undeveloped land at the edge of metropolitan areas can be described in two distinct ways. The first, and most straightforward, focuses on ownership and use characteristics of land parcels, while the second focuses on the characteristics of the total land area. The first approach considers all owners to be of equal importance and is appropriate when the purpose is to describe owners of fringe land. The second weights owners of large parcels more heavily than owners of small parcels and is appropriate when the purpose is to describe who owns the land area.

Because land parcels vary in size, the two ways of describing land often yield very different results. This is illustrated by table 9-1, which shows that although most land parcels located at the urban fringe are relatively small, a large fraction of the land area is held in quite large parcels. Although 85 percent of the land parcels in the U.S. sample and 66 percent of the Canadian parcels are less than twenty-five acres each, these small parcels represent only a fraction of all land located at the urban periphery. On the other hand, the 4 percent of U.S. land parcels larger than one hundred acres accounts for more than 40 percent of the total fringe land. The distribution is even more striking in Canada where two-thirds of the land area is held in only 13 percent of the land parcels larger than one hundred acres.

The distinction between land parcels and land area has direct policy importance. A land policy can affect most owners but little land area, or few owners and a great deal of land. It is important to be clear about which profile is being considered. Since both are of interest, owner and use characteristics are described for land parcels as well as for the total land area.

Overview of Owners and Land

The overwhelming proportion of urban fringe land is owned by individuals: 85 percent of all land parcels in the U.S. sample and 79 percent in the Canadian sample are owned by individuals, representing more than two-thirds of

Table 9-1
Parcel Size
(percentage)

	United States		Canada	
Number of Acres	*Parcels*	*Land*	*Parcels*	*Land*
1-9	62	12	36	3
10-24	23	18	30	9
25-99	12	29	20	21
100-199	3	19	9	24
200-499	1	12	4	26
500 and over	*	11	*	18

Note: U.S. sample = 448; Canadian sample = 271.
*Less than 0.5 percent.

the total land area (table 9-2). Partnerships and corporations own only about 7 percent of all parcels in the U.S. cities and 12 percent in the Canadian cities. Because of the relatively large size of their holdings, however, partnerships and corporations control 18 percent of the total land area in the U.S. and 21 percent in Canada. Family-held businesses account for about 10 percent of the land area in both countries.

The land market at the urban fringe is relatively active. Table 9-3 shows that one-third of the land parcels in the United States were purchased by their present owner since 1970, and nearly 60 percent were purchased since 1960. In Canada as well, six of every ten parcels have changed owners since 1960. About one-fourth of the total fringe land has been sold at least once in the past eight years in both the United States and Canada. At the other extreme, a significant share of urban fringe land has been held for a relatively long period. Approximately 20 percent of the land has been held by the same owner for more than twenty years.

Agriculture remains the dominant use of fringe land in the Canadian cities, but nearly half of U.S. fringe land is used solely for residential purposes or is left idle. Table 9-4 shows that almost 80 percent of the total land area in the Canadian sample is cultivated for agricultural purposes, with approximately half of this also serving as a place of residence for a farm family. Agricultural landholdings are quite large, demonstrated by the much smaller fraction of total parcels (42 percent) cultivated for agricultural purposes. About one-third of the Canadian parcels, representing only 8 percent of the land, are used solely for residential purposes, and only 7 percent of the land is left unused. In contrast, less than half of U.S. fringe land and only 18 percent of the land parcels are farmed. Residential land use is more common, accounting for half of all land parcels, although these tend to be relatively small. Nearly one-fourth of the land parcels and total land area of the urban fringe of the U.S. cities has no current use.

In summary, for the U.S. cities, a majority of fringe land is held in parcels smaller than one hundred acres; however, most parcels are less than

Table 9-2
Form of Ownership
(percentage)

| | United States | | Canada | |
	Parcels	Land	Parcels	Land
Individual	85	69	79	67
Family business	8	13	8	9
Partnership	3	8	4	6
Corporation	4	10	8	15
Other	*	1	1	3

Note: U.S. sample = 447; Canadian sample = 272.

*Less than 0.5 percent.

Table 9-3
Year Acquired
(percentage)

Parcels Acquired Since	United States		Canada	
	Parcels	*Land*	*Parcels*	*Land*
1970	34	26	20	24
1960	59	56	59	59
1950	83	80	89	79

Note: U.S. sample = 443; Canadian sample = 247.

ten acres. Landowners are typically individuals or families, although partnerships and corporations hold a disproportionate share of large parcels. One in every three owners has acquired the land since 1970. About half of the land area is cultivated for agriculture, and half is used solely for residential purposes or is left idle. For the Canadian cities, landholdings are markedly larger, with fully two-thirds of the land held in parcels greater than one hundred acres. Similar to the United States, individual and family owners dominate, and one-quarter of the land area has changed hands since 1970. A much higher fraction of the total land area is currently farmed, although a number of smaller residential parcels are found as well.

Types of Landowners

Landowners hold fringe land for many reasons: personal or business use, investment purposes, or future development. These reasons may not be mutually exclusive. For example, land purchased for a personal residence may also be considered an investment. The landowners surveyed were asked to identify the principal reason they purchased their property.[4] On the basis of the response to this question, three distinct types of land owners were distinguished.

Table 9-4
Current Use of Land
(percentage)

	United States		Canada	
	Parcels	*Land*	*Parcels*	*Land*
Residence only	50	25	36	8
Farm only	5	19	19	40
Farm and residence	13	27	23	39
Other	7	7	9	6
No use	25	23	14	7

Note: U.S. sample = 449; Canadian sample = 272.

Users acquire and hold land primarily for the purpose of using it. The archetypal user is a farmer, although there are a variety of other types of rural users such as owners of a woodlot or sand pit or people who prefer to live in a rural environment. In most cases, rural users acquired their land long before future urban use was anticipated. Users often have skills associated with their present use of the land and are likely to place high personal value on their ability to produce income from the land or from living on the land. A strong personal attachment to a particular parcel encourages rural users to hold on to the land despite increasing prices and rising development pressures.

Investors acquire urban fringe land in anticipation of earning a capital return from appreciation in land values as the potential for urban use is recognized. The significant characteristic of investors is that they neither use the land in a rural state (although they may rent the land to a farmer) nor have expertise in developing the land for urban use. Investors seek to acquire undeveloped land with a minimal equity investment, catch an upswing of land prices, and make a return many times the original down payment plus finance charges. Investors hope to sell at the earliest possible time but realize that a long wait may be necessary before earning the expected return.

Developers acquire fringe land for the purpose of developing it for urban use. Developers take the action that transforms rural land into cities. Development is often directed by large corporate actors, although there are many small-scale private entrepreneurs as well. The most striking characteristic of this type of owner is the fact that they work with institutional financing, and their time frame is dramatically shorter than the investor's.[5]

Table 9-5 shows that users are the dominant owner type in fringe areas of Canada and the United States. Fully three-fourths of all owners acquired their land primarily for personal or business use. These owners hold more than 70 percent of the total land area. Owners who acquired their land for investment purposes account for approximately 20 percent of the fringe

Table 9-5
Motivation for Acquiring Land
(percentage)

	United States		Canada	
	Parcels	*Land*	*Parcels*	*Land*
Personal use	76	71	74	73
Investment	21	18	16	12
Development	2	6	10	13
Other	2	5	*	1

Note: U.S. sample = 443; Canadian sample = 267.
* Less than 0.5 percent.

land surrounding the four U.S. cities. Investors are less important in the two Canadian cities, where they hold only 12 percent of the land. Conversely, owners who acquired land for development purposes are relatively more important in Canada than in the United States. Developers own 13 percent of urban fringe land in Canada but only half that fraction in the United States.

Users: Users are the largest owner group, accounting for more than three-quarters of all parcels and 70 percent of the total land area in both the United States and Canada. Contrary to popular stereotypes, most owners who acquired rural land primarily for personal or business use are not farmers. Although 90 percent own the property as individuals or as a family business, only a minority farm their land. Table 9-6 shows that only 28 percent of the U.S. users and 37 percent of Canadian users cultivate their land. In fact, the most-prevalent land use is residential; 42 percent of Canadian users and 58 percent of U.S. users live on their land but do not farm it. Agricultural parcels tend to be significantly larger than residential parcels, and so agricultural land accounts for a greater share of total acres owned by users than residential use. Indeed nearly 75 percent of all Canadian user-owned acres are under cultivation.

This point is reinforced by the occupational characteristics of land-owners. Only 8 percent of U.S. parcels and 26 percent of fringe land in the United States is owned by individuals who identify farming as their principal occupation. Nearly one-fifth of all parcels and land is held by those employed in business or a profession, and an equal fraction are retired. Farmers are a more-important group in Canada where they own 23 percent of the parcels and 63 percent of fringe-land area. Even so, over three-quarters of all Canadian parcels and one-third of all land is owned by persons employed in nonagricultural occupations.

Not surprisingly, given the number of retired owners and farmers, the income distribution of users is not especially high, although the median is above $20,000 (table 9-7). Almost 90 percent of users have incomes under

Table 9-6
Current Use: Land Held for Personal or Business Use
(percentage)

	United States		Canada	
	Parcels	*Land*	*Parcels*	*Land*
Residence	58	31	42	13
Farm	4	13	13	32
Farm and residence	14	30	24	42
Other	7	7	11	6
No use	18	20	10	8

Note: U.S. sample = 292; Canadian sample = 179.

Table 9-7
Personal Income of Owners Holding Land for Personal Use
(percentage)

	United States		Canada	
	Parcels	*Land*	*Parcels*	*Land*
Less than $20,000	45	44	65	39
$20,000-49,999	43	26	11	13
$50,000-99,999	1	5	3	3
$100,000-249,999	*	3	*	*
$250,000 or more	11	23	22	45

Note U.S. sample = 292; Canadian sample = 179.

$50,000. In both nations, however, a small group of users have very high incomes; 11 percent of U.S. users and 22 percent of Canadian users have annual incomes above $250,000. These wealthy owners control very large landholdings. In the United States, they own nearly a quarter of the user-held land area, and in Canada they own 45 percent.

Owners who acquired land primarily for personal or business use do not tend to be active participants in the land market. Half of the users in our sample had held their land parcel for more than twenty years. Most own only a single land property currently and, indeed, in their entire lifetime. This one property often represents the owner's chief personal asset. Roughly 80 percent of users in the United States and a slightly higher percentage in Canada plan to continue the present use of their land for the next five years. Only about 10 percent anticipate selling their land in that time period (table 9-8).

To summarize, owners who acquired property for personal use own the majority of land located at the fringe of metropolitan areas. They are also the most numerous owner group, holding many small residential parcels. Users are not typically farmers, and the land they hold is not typically cultivated for agriculture, particularly in the United States. Personal incomes

Table 9-8
Five-Year Plans: Land Held for Personal Use
(percentage)

	United States		Canada	
	Parcels	*Land*	*Parcels*	*Land*
Do nothing; hold	80	78	85	89
Develop	7	5	8	3
Sell; subdivide	12	14	7	7
Other	1	2	*	1

Note: U.S. sample = 312; Canadian sample = 195.
*Less than 0.5 percent.

are not especially high, although the median is above $20,000. Most users view their property as their chief personal asset and are not active in land-market transactions. Most would not consider selling their land and intend to continue the present use of their land over at least the next five years. These characteristics indicate a strong personal attachment to the land.

Investors: Investors comprise about 20 percent of U.S. landowners and about 15 percent of Canadian owners. As table 9-9 shows, most investors are individuals, although partnerships and corporations own a substantial share of the total land area. One-third of investment-owned fringe land in the United States and one-half of land in Canada is owned by partnerships (including syndicates) and corporations, with partnerships owning about twice the total land area as corporations in both countries. Land held for investment shows considerable variation in terms of parcel size. Most investors hold relatively small parcels; however, one-fourth of investment-owned land in the United States is held in parcels of two hundred or more acres. These large investment tracts tend to be held either by corporations or syndicates.

A large fraction of fringe land held for investment purposes is used for agriculture; 43 percent of U.S. and 73 percent of Canadian investor-held land is cultivated (table 9-10). In large part this reflects investors renting to farmers while waiting for land values to rise. This pattern is less common in the United States, where 43 percent of investor-held acres have no current land use. In contrast, only 6 percent of the investment-held land in Canada is not currently used.

Investors have substantially higher personal incomes than users. The median income for fringe-land investors in the United States is nearly $50,000, and more than one-third of investors have personal incomes above $250,000 (table 9-11).[6] Median income is lower for Canadian investors, but

Table 9-9
Form of Ownership: Land Held for Investment
(percentage)

	United States		Canada	
	Parcels	*Land*	*Parcels*	*Land*
Individual	82	53	69	36
Family business	4	13	11	15
Partnership	9	23	17	33
Corporation	5	11	4	15
Other	1	1	*	*

Note: U.S. sample = 80; Canadian sample = 33.
*Less than 0.5 percent.

Table 9-10
Current Use: Land Held for Investment
(percentage)

| | United States | | Canada | |
	Parcels	Land	Parcels	Land
Residence	33	13	49	15
Farm	6	30	24	55
Farm and residence	4	13	11	18
Other	2	3	1	6
No use	56	43	15	6

Note: U.S. sample = 80; Canadian sample = 33.

more than half of the total land area is held by persons earning over $250,000 annually. In both the United States and Canada, over 50 percent of noncorporation investors are employed in business, a profession, or real estate. These owners hold nearly two-thirds of the investment-held land (table 9-12). The property surveyed in this study represented the chief asset for only about one-quarter of investors versus 70 percent of users. Clearly a group of quite wealthy individuals owns a substantial part of the total land held for investment.

Investors as a group are active participants in the urban fringe-land market. Ten percent of investor owners (representing 20 percent of the land area in the United States and 30 percent in Canada) are very active, buying and selling land on a regular basis. Another 30 percent are somewhat less active, transacting land every four to ten years. These active investors often own substantial amounts of other fringe land, frequently in excess of five hundred acres. These large-scale investors own more than one-fourth of the investor-held land in our sample. At the other extreme, a substantial share of owners who purchase rural land as an investment own no other property.

Table 9-11
Personal Income of Owners Holding Land for Investment Purposes
(percentage)

| | United States | | Canada | |
	Parcels	Land	Parcels	Land
Less than $20,000	26	16	47	9
$20,000-49,999	29	28	14	26
$50,000-99,999	8	9	11	4
$100,000-249,999	3	12	7	8
$250,000 or more	35	35	22	52

Note: U.S. sample = 68; Canadian sample = 23.

Table 9-12
Occupation of Owners Holding Land for Investment Purposes
(percentage)

| | United States | | Canada | |
	Parcels	Land	Parcels	Land
Farmer	1	2	6	13
Real estate related	31	21	20	29
Business, professional	27	43	32	50
Retired	3	13		
Other	39	22	43	8

Note: U.S. sample = 68; Canadian sample = 24.

These tend to be individuals who acquire a small lot as a personal investment.

Investors tend to hold land for a shorter period than users; at the same time, much land investment is long term. About half of the investor-held land in our sample was acquired after 1970. However, 20 percent of Canadian investors and 28 percent of U.S. investors acquired their land prior to 1960. As a group, investors are considerably more anxious to sell their land than are users. Nearly 40 percent of U.S. investors plan to sell or subdivide their land within the next five years, and one-third of the investment-held land is currently for sale (table 9-13). Recall that only 10 percent of user-owned land was currently available for purchase. Canadian investors generally express a longer time frame, with one-third of the land area planned for sale or subdivision in the next five years and one-fifth available for sale immediately. This compares to the plans of user owners in Canada, where nearly 90 percent plan to hold their land for the next five years. Clearly, in both the United States and Canada, investors are very active participants in the land market.

To summarize, investors are typically employed in business, a profession, or in a real-estate-related occupation and have high personal incomes.

Table 9-13
Five-Year Plans: Land Held for Investment Purposes
(percentage)

| | United States | | Canada | |
	Parcels	Land	Parcels	Land
Do nothing, hold	55	48	79	63
Develop	9	10	5	16
Sell, subdivide	36	42	16	22

Note: U.S. sample = 77; Canadian sample = 32.

A substantial share of the land held for investment is owned by partnerships and corporations. Investors are reasonably active in land markets and often own several land parcels. Typically they have some explicit action planned for their property over the next five years. Canadian investors tend to continue the agricultural use of land while waiting for land values to rise, while many U.S. investors allow the land to lie idle. Nearly one in four investors has held the land for more than twenty years.

Developers: Developers are the least-important owner type in terms of number of parcels and total land area held, but they are the most active. Developers own substantially more fringe land in Canada (13 percent) than in the United States (6 percent).

Land held for development in the United States is evenly divided between individual and family owners on the one hand, and corporations and partnerships on the other (table 9-14). In contrast, corporations own more than 80 percent of the Canadian land held for development, although many small-scale individual developers are found in Canada, as well as in the United States. Canadian development corporations tend to hold very large land parcels, frequently in excess of five hundred acres. U.S. developers hold much smaller parcels on average.

Developers are quite active in the urban fringe-land market. U.S. developers typically buy and sell land at least once every three years. Large Canadian developers are even more active, with 80 percent buying and selling land on a regular basis. More than 40 percent of the developer-held land in the United States and 90 percent in Canada are owned by parties who have other land holdings in excess of two hundred acres.

The majority of developer-held land in our sample was acquired by the present owner since 1970. Most of the remaining was acquired during the 1960s, although some developers have been holding land since the 1950s.

Table 9-14
Forms of Ownership: Land Held for Development
(percentage)

	United States		Canada	
	Parcels	*Land*	*Parcels*	*Land*
Individual	41	27	67	6
Family business	15	19		
Partnership	32	23	3	9
Corporation	12	31	28	83
Other	*	*	2	3

Note: U.S. sample = 26; Canadian sample = 35.
*Less than 0.5 percent.

Two-thirds of U.S. developers plan to develop their parcel in the next five years (table 9-15). However, nearly two-thirds of the total land owned by developers is up for sale, and less than half is planned for development in the next five years. Large U.S. developers appear to be looking around for alternatives even though they originally purchased the land for development. In contrast, Canadian developers express very clear intentions to develop their holdings over the next five years. It would appear that the institutional setting in Canada provides a much more certain process and, therefore, more certainty on the part of developers.

In summary, developers own only a small fraction of urban fringe land, particularly in the United States. Many developers are small-scale individual owners, but the majority of developer-owned land is held by corporations and partnerships. Large-scale development firms are active participants in the land market and often have substantial landholdings. Most developers have held their land for fewer than eight years and plan to develop it within the next five years, although some U.S. developers anticipate selling their land.

Land-Market Dynamics

By comparing the characteristics of land and landowners in fringe areas where development pressures are relatively intense to those where pressures are less strong, it is possible to gain insight into the dynamics of the land market at the urban periphery. The evidence indicates that several distinct submarkets are found at the urban fringe, with the character of land and landowners showing sharp differences among them. The transition from rural to urban is not abrupt; it is a gradual process of replacement whereby traditional rural owners sell their land to investors and developers. This transition begins more than fifteen years before the land is actually developed for urban use. The pace of land turnover depends on the willingness of owners to sell their land.

Table 9-15
Five-Year Plans: Land Held for Development
(percentage)

	United States		Canada	
	Parcels	*Land*	*Parcels*	*Land*
Do nothing, hold	14	16	3	17
Develop	65	48	95	73
Sell, subdivide	21	36	1	3
Other	*	*	1	7

Note: U.S. sample = 25; Canadian sample = 30.
*Less than 0.5 percent.

Land Submarkets

The composition of owners and the size and use of rural landholdings differ greatly between fringe areas where development pressures are intense and areas where development pressures are less strong. Still, important shifts in land and ownership in anticipation of future urban expansion can be seen in fringe areas not likely to develop for fifteen or more years.

Investors and developers own a much larger fraction of the land area where development pressures are strong than where they are moderate or weak (table 9-16). Investors own 30.6 percent of the land and developers own 12.1 percent of the land in fringe areas under intense development pressure in the United States. By contrast, in fringe areas where development pressures are moderate or weak, owners holding land for personal or business use own more than 80 percent of the total land area. Still, even in areas where conversion for urban use is ten to fifteen years in the future, investors already hold 14 percent of the land. Developers, on the other hand, own less than 4 percent.

Investors and developers are even more prominent among recent buyers of fringe land. Where development pressures are intense, investors own nearly half of the total land area transacted since 1968, and developers own nearly 20 percent in the four U.S. cities; less than one-third of recent buyers plan to use the land personally. Where development pressures are less strong, investors have purchased about one-fourth of the acres recently transacted; two-thirds of recent buyers are personal or business users.

Table 9-16
Motivation for Acquiring Land by Development Pressures
(percentage of land area)

	United States		Canada	
	Intense	*Moderate-Weak*	*Intense*	*Moderate-Weak*
All owners[a]				
Personal use	57.3	82.1	46.0	85.3
Investment	30.6	14.1	20.3	9.5
Development	12.1	3.7	33.8	5.3
Owners acquiring land since 1968[b]				
Personal use	31.9	69.0	20.0	74.5
Investment	48.9	24.1	30.0	14.9
Development	19.7	6.9	50.0	10.6

[a]Sample size for areas of intense development pressure is 128 for the United States and 79 for Canada. For areas of weak development pressure, the sample size is 321 and 193, respectively.
[b]Sample size for areas of intense development pressure is 48 for the United States and 41 for Canada. For areas of weak development pressure, the sample size is 99 and 48, respectively.

A similar pattern is observed in the Canadian cities. Investors and developers own more than half of the total land and 80 percent of land recently sold on the market in areas where development pressures are strong but only half this amount in areas of more-distant development prospects. In comparison to the United States, developers own a larger fraction of the fringe land in Canada, particularly in areas of strong development pressure. Developers hold more than one-third of the total land area and have purchased fully half of the acres sold on the market since 1968 in areas of intense development pressure.

In fringe areas where development pressures are intense, partnerships and corporations own 22.8 percent of the land in the United States and 46.6 percent in Canada (table 9-17). They own an even greater fraction of recently sold land: 36.1 percent and 65.9 percent, respectively. In contrast, individual owners dominate in fringe areas where development prospects are less immediate. Still, even where urban use is ten to fifteen years in the future, corporations and partnerships are acquiring land as it becomes available on the market. More than 20 percent of the land sold since 1968 in fringe areas of moderate to weak development pressures has been acquired by partnerships or corporations in both the United States and Canada.

Shifts in the characteristics and motivation of owners are paralleled by shifting land use as development pressures rise. Table 9-18 shows that less land is used for agriculture in areas of intense development pressure than in other fringe areas for both the United States and Canada. Even more important, only about 15 percent of the land acquired since 1968 in these areas

Table 9-17
Form of Ownership by Development Pressures
(percentage of land area)

	United States		Canada	
	Intense	*Moderate-Weak*	*Intense*	*Moderate-Weak*
All Owners[a]				
Individual or family	77.2	84.5	53.4	86.9
Partnership	10.2	7.0	9.6	5.2
Corporation	12.6	8.5	37.0	7.9
Owners acquiring land since 1968[b]				
Individual or family	63.8	78.6	34.1	74.5
Partnership	19.1	8.2	12.2	8.5
Corporation	17.0	13.3	53.7	17.0

[a]Sample size for areas of intense development pressure is 128 for the United States and 79 for Canada. For areas of weak development pressure, the sample size is 321 and 193, respectively.
[b]Sample size for areas of intense development pressure is 48 for the United States and 41 for Canada. For areas of weak development pressure, the sample size is 99 and 48, respectively.

Table 9-18
Current Land Use by Development Pressures
(percentage of land area)

	United States		Canada	
	Intense	*Moderate-Weak*	*Intense*	*Moderate-Weak*
All owners[a]				
Agricultural	38.3	48.3	70.9	79.3
Nonagricultural	33.6	32.7	25.3	14.0
No use	28.1	19.0	3.8	6.7
Farm land personally	21.9	38.3	29.1	66.8
Owners acquiring land since 1968[b]				
Agricultural	35.4	40.4	85.4	58.3
Nonagricultural	31.3	36.4	12.2	27.1
No use	33.3	23.2	2.4	14.6
Farm land personally	14.6	29.3	17.1	37.5

[a]Sample size for areas of intense development pressure is 128 for the United States and 79 for Canada. For areas of weak development pressure, the sample size is 321 and 193, respectively.
[b]Sample size for areas of intense development pressure is 48 for the United States and 41 for Canada. For areas of weak development pressure, the sample size is 99 and 48, respectively.

is farmed personally by the new owner. Individual farmers, as commonly pictured, clearly constitute only a small fraction of landowners or recent land buyers in areas under strong development pressure. By contrast, in fringe areas of moderate to weak development prospects, individual farmers own about one-third of the land area in the United States and about two-thirds of the land area in Canada. Farmers also account for about one-third of recently purchased land.

As development pressures rise, average parcel size declines with the splitting up of large rural landholdings, particularly in the United States. In U.S. fringe areas where conversion for urban use is remote, more than a third of the land is held in parcels larger than two hundred acres; however, where development expectations are immediate, fewer than one in ten parcels is larger than two hundred acres, and more than 40 percent of the land is held in parcels of fewer than ten acres. Less splitting occurs in Canada, where even in areas of intense development pressure, about 40 percent of the land remains in parcels larger than two hundred acres. This reflects the very large size of many Canadian land investors and developers and stricter government controls on subdivision.

Recent buyers of land appear to have a shorter time perspective than do long-term landholders. In fringe areas of intense development pressure, only 41.5 percent of recent U.S. buyers anticipate that they will own their land five years in the future; 36.6 percent plan to sell before then, and 21.9 percent plan to develop the land (table 9-19). In Canada, more than 40 percent

Table 9-19
Five-Year Plans by Development Pressures
(percentage of land area)

| | United States | | Canada | |
	Intense	*Moderate-Weak*	*Intense*	*Moderate-Weak*
All owners[a]				
Continue existing use, hold	51.7	81.2	62.7	86.8
Sell	33.6	13.8	11.9	6.8
Develop	14.7	5.0	25.4	6.3
Consider immediate sale	37.3	17.4	19.2	13.4
Owners acquiring land since 1968[b]				
Continue existing use, hold	41.5	78.2	52.9	79.5
Sell	36.6	11.5	2.9	9.1
Develop	21.9	10.3	44.1	11.4
Consider immediate sale	36.8	16.0	16.2	17.8

[a]Sample size for areas of intense development pressure is 128 for the United States and 79 for Canada. For areas of weak development pressure, the sample size is 321 and 193, respectively.
[b]Sample size for areas of intense development pressure is 48 for the United States and 41 for Canada. For areas of weak development pressure, the sample size is 99 and 48, respectively.

of recent buyers in the areas of strong development pressures plan to develop their land within five years.

Dynamics of Change

Bringing these separate pieces together, we can begin to trace the transition process that occurs as rural land ripens for urban development. Prior to the time that development expectations take on clear form, rural land at the urban periphery is held in relatively large tracts, which frequently are farmed. This land is largely owned by individuals or families who acquired it for personal use (typically a farm or rural residence); often the land represents the owner's chief personal asset. These rural users do not tend to be active participants in the real estate market. Most anticipate that they will continue their current use of the land for at least the next five years; few express an interest in selling their land immediately.

As conversion for urban use becomes more imminent and certain, traditional rural users are replaced by owners who acquire land for investment purposes or, if development expectations are imminent, acquire land with the intention of developing it for urban use. A substantial proportion of investors maintain the land in agricultural use while waiting for values to rise but do not consider themselves to be farmers. The land parcel often represents only a small portion of the owner's total assets, which frequently include substantial other landholdings. Most intend either to sell their land or develop it within the next five years. A substantial number are willing to sell their land immediately if a good offer were forthcoming.

The transfer of rural land from traditional owners who hold the land for current rural use to investors and developers who value the land for its potential urban use is the cumulative result of the former group's selling their land to the latter group. This occurs when rural owners split off one or several parcels from their landholding or when they sell the entire land tract.

This transfer of ownership is illustrated by the contrast between recent buyers of land and long-term owners. As tables 9-16, 9-17, and 9-19 show, owners who have acquired their land since 1968 are markedly less rural in character, motivation, and land use than are long-term owners, particularly in fringe areas where development pressures are intense. Recent owners are more frequently corporations or syndicates than individuals or families; they are more often motivated by investment or development prospects rather than by personal or business use of the land; they typically expect to hold their land for a shorter time; fewer are farmers and more are employed in real estate, business, or other professions; more often they are active participants in the land market.

These differences between recent purchasers and long-term owners reflect increasing development pressures. Whereas long-term owners acquired their land at an earlier time when expectations of urban development were remote or often nonexistent, recent purchasers reflect current market conditions, which include the perceived opportunity for speculative profits from future urban use of the land. Consistent with this, the proportion of post-1968 buyers who exhibit urban characteristics increases sharply as development pressures intensify. Recent buyers of land in areas expected to develop for urban use within the next five years are more likely to be syndicates or corporations, to be motivated by investment profits, and to plan to sell the land within the next five years than are recent buyers in areas not expected to develop for ten or fifteen years. But even in fringe areas where development expectations are quite remote, recent purchasers of land differ in important ways from long-term rural landowners.

As more and more rural users sell to investors, developers, or low-density urban users, the cumulative effect is reflected in a shift in the composition of ownership and land characteristics. Because the normal rate of turnover in rural land is relatively slow, this transition is a gradual process. Furthermore the transition is never complete. Some long-term investors are found in areas where development pressures are weak, and a residue of rural users remains in areas of intense development pressure.

The pace of land turnover in anticipation of future urban development depends on the willingness of owners to sell their land. Interviews with previous owners who sold their land and with current owners who indicate an interest in selling their land suggest that at a given time, a surprisingly large fraction of urban fringe land is available for acquisition, particularly in areas where development pressures are intense. Owners of nearly 40 percent of the total U.S. land in areas of strong development pressure indicate that they are currently considering selling their land.

Some owner types are markedly less willing to sell their land than others. In particular, individual or family owners, personal users of the land (particularly farmers), and middle-aged owners are less willing to sell than are syndicates or corporations, owners motivated by investment or development, those who do not use the land, young owners, and those of retirement age. The resistance of the former groups to sell appears to reflect a strong personal attachment of these owners to their land. The latter owner types are more responsive to a good offer. For all types of owners, the expressed willingness to sell increases as development pressures intensify, suggesting that rising land values induce some owners to sell who would not have sold otherwise.

Family and life-cycle factors are the reasons mentioned most often by owners who are considering selling their land (table 9-20). Even in areas of intense development pressures, family factors are cited as important by more than one-third of owners expressing an interest in selling. Rising land prices are an important factor precipitating a sale for about 20 percent of fringe landowners and nearly 30 percent of those holding land in areas of intense development pressures. Rising property taxes are mentioned as a reason for selling land in areas of intense development pressure but not elsewhere. Liquidity needs often are met by selling a portion of a larger landholding rather than selling the entire parcel. Nearly a third of all fringe landowners have split off one or more segments of their land since acquiring it.

The evidence generally suggests that personal factors to a large extent determine when and which land is available on the market. However, it

Table 9-20
Reasons for Considering Sale of Land, United States
(percentage)

Factor	Total	Intense	Moderate-Weak
Family or life-cycle factors	36.4	34.9	40.4
Good offer, area ripe for development	19.6	27.3	14.8
Tax factors	16.8	31.8	5.7
Better investment elsewhere	14.7	13.6	16.7

Note: Table refers to percentage of owners who are considering selling their land. Sample size is 44 for intense development pressures and 54 for moderate-weak pressures.

Percentages may total to more than 100.0 percent since multiple responses were allowed.

appears that as development pressures intensify, rising land values and increasing property taxes induce some owners to sell earlier or in response to less-pressing personal factors than they would have otherwise.

Implications for Land Policy Design
and Implementation

The empirical findings presented here show a picture of landownership and land-market dynamics at the metropolitan periphery that challenges a number of commonly held perceptions. Land policies directed at regulating urban expansion at the metropolitan fringe that are based on these faulty images will prove less than adequate in execution and may have unintended, undesirable consequences. This section examines four widely used land policies to illustrate how our research provides insight into the expected ability of land policies to achieve their intended purposes.

Preferential Tax Treatment of Agricultural Land

Most states and Canadian provinces tax agricultural land at a lower rate than other types of property. This is accomplished by either setting an assessment below the market price or by various schemes of temporary abatement with recapture provisions.

While the rationale in the minds of policymakers implementing such programs is open to debate, the legislative history and literature on the subject suggest two major objectives.[7] First, by providing a subsidy to farming, preferential tax treatment for agricultural land is intended to help maintain the rural and open character of land at the fringe of metropolitan areas. A second objective is to assist financially pressed farmers who face increasing property taxes as the urbanized city expands into the surrounding countryside.

Property taxes typically rise in urban fringe areas as land values rise in anticipation of future urban use and as demand increases for public services, such as sewers, schools, and improved roads. Higher property taxes can create cash-flow difficulties for farmers who receive no compensating increase in the income earned from farming the land (although they do receive the benefit of appreciation in the value of the land). Rising tax burdens are believed to force some farmers to sell their land. Legislators have responded by granting tax relief for land maintained in agricultural use.

Our research raises serious doubts about the effectiveness and fairness of preferential tax treatment for agricultural land in achieving either of these objectives, particularly in the United States, where less than half of the fringe land area remains in agricultural use. In addition, in both the United States and Canada, a substantial share of the subsidy flows to owner groups other than the individual farmer the program is designed to assist.

The majority of urban fringe land in the United States currently is not used for agriculture, particularly in areas under strong development pressure. Less than half of the undeveloped fringe land in our sample, and less than 40 percent of the land in areas under strong development pressure, is currently farmed. In contrast, more than 70 percent of Canadian fringe land is farmed, even in areas of intense development pressure. While a subsidy to land used in agriculture could have some impact on the amount of land maintained in rural use, most fringe land in the United States will not be affected.

Nearly a fourth of the total urban fringe land surrounding U.S. cities in our sample is used as residential property, and an equal amount is not currently used at all. As with farmers, these owners feel the pressures of rising real estate taxes. Rising tax burdens and liquidity needs can induce residential owners to sell a portion of the total landholding. Subdividing of residential property results in higher-density development and elimination of the rural character just as much as the development of agricultural land. If the objective of the policy is to maintain the rural character, programs need to be extended to meet the reality of land use at the fringe.

The patterns of landownership and land use found at the metropolitan edge of both Canada and the United States reveal that a substantial share of the subsidy granted to landowners under preferential-tax-treatment programs will benefit not individual farmers but rather land investors. Our data show the simple view that farmers hold and use fringe land until development occurs is erroneous. In reality, much land at the edge of cities passes out of the hands of farmers into the hands of investors or developers long before development occurs. Much of this land remains in agricultural use; indeed nearly 25 percent of the fringe land currently used for agriculture is owned not by farmers but by investors and developers. This is true in both the United States and Canada. Rather than being a program to assist farmers, roughly one of every four dollars of the tax subsidy goes to investor owners who are holding the land for capital gains. These are typically wealthy investors rather than the impoverished farmers whom the policy's proponents intend to assist.

The efficiency of aiding farmers and protecting farmland by means of preferential tax treatment for agricultural land is further challenged by evidence on the factors motivating landowners to sell their land. Only 16.8 percent of current landowners in our sample who are considering selling their land said that taxes were important in their decision to sell. Real estate taxes were cited as a motivating factor less often than life-cycle or family-related reasons (33.4 percent) or the fact that they had received (or expected to receive) an attractive offer to sell (19.6 percent). Tax-motivated sales are most common in areas of intense development pressure, where they were mentioned by 31.8 percent of owners considering selling. Even here, family or life-cycle factors motivated one in every three sellers, and 27 percent of owners sold in response to a good offer. The evidence indicates that tax factors are not the major cause of landowners selling their property. Preferential tax assessment for agricultural land cannot be expected to prevent owners from selling who are motivated by other factors.

Land-Speculation Taxes

A number of jurisdictions, notably the province of Ontario and the state of Vermont, have introduced taxation schemes that seek to dampen speculative activity by imposing charges on gains earned from the short-term holding and sale of land. These charges take a decreasing proportion of the gain, depending on how long the speculator holds the land. Typically land held more than five or six years is exempt from the tax.

Legislative and popular support for these tax laws rests in large part on the misconception that speculators are responsible for rising land prices and that by reducing the returns from speculation, land prices can be held down. Widespread distrust of land speculators is aggravated by their image as nonproductive owners (essentially gamblers) who earn profits from buying cheap and selling dear.

Although it is generally true that land values rise, often dramatically, during the time that investors acquire fringe land, these increases are for the most part not the result of speculative activity. In order to push land prices above what they would be otherwise, land investors would have to assert monopolistic control. Our research shows that while some investors own very large landholdings, investors neither individually nor as a group assert monopolistic power at the urban periphery. In the United States, 85 percent of land parcels and 69 percent of urban fringe land is owned by individuals, most of whom are not wealthy. Only 18 percent of the land area is held by owners for investment purposes. Even in areas where development pressures are intense, investors own less than one-third of the total land area. In Canada, just 12 percent of the total land area is owned by investors, and only about 6 percent is owned by large corporate or syndicated investors. It is extremely unlikely that investors with this kind of market power can influence the market price of fringe land.

Some observers have suggested that speculative activity itself can raise land prices above what they would otherwise be in highly speculative markets. If investors' expectations of future appreciation in land values are influenced by recent trends, then observed rises in values stimulated by inflation or exogenous demand factors may be optimistically extrapolated into the future. The higher purchase prices and increased speculative activity that result can touch off a speculative boom, bidding prices above the long-run equilibrium level in a self-sustaining spiral. This is largely a short-run phenomenon, however, since in the long run these expectations will be proven to be too high. Competitive market forces—primarily the ability of developers to purchase land elsewhere—will tend to push prices back toward equilibrium levels in the long run.

The point is that the presence of investor owners does not itself cause higher land prices. While values are observed to rise over the period that fringe land is acquired by speculators, this, in large part, reflects the normal appreciation of rural land as expectations of future urban development are capitalized into current land values. Land prices would rise from rural to urban levels whether the land were owned by investors or whether it were passed directly from rural farmers to urban developers.[8] The primary impact of investors is not upon price levels but upon who captures the implied capital gain. In the former case, the investor, or a series of investors, captures the gain. In the latter case, the capital gain will be divided between the farmer and the developer. The astute farmer will ask a price equal to that demanded by the investor—that is, a price that reflects the anticipated future income stream of the parcel. If, on the other hand, the rural owner is not fully aware of the value of his land for future urban use and accepts a lower sale price, then some portion of the capital gain is merely shifted to the developer who captures it upon sale of the (developed) land to some urban user.

As currently formulated, speculative taxes affect only investors turning the land over in a relatively short time period. Our data show that much of the investment activity occurring on the urban fringe is very long term. Indeed, only half of the investors in our sample had acquired their land parcel within the past seven years. Investors begin to purchase rural land ten to fifteen years in advance of urban development, and many investors hold land for quite long periods. Indeed nearly 30 percent of the fringe land area in our sample acquired for investment purposes had been held for twenty years, and 60 percent had been held for ten or more years. Furthermore, only one-third of the investor owners were currently considering selling their land. These data suggest that as currently formulated, speculative taxes will not affect a major share of land investors.

Our data suggest that a land-speculation tax can reduce the amount of speculative activity by reducing the short-term profits that can be earned. This is evidenced by the somewhat smaller role played by investor owners in Toronto, which has instituted a speculation tax, than in the four U.S. cities without such a tax. Investors hold 14 percent of the fringe land area in

Toronto and 19 percent in the area under strong development pressures, compared to 18 percent of the fringe land in U.S. cities and more than 30 percent in areas of intense pressure. However, there is no reason to believe that by reducing short-term speculation, land prices will be less as a result. Indeed, the evidence from Toronto suggests that investors are simply replaced by developers. More than 12 percent of fringe land in Toronto and nearly 20 percent of land under strong development pressure is owned by developers compared to 6 percent of fringe land in the United States and 12 percent of land under strong pressure.

Subdivision Control of Rural Land

Policymakers in many jurisdictions find that by the time a local municipality imposes zoning restrictions on agricultural land at the urbanized periphery, much of the land has already been split into small parcels. To counter this, subdivision controls increasingly are being imposed at the state, provincial, or regional level. These controls restrict the subdivision of land in areas that have not yet been annexed to a local municipality but that are in the path of development.

Our research shows that regional controls extending far beyond the built-up perimeters of the city are necessary to maintain land in the large parcels associated with rural use. Investors begin to acquire rural land fifteen to twenty years before development is expected to occur. These early investors begin a process that results in the smaller parcel size found at the immediate edge of metropolitan areas. Our data show that for U.S. fringe areas, when development is five to seven years in the future, twenty percent of the land is held in parcels smaller than ten acres. Less fracturing is observed in Canada where large investors and developers tend to preserve large rural holdings intact and where subdivision controls extend far from urban centers. To prevent this fracturing, subdivision controls must be imposed far into the rural countryside.

At the same time, policies of this sort may lead to a number of reactions that are viewed as detrimental to the process of land conversion. The ability to split off sections of land is one way that landowners adjust to the liquidity problems associated with holding an asset for a long period of time. Fully 30 percent of landowners in our sample sold at least one section of their land after acquiring it. Typically the reasons for selling were entirely unrelated to future urbanization. Half of the owners report that they sold the section to obtain cash to last through a difficult period or as a result of family or life-cycle changes—for instance, to provide a house lot for a married child or upon retirement. If statewide regulations prohibit owners from selling a section, some rural owners, many of them farmers, may be forced to sell their entire parcel rather than only a part of it. By eliminating split-offs as a means of financial and family adjustment, the form of ownership and use of land may be altered in ways that are not desirable.

To be effective, subdivision regulations must extend to cover a substantial part of the rural land and must be put in place long before there is any consideration of urbanization. However, by restricting even occasional split-offs based on reasonable and compassionate grounds for financial or family problems, the regulations may hasten the turnover of land from rural owners to investors or developers.

Growth Controls

Investment in land offers the potential for large capital gains for investors able to anticipate correctly future urban development in rural areas. These gains arise because of the uncertainty surrounding where and when future development will occur. Speculative profits are essentially made by correctly anticipating the development potential of land before others do so. If future development is known for certain, then speculative gains are not possible since the future urban value of the land will be fully capitalized into the seller's asking price.

Uncertainty arises from many sources, including the likely pace of urban expansion, the diverse and decentralized land-development process, and the historically ineffective policy efforts to control urban development. Suburban development in U.S. metropolitan areas takes place in a milieu where no policy or control has ever lasted very long. This uncertainty about the nature and location of development has meant that the owners who hold the land for speculative gains are different from the owners who actually develop the land.

The evidence from Calgary, which has implemented precise and strict development controls regulating where and when urban expansion may occur, suggests that such controls can affect the mix of landowners. These controls in Calgary have greatly reduced the uncertainty surrounding the timing and location of future urban development, thus reducing the potential gains from land speculation since it is very difficult for an investor to anticipate future urban use before the general market recognizes this potential. As a result, fewer investors own land and developers are much more likely to purchase land directly from rural users and to hold land for their own development.

These contrasts in the ownership of land are clear from our survey. In the United States, 25 percent of the land under strong development pressure is held by owners who purchased the land as an investment. By contrast, only 3 percent of this land at the fringe in Calgary is held by investors. Strong development controls would seem to reduce uncertainty and thus the amount of investment activity at the urban fringe.

There is little reason, however, to believe that the decrease in speculative activity has any impact on the level of land prices or the form or nature of urban development. It is possible that the removal of investors has altered the distribution of gains among rural users, investors, and developers. These redistributional impacts may be important issues for policy debate but are very different from the issues usually raised with regard to the impact of investors.

A few final comments can be made with regard to the implementation of growth-control regulations. If the controls are flexible and subject to frequent change and variance, uncertainty returns. Greater uncertainty means that gains from investment in land, and hence investors, return again. To reduce speculative activity, the controls must be implemented rigidly and with certainty.

At the same time, the implementation of controls affects the value of land and generates pressure for flexibility and variances. Owners of land designated for future urban development will expect to share in the gains from urbanization and therefore will demand a higher price than when the future use of the land parcel is uncertain. Higher asking prices will give developers an incentive to investigate the possibility of developing other property that is not yet designated for development and, therefore, has a lower price. Also, by convincing the empowered authority to expand the supply of land available for development, developers can reduce the price they must pay for land and thereby increase the return they earn.

Thus the very act of designating particular land for development begins a series of adjustments in land prices that generates pressure to relax or change the controls. The authority empowered to set the controls will be under substantial pressures to make changes and to be flexible. However, if the authority does not hold the controls strictly, uncertainty will arise again, and investors will be attracted to acquire fringe land by the opportunity for speculative gains.

Controls can affect the market for land and the ownership of land only if they are implemented strictly without variances or exceptions. But the very act of instituting the controls alters land prices and generates pressures to modify them.

Conclusion

Land policies are based on widely held perceptions of the land market and landowners. Although these simple models are often accurate and insightful, there are several conflicts between these implicit or explicit models and the reality of land markets. The knowledge gained from this study and others like it can improve our understanding of the character of the actors and their motivation and can lead to the design and implementation of more-effective land policies.

Notes

1. Marion Clawson, *Suburban Land Conversion in the United States* (Baltimore: John Hopkins University Press, 1971), p. 102.

2. Charles S. Sargent, Jr., "Land Speculation and Urban Monopoly," in *Urban Policymaking and Metropolitan Dynamics*, ed. John S. Adams (Cambridge, Mass.: Ballinger Publishing Co., 1976), p. 23.

3. Interviews were conducted between 1977 and 1979 in Atlanta, Boston, Buffalo, Calgary, Sacramento, and Toronto. The complete study is reported in H. James Brown, Robyn Swaim Phillips, and Neal A. Roberts, "Land into Cities" mimeographed (Cambridge, Mass.: Lincoln Institute of Land Policy, 1980).

4. Owners who did not purchase their property (for example, those who inherited the land or acquired it in payment for a debt) were asked the reason that they decided to retain the land.

5. This three-part typology of urban fringe landowners was originally developed in an earlier study of rural landowners in Phoenix, Arizona. See H. James Brown and Neal A. Roberts, "Land Owners at the Fringe of Urban Areas" (Cambridge: Department of City and Regional Planning, Harvard University, 1978). Reprinted with permission.

6. Investor incomes are reported for individual and family owners and for members of partnerships and syndicates. Corporate incomes are not considered here.

7. Neal A. Roberts and H. James Brown, *Property Tax Preferences for Agricultural Land* (Montclair, N.J.: Allanheld, Osmun & Co. Publishers, 1980).

8. It is likely that the presence of owners who purchase land for explicitly speculative reasons eases and speeds the recognition of rising values since these owners are probably more aware of such changes. In their absence we might observe more that rural values suddenly jump to urban levels with a single transaction from farmer to developer rather than a gradual rise made observable by multiple intervening owners. However, the final urban price is the same in either case.

Moderator

William Doebele: My favorite story coming out of this study—a story that Jim Brown and Neal Roberts did not mention—is the fact that when they were in Phoenix, Arizona, they were doing some fieldwork and they went out to the outskirts and saw a farm with an old house. There was an old man, very dusty, wearing an old hat, driving an old tractor on this farm, which was clearly in the path of development. They assumed that he was a farmer who really didn't know what was going on. So they went up to this farmer and they said, "Sir, do you own this farm?" And he said, "Yes, I've owned it for a long time." And they said, "Do you happen to have any idea how much your farm is worth?" And he said, "Well, as of two weeks ago it was worth $2,534,000." They said, "Well, why don't you sell and retire to Florida or California?" He said, "You know, I've thought about that, but I love this place and I love driving this old tractor and I've lived here all my life. I have one child in Oregon, one child in New York, one child in Chicago. They're not going to take over the farm. If I retire, what would I do in California? Just sit around a swimming pool all day? I would be quite willing to stay here, and I will stay here until I die. Then the farm will be sold."

It seems to me that's an interesting story, not only about how rational people are, how much they know, but the fact that the life cycle, the fact of death, may be one of the most important factors in the supply of land in urban areas. This means that when we talk about the incentives as Neal Roberts did, about taxes and about other kinds of land-use controls, it may very well be that the inheritance tax, the kinds of policies that are related to death, may have a more important impact on what happens to the supply of land than many of the other instruments that we have talked about.

The other thing that comes out in their study is that what we have thought of as being a unified land market in urban areas in fact is not a single market, but it is a series of many submarkets. There are four, five, or perhaps six submarkets, with people who have very different motivations, people who have very different time spans of calculation. And the policies that we use to control land markets cannot be general policies; they must be targeted very directly to the psychological motivations of each one of those different kinds of people. In the end, laws are effective only if they change the minds of people and change their behavior. Until we understand the psychology of behavior we cannot make effective legislation.

I would therefore make my own personal appeal that all of you very seriously consider mounting research programs on the model of the Neal Roberts study so that you will understand the psychology of the buyers and sellers of land in your own countries. I believe the only way you will have effective government policies is if you do understand the psychology and the things that move people or do not move people and that you gain from the mistakes we have made in the United States where our legislators have had very false images of what motivates people and the legislative policies we have had to change their behavior have not been very effective. I suspect that's true in many countries. And I suspect it can only be corrected when we do studies like this to understand the psychology of people who own and transfer their land.

10 Urban Land-Market Studies in Latin America: Issues and Methodology

Guillermo Geisse and
Francisco Sabatini

This article synthesizes some of the main concerns shared by the members of a study group carrying out a research project on urban land policy problems in Latin America (ULPPLAN). The project includes six case studies on the cities of Bogotá, Caracas, Guatemala, Lima, San Salvador, and Santiago.

From the first meeting of the group, the participants agreed that there was a set of land-development problems affecting each one of the cities in a similar way. They also agreed that similar kinds of development problems could give rise to some generalizations valid for Latin America as a region. As expected, differences among the cities were also present in many other aspects of the land-development process. The study group believes that a systematic discussion of such similarities and differences can contribute to the theoretical knowledge on urban land problems, which have become critical in Latin America, and to the formulation of urban-development policies for each of the case studies.

The study group is aware that public agencies in Latin America are more sensitive to recommendations for planned intervention on urban land-development processes than to most other critical issues of development. To a considerable extent this is due to the contribution of international development agencies, such as the United Nations, in the denunciation of urban land speculation as a factor affecting the quality of life of the urban poor.

There seems to be increasing support for different forms of state intervention in both the capturing of land-value increases that are the outcome of public programs and in the general task of land-use planning. In practice, however, resistance is still too strong for recommendations to be effectively implemented.

One of the main hypotheses analyzed here is that most policy recommendations in Latin America seem to suggest that landowners and subdividers are the only agents in the real estate market capturing speculative profits on the form of urban land rent. This is true only in two of the case studies. In the other cities, the land market is substantially more complex. In all six cities the real estate market is becoming highly heterogeneous, especially with regard to differences in the degree of development of its various submarkets and to the kind of linkages among submarkets. At the same time cities differ one from the other with regard to the relative participation of each agent, landowners, builders, real estate brokers, promoters, and financial institutions in the appropriation of land-rent increase. Accordingly recommendations for land-development policies that neglect market heterogeneity, linkages between submarkets, and the manner by which agents are integrated and organized in the real estate market are condemned to failure.

The study group is aware that the effectiveness of policies to be recommended hinges upon the occurrence of certain changes at the national level. The study group has no intention of analyzing relations between real estate markets and national economic and political structures. However, some key linkages between the two levels are expected to emerge when comparing the findings of the six teams in light of differences between countries with regard to degree of economic development, social stratification, and political systems.

The research, however, is still in a preparatory stage; therefore, no conclusions will be offered in this paper. In any event, neither the group as a whole nor the local teams are looking for a formula to solve all land-development problems affecting the cities under study. On the contrary, the purpose of the research is to examine those forces that are persistently opposed to the kind of policies likely to be included in the cities' development plans and to bring out structural differences among the six cities in order to avoid the temptation of making generalizations in the area of policy recommendations.

Regressive Effects of Rising Land Prices

The rise on prices of urban land above average inflation is a tendency affecting almost all major cities of the world under a market economy. The social consequences of this tendency are, by and large, more serious in Latin America than they are in the developed countries of Europe and North America. In the latter, the expansion of metropolitan areas came as a gradual process that went hand in hand with the general and steady economic growth for long periods of time, thus resulting in a more equal distribution of income. In Latin America, urban concentration in large cities is a recent phenomenon. Its rate of growth (concentration) during the 1960s and 1970s has been the highest of the various regions of the world. This has taken place with slow economic growth and an increasingly unequal distribution of income. Also, increasing demands for urban land tend to be concentrated on one or two cities in the country. Land speculation and the higher costs of urbanization reduce the supply of land exactly where it is needed most. For some urban economists in the neoclassical tradition, neither land speculation nor rises in prices and profits are in themselves negative or questionable. Rather, speculation would be an expected response of those whose interests are damaged or denied by the general objectives, contents, and procedures of urban planning.[1] Under certain minimum conditions of efficiency in market operations, speculation could become desirable since it could allow for future more-intensive and productive use of land (such as multifamily houses and offices).[2] In the case of suburban land it could also help to lower the rate of urban expansion to an optimal level. Thus, according to this point of view, urban land speculation is considered a regulatory function contributing to market efficiency. On the other hand, profits stemming from land speculation are justified as a compensation for the risks involved since not all the land held back from the supply market at one time may turn out to be as valuable as expected when finally sold.[3] In sum, for neoclassical economists, land speculation is as risky as any other investment portfolio; it could result in either great profits or in substantive losses.

Both statements have been the source of criticism by scholars of the same tradition. On the one hand, visualizing the market as an unquestioned mechanism for the allocation of land could limit efforts toward identifying the main causes of existing inequalities and inefficiences in cities. On the other hand, the possibilities of losing are very small for high-income investors, who would be choosing from a wide range of investment opportunities and would have preferential access to credit and information.[4]

These criticisms of neoclassical theories are even more justified when applied to Latin America where the unequal distribution of land property of wealth and of political power has been used to influence public policies that have resulted in further accumulation of wealth and political power. The concentration of the demand for urban land in one or two cities in each country and in certain areas within these cities practically eliminates the risk for speculators and at the same time makes problems of urban inefficiency and inequalities even more serious.[5]

The regressive effects due to variations in land values are reflected in rising costs of housing for low-income groups. In San Salvador, the prices paid for land for social housing programs increased more than two and a half times between 1975 and 1977 (both included), for an annual average increase of 40 percent. These programs cover only a small proportion of the total need for low-cost housing. In some cases, land is sold without consideration of legal regulations. In these cases, it has been estimated that prices increased nearly 40 percent a year. In fact, it has been said that the average price for one of the illegal units of land in the city surroundings was approximately the same price of an urbanized unit with houses built by the Foundacion Salvadorena de Deserrollo y Vivienda Minima (FUNDASAL).[6] In the city of Guatemala, the price of land as a percentage of the total price of low-cost houses increased very rapidly after the earthquake in April 1976. In one year it increased almost 57 percent for a *tugurio* (very substandard housing) in a central area and 63 percent for self-constructed houses in an illegal development in the city surroundings. In the case of houses for the organized sector of middle- and high-income groups, the increase was only 35 percent.[7]

This is a common situation in most of the large cities of Latin America. The high price of land affects the standard of living of the poorer sectors, forcing them either to conditions of overcrowding in central areas or to do without the basic services in the city surroundings. As a result of this condition we find *mesones, callajones,* and *conventillos* (various descriptors of poor-quality rooming houses) in the rental submarkets in central areas and *pirate neighborhoods, illegal colonizations, ranchos* (derogatory terms for substandard peripheral housing), and other illegal developments in the urban fringes.

In summary, increases in land prices affect all social sectors of the city, including those in the higher-income brackets, but they are especially severe for poor families who have to allocate a higher proportion of their income for land payments, which in turn affects their basic level of consumption. In some cases, the amount paid by a poor family per unit of land is equal to that paid by a higher-income family.

Problems Related to the Demand for Land

The current rate of population growth will continue to be the immediate cause for the increasing land demand for residential use. Given the demographic size of the cities, the natural rate of population growth ensures an absolute increase in demand for land even without taking into consideration growth brought about by migrations. The expected rate of growth in the years to come will vary from 3 percent in Santiago to 7 percent a year in Bogotá and Guatemala. The population increase of low-income sectors is generally higher in relation to the total urban growth. Toward 1969, the number of persons living in *tugurios* and poor settlements reached almost 40 percent of the total urban population in Caracas and 60 percent in Bogotá.[8] In Guatemala City before the earthquake of February 1976, 70 percent of houses were *tugurios*, houses built in illegal developments with no public services, and *palomares*, poor-quality houses in old structures.[9] In San Salvador, nearly two-thirds of the population lives in three types of illegal dwellings.[10]

Increased unemployment and salaries that do not keep up with the rising costs of living and with the increase in construction prices have contributed to reducing the land and housing available to low-income groups. In this sector, a significant part of the demand is channeled in nonconventional ways: illegal sales made outside the formal market and takeovers of public and private land.[11] In both cases, the main characteristic is the absence of legal property titles. Because of the lack of legality, such buyers are excluded from public investment and service programs at the same time they are an easy target for both undesirable mediators and police repression.

Problems Related to the Supply of Land

Although there are considerable reserves of land available for metropolitan growth in these six cities, high urbanization costs and land speculation result in excess demand.[12] Public investments in urban infrastructure are not enough to cover the needs of population growth, and in many cases, these investments end up being directed to higher-income sectors. In San Salvador, for example, public investment has been directed toward areas where there is a formal housing market representing only one-third of the total city population. For the other areas, investments in infrastructure have been scarce and slow.[13] In Santiago, the municipality of Las Condes, with the highest income per person and with only 8 percent of the metropolitan population, received 42 percent of total public expenditures in street pavements and local highway construction in the city between 1965 and 1975 (20 percent when national highways across the city and metropolitan beltway are considered).[14]

In Bogotá, public investments allocated to pirate developments are almost nonexistent. On the other side the valuation tax (*Impuesto de Valorizacion*), established by the state to capture part of the increase of land value due to public investments, has led to the concentration of the benefits from these investments to higher-income areas. It is believed that only in this way would returns to investments reach a level high enough to guarantee the financing of new investments.[15] The objectives of valuation laws aimed toward redistribution thus have been overriden by the application of conventional criteria of efficiency. When efficiency criteria are applied to realities characterized by great differences in income and power, they usually bring about greater inequalities, as seems to be the case of the valuation tax.

Land speculation is a second factor affecting the supply of land in the six cities being studied. This may take the form of monopoly speculation or competitive speculation.[16]

In most of the cities, except Santiago and Caracas, a great proportion of the land available for urban development is controlled by a few families or building enterprises, a situation that has led to monopolistic speculation, making it possible for a few families to have direct control of market prices by withholding land from the open market. Much of the large amount of vacant land in Bogotá, Guatemala City, and San Salvador is the result of this sort of speculation. This vacant land is enough to house several million people.[17] Land retention is indeed an effective way for an owner or building enterprise to obtain extraordinary speculative profits.[18] It also encourages urban sprawl and spatial segregation, which affect the efficiency and equity objectives of governmental urban-investment policies.

In Santiago and Caracas, on the other hand, where the ownership of land is not so concentrated, there is a competitive type of speculation. Large middle-income sectors join high-income investors in buying land as a safeguard against inflation. In this case, the decision of buying and selling land on the part of the investor does not affect the market prices per se. Nonetheless this factor probably does contribute to a greater increase in the prices of land in areas where demand tends to concentrate in comparison to the lower-income residential areas of the city.

The social effects of either type of speculation are different, especially in distributional effects. In both cases, the study groups doubt whether land speculation has any effect at all on regulating the market.

Policies Affecting Supply and Demand of Land

Those public instruments that seem to have a great influence in both land and housing markets were conceived, originally, as distributive instruments in all six cases; however, the study groups believe that these instruments have regressive effects. Some of the most common instruments are public policies for housing development. These public actions have both an indirect effect, by way of housing-development laws, and a direct effect, by way of public programs for low-cost housing.

Among the former are tariff discounts on imported building equipment aimed at bringing down construction costs. Often these discounts seem to have been capitalized by large enterprises in the form of profits rather than reducing the price of houses. Another indirect policy has been tax exemptions on new houses for lower-income groups. Here again, these policies have also been extended to middle- and high-income groups. In San Salvador, housing-development policies did not have a significant effect on private urban-development projects for lower-income sectors.[19] In Santiago, the application of tax-exemption laws for low-cost housing has been so flexible and generous as to make it applicable to one-family and multifamily luxury houses.[20]

With regard to direct public action, actual building of low-cost houses by the state has not had a great significance for the housing supply except in Santiago during the period 1965-1973. Chile was an exception during that period as far as state policies of social interest go. But even there a number of housing developments built by the public sector for workers were finally assigned to middle-income groups. Since 1973, the total number of low-cost housing units built per year in Santiago has decreased to one-third of what it was during the period 1965-1973.

Another example of direct public intervention on land supply is the establishment of public land reservation. This policy has not been very significant though except in the case of Santiago when the Corporacion de Mejoramiento Urbano (1965-1973) was in charge. There are no other important and effective experiences in Latin America.[21]

Credit policies geared to the promotion of housing demand have been another instrument used in an effort to keep the market as the main regulator of supply and demand. State incentives for the establishment of savings and loan associations in several Latin American countries during the 1960s helped greatly in increasing the effective demand for houses, but because of low salaries and relatively high unemployment, the great majority of the urban population could not meet the basic requirements and were left out of the system.

In Colombia, for instance, only one-third of the total number of loans granted by the Central Bank Hipotecario in 1973 were for low-cost housing. This represented only 13 percent of the total amount of money lent by this bank. In turn, more than 50 percent of the loans went to houses of 90 or more square meters, using 74 percent of the total resources involved. In Chile in 1970, only 6 percent of all loans granted by the National Saving and Loans System were given to the poor sector (up to two *sueldos vitales*) while a higher-income group (five or more *sueldos vitales*) received almost five times more loans (38.1 percent).[22] This difference is considerable if we compare the unequal percentages represented by these two groups within the total population and considering that the average loan in the different cases must have been of completely different amounts.

A third example of policy affecting the relation between supply and demand in the real estate market encompasses three conventional public instruments: public investment geared to land conversion from rural to urban use, regulation of land uses, and taxes as a way of recovering operation and investment costs. The practical results of these policies are not consistent with what would be expected theoretically. This is true in almost all the cities being studied. Public investment in infrastructure is never enough to meet the need and frequently responds to pressures on the part of the speculator in order to raise the value of land temporarily withheld from the supply market.

Land-use regulations usually have resulted in the restriction of the supply of land (by setting urban limits, for example), consequently increasing the prices of land. They have also contributed to increased spatial segregation. Land-use planning usually is guided by criteria of control rather than promotion and in turn is oriented to high-income sectors. Most rules and regulations are put forward in the form of excluding or forbidding (such as limiting the size of a land unit or establishing minimum quality standards for buildings and urbanizations). The prohibiting nature of these rules and regulations contributes to rising social status and the exclusiveness of certain areas. This in turn encourages a concentrated demand for land, making its valuation process inseparable from the spatial segregation of socio-economic classes in cities. This excluding type of planning has no meaning for poorer sectors. For them, the system results in a larger informal sector and an ever-greater number of illegal urbanizations without any planning support.

Real estate taxes in all six cities have not been an efficient instrument, and for Santiago, Caracas, and Bogotá, the research teams have advanced a hypothesis on their regressive effects. The lack of reassessment and tax re-rating over long periods of time has resulted in the deterioration of the tax base. The best demonstration of the inefficiency of the tax system is the decrease in real terms of the amount being collected by the state through real estate taxes.[23] Tax increases, when they occur, are often transferred to the price of land and therefore to the consumer.[24]

Given the great difference in the rate of land-value increase affecting high- and low-income sectors, the deterioration of the tax base favors high-value areas. Thus the tax system is comparatively more inefficient in high-income residential areas than in the rest of the city. Those having a lower-value property pay relatively more. In Santiago, for example, the assessment of land values in the highest-income municipality (Las Condes) represented 75 percent of the average market value of land in 1964. In 1976, this percentage represented only 60 percent. But in poorer municipalities, both values were equal in 1964, while the first one rose over the market value by nearly 174 percent in 1976.[25]

Alternative Theoretical Approaches to
Urban Land Problems and Policies

These urban land problems have been widely acknowledged in the region but not very well understood. Authors who are concerned with them seem to agree in their opposition to narrow ideologies that rely entirely on the market's invisible hand as the main mechanism to overcome disequilibrium. State intervention in the land market has been generally accepted at least in words. Discussions among the different ideological advocates focus on such issues as orientation, intensity, and extent of state intervention in the development processes. Some urban planners envision the role of the state as a mediating function designed to prevent market imperfections affecting the poorer sectors without threatening private-property rights on land, while others see the state as a main instrument in the reinforcement of a system of social exploitation of which the land market is but a part.

Of the great number of theoretical-ideological positions with regard to land problems, two are the most widely represented in the local literature on this topic. One builds its assumptions on the neoclassic theory of exchange while aligning it to the welfare economic tradition. The other is founded on the classics of social science, particularly in Marx's contribution. Neoclassicists within the welfare economic tradition are willing to accept that land cannot be considered in the same way as other factors of production: "Property income of a given dollar value places the receiver on a higher welfare plane than labour income, because he needn't work for it." Public participation in the land market would be justified in the first place only by the fact that land value "derives from public works and spillovers, not from the owner's effort" and mainly because of the urban effects derived from imperfect market operations.[26] These criticisms—perhaps the most well known in the field of urban planning—have been adopted by international as well as government agencies. It is interesting to see the extent to which progress has been made in developing a consciousness of planned intervention in the urban land market by those who are not willing to accept it in any other market.[27]

Organizations such as the United Nations and the World Bank have not limited their actions to discussing these issues but have extended their field of action to recommendations implying active state participation in the land market. The United Nations Conference on Habitat and Human Settlements in Vancouver (1976), for example, made important recommendations in this respect.[28] Had the recommendations been applied, some of the problems related to low-cost housing would have been solved. However, none of the national governments responsible for the planning of the six cities has applied them in spite of the fact that they all signed. Actions taken by state agencies before and after Vancouver were isolated or partial. According to the evaluations made by the study groups, the results obtained do not meet their own objectives and are often in contradiction to them.

Those who hold theoretical-ideological standings in the other extreme think that because urban problems originate in the private handling of land, they cannot be solved within the capitalist mode of production. Some of them claim that not even the socialization of urban land would free land revenue from private appropriation if capitalist modes of production are maintained.[29] The appropriation of profits stems not only from the right of private property but also comes forth from the capitalist nature of production of "urban objects."[30] Therefore as long as this type of system prevails, profit accumulation on land would continue to take place even without private property of land.

Although these theoretical approaches to urban planning are very different, they are equally ineffective in dealing with the problems caused by the speculative rise in the prices of land. This is specially true for problems affecting the living standards of the poorest sectors. To say that the reason for this ineffectiveness is the lack of efficient mechanisms in the fields of legislation, taxing, zoning, and so on is not, according to the study group, a reasonable explanation.[31] The main issue is why these policies produce results different from those intended and expected theoretically. The study group agrees that answers to these questions should be attempted at two different levels of analysis. The first level refers to the land market operations within the broader context of the real estate market. The second has to do with the relationship between rent accumulation in the real estate sector of the economy and the general process of capital accumulation.

Operating Methods of Real Estate Agents

Production and distribution activities in the real estate market include land subdivision, building, financing, and marketing promotion, as well as the handling of land by landowners. Agents operating in each of these activities include in their profits part of the land revenue, and with these objectives in mind, they look for integration, divide their work, and often enter into conflicts among themselves. For this reason, the real estate market is a heterogeneous one comprising different objectives, rationalities, and types of organization among its agents, which in turn vary considerably throughout the various states of economic development and between political systems. As a result, we find market differences within the real estate market of the six cities being studied. General and specific recommendations for urban land policies seldom take into consideration these differences, and our study group believes that their lack of effectiveness lies, at least in part, in this fact.

The first reports presented by the study groups show three main sources of profit in real estate activity: land revenue, profits accrued from capital investments in building, and interest derived from finance capital.

When real estate activities are carried out separately and by different agents, it is comparatively easy to identify sources of profit and the relative importance of each agent within the real estate sector of the economy. The landowner sells raw land to the developer, who subdivides it either directly or by contract with a firm specializing in the construction of urban facilities and in the provision of services to sites. Those sites are then sold for construction of houses either to individuals willing to build their own houses by themselves or by hiring a construction firm. Credit needed at each stage is granted to the agents involved by bank or other financial agencies, such as savings and loans associations.

Policy recommendations aimed at preventing land speculation seem to be concerned only with the first stage of this process, and therefore planned intervention is geared to limit the utility gains of the landowner. Data of some of the research teams appear to support such an assumption.

Preliminary data also suggest that capital gains on land during the development of housing projects exceed by far those obtained by the landowner. The more integration of the real estate market activities, the less the participation of landowners in the appropriation of land-rent increases.

In the case of a fully integrated housing project under the control of a single agent (such as a real estate promoter), capital gains on land are expected by both the landowner (at the first step of the project) and by the leading agent (generally financial) at the moment of selling the dwelling units to the final user.

The research team for Caracas formulated the hypothesis that profits accumulated by financial agents and other intermediaries in the housing market exeed the normal rate of interest and other fees and therefore should be considered capital gains to land. Those gains are as speculative as gains being capitalized by landowners by the monopoly of land and should not be ignored by policymakers. This hypothesis will be tested in Caracas, as well as in Santiago and Bogotá. The respective research teams are aware, though, that there are theoretical aspects to be clarified and empirical difficulties to be overcome. Just as it is difficult to separate the price of land from that of the building and other improvements in a real estate property, a similar difficulty emerges in an integrated project in identifying who in the market gets the profits stemming from land-price increases. This is due to the fact that the value of land is related to its use. The use of land changes with the improvements introduced to it as a result of demand pressures, and price changes also occur.

ULPPLA intends to identify differences among submarkets within each city with regard to the way land revenue originates and is distributed in order to contribute to the formulation of adequate urban policies for each situation. For example, a landowner from Guatemala City or San Salvador undoubtedly obtains almost all the profits of the real estate sector, while in Caracas and Bogota, financial institutions and building enterprises obtain a greater part of the profits. Preliminary data presented by the Caracas study group indicate that not more than 30 percent of the real estate profits obtained from multifamily projects were received by the landowner. The remaining revenue and real estate profits were absorbed wholly as profits obtained from mediation of an openly speculative nature, by promoters, financers, and developers. A similar tendency seems to be present in Santiago, where financial institutions seem to be actively participating in the submarket of luxury houses (the only one that has been active in the past five years), obtaining profits exceeding normal capital interests. This indicates there are existing differences among cities and submarkets that cannot fall under simple theoretical generalizations and recommendations for urban policies without considering the local political and economic context.

In theory, land revenue has been considered a barrier for capitalist or productive accumulation.

Therefore it is necessary to identify the different ways of obtaining profits in the real estate market, the different and sometimes conflicting criteria and objectives of the various agents receiving them, and the manner in which they combined. But this is not enough. Some members of the study group believe that in order to ensure the validity of these explanations and the effectiveness of policy recommendations, it is necessary to understand why these methods, combinations, and criteria come about and why they differ from one submarket to another and from one city under study to another. The study group acknowledges that the answers to these questions will lead discussions, and therefore the research itself, to a more complex scenario—one that includes the relations between the real estate market and the more general economic and political structures.

Land Rents, Capital Accumulation, and Urban Development Policies

Land revenue is a form of an appropriation of part of the productive surplus; it is also the incentive with the greatest influence on the formation of urban structure.

In theory, land revenue has been considered a barrier for capitalist or productive accumulation.[32] Land revenue becomes a major factor in increasing the price of housing, which in turn increases the cost of satisfying the labor force. The study group is willing to explore the policy implications of potential conflicts between rentier and industrial capital. In some cities conflicts of this nature are likely to evolve on the side of favoring industrial capital through a more integrated control of the state over the land market.

A different situation would occur if finance and intermediating capital are the dominant forces of the national economy. If that were the case, it would not allow for any type of state regulation on land revenue since it would reduce the sphere of these speculative types of activities. This situation often occurs under power structures that allow for other ways of decreasing labor costs, such as the repression of labor.

The conflicts between subsectors of a dominant social sector (rentiers and capitalists) are rarely permanent or serious, however. The current tendency in all six countries is one of complementarity rather than of conflict since their industrial production, like intermediate and financial activities, are increasingly oriented toward the demand of higher-income groups. Such a tendency affects the spatial patterns of the residential areas. The highly selective and diversified demand structure of the high-income groups presses for greater autonomy of high-income residential areas, thus favoring spatial segregation.[33]

Furthermore conflicts between rentier and productive capital, as first envisioned by Ricardo, tend to decline because the development process itself tends to dilute boundaries and interests if either of the sectors overlaps. The way in which this kind of conflict evolves varies from one country to another. Factors accounting for such a variance seem to be related to the degree of economic development, to the internal power structure, and to the way in which local economies are integrated into the international markets.

Internal power relationships and the degree of development of national economies are not independent of the relationship existing between local economies and international markets. The transnationalization of Latin American economies, which has taken place in the last few decades, has influenced the urban structure of all six cities by way of imported technology, equipment, and design and by urban forms and standards derived from the increase in car ownership and complementary goods and services. The effect of transnationalization on the structure of the cities is rather uniform in all the six cities under study, although there are differences depending on whether the process of transnationalization has given priority to the internal market, to the use of natural resources, to the exploitation of the labor force, or to different combinations of these. National economies facing the first situation experienced an expansion of their manufacturing sector with an emphasis on urban concentration in one or two cities. This was the case of Chile between 1964 and 1970. However, in cases where the national economy's attracting factor for international capital has been its natural resources, production activity and a corresponding expansion of industrial activity related to it in these economies are likely to expand in a decentralized way, permitting financial and intermediating sectors to play a dominant role in the city.

A variety of situations in the cities resulted from the differentiated ways of the insertion of local economies into international markets. Variety also results from the degree of development during the different historical stages preceding the transnationalization of their economies and on their local resource endowments. The structure of a city in which the industrial sector is the most dynamic and has greatest relative importance in the urban economy is quite different from one in which the dominant role is taken up by the financial sector and residential areas where consumption of luxury goods is concentrated. In such cities the criterion most likely to be imposed upon the real estate market will be the one of the real estate speculator linked to finance capital.

Not all of the study groups are favorably inclined to enter in the complexities of this level of analysis. Some of them believe that this would divert them from the more-concrete problems that need immediate action. Some, however, are favorably inclined to it, believing that the analysis of the relationship between the real estate market as part of the global political economy is a necessary condition to ensure the political feasibility of the recommendations. In this case, if as a result of the analysis it would be concluded that certain planning actions are not feasible, it would be better for planning agencies to know this beforehand rather than after having spent resources on policies that may not contribute to planning objectives.

**Real Estate Agents: Behavior and
Forms of Organization**

A tendency common to all the cities is the integration of the different real estate activities, at least in certain areas of the city. With economic development and city growth, finance and construction capital generally becomes progressively more important in the real estate sector, and land revenues become more dependent on investments stemming from those sources.[34]

In all six cities this tendency occurred together with a skyrocketing increase in the price of land and with the concentration of the housing market in high-density, large-scale apartment buildings for the higher-income sectors of the population. Based on the observation of these tendencies, the Caracas research team suggests that the increases in land prices have resulted from the speculative practices of financial capital. The financial capital rather than the landowner controls this submarket, and it captures the greatest share of increases in land revenue in Caracas. The land rent estimated from the selling price of apartments in high-rise buildings in Caracas resulted from multiplying the price paid by the developer for the parcel (originally zoned for single-family housing) by the number of floors in the building. The financial and construction firms have become so powerful in the market as to manipulate zoning ordinances on their behalf, displacing landowners in the appropriation of land revenues.

The integration of the different land-development functions in a few developers has been favored by tendencies in all of the cities toward the concentration of the demand for land in high-income submarkets. Based on high-income demand, integration presents backward and forward linkages.

The first refers to building enterprises that manage land. Two factors seem to have contributed in this direction. First was the creation of savings and loan associations during the 1960s. Loans were granted for the purchase of dwelling units rather than for sites alone. The other factor is the logical tendency of building activity to increase scale production of houses. A supply of urban land that depends upon the landowner's decision to sell presents serious obstacles, which building enterprises will try to overcome by integrating land marketing into their activities.

Forward integration represents a more advanced stage of development of the real estate sector. As land increases in value and as the amount of capital required for construction increases, the financing of the supply, as well as the demand, promotion, and marketing, becomes more important.

The tendency toward the integration of the real estate market and financial agents can be found in different degrees and combinations in the six cities being studied. The criteria and ways of association of the real estate agents can be outlined in four situations.

In situation A, the landowner is the dominant agent. The main activity in the real estate market is the subdivision and private sale of the land, and the dominant rationality behind the sale of land stems from the consumption needs of the owner. This implies obvious restrictions on the supply of land in the market and the development of enterprises that are moved by the rationale of capital profit maximization. There are two different cases in this situation: high concentration of property of land available for urban uses (San Salvador, Guatemala City) that give rise to monopolistic speculations, and low concentration of landholdings (Santiago, Caracas) in which case the tendency is toward competitive speculation. Within these activities, building enterprises play a dependent role. This is true for large enterprises dependent on public-housing projects (Santiago, 1965-1973), as well as for small enterprises engaged in the building of houses for buyers of sites.

The predominance of landowner agents in cities like San Salvador and Guatemala does not seem to have a parallel in any of the other cities. The main obstacle that this situation presents to urban planning can be illustrated by a project proposed in 1973 for the construction of an urban center, integrated with the city of Guatemala, for approximately 400,000 inhabitants. The economic and social benefits that would be obtained were widely publicized by the government agency in charge, and a preliminary agreement for the purchase of 3,000 hectares of urban land was reached. The land belonged to a small number of politically influential families who did not honor the initial agreement. Their price expectancies rose as they realized that they enjoyed an absolute control of land supply. The project was never carried out, and four years later, part of the land was sold at a price ten times higher than the initial price.[35]

In cities where the landownership is more evenly distributed, it has had less influence on the city expansion. The expansion of the urban areas of Santiago up to 1940, for example, was a gradual process of subdivision of small and medium-sized rural properties, without the owners individually influencing the prices of land or the direction or the pattern of urban growth. Growth came about in an insular way, with large areas of agricultural land encircled within the urban limits. This is the case of the urbanization of the higher sectors of the city during the first decades of this century.[36] Since 1940 landowners have lost influence on the development of the city.

In situation B, building enterprises are the dominant agents. Centered on the construction of houses, enterprises often control land subdivision and urbanization works (backward-integrated enterprises). Eventually distribution and marketing of houses are integrated to the dominant activity (forward-integrated enterprises). The dominant criterion is the maximization of profits obtained from production capital. In some cases, this objective may result in conflicts with those of the landowners engaged in speculative practices.

The development of backwardly integrating building enterprises was encouraged in submarkets of middle- and high-income groups with the establishment of the housing savings and loans system during the 1960s. The financial capital available for the purchase of houses expanded housing-development projects in the submarkets and moved the building enterprises into land marketing in order to ensure the necessary land for themselves. The original landowner loses his influence and in some cases may associate with the building enterprise. Both promotion and marketing are taken up by specialized agents, who often enjoy certain privileges.

Large building enterprises integrated both backwardly and forwardly become the dominant enterprises under situations of great economic concentration. This has been the case in Chile since 1973. Housing demand in Santiago was practically restricted to high-income groups and concentrated in a few privileged areas of the city. Four to five years of housing supply was limited to luxury condominiums. Cost increases and skyrocketing land prices caused building enterprises to associate themselves with financing agencies.[37]

In some situations agents other than the builder and the landowner may dominate the real estate market temporarily during certain periods. This was the case of the urbanization firms of Santiago between 1940 and 1960 and of Lima between 1950 and 1965. These firms bought raw land at the fringes of the cities and specialized in subdivision and urbanization. In the case of Santiago financing was funded by owner down payments; while in Lima, firms relied heavily on local banks.

These were periods in which Lima and Santiago grew by major extensions rather than by small accretions to the urban area as had occurred prior to the emergence of the urbanization firms. The pattern of city growth almost exclusively depended on the activities of urbanization firms during these periods.

In situation C, financial capital interested in speculative gains is the dominant agent in the real estate market. Here again we have two cases: multifamily housing projects and suburban subdivision of land, in both cases for high-income sectors.

The real estate market in Caracas during the present decade has been clearly controlled by financial enterprises that have encouraged apartment-building projects for high-income groups. The dominance of financial capital in the market has not been accompanied by economic concentration within the construction industry, which seems to be the case of Santiago. On the contrary, the atomization of this industry in Caracas is one of its main characteristics. Furthermore, according to the Caracas research team, such an atomization has enabled the predominance of financial groups in this market. They are the promoters in charge of organizing and coordinating the various agents involved in the housing-development projects (landowners, construction firms, small subcontractors, architects, banks, brokers, and publicity agencies). Estimates made by the Caracas research team for some of the housing projects in this submarket show that approximately 80 percent of the profits are obtained by the financial agents. It is believed that the effect of these profits on the price of houses is extraordinary for the city as a whole. The price per square meter of construction rose 316 percent between 1970 and 1975, 3.15 times the increase in the cost of living. It has been estimated that 60 percent of this increase—that is, practically all that exceeds the increase in the cost of living—is due to the increase in the value of land. The value of land in Caracas increased on average seventeen times in the fifteen years.[38] The research team suggests that this is precisely the source of capital gains of the financial agent in the real estate market.

In Santiago, with the recent announcement that "urban limits" will be raised, land developments for high-income sectors in the suburban areas have begun to emerge again. This is an expected consequence of an urban policy recently issued by the central government. The policy announces the end of "rigid norms in order to encourage the natural growth of the urban areas following the tendencies of the market."[39] Purchase of large parcels of land outside the limits of the city by well-informed speculators took place before the policy was enacted formally. Even the sale of sites was announced before subdivisions were legally sanctioned.[40] The unit price of land in high-income suburban areas increased at least twice as much in six months as since the end of 1978. The price per square meter of urban land sold at the time when urbanization works were at an initial stage was approximately forty dollars. The difference between these land developments and those carried out by building enterprises between 1940 and 1960, apart from the fact that its price was considerably lower at that time, is that now the financing agents have a greater direct and indirect participation in the profits and land operations.

In situation D, the informal sector is the dominant agent. The domination criterion in this situation lies in a more or less spontaneous urban economic and social action, with or without participation of political organizations. Land occupation has occurred outside the market through illegal actions or with the tolerance of the state and sometimes even with the supervision of government agencies. Here again we find two cases: private illegal sales of land affecting a high proportion of the population in all the cities being studied and spontaneous or organized takeovers of land on the part of low-income groups with or without state acceptance.

The illegal sale of land is common in low-income submarkets in San Salvador, Guatemala City, Bogotá, and Caracas. It was also practiced in Lima and Santiago between the 1920s and 1950s. Illegal land operations consist of projects based on the selling of sites to low-income families, with the promise that they will be urbanized. Legal sales contracts are offered to the buyers once the urbanization works (infrastructure and services) are concluded because without the services, sales contracts have no legal value. Developers have found that contracts are necessary for them to obtain down payments, which are surprisingly high, and so that buyers will make timely payments. The developer usually makes a small initial investment, and very rarely the urbanization works stated in the contract are finished. Under pressure, developers often resort to false legal titles of property.[41]

Since 1960 in Lima, land takeover by low-income groups has been a way of expressing their dramatic need for land. This has led to the rise of *barriadas* (congested illegal settlements). Since then, specific policies have been developed to deal with these *barriadas* varying between repression and community-development planning. In all these cases, however, once the settlement is consolidated, urban and legal support has been given by public organizations. Legal urbanizations and *barriadas* have been taken care of by the state in a way that has created a two-faced policy with regard to the housing problem.[42]

In Santiago both spontaneous and organized takeover of urban land so-called *tomas* (takings) began around the 1940s, and they in turn gave rise to the *problaciones callampas* (slum populations). Between 1960 and 1973 these were tolerated and sometimes assisted by some public agency, giving rise to *campamentos* (encampments). Although the original owner of the land was usually affected by these takeovers, there are cases in which landowners were indirectly encouraging takeovers in order to have them later legally expropriated and paid by the public sector.

None of the agents in these situations was able to impose its objectives and rationality on the real estate market in an absolute way. In each city a combination of situations gives shape to a heterogeneous structure, different from the others. Combinations differ also among submarkets of a same city.

In view of this, the accumulation of land rents may have different effects on the general development of a city, depending upon the objectives and the rationality behind the agents' getting the higher share in each sub-market and according to the degree of integration of the various activities and agents. For example, the objectives proposed by large residential projects controlled by financing enterprises seem very offhand and often competitive with widely accepted urban-planning objectives. The popularity of these projects demonstrates the degree to which profits obtained depend on promoting consumer styles of life in capitalist-developed countries. In all six cities, and some more than others, real estate financing enterprises are playing an increasingly important role in subordinating local development objectives to the criteria of transnational enterprises, with their subsequent economic, cultural, and environmental effects.[43] Housing projects under their control have become increasingly dependent on production geared almost entirely to high-income groups and to certain exclusive areas of the city. Architectural and urban design are based both on the use of the car and in the introduction of shopping centers offering a convenient environment for the marketing of goods and services used by high-income groups.

Spatial segregation has been often criticized by urban planners because it expresses a differentiated access to natural and man-made environment resources according to income levels. Today, under the dominance of financial capital, it becomes a necessary condition of speculative real estate profits. In a political-economic context favoring the concentration of wealth and the hegemony of financial enterprises, it may be possible to find that a few financial groups decide virtually unchallenged what is the best environment for the entire city. The urban development projects under their control may be capturing external economies of urban development while the social costs related to air pollution, traffic congestion, and flooding are paid by the rest of the population, particularly the poorest.[44]

Housing-development projects oriented to high-income demand are built in the same cities where the great majority must turn to the informal sector for housing at the expense of their standard of living. Excluded from the housing market and from urban facilities and services provided by the public sector, their alternatives are to look for sites of the lowest value in the city surroundings or to the rental market in areas close to downtown.

In all six cities, besides the heterogeneous nature of the real estate markets, there is a tendency toward a two-pole dualistic urban structure. On one side of the real estate market is a highly concentrated financial sector with an increasing share of the total land revenues (situation C). On the other side is the informal sector of the poorest totally dependent on developers and renters acting outside the law, or to repression, if they decide to take things into their hands (situation D).[45]

A better understanding of the role that the real estate market plays in the dualization of the urban structure of the cities under study is needed in order for planning to be effective in ameliorating the conditions of the urban poor. Planners at all levels of decision making are beginning to realize that development problems in all six cities are related more to the unequal growth patterns of the city structure rather than to the large size of the city's population. In fact, increasingly fewer Latin American planners advocate slowing the rate of population growth in the large cities. Instead they have become more concerned with the impact of current dualistic urban-growth patterns on efficiency planning objectives and the mechanisms through which the benefits of urban concentration are appropriated by the wealthier classes while the costs are discharged on the poorest sectors. The uncontrolled real estate market is one of these mechanisms. The more planners are involved in market studies, the greater is the consensus that unequal development in the cities is not so much related to the rapid growth of the demand and of the need for urban land and housing as to institutional and economic constraint of the supply side. Otherwise, how can the scarcity of low-cost land vis-à-vis large areas of vacant land within the city limits and in the city fringe, and scattered low-density residential growth, all of which force up the social costs of urbanization, be explained?

The study group believes that some of the failures of planning agencies in the handling of urban land problems are due to planners' limited knowledge about the functioning of the real estate market. Many historical urban-planning opportunities have been missed in the cities involved. Government planning agencies in Santiago during the late 1960s and in Bogotá during the early 1970s enjoyed a considerable control of the supply side either of land or of the housing market and fell short of implementing comprehensive planning schemes for urban development. In all six cities, many actions and planning instruments intended to improve the housing conditions of the poorer sectors have been easily coopted by stronger interest groups in the market.

Finally, urban regulatory policies and instruments are scarcely differentiated according to the different areas of the city and housing submarkets. Urban planning has not been adequately adapted to the heterogeneous conditions of the urban structure and real estate market.

Conclusions

The study group believes that in the six cities under study, there is sufficient evidence to support the hypothesis regarding the regressive effect of the process of land-rent accumulation. On the one hand, concentrated financial and construction capital is getting an increasing share of the rent of land while concentrating the housing supply in the higher-income brackets. On the other hand, rent and land speculation in the lower-income zones of the central city and at the periphery of the city is responsible for raising the housing payments of the poorest up to levels that seriously affect their survival.

Speculation of land does not seem to accomplish a regulatory role on behalf of efficiency and equity in urban development. On the contrary, it contributes to an extremely low density and scattered pattern of urban growth, demanding increasingly high social costs of urbanization. Furthermore, speculative gains cannot be justified on the basis of risks affecting capital investment in land. Risks to investments in land are practically nonexistent because of the strong population pressures (at national levels) on each of the six cities and because of the uneven distribution of land-property income and political power among social groups and classes.

All of the teams report that land-development policies aimed at reducing the gap between supply and demand of housing (and land) have not proved to be effective and in many cases have led to results contrary to objectives.

Regardless of the rhetoric of comprehensive planning, which has dominated the field, policies when implemented do not relate one to another, and often planned intervention in one field interfers with public action in others. Policies are often of a negative rather than of a development character and often restrict the supply of land and enhance residential segregation. Finally, policy instruments are tied up to norms and design standards that originated in developed countries. Such norms and standards may meet the needs of the wealthiest sectors but not of the poor who comprise the majority of the city's population.

All of the teams have called attention to the increasing participation of financial capital in land-development projects. On the basis of this observation, the research group raises its central thesis: the appropriation of land rents in the form of revenues or capital gains is not the exclusive privilege of the *proprietario ocioso* ("idle landlord"), as Ricardo put it. An increasing proportion of land-rent increase is being appropriated by the financial capital and intermediaries linked to it. In the six cities, the various activities of the real estate market tend to become more and more coordinated by the financial agents through promoters. Most commonly, financial agents are interested in gaining a share of the capital increase. Their objectives and reasons become dominant in the organization of the market operations and of the spatial patterns of the city's growth.

The growing participation of financial capital in urban development is associated with an increase in the scale of the housing-development projects, with the participation of foreign capital in the real estate business, and with the concentration of the supply in housing and commercial facilities for the population in the higher-income brackets. Marked spatial segregation is no longer the result of spontaneous urban growth proper to market economies. It is becoming the result of a plan—not a public one—that exacerbates differences by selling a spatial environment geared to the selective and diversified consumption of the privileged few. Some large-scale private residential developments have borrowed the concept of "cities within the city" that Laughlin Currie envisioned as a state-led project in Bogotá. He thought that public control in the implementation of such a concept would ensure social diversification as well as urban efficiency in each city. On the contrary, private residential projects most likely to develop are the ones under the coordination of the finance capital. However, cities-within-city types of residential development are likely to be developed by the private sector rather than by the state. In this situation the private sector will develop "cities for the rich within the city"; the marketing information makes explicit that this is a privilege for only the few who can afford it.

While land-development operations and activities in high-income submarkets are being regulated by a strategy of speculation of the dominant financial capital and intermediaries, in the poor sectors of the cities, land development is conditioned by a strategy of survival. Land-development policies in the poor sectors should not be isolated from policies aimed at socializing part of the land-rent increases in the former sector. Policy instruments may differ from one submarket to another within a single city, but they should be formulated as part of one comprehensive land-development policy for the entire city.

Differences between countries should be considered in the process of formulation of land-development policies. In cases where the industrial manufacturing sector is the leading sector of the national economy, the state may be expected to take an active role in the expansion of the internal demand. One way of doing this has been the application of a high proportion of the public funds in social infrastructure (housing, urban services, education, health). Socially oriented land-development policies including all residential submarkets are politically feasible in these cases. In cases where national economic growth is dependent on external demand and national economies are open to the world market, the state is likely to give up its concern for social investment and land control aimed at avoiding speculation. In these cases, governments generally will not adopt strong land-development policies aimed at controlling the process of urbanization.

Notes

1. Lowdon Wingo, "Urban Space in a Policy Perspective: An Introduction," in L. Wingo, ed., *Cities and Space: The Future Use of Urban Land* (Baltimore: Johns Hopkins Press, 1964).

2. R.W. Archer, "Land Speculation and Scattered Development: Failure in the Urban-Fringe Land Market," *Urban Studies,* no. 3 (October 1975).

3. Orville Grimes, International Bank for Reconstruction and Development, *Urban Land and Public Policy: Social Appropriation of Betterment,* Bank Staff Working Paper, No. 179, Washington, D.C. (May 1974).

4. See Mason Gaffney, "Land and Rent in Welfare Economics," in J. Ackerman, M. Clawson, and M. Harris, eds. *Symposium on Land Economic Research,* (Washington, D.C.: Resources for the Future, 1962) 1-61; J. Brown and N. Roberts, "Land into Cities," Information Paper on the progress of the research project financed by the Lincoln Institute of Land Policy, mimeo.; David Harvey, *Social Justice and the City* (Baltimore: Johns Hopkins University Press, 1973).

5. "Precisely in these countries where the greater concentration of population brings about a greater demand for land is where speculation and misuse of land are more common." See United Nations, *Politices de Tierras Urbanas y Medidas de Control del Uso de la Tierra* (New York: America Latina, 1973), vol. 4.

6. ULPPLA San Salvador, Richard Willing of FUNDASAL, *El mercado de tierres en El Salvador: diagnostico y opciones al alcance del Estado* (1977). FUNDASAL has been able to moderate the negative effects of the rise in prices in its operations by adequate programming. However, because it is a private organization, its overall participation in the housing market is limited.

7. ULPPLA Ciudad de Guatemala, Harmes Marroquin, *Problemas y politicas de tierra urbana en el area metropolitan de Guatemala* (1977).

8. IBRD, *Sector Policy Paper: Housing* (Washington, D.C.: International Bank for Reconstruction and Development (IBRD), 1975). Quoted by Guillermo Rosenbluth, *La Vivienda en America Latina: una vision de la pobreza critica.* U.N. Economic Commission for Latin America (CEPAL), draft paper, DS 142 (Division de Desarrollo Social, 1976).

9. ULPPLA Ciudad de Guatemala.

10. ULPPLA San Salvador.

11. In Guatemala City, the destruction of over 50 percent of the low-cost houses by the earthquake encouraged takeovers of large public and private areas, and this has been increasing gradually since then. PROTUAL 1 Ciudad de Guatemala. PROTUAL 1 = Proyecto Tierra Urbana de America Latina No. 1 (Urban Land Project No. 1 of Latin America).

12. Of the six cities only Caracas and San Salvador have significant geographical barriers limiting urban expansion. This has not prevented the existence of big pieces of vacant land.

13. PROTUAL, 1 San Salvador.

14. PROTUAL, 1 Santiago, Guillermo Geisse and Francisco Sabatini, *Propuesta de investigacion sobre problemas y politicas de tierra urbana en Santiago* (1977). This has probably contributed to higher increases in the prices of land in these high-income sectors than in the rest of the city. The difference in 1965 was seven times more than in low-income sectors; in 1977 the difference was twenty-two times, according to a classified advertisement in the newspaper.

15. ULPPLA Bogotá, Rodrigo Manrique y Homero Quevas, of the Instituto de Estudios Colombianos, *Problemas y politicas de tierra urbana en America Latina: el caso de Bogotá* (1977).

16. See the distinction made by Jack Carr and Lawrence Smith, "Public Land Banking and the Price of Land," *Land Economics* 2 (November 1975).

17. United Nations, *Politicas de Tierras Urbanas y Medidas de Control del Uso de la Tierra* (New York: America Latina, 1973), vol. 4. This statement was confirmed and updated by the corresponding study groups for four of the six cities being studied.

18. In Caracas, according to the hypothesis presented by the study group, those sectors related to the production and distribution of houses would be receiving nearly 70 percent of the national surplus through land revenue. PROTUAL 1, Caracas. See also Institute de Urbanismo, Universidad Central de Venezuela, *Algunas hipotesis sobre las caracteristicas del desarrollo de Caracas* (November 1976).

19. ULPPLA, San Salvador.

20. The Decreto con Fuerze de Ley No. 2, DFL 2, approved in 1960, is a legal body in charge of encouraging through tax exemption the construction of houses within certain size and quality standards. It was originally conceived for low-cost houses for low-income groups.

21. United Nations, *Politicas de Tierras Urbanas.*

22. Rosenbluth, "La Vivienda en America Latina."

23. In Bogotá, the Impuesto Predial (property tax) per capita decreased in 28 percent in real terms between 1969 and 1975. PROTUAL, 1 Bogotá.

24. The final outcome, however, depends upon the elasticity of demand and supply.

25. ULPPLA, Santiago.

26. Mason Gaffney, *The Property Tax Is a Progressive Tax* (Washington, D.C.: Resources for the Future, October 1972).

27. According to the United Nations, land, because of its unique nature and its vital importance to human settlements, cannot be treated as any other good, controlled by individual persons and subject to the pressures and inefficiencies of the market. See United Nations, *Informe de Habit: Conferencia de las Naciones Unidas sobre los Asentamientos Humanos* (Vancouver, May-June 1976). At a national level, an outstanding example is

that of the conservative government of President Pastrana in Colombia (1969-1974). According to Colombia's National Planning Department, even when the increase in the value of land may be determining the uses of land, this would not be necessary or justified in economic or ethical terms since this increase benefits private owners. This would be weakening, in ethical terms, the market mechanisms and its incentives for production, and it would be discrediting the private-property system. Also land valuation has become one of the main sources of inequality in wealth, income, and opportunities. See Departamento Nacional de Planeacion, Ciudades dentro de la Ciudad (Bogotá: *Politicas y Plan de Desarrollo Urbano para Colombia* 1974).

28. Among the recommendations made by the conference is that greater public control of land is needed to control the rural-urban process, including expropriation and creation of state land reserves and of recovering the surplus resulting from public investment and general growth of the community. United Nations, *Informe de Habit,* pp. 64-75.

29. Luis Lander, *Especulacion en tierras como un obsteculo para el desarrollo urbano* (Caracas: Preparatory Conference of United Nations on Human Settlements, 1975).

30. Emilio Pradilla, "Notas sobre las politicas de vivienda de los estados Latinoamericanos" (mimeo). See also A. Lipietz, *La Tribut foncier urbain* (Paris: Maspero, 1975).

31. United Nations, *Politicas de Tierras Urbanas.*

32. Ricardo indicates in the case of agriculture that the rise in the prices of agricultural goods benefit only landowners through a rise in land revenue, reducing that part of the total product going to reinvestment. David Ricardo, *Principios de Economia Politica y Tributacion* (Mexico: Fondo de Cultura Economica, 1959), chap. 6.

33. According to Lamarche, "real estate capital," whose benefits are represented by land revenue, is in charge of organizing the commercial, financial, productive, and consumption (residential) activities in the metropolitan environment in order to bring down time and circulation costs of capital, in this way accelerating its accumulation. Francois Lamarche, "Property Development and the Economic Foundations of the Urban Question," *Sociology et sociétés,* no. 4 (1972).

34. In European cities, this occurred during the last century. In North American cities this has also occurred from the beginning of this century and is beginning to appear in some of the main Latin American cities.

35. ULPPLA, City of Guatemala.

36. Leon Echaiz, *Nunehue* (Buenos Ares: Editorial Francisco de Aguirra, 1972).

37. Out of a total number of thirty-six advertisements published by urbanization firms and/or building enterprises in *El Mercurio* in Santiago

(four weekend editions of April 1978, selected at random) twenty-seven were promoting luxury apartment building in high-income areas.

38. ULPPLA, Caracas.

39. Ministerio de la Vivienda y Urbanismo de Chile, *Politica Nacional de Desarrollo Urbano* (March 1979).

40. *Revista Que Pasa,* Santiago, October 5-11, 1978.

41. The prices paid in some of these urbanizations per unit of land were sometimes equal to the prices of land paid in higher-income submarkets. The information confirming this situation was found in at least two of the cities being studied. PROTUAL 1, Guatemala City; PROTUAL, 1 Lima.

42. ULPPLA, Lima.

43. For some authors, the criterion of accumulation at an international level is present in these urban development patterns. According to Browning and Roberts, in this century urban-development patterns in Latin America have been increasingly dominated by North American finance capital. The segregation of high-income groups in given areas within the city, as well as their extensive growth, has created markets for durable consumption goods and services related to the increasing use of the car and the possibility of obtaining speculative profits in the land market. Harley Browning and Brian Roberts, "Urbanization, transformacion sectorial y utilizacion de la mano de obra en Lationoamerica: una interpretacion historica desde la perspective internacional," in Jorge Hardoy et al., comps., *Ensayos Historica-sociales sobre la Urbanizacion en America Latina* (Buenos Aires: Edicionas SIAP CLACSO, 1978).

44. In all six cities, cars are the main cause of pollution and traffic jams. Although only 20 percent of the families in the cities own a car, private cars occupy 80 percent of the total street surface. Cars are the main cause of street congestion suffered by the remaining 80 percent of the population commuting by bus. High-income residential areas are not affected by congestion and pollution since they are usually favored by public investment in streets and protected by zoning ordinances and natural advantages. In some cities urbanization works in residential areas located in the higher parts of the city have affected the soil's natural capacity of rain absorption, thus resulting in floods in the lower parts of the city where most of the middle- and low-income groups live.

45. Examples illustrating this tendency can be found in all of the cities. One that is most representative is a project for several thousand houses at a cost of approximately $300 million in Santiago. This project is controlled by a national and international financing group; its purpose is to "change the consumption habits of Chileans," meaning "the client is the car." Until now, the only criticism on the part of the authorities has been with regard to the "foreign" name (Parkennedy). Their promoters justify this project on the basis of a market study. This occurs at a time when the supply of low-

cost housing is only one-third compared to the period before 1975 and unemployment during recent years has never been less than 13 percent. This situation is consistent with the growth of a rental submarket to which the majority of the middle- and low-income families have had to recur. Rents in 1974 and to 1978 increased approximately 150 percent, according to official data. It must be assumed, also, that in view of the decrease in the production of low-cost houses, the answer to the demand has been overcrowding in existing houses.

Moderator

William Doebele: Dr. Geisse's paper is particularly interesting because it has the same theme as that by James Brown and Neal Roberts: that the market is complicated. We have assumed generally in Latin America that the plus value or the betterment of these great increases in land values goes to the landowners. In fact, what Dr. Geisse has told us is that there are at least six actors in the land market: the landowners, the people who sub-divide land (who might be quite a different group), the financial institutions, the construction companies, the market companies (the people who advertise and who sell the land), and finally the users, the consumers, the buyers of the final house or unit or lot. And plus value or unearned increment or betterment does not necessarily go to the landowner; according to the country and according to the historical circumstance it may go to any one of these other actors. And in fact, what we are seeing in some countries is that the landowners are dominant and are capturing these high prices. In other countries there have been times when the construction companies have been the ones who have moved in and who are really getting the plus value. Most recently, since the 1960s, with the growth of savings and loans associations (some of which were sponsored by the AID and other international agencies) the dominant forces in the real estate market have been not the landowners or the construction companies but the financial institutions. What we are beginning to see now is that the plus value is divided and that the amount that each group gets depends on its dominant position at a particular moment. The most interesting development that is occurring now is an integration of several of these forces in a single financial institution, which will go out, will create its own land banks, will have its own sub-dividers, will have its own construction companies, will have its own marketing companies, and will become an integrated operation, which is a very different type of problem for government policy than the old situation of the landowner dividing his land and selling it directly to a buyer.

I think this might be an ominous development because when you get these large, integrated companies based on financial power, you may have a group that is even more difficult to deal with politically than the traditional landowners, who have had such political power in Latin America. The situation is very different in each country; it is something that must be studied individually in every city. But I think we should learn the lesson from Dr. Geisse's presentation that we must not oversimplify whom we are dealing with. Rather we must consider the fact that there are a lot of actors, and in many countries they are beginning to integrate themselves into very powerful entities that will be difficult to deal with for people who are trying to plan and look at the problem from the public-sector point of view.

11 Urban Land Markets in the Yugoslavian System

Miodrag Janic

Land-use policy in Yugoslavia is closely related to the socioeconomic and political structure of the country. Yugoslavia is a multinational federal socialist state composed of six republics and two autonomous regions. From a social and political point of view, the country is further divided into 510 local municipalities, which administer various activities. There are 11,568 neighborhood units as well. Although these do not have administrative power, they are responsible for organizing, initiating, and coordinating various activities important to the people in their everyday life. Neighborhood units can initiate many activities—environmental protection, mother and child care, adult care, social life, and so on.

The Yugoslavian territory has about 27,500 settlements, of which 59 percent have fewer than 2,000 people and 9 percent have more than 100,000 (according to 1961 data). Due to historical and other reasons, Yugoslavia inherited a dispersed structure of settlements, which is irrational from the social and economic point of view. The postwar process of urbanization growth has been very rapid, even dramatic; the urban population increased from 19 percent in 1948 to 39 percent in 1971. Rough estimates now show that about 50 percent of the people live in urban areas.

During the first few years after World War II, private land in agriculture was limited to 10 hectares of arable land, large estates were nationalized, and expropriation measures in towns provided land for residential, commercial and other purposes. In 1958 the government approved a nationalization law valid for 860 towns and various industrial, mining, and tourist centers in order to help them to overcome various obstacles to intensive construction and urban land extension. Since then, other legislation has been passed, designed to develop and improve the Yugoslav self-management system. In 1974 a new constitutional law was approved, followed by many other legislative activities especially those related to physical planning, land policy, environmental policy, urban land policy, and so on. The nationalization law of 1958 is outdated and has been replaced.

The Yugoslavian government is characterized by pluralization of self-government and self-management interests. Republics, autonomous regions, and municipalities were provided the basic legislative and regulative measures for urban and physical planning, housing, land-use

177

policies, and various social and environmental activities. Further decentralization of decision making provides a much wider basis for economic and political initiatives to the decision makers and to the people as a whole.

According to the Yugoslav constitution, the land is the good (resource) of general social interests and must be managed in a regional way. Because land as a natural good is limited in quantity and quality, there can be no monopoly on those lands that are of exceptional value for the society as a whole. Everybody must have equal access to such land, which includes rivers, lakes, sea, forests, and national parks. This principle is also relevant for minerals and other resources.

From an operational point of view, land management, private or social, has a structural framework in which the basic attributes should be recognized: subjects, objects, constraints, and criteria. Subjects are the decision makers who own, hold, or use the land. Landowners are dominant in rural areas where the agricultural land belongs mostly to private farmers. Landholders and users are in urban areas where the land is socially owned. Landholders are dominant in transitional types of areas, the so-called building areas, which will be transformed from rural to urban use over a period of ten years, under specified legislative and regulative procedures, defined by the local municipality according to its statute, which is based on the federal and republic constitutions. All of the self-management units in the social sector—manufacturing, commerce, construction, transportation, housing, public utilities, social institutions, and so on—can use the urban land under specific conditions. A distinction must be made between economic and other types of users because different criteria and regulations apply. The situation is the same with individuals who can use the urban land as an original farmer owner or as a potential user. In the agricultural sector of the economy, the decision makers are owners of the land, working cooperatives, and economic agricultural estates.

Objects are the things and processes that are influenced by the subjects (decision makers) with the purpose of implementing certain goals and objectives to realize some benefits. Within the framework of land-use policy, the parcel or group of parcels of land is the fundamental element. The goal of land policy in urban areas is to provide the land for various functions at the right time, at the right place, and at prices based on social and economic criteria. Social, economic, and technological changes have fundamental impacts on space. All the interdependencies in social and economic life have spatial reflections, which result in enlarging the space for urban functions with many positive and negative characteristics—positive in increasing income and standard of living and negative in decreasing some social and environmental values.

When decision makers formulate and implement land-use policy, particularly in urban areas, they are constrained by physical, economic, social, financial, technological, institutional, and other factors. Each region and city has its specific socioeconomic structure, level and quality of urbanization, size and location, and needs and requirements that should be satisfied in the process of growth and development.

Land Use in Rural Areas

Private landowners can cultivate land independently, in coordination with other owners, or in collaboration with agricultural cooperatives. Private land property is secured by the constitution and cannot be expropriated for agricultural purposes. Private agricultural landowners are obliged to use the land in the best possible way, which means that they must apply all of the necessary agrotechnical measures in order to realize the highest possible benefit. If one of the owners is not able to cultivate his land, the local community has the right to offer such land to an agricultural estate, a co-operative, or another private owner for further collaboration. This can be done only on a contract basis, which cannot last more than five years. During that period the original owner is not discriminated against and does not lose his property rights. The income from the land, minus the current costs and taxes, belongs to the original owner.

An owner might decide to lease his land for the purpose of agricultural production to other persons or organizations on a contractual basis, which must be in written form. If some of the agricultural land might be eroded by water, wind, or underground water, the municipality can undertake appropriate measures to protect it. Antierosive protection measures can take various forms; for example, special modes of cultivation can be regulated or land can be put out of cultivation.

Land Use in Urban Areas

Urban areas are composed basically of three interrelated types of land:

1. Land densely populated and equipped with physical infrastructure and social amenities within the city border or in settlements that have urban characteristics.
2. Land within the limit designated by a general urban plan that is determined and reserved for urban extension.
3. Land in other areas in which housing, commercial activity, manufacturing, and social construction are forecast for the near future.

In fact, there exist two types of land in urban areas: built-up areas, which are more or less completely constructed and covered with superstructures, and building areas, determined by the urban plan, in which different transitional forms are existing. The spatial structure of the given municipality, in terms of land-use policy, may be presented as in figure 11-1.

In building areas, dynamic transformational processes take place, with different results and consequences. Before construction begins, we need to develop studies and research work designed to propose solutions to the particular situation. The plan is the final act, and it does not mean planning.

Transforming the land from rural to urban should be done on an economically rational and socially feasible basis. By the general urban plan, agricultural land can be designated for building purposes. The detailed plan is the document that elaborates and implements the general plan. By the detailed plan, the general social interest for the land transformation from rural to urban is finally approved, as a legislative and regulatory document. Expropriation is the legislative instrument for transferring the ownership from private to social.

Urban land is used in accordance with the town (general urban) plan. The municipality is entitled to extend the urban area whenever the objective and legal conditions are satisfied in this respect. This is, therefore, a permanent process imposed by the need to extend the urban area. Each settlement

(land in hectares)

Area Unit Level	Built-Up Area (rural)	Building Area (semi)	Agricultural Area (rural)	Total
1. Parcels and groups of parcels				
2. Planning zones				
3. Neighborhood units				
4. City				
5. Municipality total				

Figure 11-1. Horizontal and Vertical Relationships of the Land-Use Structure

develops its own general plan, which extends for a period of fifteen to twenty years. In the plan zoning is proposed for each function—residential, recreational, manufacturing, commercial centers, transportation, public, and so on. The use of each location and site of urban land, with the detailed parcel and reparcels, is elaborated in a detailed town plan, which is also approved by the municipality, according to the order and priorities laid down by the general urban plan. These plans are elaborated in stages—draft and final-draft stage—and are adopted in a democratic procedure. In this way each interested party may participate in the decision making at all stages—from the preparation to the adoption of the plan. Investors and developers, workers and citizens, future holders and users of land, dwellings, and facilities take an active part in this process.

The detailed urban plan, completed before construction begins, speci-fies the use of each building site. It identifies which buildings are to be demolished because they do not correspond to the new use of the land—for instance, the construction of roads, green areas, and other public facilities. Frequently privately owned single-family houses must be demolished when housing developments are to be built in their place.

If the construction of individual family houses is planned, the detailed urban plan also determines the land sites for individual permanent uses (not for ownership of land) through public competition through tenders. Land for construction of various economic and commercial buildings and facilities is allocated for permanent use to the different decision-making units in the same way. Land for schools and for health, social, cultural, and other public buildings is allocated to the users without public tenders, only on an agreement basis. Extremely valuable and attractive locations can be allocated to those who are ready to pay maximum money through direct contract.

Each building and work project must be constructed in accordance with the detailed plan and with a building license. A municipal inspector supervises the construction and is authorized to stop the work or give an order for demolition if the operation does not go according to the detailed plan. After completion of the construction, the investor, public or private, has to obtain a permit for use from the responsible municipal body.

Each individual can own two large or three small apartments. In multistory residential buildings, individual dwellings may be owned privately. In the case of individual family houses, the owner of the dwelling unit or units is considered a direct user of land. In multistory public buildings, the owner of the apartment is an indirect user of land. In both, as well as in other cases, the owners do not have property rights of the land.

Institutional Framework of Land Use

The original land owner must be fairly compensated. Fair compensation, however, excludes the additional value of land that has resulted from different social actions—for instance, building roads and other public facilities, extending the urban areas, constructing the dams and irrigation installations, and so on.

Those who are proposing expropriation are obliged to provide money for compensation; otherwise the expropriation cannot be implemented. The level and volume of fair compensation depends on the type of assets. For agricultural land, the fair compensation is defined in terms of market prices after deducting the additional value of land. The municipality is obliged to investigate and define all of the external factors that influence the land prices to increase above the so-called normal price. Depreciation of the owner's assets must be paid as well. In order to eliminate extra value of land as a result of external conditions, the municipality is obliged to define and publish such zones of land a year before the compensation has started.

For building land, compensation is calculated per square meter in percentage from the average market price, which is based on the price of 1 square meter of housing area in respective areas. That percentage cannot be more than 1 percent or less than 0.2 percent.

For physical structures, the compensation is calculated according to its construction value, which includes the costs of materials, labor, transportation, and preparation of various technical documentation. The depreciation is deducted from this value.

For vineyards and orchards, the compensation is defined like that of agricultural land. The total value of land is increased to include that portion that will be depreciated from the period of vineyard duration, for example.

The owner living with the family in the expropriated building will receive in addition a dwelling in tenancy that has to correspond to the dwelling that was demolished.

The original owner of the raw urban land has a priority right to construct his own house on one building parcel (site area) and according to detailed plan. This priority right to build can be inherited by close relatives (spouse, children, grandchildren, parents, adopted children). The original owner of the land and the present owner of the house have the same rights and duties as any other users of land in the respective territory.

The use of urban land must be consistent with the general interest. The land use can be modified only if the general or detailed plans change and for very good and economically and socially feasible reasons. Such a change must be approved by the municipality.

Users of land in urban areas are registered in a land-registration book. Each registration book provides the number and size of parcel, position, border, building, description of activity, and name of individual user or name of the economic organization or social institution.

All land users must pay for the costs of land preparation and land equipment. These include the costs of obtaining the land compensation, demolishing the old buildings, providing the new houses for those who have to be resettled, preparing necessary documentation and plans, and installing any land equipment.

The municipality has a right to impose the land taxes on all the users of land as an instrument for redistributing surplus value of land and socializing it. Urban land rent is calculated per square meter of building area according to various criteria: location, level of infrastructural equipment, position of each location within the city or region, benefit that could be derived from land, environmental advantages and disadvantages, accessibility to the city center and other centers of activities (recreation, place of work, schools, hospitals, and churches), and transportation costs.

According to these criteria, the categorization and classification of land have been defined into two basic categories, depending on the size of the city: two or more categories of residential zones and two or more categories of commercial zones.

Collected financial resources in this way can be used only for further expansion of urban infrastructure. Rent is calculated according to 1 square meter of dwelling or business floor space rather than square meter of land. This tax is payable each month, together with housing rent or with the tax payable by the owners of family dwellings or individual flats. This urban rent tax is a special instrument; it does not replace any of the regular taxes. The urban land instrument has a special role—for instance, to take part of income that originates from favorable national conditions, from exceptional privileges of the market, or from any other exceptional privileges in income earning (that is, unearned increment). The municipality can loan this extra income to the users of land—perhaps to enlarge production, to open up new working places, or to add to the urban infrastructure.

Each municipality has created special institutions for managing the urban land.

12 The Land-Market Structure on the Fringe of Tokyo

Yuzuru Hanayama and
Tokunosuke Hasegawa

Like other large cities, Tokyo has been growing in this century. The population of the Tokyo region in 1975 was 27 million, twenty times as large as that in 1870.[1] The built-up area was 1,700 square kilometers as of 1975, thirty times as large as that in 1870. As the city has grown, there has always been a high demand for land on the outer fringe of the urbanizing area. This area has become increasingly far from the center of the city, incorporating what was once agricultural and forest land.

Within the inner zone of the city, land use is changing constantly. Skyscrapers are built one after another in the central district for commercial or administrative activities, high-rise apartment buildings and condominiums surrounding the central district are mushrooming, and some large mansions formerly owned by the very wealthy are subdivided into smaller townhouses in the suburbs. The major increment of residential land during these decades has been generated on the outer fringe, however.

Land prices in Tokyo are high. An average-sized residential lot costs about US$40,000; if there is a house on the lot, that amount should be doubled.[2] The average worker earns approximately $14,000 a year, so a house with land is equivalent to six years' earnings. Land prices have risen about 20 percent a year for thirty years, with the exception of the five years after the 1973 energy crisis. The result is that housing in Tokyo is small and sparsely furnished. The average size of newly built houses in 1976 is 80 square meters, and the average area of a lot is 130 square meters.[3]

The original landowners are farmers. They can subdivide their land and sell it directly to the buyers who want to live there, or they can organize a cooperative for land readjustment so that they can sell the land at a higher price after land improvement has taken place. But in many cases, developers stand between farmers and buyers. Thus the land-use change on the fringe of the urbanizing area happens simultaneously with the transfer of title.

Historical Background

About a hundred years ago, during the Meiji revolution, the modern land system was founded. Titles were given to citizens and farmers who in

185

exchange had to pay property tax. In those days the built-up area of Tokyo was rather small—its diameter was only 10 kilometers—though its population was already 1 million. Most land was owned by the samurai class, who had been feudalistic knights and now were bureaucrats and merchants in Tokyo. The majority leased small pieces of land from these landowners.

The city began encroaching on the agricultural area when a number of factories were built outside the old city and a mass of population immigrated from the rural region into the city, searching for jobs in the newly developing industries.

In 1923 an earthquake destroyed much of Tokyo. Shortly after suburbanization began. As the white-collar class left the city, subdivision of land was planned on a large scale and carried out by developers who bought land from the farmers and built railroads, in many cases before they even sold the subdivided lots. Land readjustment by cooperatives of landowners was popular in both the suburbs and in the city. The City Planning Act, which had been passed four years before the earthquake, was applied for the first time in Tokyo. At that time the area of Tokyo city and its vicinity was about 500 square kilometers, with 5 million inhabitants.

During World War II, a quarter of a million citizens of Tokyo were killed or injured, and more than half of the buildings in the city were destroyed. The population immediately after the war was only half that of 1940.

After the war, land reform was carried out all over Japan. The maximum was set on the farmland that could be owned by individuals and about three million sharecroppers got their land. In this process, the large-landowners and small-sharecroppers scheme, which had characterized Japan's society, disappeared. Two aspects of this land reform merit note: first, commercial, industrial, residential, and forest lands were put outside this process, and, second, the size of land plots owned by the farmers was small. The average area was about a hectare and yet it was dispersed into several small pieces forming a very complex cadastral map.

After the war, people returned to Tokyo and built huts on the ruins of the city. In 1954 the National Housing Finance Cooperation was founded to provide housing loans, but this governmentally managed finance was available only to people who already owned land. The number of private houses increased gradually, but the number of wooden-framed apartments built to meet the working class's demand mushroomed, while the public-housing supply was inadequate.

In order to make the city development orderly, a comprehensive plan for Tokyo was enacted in 1946. In 1969 the Metropolitan Control Act, designed to control city expansion, was enacted. But Japan had entered a period of rapid growth, which continued for a quarter of a century until it was stopped by the 1973 energy crisis. During this period the population increase and industrial expansion in Tokyo were so rapid as to negate the plans. The population of Tokyo and its environs grew from 10 million (12 percent of Japan) in 1950 to 27 million (24 percent) in 1975. The plans were amended often, trailing the actual trend.

Residential land was in high demand because of rapid population and income growth and family nuclearization.[4] Subdivisions characterized by small-sized houses and poor facilities sprang up on the city periphery.

Yokohama and Kawasaki, a port city and a heavily industrialized city, respectively, sprawled in the same fashion as Tokyo. Chiba and Urawa, the capital cities of Chiba and Saitama prefectures, followed them. As a result the greenbelt that used to separate these cities vanished, and a number of dormitory cities (bedroom suburbs) were generated here and there. Those cities eventually merged into a huge megalopolis, spreading without bounds.

Finally in 1968 the City Planning Act was amended. It divided land in the metropolitan area into two categories: the urbanizing area where urbanization had already taken place or was to be promoted by the governments and the controlled area where development was to be prohibited for at least ten years. In 1970 primary zoning was accomplished, and 3,161 square kilometers of land fell in the first category in Tokyo and the adjoining three prefectures.

Land Prices

The soaring land prices in Japan, especially in the Tokyo region, are probably unmatched in any other country. According to research by the Japan Institute of Real Estate, the average price of residential land in major cities increased by twelve times between 1960 and 1980. In other words, land prices rose at the rate of about 20 percent a year during this time period. The only exception is the period between 1974 and 1978, when Japan's economy suffered a recession caused by the sudden rise of the cost of oil in 1973 and the resulting world economic recession. Since 1979 land prices have been rising even faster than they did in the 1960s.

As a result, at least three problems have developed. First, newly married couples and young people who have migrated to the large cities have had difficulty finding their own housing due to rapidly increasing land prices. Although the wages of workers have increased by six times in nominal terms and four times in real terms during this time period, people who had saved in order to buy their residential lots were not able to buy them because land prices have risen more rapidly than their wages. In Tokyo and its vicinity, 30 percent of the households own no land; they live in small, wooden-framed apartments. Two-thirds of these have only one room, lacking private toilet and bath.

Second, rising land prices have brought a large windfall to landowners, almost all of whom were originally farmers on the outskirts of Tokyo. In fact, most of Japan's millionaires are these landowners, not the executives of world enterprises. In short, rising land prices have enlarged income differentials among the people.

Third, soaring land prices have prevented local governments from providing adequate facilities such as roads, parks, water and sewerage works, schools, nurseries, and public housing. A larger percentage of the public budget goes for land costs because of rising land prices. In addition, landowners want to hold on to their land because they expect higher prices in the future. Thus it is difficult for local governments to acquire the sites necessary for public purposes.

Table 12-1 shows how land prices rose over this decade. And table 12-2 gives some explanation for the rising land prices.

Stock and Flow of Land

The urbanization area in the Tokyo region is 3,161 square kilometers; the built-up area, including roads and parks, has 1,700 square kilometers. Thus almost half of the urbanization area is not built up yet. Actually 600 square kilometers of farmland and 300 square kilometers of forest were put into the urbanization areas when the new City Planning Act was implemented (tables 12-3 and 12-4).[5]

If we draw a circle with a radius of 40 kilometers from the center of Tokyo, we have about 4,000 square kilometers (excluding water) within the circle. But the built-up area within the circle covers only 1,700 square kilometers. Thus about 2,300 square kilometers are left for housing.[6]

Table 12-1
Land-Price Changes in Tokyo Area, 1968-1976
(dollars per square meter)

					Percentage Change			
	1968	*1970*	*1973*	*1976*	*1968-1970*	*1970-1973*	*1973-1976*	*1968-1976*
Outer core (10-20 km)	160	250	380	500	1.6	1.5	1.3	3.2
Inner ring (20-30 km)	80	160	290	380	2.0	1.8	1.3	4.8
Outer ring (30-40 km)	40	70	220	300	1.8	3.1	1.4	7.6

Note: Land price is the mean value of ten to twenty spots.

Table 12-2

Population Increase in Some Cities in Tokyo Area, 1965-1970
(thousands)

Categories	1960	1965	1970	1975	Percentage Increase			
					1960-1965	*1965-1970*	*1970-1975*	*1960-1975*
Outer core (six wards)	1,644	1,983	2,161	2,229	1.2	1.1	1.0	1.4
Inner ring (fourteen cities)	630	1,021	1,340	1,537	1.6	1.3	1.2	2.4
Outer ring (seven cities)	338	484	677	876	1.4	1.4	1.3	2.6

About 27 million people live in the urbanization areas. If we divide the area by the population, we get 115 square meters per person.[7] This figure appears to be fairly good for residential purposes in the urban district. Assuming family size to be three people and half of the urbanization land to be used for public, commercial, industrial, and other purpose than residential use, there would be about 170 square meters per family. In fact, however, 30 percent of all the households in the Tokyo region own no land. The reason is that the supply of land falls short of demand.

Population is more fluid than land. The flow of population in the Tokyo region can be divided into three major categories. One is the migration of population from all over the country, especially from Tohoku region where the major industry is agriculture and opportunities for employment are poor, into the core district.[8] Another is out-migration from the core district to the surrounding zone, especially to the three prefectures of Kanagawa, Chiba, and Saitama. A third is the interchange of population within the core district (table 12-5).

The first flow consists mainly of young people coming to Tokyo in pursuit of jobs, school, and marriage. In recent years about 400,000 have migrated into the city of Tokyo for these reasons every year. Most of them initially live in poor-quality apartment houses. The second flow of population consists mainly of people who have moved out to the surrounding zone where they have purchased housing. But it has become increasingly difficult to purchase housing because of the rising price of land, and as a result, sites where residences can be built are located increasingly farther from the core district. The third flow of population consists mainly of people who move from one apartment to another in small apartment buildings in an effort to improve their living standard.

Even at the fringe of the Tokyo region, residential land is in short supply because of the demand, although the amount of total land is adequate (table 12-6).

Table 12-3
Area of Tokyo Region by Category

Prefectures	Administrative Spheres		City Planning Areas		Urbanization Areas	
	Land Area	Population	Land Area	Population	Land Area	Population
Tokyo	2,141	11.7	1,629	11.4	1,041	11.3
Chiba	5,080	4.1	2,614	2.8	601	1.8
Saitama	3,799	4.8	2,620	3.7	638	2.7
Kanagawa	2,387	6.4	1,925	5.5	880	4.9
Total	13,407	27.0	8,789	23.3	3,161	20.8

Note: The units for land areas are square kilometers; those for population are millions.

Table 12-4
Land Use in Urbanization Area
(square kilometers)

Prefecture	Built-up Land	(Residential Use)	Roads	Parks	Agricultural Use	Forest
Tokyo	537.5	(408.2)	107.5	25.8	99.2	23.1
Chiba	254.7	(162.1)	54.6	4.7	119.2	73.7
Saitama	231.1	(174.1)	53.7	5.0	240.9	34.8
Kanagawa	430.7	(310.2)	67.9	14.8	141.0	99.6
Total	1,453.9	(1,054.6)	283.7	50.3	600.3	231.1

Table 12-5
Population Movement within Core District
(thousands)

Regions	Years	To Core Area	From Core Area
Tokyo (excluding core area) and adjoining three Prefectures	1966	223	439
	1976	219	407
Other regions than the three Prefectures	1966	400	231
	1976	322	288
Total	1966	623	670
	1976	541	695

Behavior of Landowners

To examine the tightness in land supply, we conducted a field survey by interviewing some four hundred landowners on the fringe of the Tokyo region.[9]

We found that the size of their land varies, but in 50 percent of all cases, it is between 0.5 and 2 hectares. Three-quarters of their land is used for agriculture; one-fifth is forest or their own residential lot; and the rest is rented for residential or commercial uses (table 12-7).

They assess the value of their land at between $500,000 and $2 million. In contrast, they estimate the value of their movable property at less than $300,000.

In three-quarters of all the cases, they rent houses or apartments, but the rental revenue is rather small—between $5,000 and $15,000 a year, which is equivalent to 1 percent of the total value of their assets but about 40 percent of their total annual income, which is between $10,000 and $15,000.

Almost all of them have sold land, but not often—about once in ten years. The amount of total land sold is only about 10 percent of the total

Table 12-6
Developed Area for Residential Use
(square kilometers)

Prefectures	1969	1970	1971	1972	1973	1974	1975	1976	1977
Tokyo	6.1	6.1	2.4	5.1	3.2	3.6	1.8	2.2	2.2
Chiba	6.3	10.1	13.2	9.5	12.4	10.7	6.9	9.7	8.0
Saitama	2.7	4.1	5.9	6.0	5.8	2.5	3.2	2.2	3.4
Kanagawa	8.3	10.5	12.1	10.4	14.9	5.4	5.8	6.9	5.8
Total	22.0	30.9	34.5	30.5	36.3	22.2	16.7	21.1	18.3

Table 12-7
Number of Farmers at Fringe of Tokyo Region, by Size of Parcel Owned

Size in Hectares	Matsudo	Kawasaki	Machida	Abiko	Total
0-0.3	3	31	28	0	62
0.3-0.5	8	27	14	2	51
0.5-1.0	31	22	29	20	102
1.0-2.0	47	15	12	48	122
2.0-3.0	11	7	4	18	40
3.0 and over	0	5	5	12	22
Total	100	107	92	100	399

land owned. Also many have used their money from the sale to buy agricultural land or other land outside urbanization areas. They seem to want to maintain the size of their holdings (table 12-8).

Three major reasons for disposing of their land stood out: building or modernizing their own houses, construction of houses or apartments for rent to increase their income, and payment of inheritance tax (table 12-9).

Chronologically the disposed land was larger in the year when the capital gains tax was relaxed than in the year when it was tightened (table 12-10).

Most of those interviewed believed that land prices will go up further or remain at the present level. They will not sell any more land even if land prices rise because they are satisfied with their lives. They will dispose of only small pieces of land, and only if circumstances force them to.

Land-Market Operation

The owners of land in Tokyo used to be small-sized farmers who could earn their living by farming and without disposing of their land in many cases. As land prices began to rise, most chose to hold on to their land and wait for prices to rise even further. Most also chose not to make any investments that would increase the productivity of their land.

In fact, many farmers have disposed of part of their land in districts incorporated into the outer fringe of the urbanizing area. They have used the revenue from the sale to modernize their own homes, to construct houses or apartments for rent for the purpose of increasing family income to cope with the rising standard of living, or to pay inheritance taxes. When they have satisfied these purposes, they do not sell any more land. Keeping it is the best way for them to increase the value of their assets as the price of land rises at a faster rate than does the standard rate of interest prevailing in the money market.

Table 12-8
Proportion of Disposed Land to Owned Land

A \ B/A	0 Percent	0-10 Percent	10-20 Percent	20-30 Percent	30-40 Percent	40-50 Percent	50-60 Percent
0-0.3	20	2	2	2	3	1	3
0.3-0.5	14	5	2	2	6	3	2
0.5-1.0	18	18	19	15	9	5	5
1.0-2.0	24	38	31	21	9	6	5
2.0-3.0	6	25	14	8	6	0	1
3.0 and over	4	11	6	2	0	2	1
Total	86	99	74	50	33	17	17

Note: A: area of land owned in 1965; B: area of land disposed since 1966. Size of land is given in hectares.

When this happens, those who wish to buy land must go out even farther where they purchase the minimum amount of land they can afford on which to build their own house. Thus the land that is left unsold on the inner side of the border rises automatically in most cases because the inner locations are more convenient for commuting to the central district. The result is that a great deal of farmland is left unsold in the districts within the outer boundary of the urbanizing area. The total area of this land is much larger than that demanded annually. Nevertheless the price of this land continues to rise faster than the standard rate of interest.

The situation can be described by a demand-supply schedule. Suppose an individual farmer want to sell part of his land for a specific purpose.

Table 12-9
Reasons for Land Disposal

Reasons	Number of Cases	Gross Sale (thousands of dollars)	Averave Gross Sale (thousands of dollars)
Living expenses	32	412	13
Building own house	157	5,903	38
Education or marriage of children	24	280	12
Inheritance tax	81	12,612	156
Building house or apartments for rent	134	8,388	63
Purchase of land	93	2,790	30
Investment for private concern	11	728	66
Investment for stock, bond, and savings	256	6,144	24
Miscellaneous	148	6,822	46
Total	938	44,079	47

Table 12-10
Chronological Change of Land Disposal

Year	Number of Cases	Area (hectares)	Gross Sale (thousands of dollars)	Average Area (thousands of square meters)	Average Sale (thousands of dollars)	Average Price (dollars per square meter)
1965	30	9.9	2,880	3.3	96	29
1966	15	1.8	516	1.2	34	29
1967	49	11.6	2,424	2.3	49	21
1968	36	7.4	1,632	2.1	45	22
1969	22	3.4	876	1.5	40	26
1970[a]	59	12.5	5,572	2.1	94	45
1971	36	4.9	3,080	1.4	86	63
1972	41	7.3	6,424	1.8	157	88
1973	34	4.6	4,672	1.4	137	101
1974	32	5.0	6,313	1.6	197	126
1975	40	5.0	10,088	1.3	252	202
1976[b]	21	1.1	2,108	0.5	100	192
1977	33	1.5	2,980	0.5	90	199

[a]In this year capital gains tax was relaxed.

[b]In this year capital gains tax was strengthened.

Because he inherited the land or bought it at a very cheap price at the time of the land reform after World War II, the cost at which he obtained the land is negligible. His supply function can be presented by

$$pqi = \pi\ i,$$

where p is the price of land, q is the quantity of land to sell, π is his profit, and i indicates the group of the specific farmer population. The function is in the shape of a hyperbola. The integrated supply function of individual supply schedules (within an area) is also a hyperbola:

$$q = \sum_i qi = \frac{1}{p}\ \sum_i \pi$$

On the other hand, the demand schedule for land by new residents is a declining curve.[10]

While the demand is weak, the price is very low, but if the demand curve shifts because of an increase in population, and intersects the hyperbolic supply curve, the price begins a rapid increase that reaches an equilibrium shown by P_A, because the demand surpassed the supply while the price was between P_A and P_B in figure 12-1.

In the process some suppliers leave the market because they have realized their profit by selling their land. Thus the hyperbolic supply curve is always coming closer to the origin. The number of demanders might have declined if the population is fixed because some of them also leave the market after they have bought housing lots. However, a continuing influx of population keeps the demand level high, and the increasing income of these newcomers makes the demand even higher.

Some of those seeking land may move to outlying areas where the number of farmers is larger and the supply level is still high. In figure 12-2 *SS* is the supply curve of the outer area which curves more to the right than the supply curve of the inner area shown by *S'S'*. Because buyers will pay more for a housing lot located closer to the center of the city, the demand curve can be shown in a declining fashion.

The price of land in outlying areas is lower than that nearer the city center. But *SS* will move closer to the upper left corner if some of farmers stop selling land because they have realized their profit, and the price will go up if population increases.

Recommended Policies

As a result of the interactions between the increase of population and the rising prices of land, large areas of farmland and forests are left undeveloped within the urbanization areas. Indeed there remains more va-

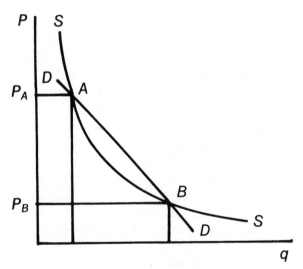

Figure 12-1. Price Shift with Increasing Population

cant land than that developed each year. Therefore, the Tokyo region has a great deal of potential for providing residences. Nevertheless much of this land remains off the market because the landowners are holding onto it in the face of rapidly rising land prices. Therefore it is necessary to devise some measures that would result in this land being available for sale.

A heavy inheritance tax is one of the most effective policies to achieve this end. As the field survey indicated, many landowners were forced to dispose of their land in order to pay inheritance taxes.

A heavy property tax seems to be effective too. Each town and city sets its own property tax rate—1.4 percent in most cases. Major cities, in addition, levy a city planning tax of 0.3 percent. Although every property is required by law to be assessed ad valorem or at the market price, for farmland, nevertheless, a preferential assessment is adopted. Even within the core district, for example, the average of the assessment value of such is only $0.50 or less per square meter, while the assessment value of residential lots adjoining those farmlands is $4,000 or more per square meter. This means that someone with a small lot of perhaps 100 square meters will pay more tax than does a farmer who owns 10,000 square meters.

Some argue that a preferential assessment should be used for farmland. One of the reasons cited is that the actual income gained from farming the land is too small for the farmer to pay property tax. Nevertheless the potential capital gain is very large.

Legislation passed in 1971 required every autonomy to abolish the preferential assessment for farmland within the urbanization area. The farmers so strongly opposed this act, however, that it has been revised.

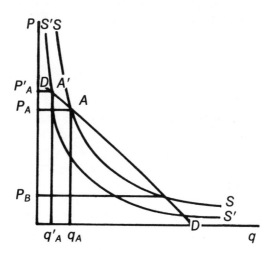

Figure 12-2. Price as a Function of Distance

Levying heavier property tax shifts the supply curve in figure 12-2 in a northeasternly direction and makes the price lower.

Some people believe that a capital gains tax can function in much the same way as the property tax. A progressive capital gains tax certainly may be useful for income redistribution, but it may even result in a tightening of supply. Indeed this has happened. Just as landowners expect the value of their land to rise, they expect the capital gains tax to be lowered. They will thus wait for the government to change its policy before selling the land.

Conclusion

Clearly land prices were boosted as a result of a concentration of population in urban areas caused by Japan's rapid economic growth. And conversely, economic growth was aided by rising land prices. Land prices that rose at such a high rate as to surpass the standard rate of interest were the best security for bank loans for investment in housing, and plant and equipment, and thus assured economic growth by providing effective demand in the macro market. This course of events reinforced the opinions of those who believed in the efficiency of the market mechanism and supported *laissez faire* policy, neglecting empirical research about the structure of land market.

But now it is obvious that the *laissez faire* policy has resulted in soaring land prices. People are thus prevented from enjoying goods or services that should be provided by the local governments but are not because of the high price of land. We therefore need to examine the land market mechanism and the behaviors of the major characters in it so that we can fashion effective policies to control them.

Notes

1. The Tokyo region is defined here as the city planning area, designated by the City Planning Act, of Tokyo and the adjoining three prefectures: Kanagawa, Chiba, and Saitama. Yokohama, Kawasaki, and 106 other cities and towns are included in it. The built-up area is almost contiguous in this region.

2. In this paper one U.S. dollar is converted to 250 yen.

3. Apartment houses are much smaller. The average number of people living in a room is 0.9, and the average floor space per head is 10 square meters as of 1975. It was reported that a delegation from the EEC in 1979 examining Japanese economic activity described the houses as rabbit huts.

4. The average family size declined from 4.7 people in 1950 to 2.9 in 1957.

5. These figures for farmland and forest were obtained by accumulating the registered area in the cadastre. But it is said the registered area in the cadastre is too small and the actual area is 1.2 times larger.

6. The urbanization area in the Tokyo region is almost equivalent to that of the core and inner ring (3,328 square kilometers) in the New York City Planning Area with 15 million people, or the greater London area (1,400 square kilometers) with 8 million people.

7. This figure is 230 for the New York City Planning Area and 240 for the greater London area.

8. The city of Tokyo consisting of twenty-three wards and 8 million people is regarded as the core district.

9. Interviews were conducted in 1978 and 1979 in four cities—Matsudo, Kawasaki, Machida, and Abiko—all located on the outer ring of the Tokyo region. Some one hundred farmer families were taken as samples for each city.

10. The demand schedule of the individual demander is not hyperbola-shaped, because he wants to buy a house as well as a lot and still stay within his means, and the price of the house is an independent variable.

13

Report on Urban Land-Market Research in São Paulo, Brazil

Emilio Haddad

São Paulo, the largest metropolis in Brazil and one of the largest agglomerations in the world, with 12 million inhabitants, is the dynamic center of the country, responsible for 40 percent of its national product. With 1.6 million people in 1940 and 4.8 million in 1960, the city has faced large problems stemming from a fast pace of urbanization in a less-developed economy, where planning is usually behind.

A chaotic process of urban development resulted in a picture of unevenness in the quality of life throughout the intraurban space. A survey of the urban conditions made in 1975 revealed that only 40 percent of the streets were paved, only 30 percent of the dwellings were linked to the sewer network, and 53 percent were linked to the water network (Kowarick and Brant 1975).

Because urban land markets have played a role in the shaping of the prevailing picture, there is an awareness that they need to be understood and disciplined. Along with the unwanted impacts on the urban structure—an increase in commuting time and favorably located lots remaining empty while people occupy the poorly supplied peripheral zones—attention has been drawn to questions of equity related to market operation. The finding that land price has made many housing projects inaccessible for low-income people has been deceptive, while speculation in land, a well-established practice, is considered a national problem.

In this environment, research concerning urban markets and related policymaking has increased. With respect to policy, over the past fifteen to twenty years a few actions have been taken, and policy mechanisms designed to affect the urban land market have been created or discussed. Bolaffi (1980) examines some of these attempted or discussed land policies in Brazil. At the local level, the São Paulo Municipal Zoning Ordinance was established in 1972 and the Greater São Paulo Metropolitan Region in 1975. At the national level, the Banco Nacional de Habitação (National Housing Bank), created in 1964, periodically imposes credit restrictions concerning housing; for example, it may impose an upper limit on loans or set differential rates of interest. Furthermore, monetary correction (rates) on loans and mortgages are prefixed by the central government, and, in the past years, have been smaller than the increases in the general consumer price index. In 1979, a national bill to control rents was approved by the Congress, indexing annual rate for rental values in renewing contracts.

Research on the urban land market—its role in local and national economies and in integrating society and the urban structure—has increased markedly in the last several years in Brazil.[1] Indeed, there has been a broad effort, theoretical as well as applied, and this paper presents only a partial account of this effort: the state of the empirical research on the structure and evolution of urban land markets in São Paulo.

My major focus is on the work carried out at the Instituto de Pesquisas Tecnológicas do Estado de São Paulo S.A. (Technological Research Institute of the State of São Paulo). The research, which emphasizes the development of an information system on property prices in São Paulo and on the design of good indicators for their measurement, has been ongoing.

Promédio System

The Promédio System is an information system on real estate values in São Paulo (EMBRAESP 1976). It was developed on a joint-venture basis by Empresa Brasileira de Estudos do Patrimônio (EMBRAESP), a São Paulo-based private enterprise working on property valuation and urban information, and Instituto de Pesquisas Tecnológicas do Estado de São Paulo (IPT), a technical research institute of the São Paulo State Secretary for Industry, Commerce, Science, and Technology. The system has been in operation on a medium-sized computer at IPT since 1976. Each month it is provided with information on around 2,000 properties in the real estate market in São Paulo.

Information Collected

For each property surveyed, a card is prepared with a broad description of the property, including, whenever possible, a photograph. The following information is then stored in the computer:

1. Type of property: Vacant lot, house, apartment, industrial, commercial, garage, rural.
2. Location: Indicated by the sector of the fiscal cadastre of the municipality and by value zone (one of seventy-six zones in which the municipality of São Paulo was divided by EMBRAESP on the basis of its homogeneity vis-à-vis the real estate market). A value zone, in most cases, may be understood as neighborhoods.
3. Zoning: According to the municipal zoning ordinance, established in 1972. Main uses in São Paulo are: Z1, low density, strictly residential use; Z2, low density, predominantly residential use; Z3, medium density,

predominantly residential use; Z4, medium/high density, mixed use; Z5, high density, mixed use (downtown area); and Z6, predominantly industrial use.

4. Area: In the case of a building, its floor space.
5. Price and form of payment (cash or installments).
6. New or used building.
7. Date of the information.
8. Origin of information: Main sources are newspaper advertising, real estate brokers, and local surveys. Official data from auctions, expropriations, and so forth are also collected.

Data Entry

The information is then entered into the computer for a consistency analysis, designed to detect errors, as well as to identify extremely deviant values for rechecking. The data are filed on magnetic tape.

Automatic Data Retrieval

The Promédio System has a procedure for selective data retrieval, according to parameters specified by the user. As an example, one may request information on empty lots, ranging in area from 300 to 1,000 square meters under zones Z1 and Z2, offered for sale between February and May of 1977, located either in Santo Amaro (value zone: 65) or Represas (value zone: 69). Further, those elements can be listed according to their total value.

Statistical Data Analysis

The system also features some programs for statistical data reduction and analysis. Those programs were structured in modular form so as to make it easy to use the statistical packages of the computer library. Built-in programs provide statistics of selected variables, such as the maximum, minimum, and mean values; standard deviation; number of cases; and the coefficient of variation of the value per square meter of land.

Some Empirical Studies on Urban Land Markets in São Paulo

Studies Carried Out with the Promédio Data File

Contribution to the Intraurban Analysis of São Paulo: This research was carried out by IPT in 1978 under a contract with the National Commission for Urban Policy and Metropolitan Regions (Comissão Nacional de Regiões

Metropolitanas e Política Urbana, CNPU). A major objective of this study was to explore the development of good indicators of the behavior of property prices in São Paulo, using the Promédio data file.

This study resulted in a proposed taxonomy of properties, the division of the municipality in homogeneous zones, and the definition of price indicators. All of these tasks are aimed at the search for market segments with a higher degree of internal homogeneity with respect to prices.

A statistical quality-control procedure $\overline{X}$-chart was utilized to access simultaneously the level of quality of the data and their variability. Results of this treatment are displayed in table 13-1, which shows a reduction of variance due to the elimination of the cases out of the limits of tolerance (80 percent of cases). Yet the analysis of these extreme cases was helpful in suggesting a review of the proposed classification.

The homogeneous zones were created with the aim of showing the influence of location on price, the correlated level of infrastructure and services provision, and the socioeconomic strata of the population. Those homogeneous zones were obtained through aggregation of the seventy-six value zones into eight clusters (table 13-2). A technique blending quantitative with qualitative considerations was employed.

A difficulty in describing the urban characteristics of the homogeneous zones derived from the fact that the official socioeconomic or infrastructural data are presented in terms of districts defined by administrative procedures like the census that generally are not very homogeneous with respect to urban land prices as the value zones are. Nevertheless, an approximation of the level of infrastructure provision, land-use patterns, and family income of each homogeneous zone was obtained with data from the Housing and the Population Censuses. The results are presented in table 13-3, which shows that the level of urban quality decreases from homogeneous zones A to G, except zone C (the downtown area). With the proposed classification, it was possible to construct a cross-section (table 13-4) and time-series of values (figure 13-2), and these have been produced since 1977.

Table 13-4 displays the range of variation of urban land prices in the municipality of São Paulo in September 1977. The figures show the variation of prices by homogeneous zones (defined in the basis of these prices) and by ordinance zones: values increase from Z2 to Z4, reflecting more intensity in land use. The zoning ordinance of São Paulo was established in 1972 and has basically confirmed the prevalent pattern of land use, so it is difficult to say to what extent zoning has been a cause or a result of the existent pattern. In São Paulo land prices vary more than fifty times from the lowest to the highest in the range of prices.

Figure 13-1 is an example of time-series data, showing the evolution of average prices per square meter of apartments in homogeneous zone D in the period between October 1976 and October 1977. The figure shows the

Table 13-1
Statistical Quality Control of the Data ($\overline{X}$-Chart), August 1976-September 1977

Homog. Zones	Zoning	Sample Size		Coefficient of Variance		Average Value		Limit of Tolerance	
		I	II	I	II	I	II	INF	SUP
A	Z1	433	362	0.42	0.26	2,461	2,186	1,143	3,779
	Z2	47	42	0.52	0.45	1,612	1,358	546	2,678
	Z3 (500 a 2,500m²)	28	21	0.32	0.11	9,340	8,029	5,526	13,154
B	Z4	52	44	0.48	0.27	3,912	3,971	1,527	6,297
D	Z1	245	210	0.31	0.20	2,035	1,824	1,222	2,848
	Z2 (-700m²)	512	434	0.58	0.39	1,949	1,732	512	3,386
	Z2 (700 a 2,500m²)	200	157	0.53	0.37	2,273	1,924	724	3,822
	Z2 (2,500 a 20,000m²)	33	28	0.68	0.55	1,798	1,652	233	3,363
	Z3 (-500m²)	114	103	0.81	0.51	2,793	2,662	0	5,681
	Z3 (500 a 2,500m²)	201	162	0.61	0.38	3,835	3,407	849	6,821
	Z3 (+2,500m²)	33	27	0.74	0.45	2,996	1,651	156	5,836
	Z4	93	81	0.65	0.43	5,149	4,153	846	9,452
	Z6	80	72	0.53	0.30	2,432	1,792	795	4,069
E	Z2 (-700m²)	533	473	0.59	0.37	1,146	942	277	2,015
	Z2 (700 a 2,500m²)	151	129	0.58	0.40	1,096	981	278	1,914
	Z2 (2,500 a 20,000m²)	74	61	0.58	0.40	898	868	227	1,569
	Z3 (-500m²)	119	109	0.74	0.41	2,241	2,195	106	4,376
	Z3 (500 a 2,500m²)	112	95	0.50	0.32	2,013	1,830	725	3,301
	Z3 (+2,500m²)	23	19	0.48	0.31	1,767	1,572	684	2,850
	Z6	135	110	0.55	0.37	1,404	1,207	417	2,391
F	Z2 (-700m²)	395	334	0.56	0.36	707	631	204	1,210
	Z2 (700 a 2,500m²)	131	101	0.54	0.32	799	697	246	1,352
	Z2 (+20,000m²)	14	12	0.77	0.76	444	233	4	884
	Z3 (-500m²)	25	23	0.87	0.36	1,408	1,512	0	2,972
	Z3 (500 a 2,500m²)	22	18	0.58	0.48	2,930	2,545	739	5,121
G	Z2 (-700)	221	192	0.80	0.55	363	330	0	734
	Z2 (700 a 2,500m²)	58	52	0.75	0.42	309	289	13	605
	Z2 (2,500 a 20,000m²)	29	25	0.76	0.66	258	224	7	509
	Z6	43	31	0.51	0.25	500	528	171	829

Source: Instituto de Pesquisas Technológicas Comissão Nacional de Regiões Metropitanas e de Politica Urbana (1978).
Note: I, initial sample; II, after-the-treatment sample.

Table 13-2
Division of the Municipality of São Paulo in Homogeneous Zones
Through Clustering of Value Zones

Zone A	Zone D	Zone E
14. Ibirapuera	6. Aclimação	40. Tatuapé
18. Jardins	7. Paraíso	46. V. Prudente
19. Alamedas	8. V. Mariana	48. V. Maria
25. Alto de Pinheiros	9. Ipiranga	49. V. Guilherme
29. Pacaembu	11. Saúde	50. Tucuruvi
30. Higienópolis	13. Aeroporto	53. Casa Verde
58. Alto da Lapa	15. Indianópolis	56. Jaguaré
61. City Butantã	16. Itaim	57. Ceasa
62. Cidade Jardim	17. V. Uberabinha	60. Butantã
63. Morumbi	24. Pinheiros	68. Socorro
	26. V. Madalena	
Zone B	27. Sumaré	**Zone F**
	28. Perdizes	
3. Liberdade	52. Santana	41. Penha
4. Bela Bista	59. Lapa	45. V. Formosa
31. Consolação	65. Brooklin	51. Tremembé
32. Sta. Cecília	66. Alto da Boa Vista	54. Brazilândia
33. Campos Eliseos	67. Sto..Amaro	70. Pedreira
35. Bom Retiro	69. Represas	71. Campo Limpo
36. Brás		75. V. Andrade

Zone C	Zone E	Zone G
1. Centro Novo	10. Moinho Velho	42. Ermelino Matarazzo
2. Centro Antigo	12. Jabaquara	43. S. Miguel Paulista
Zone D	37. Pari	44. Itaquera
	38. Mooca	55. V. dos Remédios
5. Cambuci	39. Belém	72. Parelheiros

Source: Instituto de Pesquisas Tecnológicas/Comissão Nacional de Regiões Metropitanas e de Politíca Urbana (1978).

Table 13-3
Infrastructure and Socioeconomic Characteristics of the Homogeneous Zones

Zone	Electricity (%)	Water (%)	Sewer (%)	Annual Rate of Population Change	Use of Building	Average Annual Income per Capita (Cr $)
A	98.1	95.1	86.8	2.59	88.3	8.7	4,577
B	98.9	98.4	96.8	0.21	54.0	35.0	3,374
C	99.9	99.5	98.7	−0.98	8.3	83.2	2,798
D	97.6	90.1	79.2	2.77	84.9	11.0	3,455
E	96.2	76.3	47.8	4.79	86.9	10.1	1,936
F	95.0	52.9	10.6	5.02	92.5	5.5	1,379
G	78.3	21.2	2.1	9.97	93.7	4.6	955

Source: Instituto de Pesquisas Tecnológicas/Comissão Nacional de Regiões Metropitanas e de Politíca Urbana (1978).

Table 13-4
Average Price per Square Meter of Vacant Lots in São Paulo, August 1976-September 1977
(Cr$)

Homogeneous Zones	Z1	Z2				Z3			Z4	Z6
		0-700 m^2	700-1,500 m^2	2,500-20,000 m^2	Over 20,000 m^2	0-500 m^2	500-2,500 m^2	Over 2,500 m^2	Z4	Z6
A	2,186 (.26)						8,029 (.11)			
B						2,221 (.29)			3,971 (.27)	
D	1,824 (.20)	1,732 (.39)	1,924 (.37)	1,652 (.55)		2,662 (.51)	3,407 (.38)	1,651 (.45)	4,010 (.43)	
E		942 (.37)	981 (.40)	868 (.40)		2,195 (.41)	1,830 (.32)	1,572 (.31)		
F		631 (.36)	697 (.32)		233 (.76)	1,512 (.36)	2,545 (.48)			
G		330 (.55)	289 (.42)	224 (.66)						582 (.25)
Munic. São Paulo	2,053	1,072	1,171	919	233	2,323	3,176	1,168	3,996	528

Source: Instituto de Pesquisas Tecnológicas/Comissão Nacional de Regiões Metropitanas e de Política Urbana (1978).

prices of new and used apartments by number of bedrooms. Prices per square meter are higher in the new units (as one should expect) and increase with the number of bedrooms, which means that in São Paulo larger units are also better-quality ones. A remarkable effect in this period was the increase in prices of new apartments with one bedroom. An explanation for

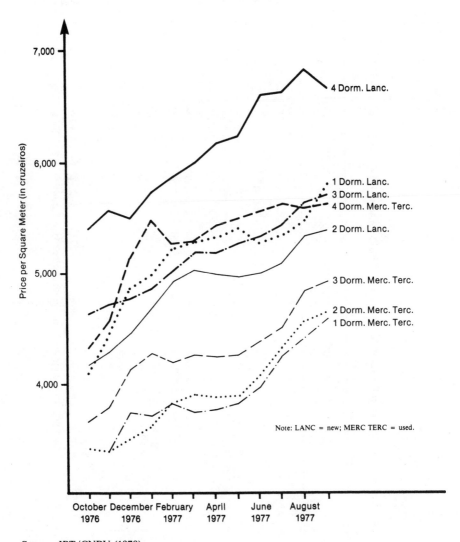

Figure 13-1. Average Values per Square Meter of Apartments in Homogeneous Zone D

this substantial rise in prices is the increasing demand for better-quality one-bedroom apartments. Single people, who traditionally lived with their parents, are now moving out to their own dwellings. Additionally, there is a new demand for one-bedroom, better-qaulity apartments for students or young professionals coming temporarily or permanently to São Paulo. During this period prices have risen in all segments, mostly because of inflation, which was around 38 percent. From February to June, the increase in prices was smaller than the rate of inflation, probably because of a governmental decision to stop financing used dwellings during this period.

Other Projects Utilizing Data from the Promédio System: Two subsequent studies have helped further to develop the research. First, an estimation of property values for a land-use and transportation simulation model (MUT) developed for São Paulo by the Traffic Engineering Company of the municipality of São Paulo (COGEP 1979a). MUT (Modelo de uso de Solo e Transportes) is a gravity-type model that uses the data from an origin/destination survey made in 1977, aggregated at the level of O/D zones, which were subdivisions of the official districts, utilized by the census. The second is a survey of the level of real estate activity in São Paulo. For both studies, a more precise division of São Paulo in homogeneous zones resulted from the improvement of the existing one (IPT/BNH 1979). This new division was defined both in terms of value zones and O/D subzones after a study of compatibility of those two forms of aggregation.

This new division in homogeneous zones has been adopted for the purpose of the stratification of the sample, as well as to aid the presentation of the results, in the survey on the level of real estate activity in São Paulo.

Other Related Studies

Survey of the Level of Real Estate Activity in São Paulo: This research has been carried out by IPT under a contract with the Brazilian National Housing Bank (Banco Nacional de Habitação, BNH). Begun in June 1978, its purpose is to survey the construction and sales of the housing units (houses and apartments) built in São Paulo, financed by the BNH, under two main credit lines, SBPE and RECON, both granted to entrepreneurs.

Indicators such as number of units sold and average prices, are published monthly. Figure 13-2 shows the number of apartments constructed and sold in the municipality of São Paulo each month between July 1979 and June 1980. These results are also provided at the level of homogeneous zones for different number of bedrooms. It is possible to compare the relationship between land prices and the construction activity at that level.

As figure 13-2 indicates, the level of real estate activity fell in this period. The number of units sold was smaller than the number of units put on sale,

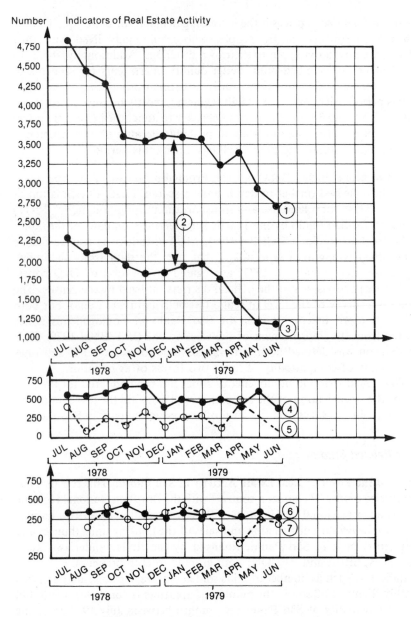

Source: Pesquisa de Comercializacão de Mercado Habitacional (1979).

Note: 1, number of units on sale; 2, number of units on sale under construction; 3, number of units on sale already constructed; 4, number of units sold during month; 5, number of units beginning sales during month; 6, number of units already constructed sold during month; 7, number of units entering stock of already vacant units during month.

Figure 13-2. Indicators of Real Estate Activity

and therefore the stock of empty apartments declined. Because of this decrease in supply, it was expected that prices would increase, leading to new investment.[2]

Starting in August 1980, this survey was made every three months. In the future, this survey will include data on the construction of units not financed by BNH. Another monthly survey on housing rental prices in São Paulo, sponsored by BNH, has been stopped since mid-1979 and may resume in the future (Pesquisa sobre Evolucão dos Aluguéis 1975).

Evolution of Land Prices in São Paulo, 1900-1978: The research carried out by IPT focuses on a fairly short time period (1977-1980) so the results do not display long-run tendencies of the land market. Therefore a complementary study is now being carried out by the secretary for urban planning (Coordenadoria Geral do Planejamento, COGEP) of the municipality of São Paulo. Based on information collected from newspaper advertising, this study has surveyed the evolution of asking prices for urban land in São Paulo since 1900. Preliminary results (figure 13-3) show the evolution of prices in real terms (in 1975 Cr$). Land prices were fairly stable from 1900 to 1932, when

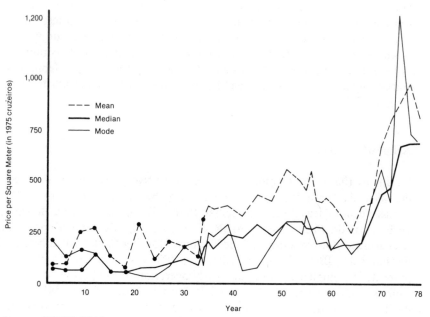

Source: COGEP (1980).

Figure 13-3. Land Prices in the Municipality of São Paulo: Mean, Median, and Mode

they started to increase. This date corresponds to the beginning of industrialization and acceleration of population growth of the city. Following a period in which prices remained fairly stable, they dramatically increased in the period 1968-1974.

COGEP, which is responsible for urban land policy at the municipal level, has carried out a series of studies to subsidize the analysis and the discussion of its proposals. These studies have stressed the question of the costs of infrastructure in the urban-development process (COGEP 1979a) and studies of land taxation focusing on both the progressive property tax and *solo criado* (created value) an adaptation of the French *plafond legal de densité*, the legal ceiling of density (COGEP 1979c).

Two other empirical studies concerning urban land markets in São Paulo are a study by Souza Lima (1977) on the fiscal equity of the property tax in the municipality of São Paulo and the survey of the stock of empty land in the greater São Paulo Metropolitan Region, now being carried out by EMPLASA, the technical body of the São Paulo state secretrary for metropolitan affairs.

Final Comments

The research described here should be helpful in the quantitative design, analysis, and assessment of policies concerning urban land prices in São Paulo. The information is useful to market analysts, builders, and valuers, as well as to fundamental and applied research. The system will be improved by the gradual incorporation of new information—for example, from other market segments, data from neighboring communities, and data from the demand side.

Acknowledgments

I want to thank the technical and administrative personnel at the Technological Research Institute of the State of São Paulo (Instituto de Pesquisas Tecnológicas do Estado de São Paulo, IPT), the Empresa Brasileira de Estudos do Patrimônio (EMBRAESP), and the Research Department (Departmento de Pesquisas) of the National Housing Bank (Banco Nacional de Habitação, BNH). Raquel S. Silva from IPT was responsible for the computer design, implementation, and early operation of the Promédio System. Luiz Antonio Pompéia and Vera Cilda Barbosa Stober from EMBRAESP participated in the conception and early development of the system. Mr. and Ms. Luiz A. de O. Ribeiro have continued to support this work. Osnei Copinski from BNH has been responsible for the survey on the level of real estate activity and has helped its development in São Paulo. Neide Oliveira and Cleide S.P. Gomes provided secretarial services.

Notes

1. In November 1978, Fundacão do Desenvolvimento Administrativo, a São Paulo-based foundation working with Development of the Administration, organized a seminar, "The Role of Land Rents in the Urban Economy," where many important contributions were presented. Other fairly recent published papers on the matter are Vetter and Rzezinski (1979); Smolka (1979); Singer (1979); and Campanário (1978). Comprehensive research has been carried out for Belo Horizonte by PLAMBEL (1978). A study of the real estate market in Rio de Janeiro was carried out by ASTEL (1978).

2. Figures for the first semester of 1980 show that those expectations have been confirmed. Increasing investment in real estate was further encouraged by the shortage of alternatives of investment prevailing in Brazil in mid-1980.

References

ASTEL. 1978. *Pesquisa sobre evolução de preços de terrenos e seu impacto na formação de preço das moradias: a experiência do município do Rio de Janeiro.* Rio de Janeiro: Assessores Técnicos Ltda./ Comissão Nacional de Regiões Metropolitanas e de Política Urbana.

Bolaffi, Gabriel. 1979. "Urban Land Policy in Brazil." *Habitat International* 4, no. 4/5/6, pp. 581-591.

Campanário, Milton de Abreu. 1978. "Economia urbana e desenvolvimento: notas introdutórias para discussão." *Revista Brasileira de Planejamento* 9-10 (September-December):41-47.

COGEP. 1979a. *Custos de urbanização.* Informações e Apoio ao Planejamento n.2; série. São Paulo: Prefeitura do Município de São Paulo/ Coordenadoria Geral de Planejamento.

COGEP. 1979b. *MUT—Modelos de uso do solo e transporte.* Informações e Apoio ao Planejamento n.1; série. São Paulo: Prefeitura do Município de São Paulo/Coordenadoria Geral de Planejamento.

COGEP. 1979c. *Política de controle de uso e ocupação do solo.* Políticas Setorias, Controle Normativo n.1; série. São Paulo: Prefeitura do Município de São Paulo/Coordenadoria Geral de Planejamento.

Cunha, Paulo Vieira, and Smolka, Martin O. 1978. "Notas críticas sobre a relação entre rendas fundiárias e uso do solo urbano." *Seminário Aberto sobre Renda Fundiária na Economia Urbana.* São Paulo, FUNDAP, November 7-8.

EMBRAESP. 1976. *Síntese descritiva do Centro de Informações Mer cado-lógicas: breve introducão ao Sistema Promédio.* São Paulo: Empresa Brasileira de Estudos de Patrimônio.

FUNDAP. 1978. *Documento preparatório do Seminário Aberto sobre a Renda Fundiária na Economia Urbana.* São Paulo: Fundação do Desenvolvimento Administrativo.

IPT/BNH. 1979. *Divisão do município de São Paulo em zonas.homogêneas.* São Paulo: Instituto de Pesquisas Tecnológicas/Banco Nacional da Habitação.

IPT/CNPU. 1978. *Contribuição para a análise intraurbana de São Paulo: Caracterização do mercado de imóveis.* São Paulo: Instituto de Pesquisas Tecnológicas/Comissão Nacional de Regiões Metropitanas e de Política Urbana.

Kowarick, Lúcio and Brant, Vinícius; orgs. 1975. *São Paulo 1975 crescimento e pobreza.* São Paulo: Ed. Loyola.

Lima, José C. de Souza. 1977. *O imposto predial na cidade de São Paulo: um estudo de inequidade administrativa.* São Paulo: Universidade de São Paulo/FEA.

PESQUISA de Comercializacão de Mercado Habitacional: Nova metodologia. 1979-. São Paulo: Instituto de Pesquisas Tecnológicas/DES/ASU.

PESQUISA sobre a evolucão de aluguéis. 1975. Rio de Janeiro: Banco Nacional de Habitação/NEURB.

PLAMBEL. 1978. *O mercado de terras na região metropolitana de Belo Horizonte.* Belo Horizonte: Superintendencia de Desenvolvimento da Região Metropolitana de Belo Horizonte.

Singer, Paul. 1979. *O uso do solo urbano na economia capitalista.* São Paulo: Universidade de São Paulo/FAU.

Smolka, Martin O. 1979. *Preço da terra e valorização imobiliária urbana: esboço para o enquadramento conceitual da questão.* Rio de Janeiro: Instituto de Planejamento Econômico e Social.

Vetter, David, and Rzezinki, Henrique C. 1979. "Política de uso do solo. para quem?" *Revista de Administração Municipal* 26:6-31.

Moderator

William Doebele: A couple of things were particularly interesting about this presentation. One is the technical aspects of studying this problem in São Paulo. The other concerns the question of life changes—death, inheritance, family changes—as being a very important factor in land markets. It was also emphasized by Jim Brown and Neal Roberts. We saw it in Japan, where one of the three factors that does make farmers sell land is the problem of inheritance taxes. This whole question of death duties is an area that we must explore carefully as planners. We have not thought about it as a land-control device, but it may be one of the most important ones, and we see it coming up here again and again.

We also saw in the Brazilian market this shift of people now wanting to have one-room apartments rather than having the typical two- or three-bedroom apartment. That will change the kind of controls and the kind of land and housing markets we have. It's one of the major changes in the United States.

Finally, Mr. Haddad made a very interesting point about government finance as being very important in what happens to the housing market in Brazil. Guillermo Geisse earlier pointed out that one of the major trends is the fact that financial institutions are now taking over land markets more and more in Latin America, creating these integrated enterprises where they have their own land banks, their own construction companies, their own marketing companies, and they do the whole thing. But essentially they are based in financial institutions. And I said that that was an ominous development because those kinds of organizations are going to be very hard to control—much harder to control, perhaps, than when you had six or seven different actors. It's all one integrated opponent.

There is, however, another interesting aspect of this integration to financial institutions controlling land markets and urban development. That is that fact that in all countries of the world, the central banking system is controlled by the government, even in the most-capitalistic countries. That means that if you have financial institutions doing this, the automatic control of the central banking system may be a way of getting at these institutions, make them in some ways more vulnerable to public controls than when you were dealing with a lot of landowners. So perhaps this development has both a threatening side and a side of opportunity. Emilio pointed out how the National Housing Bank in Brazil was, in fact, able to start using those credit controls. Again I suggest that credit controls and the use of the banking system is one of the important new land-use control devices that we all have to start thinking about. There is another approach to land problems: the land-ceiling restrictions, ceilings on what one person can own—which has been used most notably in the legislation passed by India about five years ago.

14

The Evolution of Land Values in the Context of Rapid Urban Growth: A Case Study of Bogotá and Cali, Colombia

Rakesh Mohan and
Rodrigo Villamizar

A Simple Model of Urban Land Values

That land policy is an important component in the process of public policymaking is evident. One of the key ideas resulting from the United Nations Conference on Human Settlements when it met in Vancouver in 1976 was embodied in the preamble to the recommendations for national action on land: "Land, because of its unique nature and the crucial role it plays in human settlements, cannot be treated as an ordinary asset controlled by individuals and subject to the pressures and inefficiences of the market" (Lichfield 1980). It is ironic, then, that our knowledge of the actual operation of urban land markets and of the resulting land values is highly limited. Pronouncements on the desirability of, and on the contents of, urban land policy are easy to find; facts on which these policies are based are, however, distinguished by their absence.

Our objective in this paper is to present a somewhat detailed case study of what has happened to land values in two Colombian cities during a period of extremely rapid growth when both the cities have roughly doubled their size. We believe that only when we can understand the role of land values in the urban economy and of their relationship with, and effect on, the evolving urban structure of cities during periods of rapid growth, can we begin to enunciate policies that ultimately enhance public welfare.

Much of the concern with the operation of land markets arises from the observation of rising land values that are seen as unwarranted or undesirable. Second, when land values do rise rapidly, certain lucky individuals who own land are seen to reap large windfall gains, which they have done little to earn. Such anxiety is understandable since land is a major component of the production of housing—which everyone needs—and of

The views reported here are those of the authors. They should not be interpreted as reflecting the views of the World Bank or its affiliated organizations or of Corporación Centro Regional de Población.

217

urban production facilities—on which everyone depends for their livelihood. Windfall gains or large gains are usually associated with aspects of monopoly power, and thus there is a general suspicion that urban land markets are characterized by monopolistic arrangements. An understanding of the operation of urban land markets and their relationship with urban growth would, however, reveal that these land-value increments must necessarily occur along with urban growth and more in certain parts of the city than in others. Thus, even when there is no monopoly in landownership, windfall gains would accrue to individuals who happen to own land in those parts. The latter is more an income-distribution issue than a land-policy issue.

Before presenting the empirical information on land values in Bogotá and Cali, we develop a highly simplified but useful model of land values, which will serve to put in perspective the patterns observed. Gregory Ingram has already presented a paper in this conference that places land in the context of conventional economic theory. We continue in a similar vein but pay more attention to the role of land values in ordering the internal structure of a city. The model we developed is highly simplified and might appear to belabor the obvious. Its results, however, are surprisingly powerful and help us understand the patterns we then observe.

Urban land is demanded as an asset in two ways. It is, first, a factor of production in the production of housing, factories, or public services (such as roads and parks), when returns to it come in the form of housing services or income from the produced goods. It is also demanded as what might be termed a pure asset in people's portfolios. Developed land is used as both: it usually forms the major portion of a family's assets, as well as a factor of production in housing. Undeveloped land, however, is mainly used as a pure asset. "The function of land prices is to allocate land to valuable uses" (Mills and Song 1979, p. 99). Thus, high land prices indicate scarcity, and the use of land is economized. This can also be stated conversely: when land is scarce, its price is high and its use is consequently economized. As with the prices of other goods, the price of land is important as a signal for the rational allocation of its use.

From what does land derive its value? In agricultural uses it is easy to understand that an acre of more-fertile land produces more food and is therefore more valuable as compared with an acre of less-fertile land. In the urban context it is clearly not fertility that gives land its value, but we can stretch the agricultural analogy to obtain an understanding of the value of urban land. If we consider a city surrounded by agricultural land of equal fertility that produces the food consumed in the city, will the land be uniformly valuable regardless of the distance from the city? Probably not. We can expect the price of food in the city to be the same regardless of its origin. If all the land is equally fertile we can expect all other inputs to cost the same per acre regardless of the distance from the city. The farmers farther from the city, however, have to spend more on transportation per ton of food than those nearer the city. All farmers will therefore want to locate nearer the city and will consequently bid up the value of land near the city. We will observe what might be called a land-value gradient, with land values declining with distance from the city. We can now drop our unrealistic assumption of equal fertility. More-fertile land will be more valuable than less-fertile land at the same distance; land nearer other amenities such as water sources will be more valuable as well. We now have a simple model of the value of agricultural land:

$$V_L = \text{(distance, fertility, other amenities)}$$

where V_L is the value of land per unit area. By employing minor changes in terminology, we have a model of urban land values. If we regard distance as a measure of access characteristics, fertility as merely use of site-specific characteristics, and rewrite amenities as neighborhood qualities, we can now write,

$$V_L = \text{(access characteristics, neighborhood qualities, site-specific characteristics)},$$

and we have a plausible model of urban land values. To revert to agricultural land once more, when the city expands, land near the city is converted to urban use, and distance from the edge of the city decreases for all the remaining land. We can therefore expect the value of each plot to rise. The access of each plot improves, and therefore its value rises as well. Much the same thing happens within the city as the city grows and access of plots improves.

People congregate in a city in order to take advantage of improved employment opportunities provided as a result of the concentration of a variety of activities that arise because of a concentration of people. The argument is somewhat circular but does capture the essence of cities. In general, economic activities are concentrated in or near the center of a city (we can even define the center of a city as that part of the city that has a concentration of activities). Measures of the concentration of activities include density of employment and density of residential population. Characteristically, employment densities are highest in the center of cities and decline with distance from the city center. Thus, access characteristics of land also decline with distance from the city center. If all employment in a city is in the center, access characteristics will obviously decline with distance from the city center. This is not an unrealistic representation of small cities, where almost all of the commercial economic activity is located in the city center.

As a city grows, the access characteristics of its center decline on account of increasing average distances from the city center of the residential population. Thus, commercial economic activity springs up in all parts of the city, and access characteristics of neighborhoods distant from the city center improve. Consequently we can expect residential densities, as well as land values, to increase in all parts of the city. This phenomenon is not very different from the effects of an expanding city in agricultural land values. From this simple, plausible model of land values we therefore have a number of strong results:

First, land values, population densities, and employment densities can be expected to decline with distance from the city center. Indeed, more-rigorous economic models suggest an exponential decline of these quantities from the city center.

Second, an expanding or growing city will result in the rise of land values and densities all over the city, with perhaps a proportionally smaller increase in the center because of its hypothesized relative loss in access characteristics. If the pattern of decline from the city center is exponential, we would then expect the curve to rotate somewhat, as shown in figure 14-1. If V_o is the value of land at the center of the city, $V_o A$ represents the land-value pattern at an initial time period and $V_o B$ when the city has expanded outward to B later. We are assuming here that V_o has remained constant. The slope of such a curve, or the percentage decline in land values or densities per unit distance, is a convenient summary measure describing the structure of the city. The smaller the slope of a density gradient, the smaller the proportion of people residing within a given distance of the city center. The decrease in this slope is often referred to as a measure of decentralization.

Third, with a declining slope and nondecreasing V_o, we can therefore expect a growing city to have secularly rising average land values.

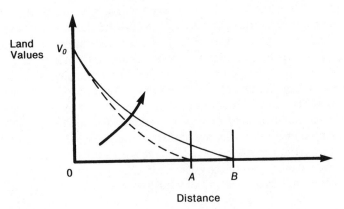

Figure 14-1. Pattern of Land Values in a Growing City (1)

Fourth, we have suggested that as a city grows, we can expect the concentration of economic activity to decrease in the center and that subcenters would develop in other parts of the city. Where these subcenters develop, because of their relatively better access characteristics (as compared with other land at the same distance from the city center), we would expect relatively higher land values. A land-value surface in a growing city therefore can be expected to change from a smooth, conical-type surface to one with ridges, valleys, and small hills.

Fifth, until now we have concentrated on the access characteristics while ignoring the other determinants of land values: neighborhood qualities and intrinsic quality of the land. In the intrinsic quality of land or site-specific characteristics, we include the level and quality of infrastructure provision and the geography of the site (for example, whether it is level, sloping, or uneven). At similar access levels, we would expect land with higher intrinsic quality to be more valuable. Neighborhood qualities are essentially externalities—positive or negative. Examples of positive externalities are the availability of good views, good neighbors, and good roads. Negative externalities include noise and air pollution.

A simple view of urban structure and land has yielded a relatively sophisticated model of the determination of urban land values. Note that I have spoken only of urban land values, not prices. Our observations so far are therefore system free. We may choose to adopt whatever price system we like in conformance with a society's preferences, but to the extent that we regard value as the opportunity cost of using a commodity, the conjectures or hypotheses of land-value patterns are general. Consequently if price is determined in a market system, we can use conformance to these patterns as one indication of the efficient functioning of the market. In a market system the price of land at time t is the discounted sum of expected returns from holding it in the future. Specifically:

$$P_o = \sum_{t=o}^{\infty} \frac{R_t}{(1 + r)^t}$$

where P_o is the price of land at time o, R_t is the return from it at time t, and r is the discount rate. Thus, the price of land today depends on the return we expect from it tomorrow. This gives another clue as to why land prices can be expected to rise with rapid urban growth. Land values, or opportunity costs, tend to rise in a growing city. In addition, as people come to expect these increases, they will tend to capitalize them today with the expectation of higher returns tomorrow. Thus, we get our sixth result: land prices can be expected to lead urban growth; that is, prices increase before the opportunity cost of the land increases.

Until now we have mainly talked about the price or value of specific parcels of land. What do we mean when we say that the price of land has increased in general? Such a statement is difficult to interpret. The observed price of any commodity is essentially a distribution around some mean, and it is, in general, not too difficult to find the mean. If a market does not contain significant distortions, the variance in observed prices is small. Thus, a statement concerning the trend of apple prices, for example, is relatively unambiguous. The key idea is that the good is homogeneous, and we can then talk about its price. As we have seen, urban land derives its value largely from its location (access characteristics and neighborhood qualities), and the value of one parcel can be different from another by an order of magnitude. An extreme view would be that each plot of land is unique and land is therefore not a homogeneous commodity whose average price we can easily discuss. Nonetheless, it is clear that if a growing city causes the land-value pattern to change from V_oA to V_oB in figure 14-1, we can say unambiguously that land values have increased in the city. If, however, the change is as in figure 14-2, V_1A changes to V_2B as the city expands, land values in the city center have declined and increased near the periphery. Now we cannot make an unambiguous statement about increasing land values in the city. Even the aggregate land values for the whole city are not very informative since the land area has also changed. Thus we need to be careful in making statements about changes in average land value in the context of rapidly expanding cities.

Changing Structure of Urban Land
Values and Population Densities

Both Bogotá and Cali have grown at remarkable rates of growth for an extended length of time. Bogotá has expanded more than eightyfold over the

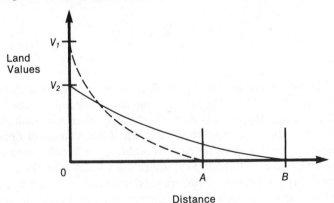

Figure 14-2. Pattern of Land Values in a Growing City (2)

last hundred years and Cali fiftyfold to sixtyfold during the same period. More importantly, they have both grown five to six times in the post-World War II period alone. Table 14-1 summarizes the growth of these cities since 1800. In comparison, in another fast-urbanizing country, South Korea, its two largest cities, Seoul and Busan, have also grown by similar magnitudes. Growth in Colombian cities was most rapid in the 1950s and 1960s and has since slowed.

Like land values, overall population densities depend crucially on the definition of a city's boundaries. According to available sources, it appears that the area of Bogotá City has been successfully redefined along with its growth, with the surprising result that overall density has remained roughly constant at 100 to 110 persons per hectare. Furthermore, according to current definition of the boundaries of Cali, the population density of Cali is also very similar. In comparison, the central cities of New York (covering the boroughs of Manhattan, Bronx, Brooklyn, and Queens) and Tokyo (each about 8 million to 9 million people) have densities of about 110 and 150 persons per hectare (Mills and Ohta 1976, p. 685); Chicago and Philadelphia about 60; central Buenos Aires 150 and central Mexico City 210 (central areas covering about 3 million people in each city); and Calcutta and Bombay about 120 to 140 (Mohan 1979). Except for Bombay and Calcutta, these comparisons are for central cities. Probably Bogotá is more densely populated than comparable Latin American cities if similar definitions are used but less so in the central city. It is of interest that its density is not very different from New York City (excluding Staten Island).

The structure of the two cities has changed with this rapid growth. Table 14-2 presents information on changing population densities by ring in the two cities from 1964 to 1978. (See figures 14-3 and 14-4). Ring 1 is the central business district (CBD). Both cities are semicircular in shape, with mountains constraining growth in the other half of the circle. Thus each

Table 14-1
Growth of Bogotá and Cali, 1800-1978

| | | Bogotá | | | Cali | |
Year	Area (hectares)	Population	Growth Rate (% per year)	Density (persons per hectare)	Population	Growth Rate (% per year)
1800	n.a.	22,000			6,000	
1900	909	100,000	1.5	110	24,000	1.4
1938	2,514	330,000	3.2	131	88,000	3.5
1951	n.a.	660,000	5.5	n.a.	284,000	9.0
1964	14,615	1,730,000	7.4	118	638,000	6.3
1973	30,423	2,877,000	5.8	95	930,000	4.2
1978	30,886	3,500,000	4.0	113	1,100,000	3.4

Source: Mohan (1979); Tabares (1979).

Table 14-2
Evolution of Population Density by Rings, Bogotá and Cali, 1964-1978
(persons per hectare)

	Area (100 hectares)	Bogotá			Area (100 hectares)	Cali		
		1964	*1973*	*1978*		*1964*	*1973*	*1978*
Ring 1 (CBD)	5	220	180	205	1.4	210	150	160
Ring 2	15	210	210	220	15	140	125	135
Ring 3	25	100	140	140	30	95	135	160
Ring 4	60	90	150	155	30	25	70	100
Ring 5	140	25	80	110	15	25	50	70
Ring 6	60	1	17	32				
Total	305	50[a]	95	115	91	70[a]	103	121

Source: Mohan (1979); Pachón (1980); Tabares (1979).

Note: All figures rounded.

[a]City area has been kept constant for all these calculations. In fact both cities grew during the period in question, and many peripheral areas included here were outside the city boundaries in 1964.

ring is semicircular. The maximum distance from the city center is about 15 kilometers (to ring 6) in Bogotá and about 10 kilometers (to ring 5) in Cali. Various features of these patterns are worth noting. First is the remarkable similarity in structure of the two cities. Growth has clearly occurred by accretion in the outer rings. The density in the CBD has tended to decline somewhat from about 200 persons per hectare. The growth has occurred on the fringes of the existing cities, along with densification of the inner rings. This process is somewhat different from the growth pattern observed in most U.S. cities as they grew in the early 1900s. "Quantum changes in the technology of urban transit imply not only a layering of incrementally lower density rings in the industrial metropolis, but also sharply lower aggregate densities in entire urban areas, the main growth of which came after 1920—in the auto age" (Norton 1979, p. 69). Thus while Bogotá and Cali have also decentralized with growth in the sense that a smaller proportion of the total population lives in any area of constant radius, they have not decentralized like many U.S. cities, where central cities have actually lost populations in absolute terms. This pattern of accretion has been very much in accordance with our hypothetical conjectures.

What has happened to land values during the same period? Good land-value data are notoriously difficult to obtain. One of the problems is that it is difficult to separate the value of land from the structure built on it. Most transactions observed in built-up cities are, however, of plots with buildings on them. We have been fortunate in obtaining a unique data set of about six thousand transactions in Bogotá covering the period 1955 to 1978 from the files of the long-established real estate firm of Wiesner and Cia Ltd. Guillermo Wiesner has kept meticulous records for almost forty years because

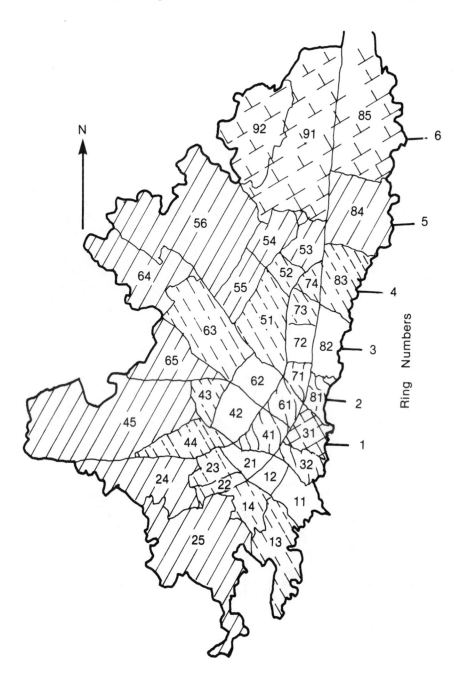

Figure 14-3. Bogotá Ring System

North

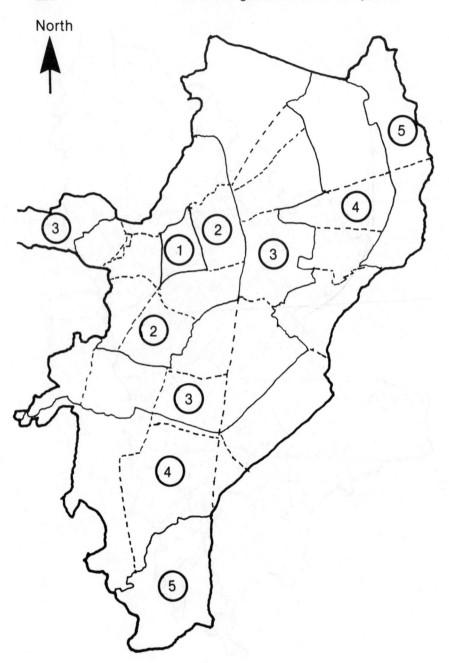

Figure 14-4. Cali Ring System

of his own interest in land valuation. We were able to choose the vacant-land-only transactions and therefore did not have to separate land values from built-up property values. This data set contains more transactions near the city center in earlier years and fewer in later years; the converse is the case for the outer rings. We have confidence in the overall quality of the data except that the land values in the CBD might be on the low side in the later years. There is little vacant land left in the center of the city; it may be that the last vacant plots being transacted have other quality problems and are therefore not representative of the CBD land values.

The data set for Cali, obtained from the Cali Municipal Planning Office, is probably of less-consistent quality since the methods of collection were different. The office has kept files on land value averages for each *barrio* or neighborhood. In 1964 there were 84 such observations and in 1978-1979 about 170. These neighborhood averages were based on direct observation, as well as interviews with local real estate agents. The compilation has been done by different individuals over this time period. We do not know the averaging procedure used within the *barrio*. Nonetheless, the overall patterns are clear, and we now turn to table 14-3, which gives a summary of the evolving land price surfaces for Bogotá and Cali from 1964 to 1978. The prices are given in constant 1978 Colombian pesos; earlier nominal values have been converted to 1978 prices by using the consumer price index. The overall pattern is that there is relative stagnation of land prices near the center and higher rates of price increases near the periphery. This is quite consistent with the evolution of density patterns. There are, however, some surprises. The Bogotá data indicate an actual decline of land prices in and near the CBD in real terms. This may be because of data problems. Nonetheless, it is clear that land prices have not risen appreciably in real terms in the center of Bogotá. The trends are better seen in figure 14-5, which shows a land price index for each ring from 1955 to 1977 in comparison with the consumer price index. Land prices have essentially risen along with the consumer price index in rings 1 to 3 and ahead of it in rings 4, 5, and 6.

The picture for Cali is broadly similar but with some differences. First, the magnitude of Cali land prices is similar to that in Bogotá. Indeed, the CBD prices seem somewhat higher in Cali than in Bogotá. Accounting for data problems, we can at least conjecture that they are unlikely to be less than in Bogotá. Their growth rates do seem to be somewhat higher.[1] That their magnitudes are now somewhat similar is consistent with their densities being similar. Mills and Song (1979) also found for South Korea that the growth in land values in the three largest cities was less than in the next nine largest. Thus, it is safe to conclude that the growth of land values is not higher in larger cities.

At this point, we need to recall the hypotheses suggested by our simple land-value model. (1) Land values and population densities do decline from

Table 14-3
Evolution of Land Values by Rings, Bogotá and Cali, 1964-1978
(1978 Colombia pesos per square meter)

| | Bogotá | | | | | Cali | | | |
	Average Distance from CBD (km.)	1963-1965	1972-1974	1975-1977	Growth Rate 1964-1978 (% per year)	Average Distance from CBD (km.)	1963	1974	1979	Growth Rate 1963-1979 (% per year)
Ring 1	0	4,250	3,900	3,100	-2.3	0	5,900	4,600	6,400	0.6
Ring 2	2.2	1,850	1,660	1,550	-1.3	1.8	1,100	1,100	2,400	5.6
Ring 3	3.8	1,350	1,350	1,320	-0.2	3.4	520	480	1,030	4.9
Ring 4	6.5	870	1,080	1,130	1.9	5.4	380	410	960	6.6
Ring 5	9.8	570	800	850	2.9	6.9	150	370	810	12.0
Ring 6	15.4	370	700	730	4.9					

Sources: Villamizar (1980); Velasco and Mier (1980). 1978 exchange rate US$1 = 38.00.

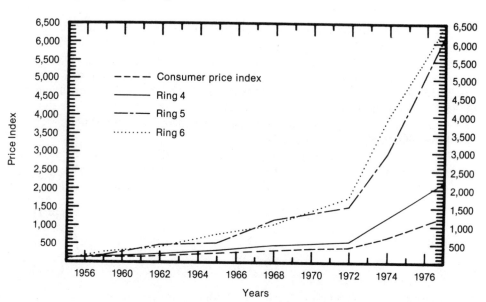

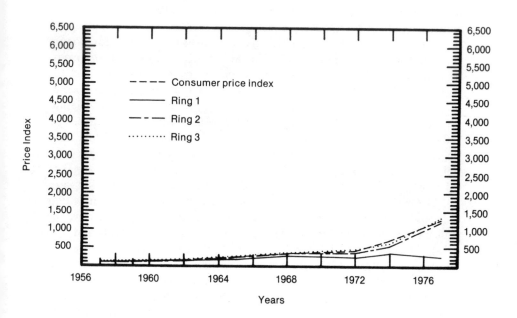

Source: Villamizar (1980), p. 16.

Figure 14-5. Land Price Indexes in Bogotá

the city center in Bogotá and Cali. (2) Land values and densities increase all over the two cities along with urban growth, but proportionately less so in the center. (3) Bogotá and Cali do have rising average land values; in Bogotá they have growth at about 3 to 4 percent per year in real terms since 1955. Recall, however, the caution with which average land values should be interpreted. To reemphasize this point, we can say with confidence that land prices have increased in real terms on the periphery, but at best, they have remained constant in the center.

We now measure the changes in land-value and density patterns more systematically by measuring the changes in density and land-value gradients. We can express the two patterns by simple exponential equations:

$$D_x = D_o\, e^{-gx} \tag{14.1}$$

and

$$V_x = V_o\, e^{-hx} \tag{14.2}$$

where D_x is the population density at x kilometers from the center, V_x is the land value x kilometers, and D_o, V_o, g and h are the parameters to be estimated from the data. In fact D_o and V_o estimate the density and land value at the center (when $x = o$, $D_x = D_o\, e^{-o} = D_o$); and g and h estimate the two gradients that can be interpreted as the percentage decrease in density and land values, respectively, per kilometer. Tables 14-4 and 14-5 present the results of these calculations.

First consider table 14-4, which gives the density gradients for Bogotá and Cali for 1964, 1973, and 1978. The unit of observation is the *barrio* or neighborhood. The table shows that g declines over time as expected for both the cities and is higher for Cali than for Bogotá. For purposes of comparison, in 1970 g was -0.08 for New York, about -0.13 for Atlanta, -0.22 for Seoul, -0.17 for Mexico City, -0.12 for Buenos Aires, and -0.08 for Tokyo (Ingram and Carroll 1981; Mills and Tan 1978). Thus Bogotá has a gradient similar to other large cities. Among smaller cities like Cali we have information for Monterrey, -0.27, and Guadalajara -0.41 (Mexico); Belo Horizonte, -0.27, and Recife, -0.17 (Brazil); Sapporo, -0.23 (Japan); and Busan, -0.13 (South Korea). We may conclude that Cali is not atypical. In general we can expect that the larger the city, the higher the income, and the lower the transportation costs (Mills and Tan 1978), the lower is g. This also implies that g depends on the age of the city (Harrison and Kain 1974). Older cities were built when intracity transportation costs were high and therefore the central cities were very dense. Consequently they had very high land values in the center. This pattern tended to persist over time. We can therefore expect that the fast-growing cities in Latin America would have relatively flatter density gradients.

Table 14-4
Population-Density Patterns in Bogotá and Cali, 1964-1978

| | Population (thousands) | N^a | D_o: Density at CBD | | | | |
			Actual[b]	Estimate 1[c] (thousands/sq.km.)	Estimate 2[d]	g^e	R^2
Bogotá							
1964	1,730	292	22	23	(20)	-0.18	0.12
1973	2,878	453	18	27	(10)	-0.15	0.22
1978	3,500	465	17	24	(10)	-0.12	0.19
Cali							
1964	640	131	21	39	(17)	-0.51	0.21
1973	930	195	16	24	(11)	-0.44	0.09
1978	1,100	193	16	29	(11)	-0.25	0.11

Sources: Bogotá barrio population data from City Study files. Cali barrio population data from Tabares (1979).

Note: Equation estimated was $D_x = D_o e^{-gx}$ where D_x is population density in people per square kilometer at distance x in kilometers and D_o is estimated population density at CBD.

[a] Number of data points in regressions.

[b] Residential population density for central business district (CBD).

[c] Estimate of D_o from equation in note.

[d] Estimate of D_o from $D_x = D_o e^{(g_1 x + g_2 x^2)}$. Other results not reported here.

[e] All estimates significant at the 0.01 level.

Table 14-5
Land-Value Patterns in Bogotá and Cali
(Prices in 1978 Col. pesos per m² and distances in kilometers)

| | Population (thousands) | N^a | V_o: Price at CBD | | | h^e | R^2 |
			Actual^b	Estimate 1^c	Estimate 2^d		
Bogotá							
1959		38	6,300	2,400		−0.18	0.56
1965	1,730	38	5,600	2,500	(2,470)	−0.15	0.55
1973	2,878	38	5,500	1,900	(2,290)	−0.08	0.39
1977	3,500	38	4,300	1,760	(2,240)	−0.07	0.35
Cali							
1959			5,000	2,240		−0.55	0.44
1963	640	84	5,000	2,030	(4,700)	−0.51	0.41
1974	940	155	3,700	1,030	(2,130)	−0.25	0.30
1979	1,100	171	5,300	2,070	(4,950)	−0.23	0.27

Sources: Mohan (1979); Tabares (1979); Villamizar (1980); Velasco and Mier (1980).

Note: Equation run was $V_x = V_o e^{-hx}$ where V_x is price at distance x and P_o is estimated price at CBD.

a Number of data points in regressions.

b Approximate average for CBD. Highest observed values are about three times these values.

c Estimate of V_o from equation in note.

d Estimate of V_o from $V_x = V_o e^{(h_1x + h_2x^2)}$. Other results not reported here.

e All estimates significant at the 0.01 level.

Now we observe the estimates for D_o: the hypothetical density at the center of the city. Column 4 gives the estimated densities in thousands per square kilometer. Column 3 gives actual observed densities. Note that central densities have remained relatively constant with a small observed decline, a phenomenon at least consistent with the behavior of land values in Bogotá. The estimated values are consistently higher. The CBD contains a large proportion of commercial economic activity and a relatively small residential population. It is therefore to be expected that estimated D_o would be higher than the actual.

Now consider table 14-5, which gives comparable land-value patterns for Bogotá and Cali. Once again, the estimates for land-value gradients decline with time in both the cities, as expected, and those for Cali are steeper than those for Bogotá. The comparability with the density gradients is remarkable (table 14-6). The estimated patterns are brought together and graphed in figure 14-6, where their comparability is evident. Recalling our simple model, we would expect land-value gradients to be similar to density gradients. Furthermore, they are consistently lower than the density gradients, as has been theorized (Mills and Song 1979, p. 109). A comparison of estimated V_o (land value at the center of the city) with actual V_o reveals that our estimates are consistently lower than the actual values. This implies that the gradient of the curve should be much steeper at the center of the city than we have estimated. Because of the high concentration of economic activity at the center, we can expect the land values to be determined much more by the employment density than by the residential density. Employment density falls rapidly from the center, and it is therefore quite plausible that land values will exhibit a similar decline. Estimated V_o therefore is quite likely to be lower than this central peak.

This brings us to a minor revision of the land-value and population-density functions. We have observed that the estimated densities were consistently higher for the CBD than the actual densities while land values are consistently lower. Indeed what we would expect is for residential densities to increase somewhat from the CBD and then decline, while land values should decline rapidly from the city center and then slow down. We have therefore attempted to fit quadratic exponential functions to the data:

Table 14-6
Changes in Density and Land Value for Bogotá and Cali

| | Bogotá | | Cali | |
	Land Value	Density	Land Value	Density
1964	−0.15	−0.18	−0.51	−0.51
1973	−0.08	−0.15	−0.25	−0.44
1978	−0.07	−0.12	−0.23	−0.25

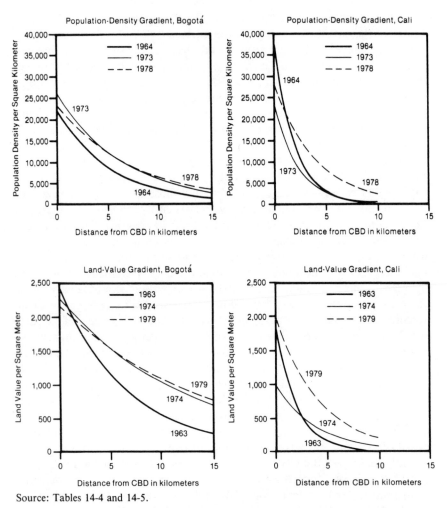

Source: Tables 14-4 and 14-5.

Figure 14-6. Changing Urban Structure of Bogotá and Cali, 1964-1978

$$D_x = D_o e^{(g_1 x + g_2 x^2)} \qquad (14.3)$$

and

$$V_x = V_o e^{(h_1 x + h_2 x^2)}. \qquad (14.4)$$

With g_1 positive and g_2 negative, the shape of the curve is as suggested above for the density (figure 14-7), while for land values h_1 is negative and h_2 is positive, which gives a rapidly declining curve, illustrated in figure 14-8).

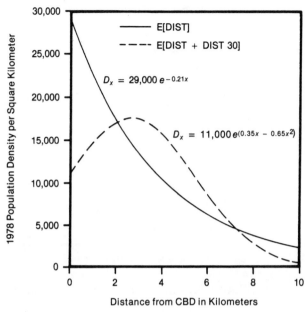

Source: Tables 14-4 and 14-5.

Figure 14-7. 1978 Population-Density Gradient, Cali

The signs of the estimated coefficients are consistent with these conditions. The quality of statistical fit improves in all cases, implying that the quadratic functions are better approximations to the actual pattern.[2]

In particular, note column 5 in tables 14-4 and 14-5. The estimates of D_o and V_o from the quadratic functions are somewhat closer to the actuals.

Therefore the land-value surfaces of Bogotá and Cali have evolved about as we would expect within the context of a very simple urban model. Land values have been highest at the CBD but have remained at a constant level in real terms over at least the past fifteen years. They have increased faster as one moves out from the city center and very much in accordance with the accretion of population that has occurred in successive outer layers of the city. The increases in real terms have been modest. Bogotá and Cali do not display a chaotic land market in this sense. If anything, the behavior of the land-price surface and of population densities is a bit too regular. Both density gradients and land-value gradients have flattened, but we must not be too hasty to conclude that these cities have decentralized in the sense of central cities losing population. It is important to note that among large European cities, this process of decentralization is of long standing. The population of central London reached its peak in 1930-1940, Paris in 1920,

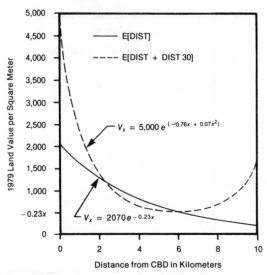

Source: Tables 14-4 and 14-5.

Figure 14-8. 1979 Land Value Gradient, Cali

Vienna in 1910, and Rotterdam, Zürich, Hamburg, Glasgow, and Amsterdam in 1950-1960 (Mitchell 1978, p. 12). All have declined since those dates, but with increasing suburban populations. To the extent that people congregate to improve economic opportunities for themselves and thereby impart higher values to land, we need to understand these processes better. With low transportation costs (despite the energy crisis) and changing manufacturing technology, there is reason to believe that manufacturing jobs are indeed increasingly moving to peripheral locations (Lee 1979), although the volume of these jobs has not yet been large enough to reduce the importance of the city center as a commercial center. We can expect greater movement of commerce and service jobs with manufacturing in the future with the obvious consequences on access characteristics of peripheral locations.

The Smoothly Evolving Land-Value
Surface: Some Wrinkles

So far we have treated the city in a relatively simple manner. The measurement of land-value and population-density gradients assumes that the city is symmetrical around the city center. In the cases of Bogotá and Cali, each city is constrained by mountains on one side, and the cities are therefore semicircular, with the city center roughly at the center of the semicircle. The cities are not, however, symmetrical otherwise. If we divide each city into approximate pie slices or radial sectors, as shown in figures 14-9 and 14-10, we observe distinct differences among the sectors (see Mohan 1979 and Terrell 1980). In Bogotá in particular, the north (sectors 7 and 8) can be characterized as rich and the south (sectors 2 and 3) as poor. Sectors 4 and 5 comprise the industrial zone or corridor. In Cali the picture is more mixed, but, broadly, the western part of the city (sectors 2, 6, and 7) is richer than the eastern part (sectors 3, 4, and 5). In general, jobs exceed the number of resident workers in the rich sectors, and the converse is true in the poorer sectors. As we might expect, the density of population is higher in the poor as opposed to the rich sectors. The question now is how these differences in land use in different sectors of the city affect population-density patterns and land values. Do density patterns and land-value gradients hold up if calculated for different sectors of the two cities?

In order to illustrate the patterns, we include computer maps of land value and population density in Bogotá, which show at a glance where population densities and land values are high: the darker the shading, the higher the density or land value. Contrary to our expectations the two maps do not appear to be too similar. (See figures 14-11 and 14-12). It is true in general, though, that in any direction from the CBD, the darker shading is nearer the center, with lighter and lighter shades as we move toward the edge of the city. Within the same ring (or same distance from the CBD) it is clear that both densities and land values are quite heterogeneous. Indeed, the denser areas appear to have lower land values than the less-dense areas within the same ring. How is the paradox to be resolved?

Until now we have concentrated on the access characteristics of land as determinants of land value and have been using distance from the CBD and residential densities as proxies for access characteristics. Now we must enrich our notions of access characteristics. In addition we have to consider the other determinants of land value mentioned in our simple model: neighborhood quality and intrinsic quality of land. By *access characteristics* we mean the proximity of land parcels to economic opportunities. We had hypothesized that large or dense agglomerations of people were instrumental in increasing these economic opportunities and that this was the reason for the clustering of population near the city center. Thus a concentration of economic activity in the center produced relatively high population densities and consequently high land values, both of which then declined with distance.

The observation that the rich live in some parts of the city and the poor in others leads us to revise some of these ideas. That more jobs are located in rich sectors means that those sectors are economically more attractive

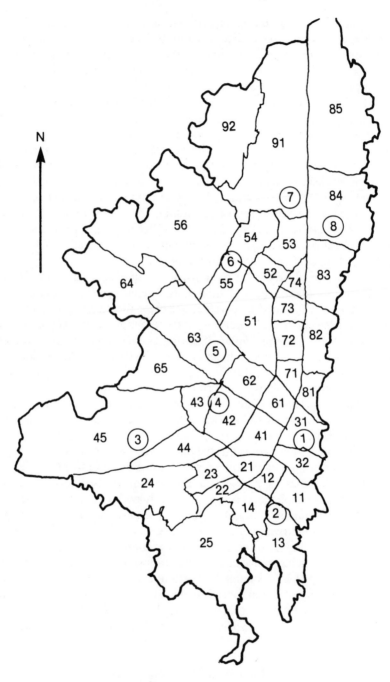

Figure 14-9. Bogotá Sector System

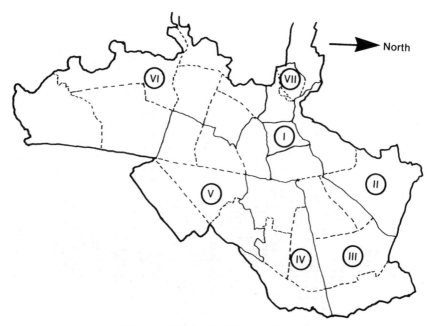

Figure 14-10. Cali Sector System

and firms have a greater tendency to locate there. Thus the lower densities of those areas are being more than enhanced by purchasing power. As a proxy for access characteristics, we have to employ the notion of purchasing power. The product of population and mean income is probably not a good measure of these access characteristics since the requirements of a large number of poor people do not aggregate; each household has meager demands so poor sectors can support only a limited number of economic activities. Consequently the rich neighborhoods have an excess of jobs over the resident labor force, and the access characteristics of these neighborhoods are not adequately measured by population densities. In addition we can expect the infrastructure provisions (such as roads, lighting, water supply, and sewerage) to be better in high-income neighborhoods, and therefore both neighborhood quality and intrinsic site characteristics are more desirable. All of these factors combine to produce somewhat higher land values than the population densities would lead us to expect in relatively rich neighborhoods.

We estimated the population-density and land-value gradients for each sector in Bogotá and Cali and emerged with striking results. Table 14-7 gives the estimates of these gradients along with the R^2 for each estimated regression. The general result is that the exponential function is still a good

N

← CBD

Figure 14-11. Population Density in Bogotá, 1978

Figure 14-12. Land Values in Bogotá, 1978

Table 14-7
Land-Value and Density Gradients in Cali and Bogotá by Sector

	Cali					Bogotá				
	Household Mean Income Index[a]	Land Value[b] g^c	R^2	Density h^c	R^2	Household Mean Income Index[a]	Land Value[d] g^c	R^2	Density h^c	R^2
Sector 1 (CBD)	163					61	−0.15	0.54	−0.11	0.06
Sector 2	212	−0.42	0.69	−0.13*	0.00	52	−0.01	0.09	−0.02*	0.01
Sector 3	84	−0.45	0.73	−0.10*	0.00	74	−0.08	0.46	−0.12	0.09
Sector 4	58	−0.42	0.69	+0.13	0.11	96	} −0.10	0.71	−0.05*	0.03
Sector 5	82	−0.55	0.77	+0.07*	0.02	103			−0.05*	0.02
Sector 6	125	−0.21	0.41	−0.26	0.16	97	−0.10	0.71	−0.16	0.50
Sector 7	219	−0.86	0.59	−0.13*	0.05	122	−0.08	0.72	−0.14	0.32
Sector 8						236	−0.07	0.55		

Source: Velasco and Mier (1980); Tabares (1979); Pachón (1980); Villamizar (1980); City Study barrio file.

[a] Percentage of mean household income for the city.

[b] For 1979.

[c] All coefficients significant at the 0.01 level except those marked with asterisk.

[d] For 1975-1978.

approximation to the pattern of land values for each sector. The population densities, however, do not do so well. The estimated density gradients are not significantly different from zero in a number of sectors. Indeed, in Cali, sectors 4 and 5 exhibit mildly positive gradients, and in Bogotá the density gradients are low or insignificant for sectors 2, 3, 5, and 6. What is common among these sectors is relatively low mean income. Note that land-value gradients are not significantly different from others in these sectors. That the population density does not vary appreciably with distance in the south of Bogotá is also obvious from figure 14-11.

To understand these phenomena, we need to delve further into the role of land values and their effect on urban structure. Gregory Ingram has emphasized the role of land as a factor of production. When land values are high, capital is substituted more for land, and the result is the construction of taller buildings. We can therefore expect to observe, on average, taller buildings in city centers and in zones where land prices are high. As land prices increase, single-family homes are replaced by multifamily apartments, and residential densities rise. While residential densities rise per unit of land area, living space per person does not necessarily decrease. These options are not open to the poor, however.

We observed previously that land prices rose more in the outer rings than in the inner ones, as expected. A further analysis revealed that the rates of price increases were no higher in the rich areas as compared with the poor (Villamizar 1980). In Bogotá, the rate of increase (adjusted for inflation) in the rich sector, sector 8, was about 2.5 percent per year between 1955 and 1977 and about 4 to 7 percent per year in the poorer sectors (2, 3, and 6). The price levels, however, were consistently lower in the poor areas. These data indicate that, although each land parcel is nonsubstitutive to some extent, there is a city-wide land market that is functioning. While land prices in poor areas continue to be lower than in richer areas, there is a catch-up phenomenon so that prices of land parcels equidistant from the city center are not too dissimilar. The natural result of this phenomenon is that while the rich substitute for land with capital, the poor substitute for land by crowding.

Figure 14-13 illustrates the structure of Bogotá by average number of floors in each zone. We can observe that much of the housing in Bogotá still has fewer than two floors, that the number of floors declines rapidly from the CBD, and that the northern part of the city, the richer sector 8, has taller buildings than other areas of the city. Table 14-8 gives other housing characteristics by residential rings and sectors. The average number of floors declines systematically by ring. It is also of interest that the average age of dwellings declines and that the proportion of single-family homes increases with distance. These patterns are very much in accordance with our expectations: capital is being substituted for land in the shape of taller

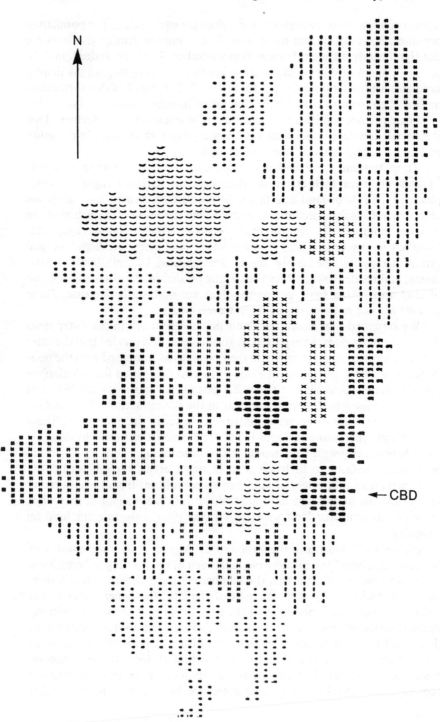

Figure 14-13. Average Number of Floors in Bogotá, 1978

Table 14-8
Spatial Pattern of Housing in Bogotá, 1978

	Mean Household Income Index	% Single- Family Unit	Average Age of Dwelling Unit (years)	Average Number of Floors	Average Dwelling Unit Space per Person (m²)
Ring 1	62	39	16	7.1	14
Ring 2	116	57	21	3.5	23
Ring 3	124	74	16	2.8	30
Ring 4	112	86	12	1.7	23
Ring 5	82	95	9	1.8	18
Ring 6	122	100	8	1.5	26
Total	100	85	12	2.1	21
Sector 1	61	39	16	7.1	14
Sector 2	53	96	13	1.4	12
Sector 3	74	91	10	1.8	19
Sector 4	96	91	11	1.9	25
Sector 5	103	72	18	3.4	20
Sector 6	97	92	10	2.1	21
Sector 7	122	84	17	1.9	30
Sector 8	236	59	10	2.9	45
Total	100	85	12	2.1	21

Source: Sungyong Kang (1980); Pachón (1980).

buildings in the inner rings; the city has grown by accretion on its edges, and therefore the outer rings have newer houses; and apartment buildings or semidetached houses are replacing single-family houses as prices increase nearer the CBD. Land prices are performing their function well, and the housing market seems to be responding as expected.

Now examine column 5 in table 14-8. There is no clear pattern of average dwelling-unit space per person except that it is low in the CBD. We would expect that living space per person would be larger in the outer rings because people would be trading space for higher transportation costs. If we now look at the sectoral pattern, it is clear that the poorest sectors (2 and 3) in the south have much less living space per person than the northern rich sectors. Thus the poor are substituting crowding for land, and the rich are substituting capital.

We now begin to understand why the land-value gradients hold up even when the cities are disaggregated into sectors and the density gradients do not. The functioning of the land market results in land values being not too different at similar distances from the center. The rich sectors have higher land values because of better employment opportunities as well as better neighborhood quality and infrastructure quality. The land values being relatively regular, the poor have no choice but to substitute for land by crowding. Even when they slide down the rent gradient and locate at the periphery, they still have to live at high densities to compensate for the land prices, which are similar to land prices in the rich suburbs. They cannot buy more space by substituting capital for land since the housing would then be too expensive. Note in table 14-8 that the average number of floors is 2.9 in rich sector 8 and only 1.4 to 1.8 in the poor sectors 2 and 3. The result is that we observe high population densities on the periphery of some parts of the city and consequently there is virtually no measurable density gradient in those sectors. The rich sectors still have a density gradient, and we can therefore observe gradients for the city as a whole as well. Nonexistent density gradients in some sectors of the city are consistent with relatively strong land-value gradients. We have therefore resolved the paradox posed at the beginning of this section. In so doing we also provide reason for caution in interpreting similarities between city-wide population density and land gradients.

There is one other important aspect of land-value patterns meriting further discussion. We have often alluded to the importance of the level of economic activity in a zone to the determination of land values. We have focused on the predominance of the CBD as the economic hub of the city. As a large city grows, however, it acquires many new competing commercial centers, which began to rival the old CBD. These alternative (or additional) economic centers in turn are strong motivating forces for residential population to decentralize as well.

We examine this process by looking at the evolving land-value peaks along key urban corridors in Bogotá (Villamizar 1980). Figure 14-14 gives a pictorial representation of this process. The street system of Bogotá is in a systematic grid conforming to old Spanish urban-planning tradition. *Carreras* (avenues) run north to south and are numbered in ascending order away from the mountains toward the west. *Calles* (streets) run east-west and are numbered from the CBD in ascending order toward both north and south. Figure 14-14 gives the trend of land prices over time at fixed ranges of key corridors in Bogotá. As an example, note the pattern of carrera 7a in the bottom right-hand corner of figure 14-14. Carrera 7a runs through the CBD of Bogotá, which is around calles 7 to 20. Observe that the prices around the old core—between calles 7 and 17—have been decreasing secularly, while those in the range of calles 27 through 45 have been tending to increase. The mid-range calles (14-26) have been relatively stable. The commercial center of Bogotá has been tending to move northward (see Wiesner 1980). Thus the position of the region between calles 20 and 45 has improved relative to the old core. Observe also the land-value peaks around calles 46 through 60 on carreras 13 and 14. This is the Chapinero area, which started to develop in the 1950s and has since been an important commercial and shopping center, competitive with the CBD.

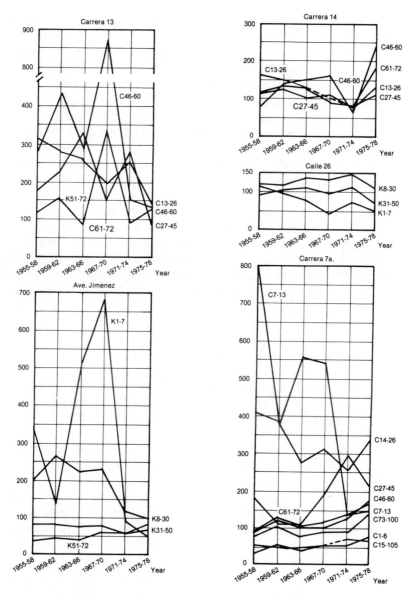

Source: Reproduced from Villamizar (1980) and data from "The Evolution of Land Values in the Context of Rapid Urban Growth: A Case Study of Bogotá and Cali, Colombia," @ Rakesh Mohan and Rodrigo Villamizar (Bogotá, Colombia: Corporacion Centro Regional de Poblacion).

Note: C = *Calle*; K = *Carrera*.

Figure 14-14.   Evolution of Land Prices Along Main Radial Corridors, Bogotá

This detailed analysis along ridges of the land-value surface reveals small hills in accordance with the access characteristics that go with higher levels of economic activity in the developing subcenters of a rapidly growing city. Because of such developments, the gradient of land prices decreases as a city grows. The relative importance of the CBD declines, and secondary gradients develop around the subcenters. We therefore confirm the fourth result from our simple urban model: as a city grows, the smooth land-price surface centered around the CBD develops wrinkles as ridges, valleys, and small hills around the new subcenters that are observed in Bogotá.

Mills and Song (1979) found that in Korean cities, commercial land values were always higher than residential land values in the CBD, as well as in the rest of the city at equidistant points from the center. The evidence we have presented is consistent with their findings. Indeed, at equal distances from the CBD, the proportion of area covered by commercial activity in any neighborhood is a good predictor of the level of land values in that area. These results are quite consistent with our expectations about access characteristics of neighborhoods and, moreover, with the observed higher land values in richer areas of the city. Commercial activity locates itself in the rich areas of the city.

Rising Land Prices: Should We Worry?

A detailed examination of land-value and density patterns in Bogotá and Cali has revealed that the evolution of these patterns has been neither chaotic nor unpredictable. Land values have responded to the rapid growth of these cities much as they might be expected to in a market economy. Growth in land values has been the greatest at the periphery of these cities and least at the center. Furthermore, land values in poor areas have increased as fast as, if not faster than, those in rich areas.

These results are somewhat surprising in the presence of a widespread impression in Colombia, as in other developing countries, that land prices in cities have been growing in recent times at undesirably high and unwarranted rates. The paradox of our results is that these impressions are not necessarily misinformed. People tend to focus on the growing or developing parts of cities. It is undeniably true that these areas experience the greatest magnitude of change, as they should in a market economy. It is also true that many people make large windfall gains in these areas. The issue to worry about, then, is income distribution. Does the land market operate in such a way that it widens the already high levels of inequality that exist in many poor countries?

The answer to this question will depend on the specific circumstances in every city or country. We have little information on the concentration of ownership of land in these cities. Ingram has presented some information on the concentration of developers in the legal housing market in Bogotá. He concluded that there does not appear to be a high level of concentration in this market. Elsewhere (Carroll 1980) there is also evidence that the illegal housing market is not concentrated. The process of development at the edge of a city, where the largest rates of price increases are observed, appears to go through a number of stages. When land is in agricultural use, we naturally expect plots of land to be much larger than characteristic urban plots. In Bogotá and Cali, many tracts of land at the edges of the two cities were certainly very large. In such situations there is an element of local monopoly power, but the land offer price cannot be too much out of line as compared with other comparable areas; otherwise the developers would move there. The norm in Bogotá is that the original owners sell to developers (illegal or otherwise), who then subdivide the tracts and sell to individuals for housing. Alan Carroll has shown that there is little evidence that the intermediary developers make excess profits as compared with usual rates of return on investment in Colombia. He does show, however, that some do make very large profits; these are, perhaps, the more-visible ones. Despite the windfall gains that occur at various stages of the development of peripheral locations around a city, it is very likely that the process of subdivision leads to much more equality in the ownership of land. To the extent that the new owners are relatively poor and that the process of a city's growth is such that it is accompanied by large land-value increases at the periphery, there is a high likelihood that much of this increase accrues to the poor. This may be the case despite large windfall gains that may accrue to the original owners.

These ideas are somewhat speculative, but we do have adequate information that is at least suggestive in these directions. Illegal housing activity consistently appears to account for about 60 percent of all residential housing construction in Bogotá (Kang 1980); land values have risen as much (or more) in poor areas as in rich areas; the proportion of owner-occupied housing increases as one moves toward the periphery; while the poorest do not in general live on the periphery, the outer rings are somewhat poorer on average. Consequently, urban land is probably one of the few assets that the poor have relatively better access to.

These remarks are not meant to imply that all is well in Bogotá and Cali, but we do imply that things may not be as bad in the land market as is often supposed. Indeed our evidence on density patterns indicates that all is not well. The extremely high densities in poor areas, especially peripheral areas, mean that the only way that large numbers of the poor can afford to live in the city is under extremely crowded conditions. Health problems result from such crowding, which is often accompanied by poor infrastructure provision. The choices in these situations are difficult. The more infrastructure that is provided, the higher the resulting price of land; and consequently higher density (crowding) would result. On the other hand, without infrastructure provision, health problems would increase, despite less crowding. Much higher densities were observed in American and European cities before the advent of mechanized transportation, and their health problems were also worse. In the early stages of industrialization, the net natural-growth rates of European cities were often negative. They were able to grow only because of high in-migration rates (Toynbee 1970; Weber 1967). Because of general sanitary improvements, conditions in cities in poor countries are clearly not as bad, but we should be alert to the dangers of overcrowding. In that sense, we should worry about high land prices, but the source of our concern should be clear. If it is the access of the poor to shelter that we are concerned about, policy measures should address these problems directly. It may be that subsidized or free access to land in the nature of squatters' rights is the best solution to this problem. It should then be recognized as such, and the opportunity cost of that land should then be viewed as the cost of such a policy. Cognizance should also be taken of the price of land as a signal for the allocation of resources.

This is not the place for a discussion of appropriate land policies. Our objective has been to provide an understanding of the role of land values in the growth of cities by providing evidence from two rapidly growing cities in Colombia. We hope that similar empirical work can be accomplished in other cities so that appropriate urban land policies can be designed. Objectives of these policies should be made clear. Are urban land policies concerned with appropriate urban structure, with providing access to housing for the poor, or with achieving a better income distribution? What must be remembered is that land-price controls can obscure the value of land, but they cannot change it.

Acknowledgments

We are indebted to a number of individuals for the availability of unusually rich sets of data that have been utilized in this study. Guillermo Wiesner of Wiesner and Cia. Ltda., Bogotá, painstakingly compiled data from six thousand land transactions covering all parts of Bogotá from 1955 to 1978. We are grateful for his labors and for sharing this information with us. Julián Velasco and Gilberto Mier were kind enough to include the raw data in their paper on land values in Cali. We thank Planeación Municipal of Cali for making available this document (Velasco and Mier 1980) and the population data in Tabares (1979). The industry of José Fernando Pineda resulted in *barrio*-level population data for 1964, 1973, and 1978 for Bogotá. This paper would not have been possible without his help. We have also benefited from discussions with Gregory Ingram and Alvaro Pachón. We thank Leslie Kramer and Sungyong Kang for arduous and timely research assistance.

Notes

1. The data for Bogotá for the last period are an average for 1975-1977, while those for Cali are for 1979. If it is true, as some believe, that there has been an inflationary spurt in land values in the last two years, absolute values in Bogotá would not be less than those in Cali.

2. We do not present the detailed results here. Note that the quadratic functions are not without their own problems. The estimated curve in figure 14-8 for land values starts rising after 6 kilometers, which is not borne out by the data.

References

Carroll, Alan. 1980. "Private Subdivisions and the Market for Residential Lots in Bogotá." Paper No. 7. Washington, D.C.: World Bank, City Study Project.

Harrison, D., and Kain, John F. 1974. "Cumulative Urban Growth and Urban Density Functions." *Journal of Urban Economics* 1:67-98.

Ingram, Gregory K., and Carroll, Alan. 1981. "The Spatial Structure of Latin American Cities." *Journal of Urban Economics* 9, no. 2, pp. 257-273.

Jackson, Kenneth J. 1975. "Urban Deconcentration in the Nineteenth Century: A Statistical Inquiry." In Leo Schnore, ed., *The New Urban History*. Princeton: Princeton University Press.

Kang, Sungyong. 1980. "Housing Stock in Bogotá: A Descriptive Study." Mimeographed. Washington, D.C.: World Bank.

Lee, Kyu Sik. 1979. "Intra-Urban Location of Manufacturing Employment in Colombia." Paper No. 5. Washington, D.C.: World Bank, City Study Project.

Lichfield, Nathaniel. 1980. *Settlement Planning and Development: A Strategy for Land Policy*. Vancouver: University of British Columbia Press.

Mitchell, B.R. 1978. *European Historical Statistics, 1750-1970*. New York: Columbia University Press.

Mills, Edwin S. 1972. *Urban Economics*. Glenview, Ill.: Scott, Foresman and Co.

Mills, Edwin S., and Ohta Katsutoshi. 1976. "Urbanization and Urban Problems." In Hugh Patrick and Henry Rosovsky, *Asia's New Giant*. Washington, D.C.: Brookings Institution.

Mills, Edwin S., and Song, Byung Nak. 1979. *Urbanization and Urban Problems: The Republic of Korea 1945-75*. Cambridge: Harvard University Press.

Mills, Edwin S., and Tan, J.P. 1978. "A Comparison of Urban Population Density Functions in Developed and Developing Countries." Paper presented at the Annual Meeting of the American Economic Association, Chicago, Illinois, August.

Mohan, Rakesh. 1979. "Population, Income and Employment in a Developing Metropolis: A Spatial Analysis of Bogotá, Colombia." Paper No. 6. Washington, D.C.: World Bank, City Study Project.

Norton, R.D. 1979. *City Life Cycles and American Urban Policy*. New York: Academic Press.

Pachón, Alvaro. 1979. "Urban Structure, Modal Choice and Auto Ownership in Bogotá 1972." Intermediate Paper No. 31. Washington, D.C.: World Bank, City Study Project.

_____ . 1980. "Automobile Ownership Bogotá and Cali, 1972-1978." Mimeographed. Washington, D.C.: World Bank, City Study Workshop.

Tabares, Henry. 1979. "Población de Cali: Series Históricas y Características." PIDECA Document No. 3. Cali, Colombia: Planeación Municipal.

Terrell, Katherine. 1980. "Workers of Cali: Who They Are, What They Do, and Where They Live." Intermediate Paper No. 37. Washington D.C.: World Bank, City Study Project.

Toynbee, Arnold. 1970. *Cities on the Move*. New York: Oxford University Press.

Velasco, Julián A., and Mier, Gilberto R. 1980. "Valores y Características de la Tierra en Cali." Mimeographed. Cali, Colombia: Planeación Municipal.

Villamizar, Rodrigo, A. 1980. "Land Prices in Bogotá between 1955 and 1978: A Descriptive Analysis." Paper No. 10. Washington, D.C.: World Bank, City Study Project.

Weber, Adna F. 1967. *The Growth of Cities in the Nineteenth Century*. Ithaca, N.Y.: Cornell University Press.

Wiesner, Guillermo. 1980. "Cien Años de Historia de los Precios de la Tierra en Bogotá 1878-1978." CCRP City Study Paper No. 3. Bogotá: Corporación Centro Regional de Población.

Moderator

William Doebele: Academics have not done a great deal of research on land markets, so I think it is fascinating that Dr. Mohan mentioned the use of brokers as a means of getting data very quickly. One of the characteristics of many developing countries is that one of the small occupations engaged in by thousands of people is the real estate business. This was very useful to us in some work we did in Korea. These brokers have a wealth of information about land prices. Sometimes you have to double-check them to make sure that the information is correct, but given the lack of systematic academic research, you might think about dealing with these people who deal with land every day and see if you can't very quickly get some data and then use other means of checking them.

If I understood correctly, the peak growth in Bogotá and Cali was in the 1950s and 1960s, and there has been some slowing recently. There were also some comments that the smaller cities are now growing more rapidly in Colombia than the larger ones. We have here phenomena in the process of change, and we are beginning to get some data about them. It is certainly true that the pattern of urbanization is changing and that the extrapolations that we have believed in for about twenty years may no longer be the case.

15

Transportation Investment and Urban Land Values: Emerging Empirical Evidence

Marcial Echenique

By investing in transportation, public authority can bring down the average urban land prices. It is assumed in this analysis that the economic system from which the conclusions are drawn is a mixed system where the land is in private hands and most of the investment in infrastructure is provided by the state. The framework of analysis is a neoclassical economic one, where the existence of a competitive market, with no monopolies, is assumed.

First, it is important to clarify why it is an intrinsically good objective to reduce average land prices. It has been argued that from the economic-efficiency point of view, the changes in land values do not alter the total welfare of the community because the land values are only transfer payments from users of land to landlords. The changes have distributional consequences only as low-income groups may be transferring money to the high-income groups (landlords).

This argument ignores an important fact, however: that as the price of land increases, there is a reduction of land utilization, increasing the density of development. Higher-density development in general is more expensive (Stone 1970). And the construction of a higher-density form of buildings demands more-expensive materials (for example, to prevent fire hazards and reduce noise transmission), and it requires skilled labor and higher levels of statutory controls. This has important consequences in developing countries, where plenty of unskilled labor is available but there is a lack of capital. The obvious solution for fast building in the developing countries is the maximum utilization of self-help. Increases in density can considerably hinder the ability for self-help, increasing the capital cost of housing and of other types of buildings.

Lower density of development also allows lower standards of services, such as septic tanks rather than public sewers and lower-quality roads, which may compensate for the more-extensive networks of water and energy supply as well as transportation. In low-density development, land may be less costly to appropriate for public uses such as recreation, education, and transportation, offering, therefore, more flexibility for future changes.

Changes in land values have important distributional consequences: increases in land values reduce land consumption, but not by the same proportion (land tends to be relatively inelastic). The implication of this increase is that people will be spending more on housing with an obvious reduction in other forms of consumption, such as food and clothing. The result of this is a transfer from land users to landowners, which is retrogressive because landownership tends to be concentrated in higher-income groups.

From the environmental point of view, high densities tend to create worse conditions: lack of clean air, lack of vegetation, and congestion, among others. With lower densities, it may be possible to encourage market gardening as a way of supplementing low incomes. There are examples of efficient production of agriculture in terms of productivity per acre on the fringes of urban areas and in allotment gardens, which may compensate for the reduction of agricultural land.

In this paper, then, I argue that to achieve the objective of lowering average prices in a competitive land market, it is necessary to increase the supply of land. The most direct way of increasing the supply of land is to reduce the cost of transportation.

Demand for Land

The individual schedule of demand can be represented by a graph where the quantity of land that an individual is prepared to buy depends on the price of the land (figure 15-1). The figure shows that if the price falls from p_1 to p_2, the individual will increase the quantity of land consumed from q_1 to q_2. The slope of the demand line represents the elasticity of demand with respect to price. Inelastic demand means that the price will not influence the

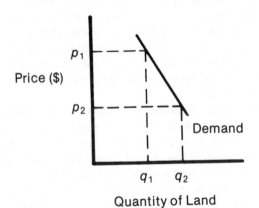

Figure 15-1. Demand Function for Land

quantity of land consumed (the slope in the graph will be parallel to the vertical axis). An elastic demand means that small variations in price will change drastically the consumption of land (the slope in the graph will be nearly parallel to the horizontal axis).

Usually the demand function is a curve rather than a straight line and can be represented by a power function (for example, Cobb-Douglas function)

$$q = p^{-\lambda}$$

where q is quantity of land consumed, p is price of land, and λ is elasticity. In the case of Tehran (Applied Research of Cambridge 1977), the elasticity of demand with respect to price varied between 0.56 and 0.49 from the lowest income group to the highest income group. In the case of Caracas (Feo et al. 1975), the elasticity was estimated at around 0.70 for all income groups. It can be concluded that if the land price doubles in both cities, the amount of land consumed will diminish by some proportion but not necessarily by half, with the consequence that individuals will be paying more in total (as the total cost of the land is equal to the land price times the quantity consumed), with corresponding decreases of consumption in other goods.

The individual schedules of demand can be added to create a total aggregated demand for the city. The graph will have the same pattern, but now for a given price the quantity demanded by the whole population will be larger (the horizontal axis will have another scale).

In the urban land market, there are considerable shifts in demand. This occurs when the demand curve moves upward (or downward), as shown in figure 15-2. The main reasons for shifts in demand are increases in the population of the city (which create a larger quantity of land demanded because there are more people in the city), increases in real incomes (which

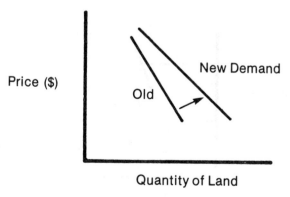

Figure 15-2. Shifts in Demand

increase the quantity demanded for the same price), and changes in the prices of other goods and services (which leave more spare income available). The first reason is typical of developing countries with high rural-to-urban migration. The second reason, where increases in real incomes lead to increases in the demand for land, can be observed in most countries where the higher-income groups tend to live at lower densities. In both Tehran (Applied Research of Cambridge 1977) and Caracas (Feo et al. 1975), the elasticity of demand with respect to income has a positive value of 0.5. This means that with a doubling of incomes, the demand for land goes up by 41 percent (figure 15-3).

It is interesting to note that the rather inelastic demand with respect to income in both cities as compared with more-developed countries may be due to the severe constraints in those cities. In Tehran there has been a policy of restriction of land supply due to the implementation of a greenbelt policy, and in Caracas the geographical constraints imposed by the mountains surrounding the city have limited the supply of land. In the Tehran region there was substantial shift in the demand between the years 1971 and 1976 due to an increase in population and an increase in real incomes, which ranged from 1 percent for manual workers to 13 percent for managers.

It is possible to transform the demand function into a density in relation to price of land. Because density is equal to persons per unit area, the graph can be transformed to relate prices to density (figure 15-4), which shows that an increase in price necessarily implies an increase in density, and vice versa.

Supply of Land

The individual producer of land (for simplicity, the producer here includes the developer and land landlord) will supply land depending on the price. The higher the price, the more land he will be prepared to sell.

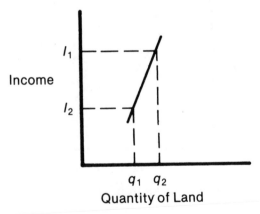

Figure 15-3. Elasticity with Respect to Income

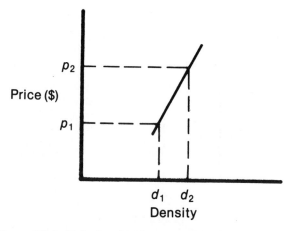

Figure 15-4. Relationship between Density and Land Price

Figure 15-5 shows that if the price rises from p_1 to p_2, the producer will increase the supply from q_1 and q_2. The slope of the supply line represents the elasticity of supply with respect to price. Inelastic supply means that the price will not influence the quantity of land produced (the slope in the graph will be parallel to the vertical axis), as shown in figure 15-6.

Traditionally in economics it has been assumed that the supply of land is inelastic. Because land can rarely be produced (only in cases of land reclamation is it possible to produce more land), it has been assumed that the quantity of land in the market is fixed and independent of the price. This assumption produces a number of important consequences in terms of land policy. This assumption is not true in urban areas, however. There the

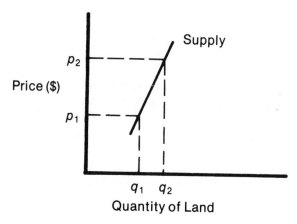

Figure 15-5. Supply Function for Land

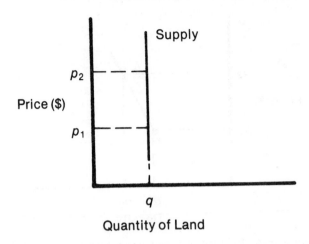

Figure 15-6. Inelastic Supply of Land

amount of land brought into the market is not fixed in the long run and
depends fundamentally on the availability of transportation. Most goods
are relatively inelastic in the short run. With a substantial increase in demand and a fixed amount of supply, the price necessarily goes up. The increase in price encourages suppliers to produce more goods to satisfy the demand. The big difference between the production of land and the production of other goods is that in the former the landowner incurs practically
none of the cost of the production of land, while in the latter there are
usually substantial associated costs.

Most of the cost associated with the supply of land is met by public
agencies. The public agencies provide the transportation and other networks, such as water, sewerage, and energy, necessary for the development
of the land. In foregoing the rent of the land in agricultural use, the
landlord loses money and also incurs some expenses associated with the provision of local roads and basic urbanization, the standard of which may
vary from country to country. For the individual landlord, the supply curve
tends to be more inelastic.

As in the case of the analysis of demand, the individual suppliers can be
added together to form an aggregated supply function of land with respect to
price. The shape of the function will be of the same form, but the horizontal
axis will have another scale to reflect the total quantity supplied by all
landlords.

There can also be shifts in supply. These occur when there is a reduction
(or increase) in the cost of supplying land. Figure 15-7 illustrates a
downward shift in the supply curve.

Shift in the supply of land, as illustrated in figure 15-7, can occur when more land is brought into the market by a transportation investment by the public agencies. Typical examples throughout history have shown that the introduction of new forms of transportation, such as suburban railways or subways, reduces the cost of transportation per unit distance (the cost of transportation includes the time associated with the travel). Therefore the area of the city within the same average cost of transportation extends from the center producing as a consequence an increased supply of land in the market, and the downward shift of the supply curve can be observed.

Equilibrium Price

The interaction between supply and demand determines the price of the land; this can be represented by the typical Marshallian cross in figure 15-8. The equilibrium price is p, and the quantity of land supplied and consumed is q.

In welfare economics (Samuelson 1967), the consumer surplus is defined by the triangle Apo in figure 15-8, and the producer surplus is defined by the triangle Bpo. Surplus is defined as the difference between what a consumer is willing to pay and what he is actually paying. In the case illustrated in figure 15-8, at least some users of land are willing to pay up to price A for the land, but they are actually paying price p. Therefore there is a gain for them, or a surplus, represented by the quantity of money $A - p$. Other users are willing to pay less and less, until there are some users who are paying the exact amount of money that they are willing to pay. The area of the triangle Apo then represents the savings all land users are making as they are paying less than what they are willing to pay. It is also true for

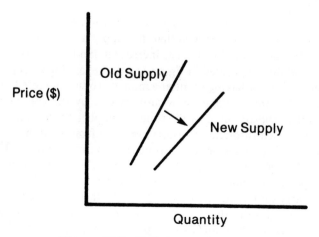

Figure 15-7. Shift in Supply of Land

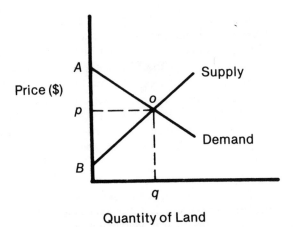

Price ($)

Figure 15-8. The Equilibrium Price

the producers of land that they are receiving more than they are willing to receive from selling their land. In the case illustrated in figure 15-8, some landlords are willing to sell for price *B* but are receiving price *p*. Therefore they are receiving a surplus of *p* − *B*. Other producers are willing to sell for more than *B*, until there are producers receiving the same price as they are willing to sell for (point *o*). The area of the triangle *Bpo* then represents the benefits that the landlords as a whole are receiving.

In policy evaluation, when policy 1 is compared to policy 2, there may be a difference in the equilibrium price (p_1 and p_2). The benefits to users of land and producers can be estimated by comparing their difference in consumer surplus (figure 15-9).

If in a fast-growing city there is a large shift in demand from one time period to the next and it is assumed that the supply is inelastic, as illustrated in figure 15-10, there could be a large increase in land price from p_1 to p_2.

In the condition illustrated in figure 15-10, the landlord receives the increase in price without having spent any money producing more land. It has been argued that this increase of wealth created by the community as a whole should be appropriated by the state. A number of alternative policies have been proposed throughout history, ranging from betterment levies to nationalization. The levies or taxes proposed have ranged in Great Britain from 70 to 100 percent of the gains. The effect of the 100 percent tax is to shift back the new demand curve to the old demand for producers, and the consumers carry on paying the new p_2 price. In fact, because the supply is not completely inelastic, the net effect of the tax is to maintain the same level of supply as before, reducing the opportunity of increasing the supply.

In figure 15-11, the government has levied a 100 percent tax on the

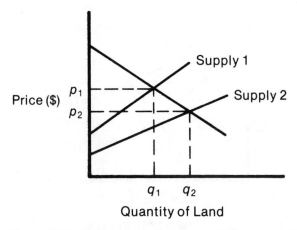

Figure 15-9. Difference in Surplus in Policies 1 and 2

landlord as if the supply was inelastic. The tax levied is $p_3 - p_1$. The result is that the producers do not bring more land onto the market and the quantity supplied remains at q_1. If the tax was not levied and the supply was not inelastic, the new equilibrium price would be p_2, with more land in the market, q_2. The difference in benefits resulting from a policy of taxation as compared with a policy of not taxing the gains can be estimated by the difference in surpluses. For the users of land, their loss is the area of the

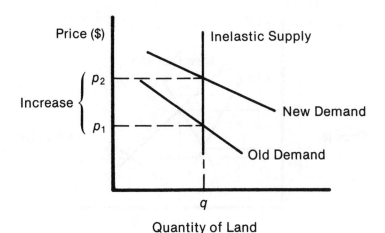

Figure 15-10. New Equilibrium Price with Inelastic Supply and Shift in Demands

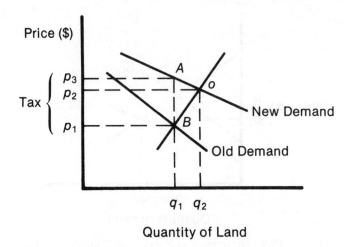

Figure 15-11. Effect of Tax on Land Values

trapezoid defined by the points p_3Aop_2. For the landlords, their loss is the area of the trapezoid defined by the points p_1Bop_2. The government receives money from both users and producers defined by the rectangle p_3ABp_1. The total net effect is a loss to the community as a whole of the triangle ABo.

If the government invested instead in infrastructure to bring more land on to the market, the net gains could be considerable, as shown in figure 15-12.

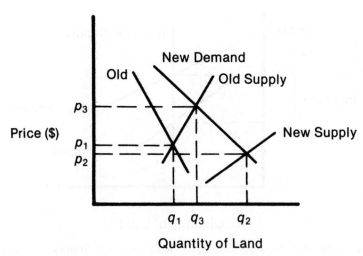

Figure 15-12. Effect of Shift in Supply and Demand

The total net gain for consumers and producers must be greater than the cost to the government of supplying the infrastructure. The implications in terms of equity can be considerable because users of land will be paying less for the land. The landlords may be receiving more than previously but less than what they would have received if there was no shift in the supply.

Spatial Prices

The previous analysis holds true in aggregate; however, the actual prices paid in specific parts of the city may differ considerably from the average aggregate price. The individual equilibrium price is different because there will be a different demand function for each specific parcel, as well as different supply functions.

If a theoretical city is considered to be of a circular form with its business district in the center, the area of land increases with increasing distance from the center. If all other factors affecting land prices are held constant, the equilibrium price must reduce with increased distance from the center because more land will be available (figure 15-13).

Land prices generally decline from city centers. This is clearly the case in Tehran and Caracas. In Tehran in 1976, an average rent in the city center was 1,500 rials per square meter per month, and toward the periphery an average rent of 200 rials per square meter per month was common. In Caracas in 1966, the average price of residential land in the city center was 710 bolivars per square meter, and on the periphery the value declined to 39 bolivars per square meter.

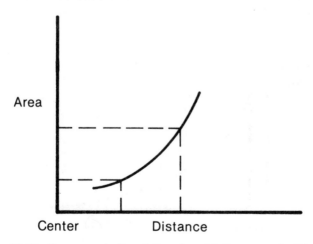

Figure 15-13. Increases in Land Supply with Increases in Distance

A number of empirical studies demonstrate that this is the case in a great number of European, American, and Asian cities. The studies by Clark (1967), Muth (1969), and Mills (1972) show a decline in density from city centers. Using the relationship between density and land prices shown in figure 15-4, it is possible to assert that land prices must decline in those cities with increasing distance from the city center.

The formulation of this phenomenon can be expressed as:

$$D = Ae^{-\beta d}$$

where D is density (or price) at distance d from center, A is constant, β is parameter, and d is distance from the city center. Figure 15-14 shows the relationship between distance and density. The constant A is the maximum (notional) density at the center, and the parameter β regulates the rate of decline of the density with respect to distances from the center.

The constant A is clearly related to the size of the city because a bigger city in terms of population will have a bigger aggregate demand, generating a higher land value and therefore a higher density. The parameter β is related to the availability of transportation and the level of income of the population. The transportation cost in general increases as distance increases but at a decreasing rate. The reason is that at the center, or near it, there is more congestion, increasing the cost of transportation per unit distance (Evans 1974). (See figure 15-15.)

For the user of land, the higher transportation cost associated with an increase in distance from the center must be compensated for by increases in the consumption of land if it will retain the same utility (or alternatively, with cheaper overall land cost, which will make more income available for other expenditure). These fundamental concepts are the basic ideas in Alonso's (1964) theory of location.

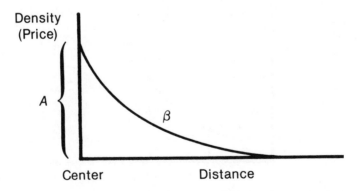

Figure 15-14. Decline of Density with Distance from City Center

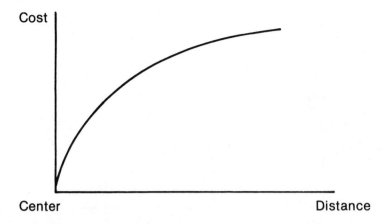

Figure 15-15.   Increase in Transportation Cost with Distance from City
                    Center

The spatial analysis shows that with an increase in the demand for land
(a shift) due to increases in population or incomes, the land-value and density
gradient must shift upward, as illustrated in figure 15-16. If there is an increase of supply (a shift) by investment in transportation and other services,
the land-value and density gradient must pivot at a given distance from the
center, reducing the land prices overall, with a substantial decline in the
center and increases in the periphery (see figure 15-17).

The two effects can be observed in the history of many cities. One of

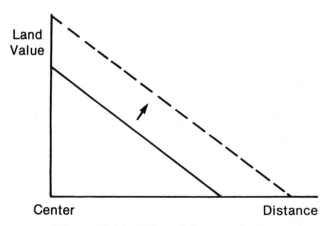

Figure 15-16. Effect of Increase in Demand

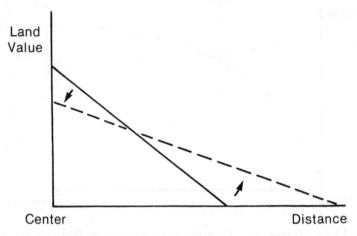

Figure 15-17. Effect of Transportation Cost Reduction

the most striking examples is the case of London from 1841 to 1939 (Clark 1967). (See figure 15-18.) While the population increased over four times in the hundred-year period, generating a considerable shift in demand, the urban area increased more than sixteen times. The average gross density fell to nearly one-third of the density of the starting period. By using the relationship between land price and density, the average price of land must have

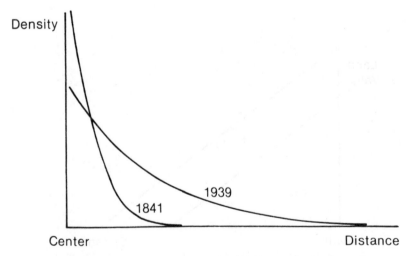

Figure 15-18. Changes in Density in London, 1841-1939

come down, with respect to average incomes, to one-third or one-sixth of the previous value. The first estimate will be the case if the price elasticity (λ) of demand is around -1 and the second if it is around -0.5.

During the one hundred years, an enormous amount of transportation development took place: suburban rail lines, the underground, trams and trolley buses, and the rapid expansion of public buses and private cars. This example clearly confirms that it is possible, with transportation investment, to reduce in real terms the value of land, despite considerable shift in demand.

Similar cases can be demonstrated in the United States (Mills 1972) and other developed countries (Clark 1967). In the case of São Paulo (Echenique 1980), the first sign of this process is occurring because the CBD has not grown since 1968 in terms of employment or floor space, and population is declining in the central districts. The process has been accompanied by an increase in transportation investment in the periphery and a process of decentralization of the CBD. This is also occurring in other Latin American cities.

Policy Implications

The first implication is that increases in transportation investment, which effectively reduce costs of transportation to the periphery, bring a new supply of land into the market, lowering average land prices. In a circular city, as illustrated in figure 15-19, a reduction of one-half of the cost of travel from the CBD increases the supply of land by four times. Another advantage of this policy is that it increases the number of potential suppliers, with consequent increases in competition, breaking the monopoly power that central landlords may exert over the market.

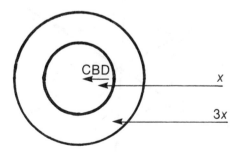

Note: CBD = central business district.

Figure 15-19. Increases in Land Supply by Reduction of Transportation Cost

The second implication is that because the transportation provision is not homogeneous but is developed along radials (such as suburban trains and bus lines), the pattern of urbanization should follow the lines of equal cost, as shown in figure 15-20. The actual distortion from a circle into a star shape will depend on the relative cost of the main radials versus the secondary network cost.

The third implication is that any restriction of the supply of land in the periphery will produce an increase in land values. This has been illustrated for the case of London by Hall et al (1973). Following the introduction of a greenbelt policy in the 1950s, land prices inflated. This has also been demonstrated in the case of Tehran (Applied Research of Cambridge 1977). It was calculated in that city that the positive gain of releasing the greenbelt more than compensated for the increases in transportation cost. In fact, the greenbelt policy with satellite cities, as has been the policy in Great Britain and also Tehran, further increases land values (see figure 15-21).

If the intention is to protect nonurban land for agricultural or recreational use in the region around the city, it would be better to follow the pattern of accessibility produced by the transportation network and protect the nonurban land with a green-pocket system, as illustrated in figure 15-22.

The fourth implication is that it may be desirable to encourage the development of secondary centers in the urban region. This produces a reduction of transportation cost on aggregate and therefore a reduction of land values. Figure 15-23 illustrates the point.

If the policy of transportation investment is followed with the development of secondary centers and protection of certain areas by a green-pocket policy, the resulting landscape will produce lower land values in aggregate. The resulting pattern is illustrated in figure 15-24. The development of

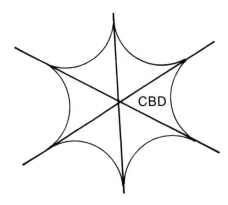

Figure 15-20. Effect of Cheaper Transportation on Main Radials

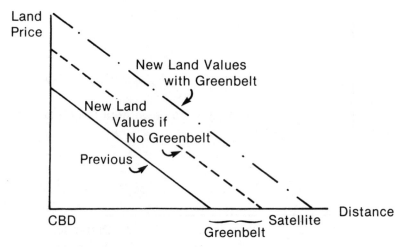

Figure 15-21. Effect of Greenbelt and Satellite Towns

secondary centers has occurred in most Latin American cities, notably in São Paulo, Santiago, and Caracas.

Conclusions

Investment in transportation leads to a necessary reduction in land prices in competitive markets. The implication in terms of individual expenditure is that the users of land will be able to reduce the density of development,

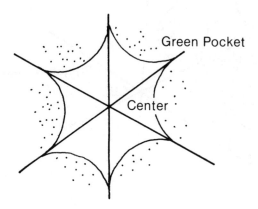

Figure 15-22. Green-Pocket Policy

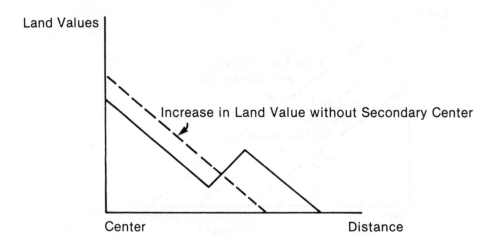

Figure 15-23. Effect of Secondary Centers on Land-Value Surface

bringing a reduction in construction costs. This reduction of costs implies a bigger proportion of individual incomes expended on other goods and services rather than housing. From the distributional point of view, it encourages more equity in the incomes of different social groups.

The policy implications of these arguments are that transportation invest-

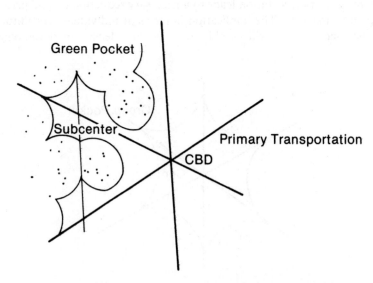

Figure 15-24. Pattern for Development

ment should be provided; the pattern of urbanization should follow the lines of transportation provision; the restriction of land through greenbelt policies should be avoided; the development of secondary centers should be encouraged.

The question of financial resources for transportation investment by the public authority has not been addressed in this paper. The increase in wealth in the community as a whole, produced by the investment, shows that it could be recouped through general taxes such as the income tax or property tax.

References

Alonso, W. 1964. *Location and Land Use*. Cambridge: Harvard University Press.

Applied Research of Cambridge. 1977. *Tehran Development Council Secretariat—Land Use—Transport Pilot Model Study*. Cambridge, England.

Clark, C. 1967. *Population and Land Use*. London: Macmillan.

Echenique, M. 1980. *SISTRAN: Transport Study of São Paulo Metropolitan Area*.

Evans, A.W. 1974. *The Economics of Residential Location*. London: Macmillan.

Feo, A.; Herrera, R.; Riquezes, J.; and Echenique, M. 1975. "A Disaggregated Model for Caracas." In *Urban Development Models,* edited by R. Baxter, M. Echenique, and J. Owers. Lancaster: Construction Press.

Hall, P.; Gracey, H.; Drewett, R.; and Thomas, R. 1973. *The Containment of Urban England*. London: Allen & Unwin.

Mills, E.S. 1972. *Studies in the Structure of the Urban Economy*. Baltimore: Johns Hopkins University Press.

Muth, R. 1969. *Cities and Housing*. Chicago: Chicago University Press.

Samuelson, P. 1967. *Economics*. New York: McGraw-Hill.

Stone, P. 1970. *Urban Development in Britain: Standards, Costs and Resources, 1964-2004*. (Cambridge, England: Cambridge University Press).

Moderator

William Doebele: There are two points that Professor Echenique made that I would like to underline. As long ago as 1952, Colin Clark, the British geographer, made a study of some seventy cities in the world and their land prices. He tried to discover why certain cities have low land prices and certain ones have higher land prices. The factor that explained a great deal of the difference in land prices in cities was the amount of transportation investment that had been made by that country. For example, in the United States, for one hundred years, we have had the lowest urban land prices of any other country in the world. And Colin Clark, at least, and Professor Echenique would argue that that is because the United States has always made the largest investment in urban transportation.

An interesting implication of this is not only that we can lower land prices, but it might be possible, if we have more data, to work out some specific figures in terms of saying that if you invest, let us say, $5 million in the transportation system or $10 million in transportation, you could lower—let us say, a factor of 3—by $30 million the total price of urban land. That would mean that it appears, if we had enough data developing this theme, that transportation investments would have very high leverage to lower land prices and that a dollar spent for transportation would in fact result in many dollars saved in land prices. In addition, we would have social equity distribution effects. We are not yet at a point where we can make those kinds of calculations, but this is an area of research with tremendous promise.

Another point that Professor Echenique made very quickly, is that the capital gains tax, taxing the capital gains on land sales, is one of the most popular instruments that has been suggested by planners and people like ourselves. Professor Echenique argued that capital gains taxation results in a net social loss; it can result in a loss to the sellers and to the buyers. It results perhaps in the gain of government taxation revenue, but looking at it from the total social point of view, capital gains taxation of land transactions can result in a net loss.

16 Monitoring Land Prices in the United States

James E. Hoben

Changing Conditions and a Land-Price Spiral

Historically the United States has pursued linked economic and land-expansion policies that provided abundant supplies of low-priced lands. Examples of these policies include early land grants by European kings; government-supported plank roads, turnpikes, barge canals, and land grants to railroads; the Homestead Act; the state and interstate highway programs; federally financed irrigation; federal and local financing for water and sewer systems; and attractive financing for land and housing after World War II. The nation developed westward, and people moved from cities to the suburbs and farther. There was an ever-increasing supply of accessible and serviced land to meet expanding demands. Plentiful and low-priced lands have been an unrecognized, yet crucial, factor in the achievement of such national objectives as affordable housing, inexpensive food, and reasonably priced services and durable goods.

It now appears that national and local government land-expansion policies may be reversing. People are increasingly skeptical about growth, especially residential, because of its fiscal and environmental costs. Even economic-development proposals are subjected to unprecedented scrutiny. A combination of conservation interests, fiscal restraint, and a desire to conserve energy have set a stage for a potential era of scarce developable lands. A direct consequence appears to have been and will be a reduction in land for urban uses and accelerated inflation in land prices. The nation's economic and social gains and its future objectives could be easily undercut by a lack of attention to land-price changes. One example of a threat to a national objective is single-family home ownership. The price of housing for the last several years has been increasing faster than incomes. Although data are spotty, it appears that land as a component of housing costs has been one of the two major inflationary elements (the other is financing). Land-price information is essential for public-private systems that would ensure adequate affordable supplies of developable lands in conjunction with ensuring decent, suitable, and economic environments and services.

The evidence of the changing conditions is plentiful. Federal spending, minus that for welfare, health, and social security, has declined in real terms since 1978. Monies for infrastructure for land use have dropped even further. For example, federal highway dollars are a fixed number of cents on a

275

gallon of gasoline. Highway costs have risen sharply and gas consumption has flattened out. Funding by the Environmental Protection Agency (EPA) for sewer and wastewater treatment does not keep up with the annual inflation in costs to meet the 1983 water-quality standards, much less begin to remedy pollution problems. Few EPA dollars are available to subsidize new facilities for expanding populations. On the state and local level, expenditures for capital facilities have dropped from roughly 29 percent in 1965 to 19 percent of total state and local budgets in 1976. Also voter approvals of general obligation bond referenda have dropped from 50 percent in 1968 to 10 percent passed in 1975. Local and state tax and expenditure limits have spread quickly and further threaten government services.

Increasing numbers of cities have failed to maintain or replace their existing infrastructure, which is vital to the continued uses of already-urbanized land. New York City is several billion dollars in arrears on maintaining its streets, bridges, water, and sewer lines. The replacement problem affects sunbelt cities as well. For example, Albuquerque and Sante Fe are both falling behind on street and water-system maintenance. The effects of these infrastructure problems reduce the development potential of vacant serviced urban lands.

Local governments are adopting stricter growth controls. A growing number of governments are restraining the amount of land and growth they will accept by defining growth-boundary limits, refusing annexations, reducing capital investments, and reducing permitted development densities. Land regulations have increased in number and costliness, and developers are being required to pay ever-larger proportions of land-development costs once paid for by the community at large.

At the same time, there is a rising demand to preserve agricultural lands. Farm products increasingly are viewed as a national resource and are an important part of our national exports. The National Agricultural Land Study is underway, conducted by the President's Council on Environmental Quality and the U.S. Department of Agriculture, with support from several other federal agencies, to ascertain how agricultural lands may be best protected. There have already been several attempts to pass national legislation to protect agricultural lands. Over thirty states have passed agricultural land-protection bills. A growing number of local governments are adopting strict agricultural zoning to prevent agricultural land conversion to urban uses. Others are engaged in programs to purchase agricultural land-development rights to prevent future development.

Against this background of declines in developable land supplies, there is a continued strong demand for land. Zero population growth has not reduced land demand. John Pitkin of the Harvard-MIT Joint Center for Urban Studies projects that the nation will have to house between 8.8 million and 9.2 million new households in the next five years, which is a 15 percent increase over the household formations of the previous five years. Twenty-seven million new households must be accommodated by the year 2000.[1] Simultaneously, people continue to want to live at lower densities. The demand for housing in the suburbs, exurbia, and a new trend of growth in nonmetropolitan communities is strong. All of this constitutes a strong cumulative demand for new developable lands.

Another important land-demand factor is an apparent increase in land purchases as an inflation hedge. Monies invested in the stock market and other intangible assets have been reinvested in land, housing, and other tangibles. Foreigners are adding to the land-demand factor because they perceive a potential for substantial increases in values.

Some statistics, although sketchy, provide a hint of the potential importance of the changing conditions. U.S. lands have been inexpensive compared to those of other developed nations. This is the result of abundant quantities of land and public policies designed to ensure developable supplies. For example, George Reiguluth of the Urban Land Institute (ULI) found in a study, "Effects of Alternative Metropolitan Development Patterns," that the average price for a single-family home site in Los Angeles in 1974 was approximately $8,000, while in Toronto it was $20,000, and in Tokyo, $70,000.

The effects of a possible decline in developable land supplies combined with a continued strong demand for land appear to have already produced a major inflation in residential land prices. In the two decades of the 1950s and 1960s, the average price for a single-family lot increased by 100 percent while the consumer price index (CPI) increased 30 percent. In the 1970s single-family lot prices increased by between 600 and 800 percent, while the CPI rose approximately 100 percent.[2] Other crude data collected by the ULI in 1980 show a pattern of rapid increases. The ULI found that the price for uniformly defined improved single-family lots in twelve standard metropolitan statistical areas (SMSAs) rose by 97 percent between 1975 and 1980, while the CPI rose only 45 percent.[3] Reflecting the higher land costs, the ratio of land to single-family housing costs has risen from 12 percent in 1950, to 20 percent in 1970, to 25 to 30 percent in 1980.[4]

A final fact from Japan presents an extreme example of the connection between radical land-price changes and restrictions of land supplies to demands. Japan, an island that is predominantly mountainous, has had a limited supply of land. It has recently experienced tremendous economic growth and commensurate pressures for urban lands. Under a constrained supply situation, the Japanese experienced between 1955 and 1979 a thirty-five fold (3,520 percent) inflation in residential land prices while the CPI rose only fourfold.[5] These land-price increases have produced major inequities in society, all but eliminating the possibilities of home ownership for the Japanese middle class.

The changing conditions in government policies affecting land supplies and the crude samples of land-price changes provide a basis for a belief that the 1980s will be a different era for various sectors.

Land-Price Users and Uses

The users and uses for land-price data and an index or indexes are numerous and diverse. There are users for micro (regional and small area) and for macro (national and interregional) land-price data. The range of needs spans landowners who need small-area land-price indexes for negotiating land leases, to national policymakers requiring land-price data to improve the modeling of the gross national product. Federal agencies need both micro and macro land-price data.

Micro Land-Price Data Needs

Local and Regional Governments: Uses for land-price data include indicators of problems of oversupplies or undersupplies of developable lands. Such data would aid in arriving at decisions on infrastructure investments, zoning changes, setting of urban-development boundaries, and agricultural-preservation policies. Also improved land-price estimation techniques and land-price indexes would assist real-property assessors to produce more-accurate, and thereby equitable, land valuations. Data would also be vital for the research and the design of antispeculation tax systems.

Private Sector: Here possible users and uses are wide ranging. Land-price data would provide builders a better basis for projecting their future land costs and could improve their market analyses. Land brokers and real estate organizations could operate more efficiently. Landowners would have a better basis for the negotiation of land lease contracts. Developers and lending institutions could improve asset estimations, helpful in determining financing. Corporations would have some benchmarks against which they could estimate land values in compliance with the Security Exchange Commission's new requirements for such data.

Academia: Housing, Urban Economics, and Public Finance: Needs include improved research on land-capitalization behavior, the production of improved urban simulations, and better projection models for housing supply, land-use changes, and tax yields. Researchers attempting urban-policy analyses or projections are severely handicapped by a lack of land-price data.

Micro and Macro Land-Price Data Needs

Department of Housing and Urban Development: Several needs include housing-policy analyses, urban-policy analyses, and improved urban-development planning and management.

Housing analyses require land-price data in order better to understand and model housing-supply functions and prices. Land-price data are required to assess the impacts of regulations affecting land and, in turn, housing prices. If land-price indexes were comparable nationwide, they could be used with residential sales data to assist with the setting of variable insured mortgage limits or variable limits for section 8 new housing.

National urban-policy analyses require longitudinal intercity and intracity land-price information to identify the relative competitive advantages and changes in economic activity in central cities, suburbs, and exurban fringes. Urban economic health could be partially assessed by monitoring changes in land prices. Price information could provide signals on the impacts of national urban policies.

Community Development Block Grants (CDBG) and 701-assisted local land planning and management require land-price data.

Department of Transportation, Federal Highway Administration, and Urban Mass Transit Administration: These agencies need land-price and index data to serve as a preliminary indicator of potential shortages of lands with transportation services. Other uses include approximations of right-of-way acquisition costs and use in calculations of land capital gains for joint-development negotiations or value-capture schemes.

Environmental Protection Agency—Water, Sewer, and Waste Treatment Programs and Environmental Regulations: The EPA needs land-price and index data to serve as a preliminary indicator of potential shortages of lands with water and sewer systems. Land prices could be utilized in analyses of proposed modifications in environmental regulations.

Macro Land-Price Data Needs

Department of Labor, Bureau of Labor Statistics: This department needs land-price indexes for analyzing price changes as a good evolves through the economy from primary to end-use markets. Indexes are also needed as deflators in productivity analysis. The treatment of land, as well as housing, in the calculation of the CPI needs to be reworked.

Federal Reserve Board and the Department of Commerce, Bureau of Economic Analysis: Here the need is for land-price and value data for improved calculations of national accounts of saving, investment, and borrowing. A major concern is the amount of wealth concentrated in land versus productive capital plant. Other uses are for calculations of land as a production cost and refinements in replacement cost accounting. Data are needed in constant dollars and on an annual basis for various categories of improved and unimproved real estate.

Department of the Treasury: The Treasury could use land-price and quantity data for analyzing the impact of the capital gains tax cuts provided in the Revenue Act of 1978, an analysis mandated by the act. Representative information is needed on the dates of land purchases, prices, and value accruals. In addition to assessing the impacts of changes in capital gains taxation, such information would aid the Treasury in judging the correctness of estate valuations and corporate declarations of land gains and losses, which are believed to be understated.

U.S. Congress: Members of Congress and the Congressional Budget Office need measures of the performance of the land market compared to the CPI and the producer price index. Land-price indexes would be useful for evaluating existing programs and proposed legislation affecting land ownership, availability, and prices.

Challenges to Collecting and Indexing Land Prices

Attempts to measure land prices and to construct indexes must cope with five challenges: the heterogeneity of land, the limited number of land transactions (sales), the limited information on land quantities, problems of weighting, and limited budgets.[6]

Heterogeneity of Land

Land is heterogeneous. It is hard to classify and compare relative to other goods such as steel or agricultural commodities. Each piece of land has numerous attributes, which distinguishes it from others. There are five key attribute areas.

Location: Locations affect prices. For example, prices vary widely according to how close land is located to a central business district, to roads, sewer and water services, transit, jobs, recreation, and so forth.

Property Rights: Land carries with it varying bundles of use rights. The greater the bundle of rights (that is, the alternative uses to which property can be put) and the greater the value that society places on these various uses, the higher the price will be.

Site Characteristics: Land has site characteristics such as size, shape, subsoil conditions, and climate that affect prices.

Externalities: Features surrounding land such as neighborhood character, crime, qualities of public services, and environmental conditions of air quality, congestion, or noise affect prices.

Regulation: Government zoning or other regulations also affect prices.

The complementary, offsetting, and overlapping effects of these five attributes make it extraordinarily difficult to delineate land types and submarkets. The price of land is not easily separated from that of other factors.

Limited Numbers of Land Transactions

Land prices are established through trading in a marketplace; however, there are very few transactions for many types of land and frequently none for substantial time periods for whole groups of land types.

Because of the heterogeneity of land, the sale price for one piece of land often cannot be ascribed to another. Further, many land transactions are not arm's length which result in unrepresentative land prices. Reliance on surrogate data such as an assessor's valuations is highly questionable, if not impossible, under today's practices. Assessors, like anyone else, usually cannot rely on comparable sales. They cannot use their replacement formulas for valuing land, and their income-capitalization methods have limited applicability. None of the assessor's three methods of real property valuation is reliable. There is also a proclivity by assessors not to assess vacant lands at full market value because this would burden vacant lands in farm, forest, or other open uses which are viewed as valuable open space. Finally, assessors' appraisals are frequently out of date by many years.

Limited Information on Land Quantities

There is little or no information on the quantities of lands by their key attributes. In urban areas, regional land-planning agencies have maps showing the extent of urbanization, and a few have computerized parcel records by a few simple land-use categories. The agencies have no, or at best very poor, information on vacant lands, by ownership, availability of services, or regulatory conditions. The lack of land-quantity data by specific attributes makes estimates of aggregate land values exceedingly suspect.

Problems of Weighting

The formation of an index implies the combining of all observed prices to create a single index. The lack of information on many land-type prices and absence of information on quantities of land types makes it impossible to know how to weight and sum prices. This makes an unambiguous price index an impossibility.

Limited Budgets

To date, there has been very little funding to study land prices and to experiment with indexes. The shortage of funds is likely to continue.

Thus land-price monitoring and the development of indexes have been severely limited. There have been only a few significant efforts. In 1933 Homer Hoyt published a report on one hundred years of land-sales data for Chicago. In 1968 Grace Milgram published a study of seventeen years of land transactions for Philadelphia. A year later, Milgram published a report on an effort to construct a land-price index for San Juan, Puerto Rico. Limited numbers of transactions were a major problem for both researchers. Because of the costliness and limits of transaction-based systems, no regularized land-price monitoring systems were established. Recently, other researchers have combined land-transactions data with land attributes and multiple-regression techniques to produce hedonic models of land prices. Paul Downing, for example, attempted to develop land-value indexes for the city of Milwaukee for the late 1960s and early 1970s. Downing's and similar work by others have helped to identify the factors underlying land values; however, the hedonic research has also been hampered by a lack of good transaction data for many land types in specific locations. To date, the accuracy of hedonic price projections has not been encouraging. Hedonic methods are also very costly. Downing estimated that the construction of land-value and price-estimation models and a land-value map for a city like Milwaukee would cost approximately $100,000; updating would cost $40,000 annually.

The Department of Agriculture (USDA) has employed a third method of land-price collection; it asks farm and ranch land owners to price their own lands. USDA has used owner price data along with data from farm and ranch land realtors to produce an annual index for such land at the state level. The USDA system is continuing.

A review of existing data sets in 1979 by a federal interagency working group on land prices found no data series that can be easily modified to construct micro/local or macro/national land-price indexes. Data sets that include some information on land such as the Census of Governments' property sales and assessment survey, the Federal Housing Administration (FHA) single-family insured mortgage insurance program, or the National Association of Home Builders (NAHB) Home Owners Warranty program cannot be factored or altered to produce land-price indexes. Present data sets have a number of limitations: price data but no area or amenity controls, limited samples of only one type of land without amenity controls, gaps in data (perhaps only one price range or one type of location), and noncomparability in location and timing.

Proposal for an Experimental Metropolitan Land-Price Monitoring System

It is proposed that an experiment be conducted to develop an inexpensive means to respond to micro metropolitan land-price data needs. It is recommended that a metropolitan area be selected for experiment to design and test a framework for monitoring land prices and to design and test inexpensive methodologies for collecting and indexing land prices. If successful, the product of the experiment would be a prototype metropolitan land-price indexing system, which would provide information on the absolute and relative change in land prices. Also a guide would be produced for the replication of the price-monitoring system by regional or local bodies in other SMSAs.

The users for the micro land-price data would be academics, private enterprise, local governments and regional bodies, and selected state and federal governments. The potential uses are varied and wide-ranging, spanning research on land as an element of housing price and the operation of land markets; improved data for public decisions on public land regulation or provision of infrastructure; and improvements in real-property valuations for taxes and private uses for land-location decisions, investment planning, or lease negotiations. An experimental prototype would not equally satisfy all users and user needs, but it would provide basic constructs and methodologies that could be refined to meet more-precise land-price data requirements.

In order to control the costs of the initial research, several limits are proposed for the experiment: number of experiments, geographic area, type of land to be priced, and exploration of data-collection methodologies. The proposal is for one metropolitan area. This will permit the development of a workable monitoring framework and data-collection technique. It will not permit intermetropolitan land-market comparisons. If feasible methodologies are developed, these can follow.

The proposal recommends the selection of a small- to medium-sized metropolitan area, a limitation designed to keep down costs. The study area should include the SMSA and the first ring of rural counties or townships so that price data can be collected for respective central business districts, city and suburban infill, and developing fringe lands. The coverage would dovetail with the USDA collections of nonmetropolitan farm and ranch land prices. The USDA data series omits land prices in areas of urban influence.

The experiment would focus only on vacant lands because they constitute a critical cost component for housing and businesses and would be a good test for the data-collection methodology. Vacant land would be classified in terms of conversion stages from unserviced (unbuildable) to developable (buildable) lands. This classification reflects current knowledge that rural lands pass through several owners and improvement stages before they are developed. Because one of the uses of land-price data will be to develop a better understanding of the behavior of land markets, an attempt will be made to relate the definitions of vacant lands for pricing with those definitions used in land-supply information systems.

The experiment would examine different methods of defining homogeneous submarkets to serve as a framework for price monitoring. A choice exists to subdivide an SMSA into small areas by superimposing uniform geographic grids, rings, and sectors or to identify small areas in terms of homogeneous submarkets. The former is considered artificial and likely to mask wide market discrepencies. The latter is favored because it builds upon what is already known about the impacts on land prices of location, development rights, and amenities. The latter is also favored because it is critical to a promising data-collection methodology to be tested. Specific challenges for the design of the price-monitoring framework are to select market data that are readily available, are updated regularly, and are more or less universally available (in all SMSAs), to define submarkets that can be compared from year to year, and to be able to plot the submarkets geographically.

The experiment would focus on testing and establishing the credibility of relying on land-price estimates by panels of land experts. The expert estimating technique will be tested against other pricing systems, such as reviewing land sales, factoring real estate assessments, and constructing hedonic projection models. This experiment will utilize the results of prior experiments to develop land-price maps from transaction data or using hedonics but will not include new hedonic modeling efforts. Although hedonic research is not proposed for this experiment, land-price maps produced by the experiment could be very valuable for later hedonic price research.

The proposal for price estimation by land-market experts was initially formulated by James Brown of Harvard University and unanimously recommended for research by the participants of the Urban Land Market symposium, held in February 1980. Against the limitations of relying solely upon sales data or trying to construct mathematical estimation models, the expert panel technique holds the promise of being inexpensive, quick, and easy to administer. The crucial research question is the design of a workable methodology and testing of its accuracy.

A number of precedents indicate that the expert panel, while seemingly unscientific, may be reliable. A private firm in Chicago, George C. Olcotts and Co., annually interviews real estate brokers to produce its *Land Value Bluebook of Chicago and Suburbs*. Land values are expressed as front-foot or square-foot values and are available at the block-face level. Olcotts collects transactions data from realty magazines to verify the expert estimates. The USDA produces a farm and ranch land price index by surveying owners and farm real estate agents. The price data are available only at a state level. ULI conducted a modest test of the expert estimation technique in the summer of 1980. It developed descriptions of representative raw and improved land parcels for housing and conducted a survey of land experts in twelve SMSAs. ULI received a 35 percent response, and there was a fair degree of clustering in the price estimates for each SMSA. Perhaps most encouraging is the Japanese experience. Japan has been operating a national system of land-price indexes for over ten years, covering all its urban areas. For 1,000 districts, the Japanese estimate land prices for four land-use types: two residential, one commercial, and one industrial. Appraisers price approximately 15,000 representative land tracts annually.[7]

A final aspect of the proposed experiment is an issue of whether a single metropolitan land-price index can be developed. This is believed infeasible at this early stage. It is recommended that research focus on developing indexes for representative land types first. The problems of land heterogeneity and unknown land quantities make it exceedingly difficult to know how to weight various land prices and produce a single index. Some limited research could be directed to explore ways of constructing an unambiguous single index.

The research steps for such a program follow. The step descriptions include a preliminary specification of substantive criteria and key analyses to be performed.

Preparation of Final Research Design

Comments on this paper, especially on the proposed experiment, would be incorporated into a final research design. Added to it would be a schedule and assignments of key responsibilities. A final budget would also be developed.

Selection of a Metropolitan Area

A metropolitan area, preferably a medium- to small-sized area, must be selected. A solicitation of interest should be extended to metropolitan planning organizations for participation. Preliminary criteria for the selection of a metropolitan site follow:

1. It should be experiencing growth.
2. The metropolitan agency and/or local governments should be attempting to manage their land development.
3. The metropolitan agency or a majority of the local governments should have information on the location of vacant lands, land plans and zoning, measures of accessibility to employment centers, and information on socioeconomic patterns and public facilities. Preference would be given to areas already working on methods to quantify developable land supplies and demands.
4. The metropolitan body or local governments should have automated real-property sales and assessment records that are easily accessible for land-price data.
5. Real estate development organizations must be willing to participate in the experiment.
6. There must be a willingness to cost share in the experiment.

A HUD-chaired panel will select the site with the best combination of desirable features.

Definition of Representative Land Parcels

Sets of representative land parcels must be defined. The representative parcels must cover the types of land that are important components in housing production and business. They must represent combinations of key site characteristics, bundles of rights, and government regulations. Realtors, builders, and local government officials should be consulted on the definition and selection of the representative parcels. A choice will have to be made as to whether the representative parcel types are to be hypothetical ones, which represent a cluster of similar parcel attributes, or actual land parcels. The representative parcels must be defined so that examples can be identified in land-transaction or assessment records. The experiment should attempt to determine which definitions of representative parcels are most useful and easy to work with. In the end it would be desirable to identify ten or fewer representative parcels to illustrate a workable system. Example representative land parcels might be:

S.F., zoned detached 3-5 DU's/AC, 3.0-25.0 acres, rectangular, no slopes, with services to the site and no services within one mile.[8]

S.F., zoned attached 10-20 DU's/AC, 1.0-5.0 acres, rectangular, no slopes, with services to site and no services within one mile.

Multifamily, zoned 25-40 DU's/AC, 0.5-2.0 acres, rectangular, no slopes, fully serviced and unserviced.

Commercial, zoned FAR 1.3, 0.25-1.0 acres, rectangular, no slope and fully serviced.[9]

Industrial, zoned for light to medium uses, 1.0-10.0 acres, no slopes, with services to site.

Rural, farm zoned, no services, 25-100 acres, rolling.

It would be highly desirable if the representative parcel could be identified in communities across the country. This would permit intermetropolitan comparisons when other metropolitan monitoring systems were established.

Submarket Stratifications

The metropolitan area must be stratified into relatively homogeneous submarkets. Several different sets of submarkets should be identified as part of the experiment to establish which definitions would best serve urban political and economic information needs and permit the most consistent price estimations. The subarea definitions must reflect land location and external attributes. Possible distinguishing measures might be distances to key places, densities, incomes, and service availability. Realtors would be consulted for guidance on submarket definitions.

The number of submarkets must be kept small—not to exceed ten and preferably fewer. An example set of submarkets based on urban service availability (sewers, water, roads, and schools) and urban density is shown in figure 16-1.

Whatever submarkets are defined, it would be desirable if they were based on data that are available for all communities in the country. In this manner submarkets could be comparable across cities and metropolitan areas.

Collection of Transactions Data

A search should be conducted for all land transactions (sales) fitting the representative land-parcel descriptions for a prior year. Potential private

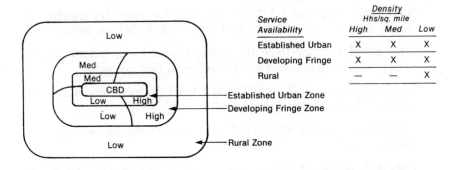

Figure 16-1. Example Set of Submarkets with Seven Subareas

sales should be screened out. In parallel, assessment rolls should be culled for assessment data on representative parcels. The assessments should be factored to market levels. The representative panel sales prices and factored assessments should be located by submarkets. A map and tables should be prepared showing sales and assessed prices by submarkets.

When parcel-price or assessment data are recorded from sales or assessment records, other available land-attribute data should be collected to facilitate future price modeling using hedonic techniques.

Collection of Expert Opinion Data

A panel of land-price experts on land values must be selected, drawn from land brokers, developers, appraisers, assessors, and real-property loan officers. Members of the panel must be familiar with actual land transactions, as well as the asking and bidding prices for land in all submarket test areas. It is important that the panel composition be balanced to avoid potential biases. Prices estimated by land developers may tend toward the high side, while prices given by assessors or appraisers may tend to be low. If the SMSA is large, there may be a need for several panels, with each expert on a portion of the SMSA.

The panel(s) should help to develop the definitions of the representative parcel and submarkets. It is possible that there will be more than one set of representative parcels and submarket definitions as part of the experiment to find the most satisfactory price framework. Once the definitions are agreed upon, each panelist would be asked to provide a best estimate of the price per square foot for each standard land parcel occurring in each submarket. The panelist would be asked to identify the average parcel size in square feet. Prices per square foot would be calculated. Estimates would be requested for 1980 and for 1975. The request for 1975 estimates would be part of a secondary experiment to establish preliminary measures of land-price changes. Price estimates would be requested annually in the future to maintain a time series.

If there were seven standard parcels and seven submarkets, each panelist would estimate prices for forty-nine pieces of land. Estimates would be made secretly and would be recorded, tabulated, and discussed. Following the discussion the experts could make price revisions and final average price would be calculated. A subsequent experiment would test the feasibility of mail out-mail back price surveys as a complement or replacement for panel meetings.

Analyses of Data Quality and Patterns

There is no certain way of knowing whether a transaction price, an assessed value, or an expert's estimated price is accurate. Arm's-length transaction prices would seem to be the most accurate, but there is error. *Arm's length* is a subjective concept, and prices reflect a combination of situational specifics of the property, buyer, seller, time of transaction, and the prevailing economic climate (for example, cost of money and future expectations). Confidence levels in prices may be established by examining the pattern of estimates and comparing these with one or more prices for specific standard land parcels by submarkets. For example, if prices are clustered, the probability is higher that the land is accurately priced.

A first analysis should be of price patterns from a single data source such as transactions, assessors, or experts. Analyses should be conducted for standard land parcels by submarkets. A second analysis would be a comparison of data from the different sources to define confidence in non-transaction data sources. Major questions are whether experts can consistently estimate prices, whether such estimates can be used to replace reliance on sales data, and whether estimates can be extended to land types and locations for which there are few sales. The analyses should be subjected to statistical tests to establish confidence levels.

Definition of Indexes (Formats)

The formats for land-price indexes must be defined. A system of absolute and relative index numbers should be designed. Assumptions, limitations, and caveats must be clearly stated.

Cost and Administrative Comparisons

The costs and administrative ease of developing price data for representative parcels and submarkets using the expert panel or other means must be defined. Also analyses must be made of the transferability to other SMSAs of the best method for collecting and indexing land prices. This will require establishing the availability of necessary data and experts in other SMSAs. A method of unit costs might be developed so that the costs for setting up similar systems in other areas can be estimated.

Report and Methodology Guide

A report would be prepared on the results of the experiment, detailing the experiments conducted and the results and providing statistics on operational costs and accuracy. Also a methodology guide would be prepared that would set out the necessary steps for establishing and updating a metropolitan land-price monitoring system.

Resource Requirements

The resources required to conduct the experiment in a cooperative metropolitan area cost approximately $225,000. The costs might be split between the federal and local governments and the private sector. The funds are needed to pay for a project manager; hire clerical staff to collect and process parcel, price, and market-area data; retain a statistician; pay the services and meeting costs of real estate experts; pay for computer time for manipulating automated records and analyzing land-price data; and meet other incidental costs. It is expected that cash contributions, work space, some data processing, plus help with locating vacant lands and delineating submarket areas will be provided by the metropolitan body. The experiment should require eighteen months to produce the final guide for establishing a land-price monitoring system.

Conclusions

It is hypothesized by a growing number of organizations that many U.S. urban areas are undergoing a decline in the supplies of accessible, serviced, and developable lands at the same time they are facing a surge in land demands for new and shifting households and businesses. Conditions are ripe in many regions for a further acceleration in the apparent rates of already alarming land price inflation. There is a growing need to develop a means to understand the operation of regional land markets that affect development changes in cities and rural areas and that are important factors in the costs of housing, businesses, and public services. The users for micro regional and submarket land-price data are numerous. There are also major national needs for macro aggregated land-price data.

There are significant technical challenges to the development of regional and submarket price indexes. It also appears that there are feasible methods for overcoming those challenges. A proposal has been made to set up a system to monitor the prices of vacant developable land supplies in metropolitan areas. A framework for following prices by types of vacant land and location has been suggested with variations for testing. Finally a possibly inexpensive and easy-to-administer price-collection methodology using land market experts has been proposed for testing against other methodologies. The product of the proposed experiment would be a proto-type metropolitan land-price monitoring system and a documented guide for the establishment of similar systems in other metropolitan areas. The pro-posed experiment might cost approximately $225,000 with contributions coming from the federal and local governments and the private sector.

Acknowledgments

I am indebted to the participants of the symposium on Urban Land Markets: Prices, Supplies and Public Policy Effects held in Washington, D.C. in February 1980. The symposium was sponsored by the Department of Housing, and Urban Development, the Department of Transportation, and the Environmental Protection Agency and managed by the Urban Land Institute. Contributions to the symposium by Michael Goldberg and James Brown were especially valuable in the development of this paper. Many of the recommendations contained in this paper were developed by the sym-posium participants. A report on the symposium, *Urban Land Markets,* is available from the Urban Land Institute.

I also drew material from the Federal Inter-agency Working Group on Land Prices, a group of representatives from the federal Departments of Commerce, Labor, Treasury, Agriculture, Interior, and HUD, the Con-gressional Research Service, and several public interest groups interested in collecting land-price data. The group was created in the spring of 1979 by the Department of Commerce, Office of Federal Statistical Policy and Stan-dards, in response to a request by Congressman Henry Ruess for a federal study of land-price-data needs.

Finally, thanks are given for encouragement and guidance to Tom Black of the Urban Land Institute, Grace Milgram of the Congressional

Research Staff, and Walter Rybeck of the U.S. House Committee on Banking, Finance and Urban Affairs.

The views and recommendations expressed in this paper are mine. They are not necessarily the opinion or policy of the U.S. Department of Housing and Urban Development.

Notes

1. U.S. Department of Housing and Urban Development, "Projections of Housing Consumption in the U.S., 1980-2000, by a Cohort Method," Annual Housing Survey Study Number 9 (Washington, D.C.: Government Printing Office).

2. These figures are taken from FHA data on the 203 single-family insured mortgage program. Lot sizes and amenities are not constant over the years. Therefore perhaps half of the lot-price increases are attributable to larger, higher-quality lots, a trend over the specified period.

3. ULI land-price survey for twelve SMSAs collected by Black and Miller in summer 1980.

4. ULI estimates.

5. Japan Real Estate Institute.

6. Michael Goldberg provides for the discussion of these factors in his "Developing an Urban Land Price Index Model: Models, Methods, and Misgivings," in *Urban Land Markets* (Washington, D.C.: Urban Land Institute, 1980).

7. In 1969 the Japanese adopted the national land-price publication system. The land-price data have been actively used in national and local efforts to moderate land-price inflation and its impacts on the economy.

8. S.F. = single family; DU/AC = dwelling units per acre.

9. FAR = floor area ratio.

Part III
Third Session

Introduction
to Third Session

Charles Haar

This Congress has been dealing with many of the issues of land development and land policy that concern us, and it has been fascinating to look at these issues from the perspectives of our different disciplines and from the perspectives of our different countries, and to see what makes sense or what the future may hold for us or what we can learn from each other. We have already looked at many of the models that researchers and the academy have been developing in order to understand more about what motivates people in terms of their investments, in terms of the capital markets, in terms of bringing land into urban use.

Now we will look at how some of these components fit together. After all, when we talk about land and land policies, we tend to think in legal, economic, or sociological terms rather than in terms of the whole, what puts it all together. So the arrangers of this conference have attempted now, to look at the city, to take into account the great movements of the past decade in terms of the environment, the movements for water and air control, the movements for an understanding for the externalities imposed by the individual developer and by the individual parcel of land, and try to bring into play in our land policies and our governmental functions a broader outlook, a broader aspect, dealing not only with the physical, but dealing with the environment—dealing with human beings—dealing with how they are living, playing, working on the earth's surface.

17 Cities Fit to Live In

Alfred A. Wood

People have always altered their towns and cities. Their needs have been changing throughout history, and this has been shown itself by modification of the urban fabric. In the Middle Ages and during the Renaissance, these changes were relatively slow and in tune with the tempo of life. During the nineteenth century, the industrial revolution, particularly in Great Britain, produced rapid and violent changes in towns, large new cities developing quickly as workers from the countryside crowded into the urban areas for the higher wages that industrial employment offered. This rapid change has continued into the twentieth century. Larger populations have had to be housed and employed, and the advent of easy transportation, initially public and later private, facilitated the urban sprawl, which has become at once one of the characteristics and the greater problems of today. What is true of Europe is equally true of North America and the great cities of South America and the Antipodes, especially those without effective public transportation.

All this has had the effect of turning our cities inside out. Those who could afford to do so left the inner city for better surroundings in the suburbs or villages outside the built-up area, a serious social loss to the increasingly deprived inner areas. Industry has also tended to reorganize, finding locations offering more space, better roads, and sites closer to much of its skilled labor force. Commerce too, and in particular shopping, followed the exodus to be closer to the higher purchasing power of the commuter settlements and to be free of the unpleasant environmental conditions for shoppers and growing congestion created by increased downtown traffic.

In addition to these trends, there has also been planned dispersal, partly by the development of large public-sector housing developments on peripheral sites intended to rehouse those living in slum areas in the inner city. There is little doubt that these forces of dispersal have had a devastating effect on the inner areas when added to the problems of obsolescence that already affected those districts, and there is a growing recognition that peripheral sprawl and inner-area decay have a direct relationship. (There are also major energy implications.) In the midtown areas of Detroit, something like 40 square miles lies underused and largely derelict. The sight of vast used-car lots, empty factories, fenced-in parking lots, waste land, decaying and dead housing areas, and boarded-up shops is familiar enough in too many European cities. The enormous scale of this daunting dereliction has a macabre fascination and provides us with a warning that we must heed. Not entirely a town planning and economic problem (there are obvious social factors at work), the fact is that this tremendous decay is exacerbated by the forces of dispersal. The new freeways and the thriving suburbs are the means and the end of people voting with their wheels. It has been paralleled in many European cities where the option of peripheral expansion has fueled the fire of inner-area decay.

Energy Dimension of Decay

Western nations based their nineteenth-century industrial democracy on the twin planks of relatively cheap labor and relatively cheap materials. Cheap labor gradually disappeared in the 1940s and 1950s, and during the last few years labor cost has become the major element in every article and service. Cheap materials stayed with us rather longer. It was only in October 1973 when the oil-producing countries flexed their economic muscles that we realized the second plank had been taken away. The disappearance of cheap oil affects every aspect of life and will, I believe, force us to reconsider our life-style in a fundamental way. In one way the oil nations may do us some good if the cost of oil makes us reappraise our resources and hence our planning attitudes. Since 1945 we have based our whole economy on cheap and plentiful energy, and this has affected our planning policies. Almost our every action has been to make personal mobility easier and the use of a private automobile to an increasing extent obligatory.

We have demolished old housing and rehoused the former occupants in new housing on the periphery of our towns and cities. Apart from the social damage of overenthusiastic slum clearance and its resultant decay (based on the idea that comprehensiveness was better than an incremental approach), the use of energy generated by these policies applied in both the public and private sectors has never been considered to be the damaging factor that I believe it to be.

We have similarly dispersed employment from our central areas that could be served by public transportation and allowed the development of suburban offices all too often in locations where use of the car is the only means of access.

There has also been a move toward the development of shopping centers and malls to replace the general corner store in residential areas. In the desire for increased catchment for each shop, a greater length of journey for the shopper is imposed. The paradoxical situation is that more restricted journeys for the few (the suppliers) means greater journeys for the many (the shoppers). Who really benefits?

The same trend toward what the economists call economy of scale has led to the development of hospitals in larger and no doubt better-equipped units, and schools have been similarly grouped. Indeed the new universities, for academic and other reasons, have appeared on the edges of our towns and cities in campus forms instead of being part of the fabric of our university towns as was the case in the past. All of these trends may have been sensible from the point of view of the developer, the mall-store owner, or the supplier, but I wonder if it has been so sensible overall?

According to the British Institute of Fuel we can look forward to between thirty-two and thirty-six years supply of oil if it is used at 1971 consumption rates but only sixteen to eighteen years if the present increase of usage is projected into the future. Indeed all other fuels show extremely limited reserves, with coal being in the best position at up to 150 years with economic usage.

In a similar way, reserves of copper, lead, bauxite, silver, tin, and zinc are all very limited (below thirty-six years according to the Organization for Economic Cooperation and Development) and all vulnerable to the same pressures that have been applied to oil. Instability in Africa and Asia highlights the difficulties that face Western consumers.

It seems to me that the message is very clear for those who will heed. Although it is easy to be pessimistic about resources, it is important not to overcompensate by way of mindless optimism—a process that seems to be happening to North Sea oil, seen as the cure for British economic ills in the 1980s. It is conveniently forgotten that borrowings abroad will have to be largely paid for with that oil and that the inevitable remedial action must be a reduction in consumption. However, President Carter's difficulty in attempting to convince Americans that there is an energy crisis underlines the problems faced by all policital leaders attempting to follow prudent energy policies. We all tend to hope that something will turn up to make the problem go away, even when we know the facts well.

We have proved to be better takers of resources than givers but unaccustomed as we are to conservation, we nevertheless will be put into the position of having to be economical with the world's resources. Considerations of this kind must condition our approach to urban restoration.

Clearly, if only from the energy point of view, we must reexamine our plans and policies to take account of our changed situation. This reappraisal must include consideration of transportation plans, settlement patterns, housing locations, and so forth in order to aim for a much lower energy-consuming society, which will extend the period during which resources will continue to be available to us and will inevitably lead to a reduction in mobility. We must also begin to plan for the maximizing of renewable resources. Agriculture and forestry will probably emerge as being more important than central-area redevelopment, and new buildings must be designed on an energy-conserving basis. Surely we must renew the inner areas rather than allow green fields to be used, particularly at a time when population estimates are declining in many Western countries, the birthrate is starting to fall in some, and for the first time in over a hundred years we have the prospect of relative population stability.

Urban Traffic and Transportation

The private automobile has become a virtually indispensable convenience for many people and has certainly widened the horizons and range of activity of many of its owners. Moreover, present patterns of manufacture and distribution rely on the growing use of goods vehicles, increasing year by year in size, capacity, and impact on our surroundings. Indeed the present economies of many countries of Western Europe rely heavily on the automobile industry. In spite of past and future increases in fuel costs (inevitable with shrinking supplies), demand for car ownership has continued to grow, although at a slowing rate.

Whether or not different forms of energy are developed and translated into new methods of propulsion is in many ways irrelevant, because it is the very numbers of vehicles that create the problems. The effects of the growth in traffic are obvious to even the most dedicated of vehicle users. Most of our towns and cities are suffering from the impact of modern traffic. Danger to life and limb, damage to buildings, noise, fumes, and visual intrusion are universal and are adding to the problems of retaining character in older towns. It has become increasingly difficult to find occupants for townhouses on busy routes. A fine house on a main street used to be a very desirable place in which to live, but now such a location would be intolerable for many people. The enduring pattern of streets in old towns is at once the key to their charm and the reason for their present-day traffic problems. Motor vehicles can penetrate into the confined streets and spaces of our towns; parked vehicles in market squares or formal spaces obstruct fine buildings, clutter the townscape between them, and obstruct the movements of people on foot. Continuous streams of traffic overwhelm the town and utterly destroy the sense of history. Harassed highway authorities, usually under great pressure from motorists and traders to relieve congestion and speed the flow of traffic, have often resorted to new road building in sensitive areas or street widening in historic thoroughfares, with a resultant loss of charming buildings or damage to attractive areas, and have created planning blight in the small shopping streets on the fringes of old town centers. Even where there has been little new road building, traffic measures of themselves can be damaging to the environment. Signs to indicate restrictions, one-way systems that very often allow an increase in volume and speed, and the paraphernalia of conventional traffic management add to the overall visual damage. The pedestrian suffers too; town centers are no longer places to be enjoyed by people on foot, and there are few areas where shopping can be the civilized pleasure that our grandparents knew. An excursion to the traffic-dominated central area of many towns and cities is an unpleasant, frustrating, and tiring business for many people. But cities are by their nature places of congregation and congestion; they have to support life and must be accessible to people and goods. A free-standing historic town set in a rural hinterland with little public transportation needs to accept a different proposition of traffic access as compared with a metropolitan area with a good public transportation system.

The dilemma is to avoid the danger of towns' becoming amiable but dead museums on the one hand or relentlessly destroyed by the onslaught of modern traffic, and to steer a sensitive course between damaging extremes. The fact that many people have rebelled against some of the physical changes that have occurred in towns, too many high-rise buildings, depressing housing projects, too much traffic, the sterile architecture of too many new buildings and that coupled with their negative wishes they have shown an increasing desire to retain those buildings and amiable eccentricities that make their town different from all others, indicate a pressing need to develop sensible and sensitive management of our surroundings in older urban areas.

In the future it will probably be no longer possible and certainly no longer desirable to redevelop our cities on the multilevel basis once considered necessary in order to accept as much traffic as possible. The move away from the "throw-away" society and the need to retain historic buildings and areas of character implies that future attempts to improve town-center conditions must be made on the basis of providing a sensible coexistence between conflicting road uses without contrived changes of level and with minimal alteration to the urban fabric.

The bus, the tram, the delivery truck, the private car, the bicyclist, and the person on foot tend to get in each other's way, and means must be found to deal with these conflicts by way of relatively low-cost environmental measures that will allow the city to function as a living, intricate organism.

Accessibility

There can be no standard solution; all towns are different. But it is possible to indicate certain principles that might be observed. Car access to central areas should be limited to the periphery of the central shopping area, which itself may well be improved by restriction or removal of traffic, given relatively short distances from a parking lot to stores, say no more than three-minutes walking time. There should be arrangements to allow vehicles for the disabled to be driven into otherwise traffic-free zones, and there must be attention to safety and convenience at the junctions with the general road system.

Because there must be a general presumption against major new road building or street widening, vehicle access to the town center will be by way of existing streets. Particular attention should be paid to the environmental capacity of those streets to accept the volume of traffic intended. This may well be somewhat below the overall crude capacity of the street system and must be judged against the function of buildings in the street and sidewalk widths and could well condition attitudes to parking-lot capacity served by the street, routes for public transportation, or access requirements for delivery trucks.

As much as possible, it is probably sensible to try to separate car, public transportation, truck, bicycle and pedestrian routes by means of selective traffic measures. Street and surface car parking should be reduced as much as possible, particularly in environmentally sensitive areas. There should be measures to discriminate in favor of shoppers and those who live in the central area, with commuter parking located farther out. The manner in which multistory parking lots are insinuated into the fabric of the town is crucial to their environmental acceptability. Generally a good rule to observe is that small lots, possibly tucked behind other buildings, are easier to absorb and have less impact on the surrounding streets.

Improvement of the surroundings by traffic reduction can be the means of retaining existing housing in town centers or reintroducing residential use for a broad range of people, but it does imply that special measures must be taken to ensure relatively easy vehicular access and parking space for residents close to their homes. This is not incompatible with overall traffic common sense and provides another example of the need to separate conflicting road-space requirements.

Access for bicycles may become more important in the future. It is probably necessary to allow bicycle access and provide safe storage in traffic-free areas and to develop a network of quiet, though not necessarily completely segregated, routes between the center and outer districts and between districts. Generally mopeds are not entirely compatible with bicycle routes and should not be given the same advantages.

Access on foot is an important traffic consideration in every town. There should be attention to the need to link nodal points by safe pedestrian routes, to link the center with the surrounding residential districts, to link districts, and to provide convenient accesss to schools, colleges, cultural features, local shops and factories. There should be a real attempt to avoid excessive detours for the person on foot or daunting changes of level for traffic-grade-separation reasons. Unpleasant pedestrian underpasses merely provide the mindless aerosol vandal with a quiet free gallery and can be a nuisance for the ordinary person on foot. Overall the aim should be to give the person on foot as much advantage as possible over other road users where the nature of the zone indicates that pedestrian priority is an overriding need.

Access for delivery trucks to stores can be provided in a number of ways. Access-only routes can be designated in the environs of the town center and within the center limited-time servicing, selective permits, trolley servicing, or unlimited access are all techniques that may be employed. It is probably environmentally damaging to provide rear access to existing premises by extensive modification of the area and, to judge by many towns with traffic-free central areas, certainly not always necessary. If rear access is a fundamental requirement, it is probably acceptable if it can be provided by existing routes without widening the spaces that provide a sense of enclosure in the minor street network.

Public transportation should have easy and short access to the town center and between districts and as far as possible should have priority over other road users, a priority that might be shared with taxis. It is sometimes possible to allow public transportation to traverse part of a pedestrian area and to designate special bus-only or tram-only streets. For pedestrian-safety reasons, speed-control devices may be necessary in bus-only streets. The location of public transportation routes and the location of stops should be aimed at passenger convenience. This is merely to state the obvious, although the obvious is by no means commonly observed.

Public-transportation schemes for old towns must consist of an overall package of measures that will include bus or tram priority, traffic restraint, transportation interchange stations, park and ride, links with traditional pedestrian routes, and so forth. The overall approach must vary from town to town, but the main principles of trying to ensure sensible and, as far as possible, separate access for different road users is clearly a requirement. Discussions with interested parties as well as general public participation are important first steps in dealing with traffic matters.

The difficult task of public participation is perhaps best tackled by the authorities' publicizing their proposals as widely as possible and making it clear that if the plans do not seem to be achieving the desired results after a period of experimentation, the project will be modified or discontinued. It is not failure to admit that a mistake has been made.

Shopping in Comfort

There is a great deal to be learned from the experience of the many European towns and cities where great environmental and commercial improvements have been achieved by the development of traffic-free areas. These foot streets, for the most part, have been created by closing existing trafficked streets to motor vehicles for the major part of the day, or even permanently, very often in situations where no rear servicing was possible. On the Continent, pressure for these pedestrian streets very often came from commercial quarters. This often occurred after initial fears that local shopkeepers would lose trade if traffic were excluded from their street, fears that proved to be groundless in the vast majority of cases.

The idea of converting existing trafficked streets to pedestrian-only use is by no means new, especially in Germany. Limbecker Strasse in Essen was closed to vehicular traffic in 1927, and in nearby Cologne, Hohe Strasse and Schildergasse were converted to foot streets on a limited time basis (there were almost no facilities for rear service access) just before World War II. After 1945, there was a renewal of interest in foot streets, and those in Cologne were restored as traffic-free zones in 1949 and in Essen, Limbecker Strasse and Kettwiger Strasse formed part of a major pedestrian area developed in the city from the early 1960s.

Now there are more than 350 towns and cities in West Germany with extensive traffic-free central areas, the great majority of them created without the extensive road building often represented as being necessary to accommodate traffic displaced by street closure. One hundred more traffic-free areas are planned for the near future. Now nearly every West German city of over 100,000 population has all or a major part of its central area devoted to pedestrian use.

The tragic Olympic Games in Munich in 1972 had a happier side: they drew the attention of a wide international audience to the virtues of a city center without traffic. Visitors to Munich found themselves enjoying a civilized quality of life, which can be created when the heart of a great city is given over to the person on foot and when public transportation is arranged to complement the new role of the center.

Consideration of the factors affecting traffic-free areas will include function, character, comfort, and aesthetics, as well as the question of access and public transportation.

The choice of the area to be closed to motor traffic is to some extent dictated by opportunity, but it also must take into account the potential commercial and physical attractiveness of the streets. Those streets with the strongest attraction to shoppers are clearly good candidates, but there must be equal attention to minimize commercial disadvantage in areas just outside the traffic-free zone. There should be sensitivity to the need to retain desirable trades in the area: the small shops, craftsmen, cafés, and so forth. A liberal attitude to forecourt and kerbside trading (that is, street vendors) can be a significant help in creating a lively street.

It will be possible, too, to improve the environment by introducing recreational features into a foot-street system: encouragement of street cafés, proper seating, and the exploitation of water and vegetation are important. The aim should be to exploit the particular character of the area so as to create a zone that is unique to that town. As a craftsman works with a piece of wood, so should the designer work with the grain of the area. Conservation of buildings of character and features that can best be described as amiable eccentricities should be considered part of the process of pedestrianization. New uses for old buildings will also help to emphasize the local character of the area. As much of the town's visible history as possible should be brought into the foot-street system, employing statuary as part of the visual experience. Lighting can play a part in emphasizing important buildings and the townscape too.

One of the main benefits to be derived from pedestrianization is the relaxation that can be brought to the town center, which then becomes a sort of open-air living room. The spaces require furnishing with this in mind. There must be plenty of seats, well designed and preferably with backrests and armrests. There is a great deal to be said for individual chairs, which Munich uses. A sensible and sensitive planting scheme can add greatly to the sense of relaxation. Seating areas generally should be protected from the main pedestrian routes and should cater both to those who like sun and those who prefer shade. They must allow the occupants to indulge in a favorite human activity: watching the passing crowd.

Safety from traffic is achieved without difficulty in most traffic-free areas, but there must be special attention to the problem if public transportation or other vehicles use the foot-street system. Speed-control devices may be considered to protect the pedestrian from unexpected traffic. Protection from crime is usually achieved by increased pedestrian activity, and as Jane Jacobs pointed out years ago, the value of residential eyes on the street can be of great benefit. Banks have found it advantageous to be included in a traffic-free area because the presence of a getaway car outside their premises on a foot-street is exceedingly obvious, and thus the site becomes safer than a conventional position in a trafficked street.

The need for shelter must be related to climate, and in some countries it may be sensible to consider constructing free-standing canopies linking the frontages or even as in Gotgatan in Gothenburg providing a roof to cover the whole street. Access to existing roofs must be allowed for, however, in case of fire. In both cases it is important to consider whether the appearance of existing buildings will be devalued by the shelter provided. Bus stops should have weather protection, as should street cafés. And in some climates the sun may have to be considered as an enemy.

There should be well-sited and signed lavatories, mailboxes, telephones, luggage lockers (in large areas), storage for bicycles, and a spectrum of facilities for food and drink. Any automatic vending machines should be sited at nodal points or grouped by existing shops. The larger schemes might even provide supervised child care in a small play area.

Although there is perhaps no longer quite the same degree of commercial opposition to traffic-free streets, it is nevertheless as well to recognize that discussion concerning such areas can be complicated and protracted. In Norwich fifteen separate and interested groups were consulted at three stages: twice during the preparation of the scheme to close London Street to traffic and once during the experimental closure period. In subsequent street schemes, discussions were generally less difficult or lengthy, but the same groups were involved and inevitably the process took time.

Inner-City Decay

Usually (but not always) located immediately around the city center, inner-city decay is easy enough to recognize, although the reasons for decline may vary from city to city. Usually the obvious physical characteristics are run-down, ill-maintained housing, often occupied by the unskilled and their families or immigrants. The shopping areas with unoccupied space on the upper floors show environmental decline, often with a reduction in the type of shops useful to the population accompanied by an increase in service industries, gas stations, and the like. In general, land tends to be underused, there are often vast areas of dormant land owned by public authorities, and there are brick-strewn gaps in the urban fabric caused by demolition without replacement, many used as parking lots. Open space and small-landscape features are often ill maintained and sometimes have a dreariness that is daunting even to the insensitive. I often think that the two dullest words in the English language are *recreation ground;* the connotations of boredom, dull landscape, worn grass, wire fences, and an atmosphere of despair combine to describe local parks in far too many inner areas. (Recreation planners all too often believe that if they provide so many acres of open space per 1,000 population they have catered for the needs of the people.)

The inner areas are probably predominantly the zones where employment prospects for the resident population have declined radically in the last few years. The old nineteenth-century intermixture of housing and factories has suffered most from age. Some industries have moved to find more space for their processes and better access for their transportation arrangements, predominantly by road today. Other industries have quietly died, overtaken by unassailable competition or in some cases because their unpleasant characteristics (noise, fumes, and smoke) attracted the unwelcome attention of town planners or public-health authorities. In many areas there is land made derelict by the industrial processes carried out previously.

The impact of traffic is usually devastating: commuters in their cars finding short-cut routes through residential streets, a phenomenon known in Britain as rat-runs. Delivery trucks servicing the factories that remain in the inner areas add to the unpleasant environment; often, too, they are parked overnight on cleared sites in residential areas. Public transportation, necessary for a higher proportion of people than in outer areas (car ownership is usually low), is generally confined to the major radial routes passing through the zones.

The inner areas, too, are the districts where the redevelopment of older housing and its replacement (if it has been replaced) has led the development of large districts where there is only the one class of tenure. It could be said that large areas of public housing lead to increased division in the city as a whole.

There is also the danger of treating the problems of inner cities as self-contained issues whereas it is clear that they are closely associated with planning policies for the city as a whole. Equally it is easy to forget that cities have always changed, and there can be a natural but misplaced desire to attempt to return the inner-city areas to their nineteenth-century role (but in architectural modern dress), forgetting that the forces that shaped these areas have changed. In considering remedies, it will probably be necessary to reverse some of the forces of dispersal but at the same time accept that the reduction of population that has occurred can be the means for improving the surroundings for those who remain and as the magnet to attract the return of other social groups. In short, inner areas must be given self-confidence in order to obtain investment from house owners and companies.

Inner-City Revival

Changing Attitudes

The most important factor in the current situation is the emergence of two evolving concepts. First, social thinking has shifted away from questions of morals and health to a broad-based idea of "the standard of living." This is a remarkable change because it is totally divorced from nineteenth-century utilitarianism. Instead of looking at poor areas from the standpoint of their effect on the welfare of middle-class society, we are more concerned with the welfare, opportunities, and future of the people living in them. Second, the concept of conservation, which was behind much of the theory and practice of town planning, has developed rapidly in the past ten years to unite a wide group of disciplines. The idea of controlled change and recycling appeals to a society disappointed by the physical effect of redevelopment and concerned over gloomy economic prognostications. For the first time, we view our cities as economic, cultural, and social resources and find dereliction and waste devaluing the environmental currency of our urban areas. I believe the concept of creative conservation to be a valuable framework for marshalling our forces in order to make inner areas agreeable places in which to live and work. An examination of the inner-area problem through this concept will help to illustrate the point. The urban poor (in relative terms) have always been with us, and in the past all manner of approaches, from the Victorian evangelistic to the massive comprehensive clearances of the 1950s and 1960s, have been adopted. Perhaps it is time to take a new approach. Now that conservation ideas and techniques have been tried and tested, the time seems right to see if such actions are appropriate for inner areas.

Conservation

Conservation has always been the basic tenet of planning. The idea of the greenbelt to conserve rural Britain is perhaps the strongest thread in postwar planning. Conservation of buildings of historic interest and architectural value has been a developing planning theme in Europe and North America in the last fifteen years or so, but more recently planning has also started to absorb the conservation ideas of other disciplines—particularly concerning energy, resources, nature, and the general environment. Most of the practical developments relevant to cities have occurred in the field of conserving buildings. Hard lessons have been learned, and probably the major constraints are now institutional and financial rather than theoretical or practical.

There are indications that other fields of town planning are becoming concerned with building conservation. Rehabilitation and conversion of older industrial premises (with a direct bearing on inner-area problems) now occupy adjacent columns in the new-style refurbishment supplements to those reporting the conservation of historic buildings. Conservation concepts of this kind unsentimentally examine the resource opportunities of individual buildings and of areas; they are aware of the economic facts of life (the need to find viable new uses has taught this); they look to the future in a way that has not always occurred in everyday city planning (it could perhaps be said that until the economic dream world of the 1960s and 1970s was overtaken by the energy crisis, the future was seen as an amiable and growing extension of the present); and by uniting the disciplines of energy, resources, aesthetics, and ecology with a common conservation objective are more likely to produce an acceptable basis for regeneration. In addition there is a parallel in social issues in the inner areas because actions for improvement of decayed zones must concern themselves with the use and development of human resources, preservation of community ties, and enhancement of cultural and educational opportunities.

The Worn-Out City

It has been said that the scale of urban decay today as compared with the past can be partly explained by changing ideas and standards and partly by the fact that cities are simply bigger. I believe that there is more to the problem than this and that the present situation can equally be said to be the result of waste and mismanagement. The throwaway society has a great deal to answer for.

Modern planning has tended to be concerned with growth in the economy and growth in private and municipal wealth. Now that this growth has ceased, we may justifiably view the past twenty years as a missed opportunity, for we failed to control the two major forces of growth: concentration at the city center and dispersal of private housing and industry. In allowing concentration, we have created congested city centers of inhuman scale with largely inadequate architecture. In energy terms, these centers have been costly to build and are expensive to operate. In allowing dispersal, we have consumed land of great agricultural and aesthetic usefulness and often pandered to the lowest level of design: low-density speculative development.

Separately each of these trends represents considerable waste. When they are taken together, this wastefulness is multiplied. In terms of land and buildings, concentration and dispersal have left a swathe of neglected, underused, and decaying cities that we now call the inner areas. Cities are now voracious users of energy because their development implies necessary commuting. This commuting has dictated massive investments in road infrastructure and has led to environmental conditions that render parts of the inner area almost uninhabitable, thus making the task of attracting people to return yet more difficult.

Despite these two trends, we have not totally ignored the worn-out parts of our cities. However, I suspect that our attentions to them have in part compounded the inner-area problem and hastened their decay. We have tackled the problems of housing, industry, and shopping as a matter of replacement rather than one of husbanding resources for the future. For administrative convenience and tidiness, we have cleared away large areas of housing and their attendant small industrial concerns to the extent that there has been a major decline in employment and wealth creation in the inner city.

The Inner City: A Different Approach to Action

Ideally we need to overhaul the organizational framework for dealing with inner areas. For many reasons, most of them political, this is unlikely to occur, but we could alter our approach to make the best of the present system.

The first essential is for government, in its widest sense, to establish clearly what direct action it can take and what partnerships it can set up and to stop interfering elsewhere so that other people can act with maximum freedom. Development control must continue to prevent the worst excesses, but if we are able to make inner areas more attractive to industry, our policies and procedures must be more responsive to its needs.

Public authorities can relinquish interest in land and buildings in a number of areas and give them to groups who can develop, use, and repair them. If this results in some revival, is that not profit enough? Certainly strict adherence to conventional wisdom will not yield any creative initiatives.

Land Resources

Land is the most basic resource, and its use is central to the development of the conservation approach to inner areas. In the absence of a proper market, owners often value their land too highly; we must establish its true value. Local authorities could release land in their ownership perhaps by using *dutch auction* methods (lowering the price each day until a sale is made). In some cases, sites may well have a negative value; authorities might have to pay developers to take them.

In Great Britain and in other European countries, public bodies, including local authorities, own large areas of land, particularly in inner areas. In the Birmingham Partnership area, for instance, 77 percent of all vacant land is publicly owned. In many cases, this land is no longer required for the use for which it was purchased (such as major road schemes now abandoned). Local authorities are unlikely to be able to develop much of this land in the near future, and if it were released for private development, not only would it be developed quickly, but it would also help to bring down the market price of inner-area land.

In Great Britain, local authorities are not the only public bodies owning land. British Rail has been able to release some former sidings for development, but there have been major problems in releasing land owned by the Gas Corporation. The sites of former town gas plants that are now redundant are in some cases being held in reserve in case they are required after North Sea gas is used up. This is a curious attitude; coal gas is surely more likely to be made at or near the coalfield and piped around the country by the gas grid that was one of the benefits of North Sea gas. Dormant land in public ownership is incompatible with the urgent need to use land creatively, and it has a disastrous effect on the surroundings of inner areas.

Many sites are difficult to develop because of physical constraints. Derelict land can be a major influence in inner areas. Although in some cases it does provide valuable opportunities for informal recreation, the use of derelict land, often with hidden mineshafts, deep quarries, or dangerous chemicals, as unofficial adventure playgrounds can be extremely dangerous. Its presence also has a negative effect on the environment of surrounding areas. Although the influence of derelict land varies in different areas, it is perhaps the biggest single environmental factor affecting industrial towns. Helped by government grants for reclaiming derelict land, my authority has already carried out a great deal of reclamation in collaboration with the districts; about a thousand acres of derelict land and waste land have been reclaimed since 1974. Apart from the improvement to the environment, land can be released for development in some but not all cases, but in any event improvement of our surroundings is crucial to restoring confidence. In West Germany reclamation of large areas of land in the Ruhr has had an important effect on the surroundings of many millions of people and has probably been one of the factors in the successful industrial regeneration of the area.

Industry

The older industrial buildings of the inner areas represent a material (and often aesthetic) resource, which we must use. The idea that old property leads to inefficient modern production has never been empirically tested but is probably only true of the largest industrial processes. Since it is the loss of the smaller firms, and hence diversity, from the industrial structure that has led to an inability to adapt to economic circumstance, there is every reason to pursue policies of conservation in the older industrial areas to provide much-needed small factory units. More people may well be earning their living by craft skills in the future.

With skill a great improvement could be wrought in the appearance of some industrial areas and, perhaps more importantly, improve their efficiency. Industrialists are rarely worried about external appearances; the days are gone when some prestige was attached to handsomely built factories, and we must reconcile ourselves to this fact. The problems of the older industrial areas have developed through the way that modern methods of distribution have been accommodated. Although inner areas are generally easy to get to, moving about within them can be very difficult. We must therefore concentrate on improving local traffic conditions within industrial areas, minimizing on-street parking, and encouraging individuals to provide off-street loading facilities. Although small firms are justifiably objects of some concern, their potential for providing jobs for the unskilled (the category in which most unemployment exists) is limited. We must therefore try to ensure that some of the major tracts of land in the inner areas are used by major employers. The gain in jobs from providing new, small units could be offset totally by the departure of one larger employer.

Urban Transportation

More-efficient traffic management has been identified as an issue affecting the location of industry in the inner areas, but transportation planning has had a more extensive and profound influence on the inner areas. There is a distinct emphasis on radial movement from city center to suburbs. This has led to major road building, which has destroyed many local inner-area centers or made their surroundings intolerable. Rarely has there been any remedial work along the frontages of these routes, and most people derive their grim view of inner areas from journeying along these highways. In addition the blighting effect of long-term proposals has been at its worst in the inner city. We must repair this damage as best we can and try to remove the uncertainty of often overgenerous road-widening lines.

To improve movement within the inner areas, we must strengthen the system of ring routes. At present we have systems of inner and outer rings around most cities, which seem to be of little direct value to the area of concern between them. This is true of the orientation of bus routes also. In most cities it is easy to commute to the center but difficult to get to work off the radial routes. There is room here for imaginative experiments with public transportation. Orbital routes, fixed-fare minibuses on fixed routes, and variations on the dial-a-ride systems modified for inner areas are examples of some possible approaches. The environmental impact of traffic is at its worst in inner areas. The intimacy of industry and housing means that the traffic generated by one interferes with the other. In the past this has been taken as justification for strict zoning, but in the inner city there is a strong case for maintaining a degree of coexistence. We must depend to a greater extent upon skillful traffic-management schemes to improve the environment of housing areas and the efficiency of distribution since this would encourage investment in both sectors.

Housing

The housing-improvement program has been gathering experience over almost ten years now and has brought about a recognition that there is a valuable resource in existing housing in the inner areas. The imaginative homesteading in Baltimore has paid off handsomely and could be copied to advantage in many other places.

We must also concern ourselves with the insensitive alterations to fine old houses by both local authorities and private individuals. At the street or area scale, there is rarely any coordination of repairs and "improvements," often with disastrous visual consequences. The administrators who allocate grants are not trained in aesthetic matters, and this may mean that the money spent on environmental improvements can be lost if the overall character of the buildings changes. There should be advice available to owners so that repairs can be carried out sympathetically. There are many advantages in living close to city centers, and there is also a market, I believe, for new private housing in the inner city.

In some cases the emphasis is likely to be on low-cost housing for sale, but given the right circumstances we should be able to attract higher-quality housing. Fine nineteenth-century parks, which may be found in the inner parts of many cities, might form a focus for such development. We could also provide new urban parks of high quality to stimulate development. Few new parks have been developed since the last century, but these could make adjacent land attractive to developers. This has happened in West Berlin with the restoration of the Tiergarten. Most inner cities possess features that can form a basis on which to build interesting and civilized surroundings to stimulate a return to city living.

Shopping in Inner Areas

City-center shopping has been transformed in recent years by pedestrianization, landscaping, and new forms of retailing. The often-substantial inner-area shopping centers have, however, been as neglected as other aspects of those areas and have borne the brunt of traffic problems. There is a presumption that people must commute to shop as well as to work, but I see no reason why the benefits bestowed on our central shopping areas should not be applied, albeit on a smaller scale, in local centers.

Townscape Resources

One of the saddest things about some inhabitants of the great industrial cities is their often-scant regard for their inherited surroundings. Either there is the apologetic view that there is nothing worth saving (rarely true) or a more downright and philistine attitude, which feels that progress is made when an old building is pulled down. The fact is that there is much to conserve creatively and improve in our industrial cities and not just the major nineteenth-century buildings of the railway kings, the coal dukes, or the textile barons. Many people recognize the value of the minor classics in our streets: the pub carefully designed to follow the curve of a corner (rarely done today), the clock in the marketplace to mark perhaps the relief of Mafeking, or the thousand amiable eccentricities that make each town different from all others. Conservation is not just the province of the special-interest group, but good commonsense management of our surroundings to ensure that we make the best use of what we have already got and that we retain individuality in our surroundings at a time when standard buildings are making all our cities look much the same. Conservation has a considerable role to play in our inner areas, in particular to retain, improve, and reuse the many solid nineteenth-century buildings. We are now beginning to value the architecture of that period more highly. I am not concerned so much with grand architecture but with the style and form of ordinary housing and local buildings. These provide a domestic scale and a richness of design that has been missing from much of the architectural dandruff that we have suffered since 1945.

In some ways town planners have directly contributed to the present state of the inner cities by imposing the dead hand of restriction. If they miss that task, there is now a new role of restriction. Whatever positive action we can take and encourage others to take in the inner city will be wasted while easier and more-profitable opportunities are freely available elsewhere. The inner areas need time and assistance before they can compete freely with green-field sites outside our cities; therefore opportunities for development on such sites must be restricted to a minimal level. This requires sympathetic action by authorities, which are often not responsible for inner areas themselves. Altruism is not a common local authority virtue, but it is clearly needed now.

Finally I must acknowledge that the role of the planner is concentrated on the physical fabric of inner areas, and while we all hope to be able to influence economic and social events through physical action, I do not pretend that the approach I have outlined will in itself solve all of the wider social problems of our cities. Action by other agencies is also essential, but given this I believe that our inner areas do contain the seeds of their own regeneration. It is our task to see that the revival of our cities does take place and to provide the opportunities for others to carry out their work to ensure that we can make all parts of our cities decent places in which to live.

In a world that has change radically in the last few years, growth is no longer the factor that it was. We must develop a sensitive, intricate, street-by-street entrepreneurial approach to the regeneration of our rundown areas, recognizing that while there may be very little new growth, that is no excuse for bad husbandry of our inner cities.

All of us were perhaps irritated by our parents when we were young when they told us that "a stitch in time saves nine" or "waste not want not." Our parents were right. Let us demonstrate by our actions that we can hand on to our children cities that have been carefully tended by good housekeepers.

18 New York City as a Case Study in the Problems and Opportunities of Improving Urban Environments

William H. Whyte

New York City has been the leader in the use of incentive zoning in the center city. In this most concentrated of cities, incentive zoning has prompted the creation of more new open space on plazas and small parks than all other large cities of the United States combined. New York is now the most sittable city in the country. But there have been other consequences not so good and some important warnings.

Incentive zoning has run into trouble. There has been considerable clamor from civic groups for a thorough overhaul of it, and the Planning Commission has been conducting a major study. Some of the issues raised concern matters of fact: the kind of buildings that incentive zoning has shaped and the effects on market values. But the most important ones are concerned with values: How big is too big? What is an hour of sunlight worth? Does the provision of one kind of amenity compensate for the loss of another?

On one point I feel quite certain. The crux is evaluation. If you are going to innovate, you had better be sure you check up on what you have done. You must go out and look—on the ground, on the street—to see what is working and what is not working. It is from want of this, I hope to demonstrate, that incentive zoning has taken some odd turns. And if there is to be redemption, it will be in the evaluation.

In its earliest form, zoning was tied to the provision of light. In eighteenth-century Paris, the height of buildings was limited to a multiple of the width of the streets—low on narrow streets, higher on wide streets. When New York City instituted zoning in 1916, the same principle was applied. As buildings went higher, they had to conform to a sky exposure plane, a specified angle slanting back from the street—sharply on narrow streets, less so on wide ones. When a building was set back enough so that the tower covered no more than a quarter of the lot, it could keep going straight up. A number of buildings did this, most spectacularly, the Empire State and the Chrysler buildings. But the more-customary result was the ziggurat, a building that looked like a series of successively smaller boxes put on top of one another.

By the late 1950s, it was evident that a comprehensive overhaul of the zoning code was badly needed. Over the years, it had gathered a host of exceptions and ad hoc provisions, in the process more than doubling in bulk. Most important, the zoning had been much too permissive on density. As sketches circulated by reform groups showed it, New York would be a solid mass of towers if building continued on to the legal limits. Clearly, some downzoning was in order.

The Planning Commission thought so and in the proposed new code sharply reduced the density to be allowed. It did this through the device of the floor-area ratio (f.a.r.). This was the multiplier the builder could apply to his lot size to get the total amount of space he could build. For commercial districts this was to be set at 15 f.a.r. This meant that a builder could put up the equivalent of fifteen stories the size of his site. He could mass them in a squat building or go up higher with smaller stories. Height and setback regulations were retained, but there were no height limitations. In practice, however, the f.a.r. did impose a ceiling. Towers can become uneconomic as they poke up higher and slimmer. Given the size of most office-building sites, somewhere around thirty to thirty-two stories is the practical limit for buildings of 15 f.a.r.

By eliminating the sky-is-the-limit feature of the old zoning, the f.a.r. greatly limited the theoretical bulk that could be put up in the city, but it would not unduly limit builders. Fifteen f.a.r. is a lot of building. Builders had been doing quite well putting up buildings of that size, and there was empirical justification for setting it as a limit. There was to be, furthermore, a sweetener. By downzoning, the planners had gained leverage to upzone, with strings.

They would do this with the incentive bonus. The first application would be for plazas. The planners had been much impressed by the plaza of the recently completed Seagram building. It was handsome, introduced lots of space and light, and made possible a sheer tower far more elegant than the old setback buildings. To prod builders into providing comparable spaces, they were offered a proposition: as a quid pro quo for a plaza, they could increase their total floor space by 20 percent, raising the f.a.r. from 15 to 18. Builders liked the idea. Many did not much like the zoning, and opposition was strong. But the bonus swung enough of them over to gain a critical margin of support.

There was one flaw, a philosophic one. The exception begged the question of the rule. If 15 f.a.r. was the right limit, how could 18 f.a.r. be? Did not the invitation to exceed the limit undercut the validity of it? Planners thought the answer was in the offset. They conceded that the extra density might be a disadvantage but believed that the amenity would compensate for it.

Others thought so too. Civic groups saw the 1961 zoning as a great forward step and were not inclined to nitpick over theoretical problems. Nor were the builders. Hailed on all sides, incentive zoning was off to a promising start.

Almost without exception, every builder who proceeded to put up a large office building took advantage of the bonus. This could have been viewed as an alert. When a building rents very easily, real estate people take it as a sign that they set the rents too low, and the Planning Commission might well have concluded that it had underpriced the bonus. There were some speculations to that effect, but the commission was not troubled. Even if it was giving builders perhaps a bit too much in extra bulk, what was more important was what it was getting from them for the public.

That is where the problem was: the plazas themselves. Most of the new ones were sterile, empty spaces that were not much use except for walking across. The lessons learned from them led to a stiffening of the plaza-zoning provisions, but this was to be a long time coming.

What had compounded the plaza problem was the inability of the planners to see that there was a problem. During the ten years after 1961 more new office space was constructed in New York City than in all the other cities of the country combined, and over a tenth of this space had plazas. During this time, the planners undertook no assessment of the plaza bonus or of the plazas themselves. They were busy forging new incentive bonuses and special districts zoning.

The Planning Commission had set up the Urban Design Group and spun off similar groups to work on midtown and downtown development. They were staffed with an outstanding group of young architects and lawyers, who went about their work with imagination and elan. I had an opportunity to appreciate this, for I was working at the time on drafting the text of the commission's plan for New York City. With some enthusiasm I prepared a section on the innovative work of the Urban Design Group and all the new amenities it was leading to.

But one thing puzzled me. In all that large staff, there was no one whose job it was to go out on the street and look. How were the plazas working? The new arcaded sidewalks? Checking these things out could greatly cut down the time lag between trial and lesson and would seem particularly important for urban design. In a preliminary draft of the plan, I proposed an investigative unit to do just that. There was no enthusiasm at all for the idea.

Several years later, with some foundation grants, I set up an independent research group, the Street Life Project, to do such evaluation. One of our first jobs was to study the use and nonuse of plazas. The commission chairman, Donald Elliott, agreed that our findings indicated an overhaul of the plaza zoning was in order. If we would come up with stiff guidelines, these would be written into the code.

Our findings were basically simple. The first, for example, was that people tend to sit most where there are places to sit. The recommendations eventually adopted were simple also: make the place sittable; relate it closely to the street; don't sink it or elevate more than a few feet; provide more trees on the street and within the space; provide food via kiosks, takeout windows, and the like; make the places easily accessible to the handicapped; require a performance bonus from the builder; make the optional provisions retroactive to existing plazas.[1]

Amendments to the zoning code were adopted in 1975. Since then there has been a marked improvement in plaza design. The guidelines did not at all limit architects as opponents charged they would. There has also been a rehabilitation of a number of previously dead spaces; a good example is the new open-air café of the plaza of the New York Telephone Company. The plaza standards were also useful in setting standards for interior spaces. The ratio for sitting space—1 linear foot for every 30 square feet of open space—has worked well as a minimum. So too has the provision for movable chairs, credited as two and a half feet of sitting space.

With plazas so much the rule, planners had become increasingly interested in other kinds of spaces that might provide bonuses—from sidewalk widenings to recessed, arcaded sidewalks, to shopping arcades within buildings, to through-block circulation areas. This progression from street to interior culminated in covered pedestrian areas, atriums and galleries that were hailed as a great forward step in urban design. The commission's heart seemed clearly in them.

Unhappily for the commission, two of these spaces failed, and very visibly. The builders pocketed the extra floors of rentable space but did not put the shops in the spaces that they said they would. The commission chastized the builders, but there was not much that it could do about it. When civic groups inquired, the commission would say that it was working on the problem.

Civic groups were also restive about the size of the buildings: they were getting bigger. An f.a.r. of 18 now was "as of right", and not a ceiling but a floor. With great ingenuity planners and builders combined different kinds of bonuses, air rights, and special district provisions to create super-buildings of up to 21.6 f.a.r. The elaborately detailed legislation made up for them would have been termed *spot zoning* in earlier days; now it was called *sophisticated zoning* or *fine tuning*.

In the late 1970s the process seemed to accelerate. To the dismay of community planning boards, a number of these superbuildings were launched one right after the other. Civic groups were now alarmed and called for a major overhaul of zoning and development policy. A defensive Planning Commission agreed, and with $100,000 in privately contributed funds commenced a study in early 1979.

The pace of building seemed to quicken. The tallest new one of them all was approved; then a number were announced for some of the few sites left on Third Avenue. One of them was for a structure squat and big that would cut off some of the key early-afternoon sunlight from the neighboring Greenacre Park. It would have this effect not by design but through sheer inadvertence. The planners did not know it would cut off the sunlight in that way and looked on those who warned that it would as adversaries. The commission approved the project.

It was a last straw for the community board people and the civic groups. To them the Planning Commission had become the adversary, more so than the builder. Before the final tribunal, the Board of Estimate, they asked that it overturn the Planning Commission's decision and deny the bonus for the extra bulk. In an unprecedented move, the board voted unanimously for a denial.

Why has incentive zoning come to this pass? There are several possible explanations. One, which might be termed the extremist position, is that incentive zoning is a bad idea bound to self-destruct. The moderate position is that the idea is a promising one that has been flawed in the application. Tightening up is in order; throwing the baby out with the bath is not.

I think the extremist position is the right one. Like many other people, I thought the flaws could be corrected, and I scanted the argument of those who warned about making rules to be broken, but they were right: the exceptions have been destroying the rules.

There are positive lessons to be learned, and not just for New York. The problems are writ large there because of its scale, but they of a kind that can affect planning bodies everywhere. On the positive side, incentive zoning has accomplished much. It has created a lot of open space that would not otherwise have been, and in the heart of the central business district. It has led to the creation of several excellent indoor spaces. One of them, Citicorp, is an outstanding popular success. And it has led to a marked improvement in the provision of simple amenities, from places to sit to public toilets in interior spaces.

The costs? Some critics of incentive zoning fasten on the value to the builders of the extra floor-space bonuses. It is very great—in the hundreds of millions. And the very alacrity with which builders seize the bonuses indicates that the city has been asking too little for what it has been getting in return. Worse, in cases where builders have not delivered the promised amenity, the city has complained and little more.

But the real cost of incentive zoning is the loss of amenities, especially in the loss of sun and light. It is a loss rarely counted. Planners' stock excuse is that there are so many shadows already, a few more floors here and there will not make much difference. But they do.

Fifteen f.a.r. is no magic figure, but it does seem a critical threshold in New York City. It is when buildings go beyond this—to 18 and 21.6 f.a.r.

and to forty, fifty, and sixty stories—that the shadows grow so big, and the abandonment of the old setback requirements almost guarantees darker streets. It is not only loss of direct sunlight that hurts but the loss of secondary light. For all practical purposes most of the light in midtown New York after 3 P.M. is reflected light, but nothing whatsoever in the zoning touches on this vital factor.

Do the amenities provided as bonuses offset this loss of light? It is hard to quantify the loss and assign it a value, but I believe it indicates that there is no fair offset. As a matter of logic, furthermore, could there be one? A particular amenity does not necessarily compensate for the effects of the extra bulk of a building. These effects and the amenity may be independent of each other. No matter how pleasant an atrium might be for those who use it, it does not itself temper the shadows cast by the extra bulk of the building, on the area to the north. By making the shadows possible, indeed, the bonus may do more harm to some people than it does good to others. And suppose it was not even a good atrium? The offset concept is a sloppy one, rather like robbing Peter to pay Paul but without conceding the robbery.

Another cost is the vitality of the street. The increasing trend to the bonusing of off-street spaces can siphon away activity from the street and internalize it in spaces that are legally public but not quite public. The effort to use through-block circulation areas as an alternative to streets is misguided. The through traffic in these corridors is only a fraction of that of the streets. People like the street, congested or not.

For future zoning policy I suggest the following for New York City. First, withdraw the incentive bonus for most of the kinds of spaces for which it has been given. An exception is the small, Paley-Greenacre type of park, either adjacent or off-site. These are a proven amenity, and satisfactory legislative guidelines are in hand. Second, reestablish an f.a.r. of 15 as the rule. Politically, this may be impossible now, and economically there is sure to be an outcry from real estate people that higher f.a.r.s are built into the price paid for sites. But a start has to be made somewhere, and at the very least the smaller-scale side streets should be downzoned.

I am not suggesting 15 f.a.r. as a happy mean. That is lot of bulk, and in other contexts it could be excessive. The general point I am making is that once you go beyond a certain limit by creating special exceptions, they become the rule, and you will have difficulty getting back to the old limit.

Third, mandate basic amenities. Instead of giving prizes to builders for doing what they ought to do, they should be required to do it. They will not be the worse for this effort. It costs no more to make a ledge low enough to sit on than one too high.

Fourth, establish new height and setback regulations incorporating the concept of the solar-zoning envelope. Much of the loss of sunlight is quite needless, even at current f.a.r.s. To judge by the setback patterns common in midtown Manhattan, you would deduce that the sun rises in the east and then traverses a full circle before returning to the east to set. But it doesn't; it sets in the west. Further research on such points is not needed. With available knowledge, we can develop zoning controls that recognize sun patterns and make the most of them. If, for example, the setbacks are sloped down toward the north, the amount of shadow cast by a building of a given bulk can be minimized. Similarly there are ways for maximizing the bounce light from buildings that can be so critical to the ambient light of an area. We ought to get busy on these matters.

Fifth, put a moratorium on the creation of any new special districts, ad hoc legislation for bonusing particular buildings, and similar exceptions that beggar the rule. (And stay away from the use of the euphemisms of *fine tuning* and *sophisticated* to describe them.)

Finally, evaluate. It sounds so obvious, so noncontroversial, but it is not being done, and this is the besetting problem of incentive zoning. What is needed is a systematic, full-time effort by the Planning Commission to look at what is working and what is not working.

Evaluation is needed elsewhere just as much. To my knowledge there is still no one in any U.S. planning commission who has the job of going out and looking. Consider the flowcharts so beloved by the profession. For all the to-do about feedback and phases and arrows pointing this way and that, there is not even a dotted line for going out and looking. There is no training in either architectural or planning schools for looking; there is no place for it in the tables of organization or in the administrative routine of our planning organizations. They are too busy for it.

Am I wrong? I conclude on the hopeful note that some of you will be able to show that I am on this charge quite wrong, and if not now, perhaps at a future congress.

Note

1. I have provided a detailed account of this in *The Social Life of Small Urban Spaces* (Washington, D.C.: Conservation Foundation, 1980).

**Part IV
Final Session**

Introduction to
Final Session

C. Lowell Harriss

C. Lowell Harriss: Over the world today, there are hundreds and hundreds of millions of people who are living better than their grandparents did. There are also many who are not living as well as they could. With the increasing population, the problems and the opportunities that will face us will be turned for better or for worse depending upon what human beings do. Of course, some things that happen are the result of nature—sun, wind, hurricanes, good climate—but virtually everything that is accomplished is accomplished by human beings acting with the resources that they have inherited from nature and from past accumulations, passing on to their successors the resources with which to work. Among these resources are land and the institutions or the ways in which land is used. In this regard, we come from many, many different areas, regions, cultures. We make different kinds of uses of the land. There are certain characteristics about land that require or call for special attention, different from other kinds of resources. One of these characteristics is the essential irreversibility of some decisions about land. Once a decision is made about how a certain area is going to be used, that decision will tend to commit the use for a substantial period, perhaps essentially forever, in an economic sense, or for substantially very long periods of time in the future. The right choice, to the extent we can make it, will mean a great deal not only for us but for our children and their children.

We face the problems and the opportunities of trying to learn what opportunities will be open and how we can make the best use of them. For such purposes, getting together on occasions like this will enable us to learn something about what has been done elsewhere. What has been done elsewhere is not necessarily the best or the worst for that particular culture. If it is good for them, it is not necessarily good for others, and vice versa. But there is a great opportunity to learn from such experiences.

Two issues seem to have received rather less attention than they should here. One of them is the discussion of what I would call the political process—government—as a way of human actions, as contrasted with market process. There are many things to be said about these often-contrasting and sometimes conflicting methods of organization, of trying to choose objectives, and decide then who is to carry out whatever the policies are, and toward what goals.

The other thing that, at least from an American perspective, seems to me to have deserved more attention is inflation. Within relatively few years in this country, the outlook toward the purchasing power of money, the worth of the dollar, has changed rather significantly, and I suggest that a great many problems associated with land and the use of land have been altered because of the changing attitudes toward inflation. Institutions that might have served us relatively well in the past must be reexamined in the light of an expectation that the purchasing power of money, the worth of the dollar, will not be stable, an assumption which, throughout much of our history, could have been made.

In closing these brief remarks, I think I should draw attention to a man whom I never had the pleasure of knowing, but who made this and many other things possible, John C. Lincoln. Mr. Lincoln was a creative businessman, an inventor of physical things and also of ways of operating business. His achievements over a long life were enormous. He started certain things, and as time passed he changed them. I think that he would take a great deal of pride in what has been happening with the Lincoln Institute; and this particular Congress is a result of all kinds of excursions, bringing a novel, creative assembly and use of resources.

Matthew Cullen: Before beginning the reports of the workshops, I would like to read a wire we have received from Patricia Harris, secretary of health and human services of the U.S. Government and the former secretary for housing and urban development, who we hoped would have been able to be here. Regrettably, she was not, and in lieu of that she has sent the following message:

> I regret that it was not possible for me to accept your invitation to come to Boston but I am pleased to have the opportunity to say a few words to you. Land policy is a subject of special interest to me and I am encouraged to know that such a distinguished group of representatives from nations in every part of the world has gathered to share information and plan strategy for the future.
>
> Here in the United States we are especially interested in land policy issues because we are witnessing a number of trends which have important implications for current and future land utilization. Decentralization of our population, the movement from the central city to suburban areas, and for more established regions like the Northeast and Sunbelt began after World War II and still continues. Furthermore, there is evidence that this trend is accelerating as people now move from metropolitan areas to rural ones. Several other developments are interacting with this trend, among them the increasing cost and diminishing availability of energy supplies and growing environmental concerns. These developments have resulted in a number of problems of special interest to those involved in land use policy. The increasing isolation of the poor in central city areas, energy-inefficient urban sprawl and pollution issues which are underscored by the fact that every city east of the Mississippi River has an air quality problem. As you well know, these problems are complex. They lend themselves to neither simple nor im-

mediate solutions. Still, it is important that we make every effort to sort out priorities and develop a clear and workable strategy.

While I was Secretary of Housing and Urban Development I chaired the Urban and Regional Policy Planning Group which produced the first President's Urban Policy Biennial Report in 1978. The 1980 Report is soon to be forwarded to the Congress and while it contains much new material, its central focus remains the same: the need to promote an energy-efficient, environmentally sound land development pattern for this country. This will require the active participation of federal, state and local officials, as well as experts and interested parties in the private sector. And HUD has established an advisory group so constituted to help establish priorities and strategy. One key element of our policy must be a thorough evaluation of the effect that all federal programs have on land policy and we have begun that task under an Executive Order signed by the President. Our nation has long understood the value of land resources. Historian Bruce Cabot, describing the pioneers who once settled the New World once wrote, "Probably no single word had more importance on revealing connotations than the word land. Land was talisman, polestar, magnet, key, the ultimate social security, in every sense of that phrase." The same holds true for us today, except that land is even more precious and its proper utilization is even more important. As I said at the outset, this is a complex subject, but a critically important one which we must not be afraid to tackle. I congratulate you on your work, and best of luck as you return home.

19

Workshop Reports

Adrian Flatt,
Neal Roberts,
Pierre Laconte,
Joan Youngman,
Fran Hosken,
Darshan Johal,
David Gouveneur,
Marsha Goldberg, and
Herman Felstehausen

Workshop I: Achieving Effective Systems
of Land Cadastres, Evaluation, and Title Registration

Adrian Flatt: The first task of this workshop was to unscramble the jargon in our title. We found that there were many different interpretations of the word *cadastre*. One participant referred the question to his wife who came up with perhaps the most plausible definition: "A cadastre is halfway between a catastophe and a disaster."

The premise of the workshop is that land-information systems are a necessary prerequisite for the development, implementation, and assessment of land policy. This has been reinforced by a sense of urgency expressed at this conference with respect to land-price monitoring, an important output of the land-information system. Our discussion focused upon the parcel-based cadastre, which like the geographically referenced cadastre, is only one of many kinds of land-information systems.

A precondition for implementation of an effective multipurpose cadastre is a certain method of identification of land parcels. As such, analysis of the base of the land-information system reveals its fundamental parts: the reference base which is a measure of the land, the map base which is representative of the land, and the cadastral overlay. This three-part base is connected by a series of linkage mechanisms to many files of information, such as title of the land, its value, administration, infrastructure, environment, and other aspects. These files of information provide the multipurpose utility of the cadastre.

There are two general categories of criteria for establishing the effectiveness of land-information systems. We must consider first the needs for an assessment of the system such as the user community, including the important and often-overlooked constituency of the general public, the types of information that should be assembled, the quality of information, and

329

implementation priorities. Second, we must consider the responses of those needs, including not only the system's design implementation and evaluation but also its technological assessment and socioeconomic impact.

The participants subscribed to the notion of the value of a multipurpose information system whose implementation might best be achieved by federal jurisdictions, which would devise strategies appropriate to their unique sociopolitical conditions, especially where a division of power exists. In nations such as Swaziland, a national strategy could be formulated to execute cadastre implementation. In developing countries, it might be a more advantageous stage right now to think about implementing land-information systems. In nations such as the United States, implementation of such systems may depend upon local governments aided by fiscal inducements.

The case of Tegucigalpa, Honduras, illustrates the effectiveness of the land cadastre in achieving multipurpose benefits such as infrastructure improvements and an expanded tax base as by-products of a system originally designed for title registration.

Workshop 2: Public-Land Ownership

Neal Roberts: In the "Financial Resources" workshop, Bill Doebele was talking about how Third World countries can approach the problem of development. He said there are various ways to study it: you might look at special assessment taxation districts, and then he described readjustment districts, or you might just have the cities own the land. What struck me about this is that the basic problems in each of the workshops tended to overlap: the basic problems of cities expanding.

In our seminar we concentrated on the use of government ownership to allocate land use and integrate public infrastructure with various other uses. The workshop concentrated on the use of ownership in the process of urbanization rather than either rural or preservation context. The case studies provided the participants in the workshop with a variety of examples of ownership mechanisms, and these laid the foundation for a rather spirited, some would say ideological, debate on the subjects of why a government should ever own land, how good a land manager a government is, and whether a government should pay property or other taxes on the land it owns.

Our first speaker, Peter Heimbürger, describing the Swedish use of ownership to coordinate urbanization, accented how well it works in Sweden and also showed how hard it might be to replicate it in other settings. He highlighted the historical development of the widespread use of public ownership and briefly showed how thoroughly the tool is integrated with other national and local policies. His paper concentrated on the experience of Stockholm, which has purchased large amounts of land out-side its own boundaries. He also pointed out that the municipal govern-ments did not expect the economic and demographic changes of the 1970s, which resulted in the production of too many of the wrong type of housing structures—high-rise flats. That's not to say that it's not working in Sweden or Stockholm but rather that, even with the best of well-laid plans, it doesn't quite come out the way you might hope it would. Professor Heim-bürger was an advocate of this type of approach but stressed that to be ef-fective, public ownership must be developed at the local level by govern-ments that have adequate financial resources, the ability to hold land for long time periods, that buy early before urbanization, and that coordinate the purchase with adequate regulatory powers. So it's not just one tool, but is a combination of tools directed toward this expansion.

Our second speaker, Professor Janic, described the land market in the socialist country of Yugoslavia and detailed his methods of studying that market. Even in a country with wide-ranging ownership powers, it was shown that many of the same problems of urbanization still exist with an in-adequate coordination of uses throughout the city.

Professor Tempia dealt with France's use of the public-ownership tool to create new development. This has been accomplished through a series of land agencies and new-town development corporations. Professor Tempia stressed that the experience with the tool varied widely and depended a great deal upon local politics. While there have been numerous examples of land agencies developing and urbanizing land, there are also many cases where the land purchased was not put to its intended use. This was usually the result of conflict or lack of coordination between the land-buying agency and the land-planning agency, causing arguments about whether they wanted housing or industry. He also pointed out that the financial base of the French municipalities made large-scale purchasing sometimes quite a problem. Other members of the French delegation disputed Professor Tempia's conclusions that land agencies have much of a role to play, so there is never only one view. In any event, we see from the French experience that there is that tool, which is looked at as just one of many. A varied group of land-allocation mechanisms is present there.

The final paper, delivered by Joan Towles, dealt with the U.S. federal government's ownership of land, its ability to manage that resource effec-tively, and the question of whether the government should pay local property taxes. She described the large amount of land in public ownership (nearly a third) and then made a strong case for the imposition of property taxes on federal land. This would both be fairer to local taxpayers in jurisdictions with large amounts of land and would result in better land management by the federal government. Ms. Towles implied that the federal government is not an effective manager. One of the problems is that it lacks an internalized accounting system to determine whether a good piece of land is being wasted or a bad piece of land is being put to intensive use. The fifty-five ad hoc systems of payments in lieu of taxes were described as being inadequate.

After these papers, debate focused on whether the government should ever own land in the first place or intervene in the private market. The various commentators stressed that the public sector makes mistakes and that planners do not have adequate information to make all of the allocative decisions. The use of charges or tax payments on government owners was advocated as a means of forcing some type of accounting system on those governments. Similarly, the use of nonmarket disposition mechanisms, such as queues or rationing, was said to be ineffective. Critics pointed to the misallocation in Stockholm, the lack of coordination between purchase plans in France, and the mismanagement of U.S. public lands as examples of public inefficiency.

Advocates of public ownership or government intervention stressed that ownership gives timing control, as well as negative controls against bad development. They said that private markets are not very good at allocating uses in urban areas, particularly when the government owns much of the public roadways and infrastructure and and must provide many services. There was also stress put on the fact that at least if you have ownership, you don't have an unearned increment problem. If there is increase in value because of urbanization, the government will get some large part of that by simply owning that land.

Various members of the audience then contrasted ownership with other tools such as regulation or the use of site-value taxation. Critics of public ownership gave numerous examples of public owners' leaving land vacant and unproductive. The advocates of ownership cited the similar misallocation that occurs in the private market.

So by the end of the day, what we had seen is that there is a tool there; it can be used in a variety of circumstances; and underlying the use of that tool is very much an ideological debate: what role the government should play. Finally, members of the workshop agreed that the problem that should be looked at is one of land use. Once that has been clearly focused on, then ownership is one of the tools to deal with that problem.

Workshop 3: Public-Private Codevelopment

Pierre Laconte: The workshop concentrated on the definition of public-private codevelopment: where there is an input by the public authorities and an input from the private sector to achieve some planning goals. It was examined in several industrial free-market economies.

First we saw a case from France. Professor de Lanversin told us that codevelopment takes place within the framework of overall planning in France. The framework consists of structure or area plans (*schema directeur*), where the authorities project the future urbanization at regional scale, and the detailed zoning plans (*plans d'occupation des sols*). He explained, using an interesting case study, how development was achieved by a joint effort of developers and the municipality in order to achieve a planned unit development. The overall lesson that came out of the case was that codevelopment had been a tool for developers and builders to get land below the market price and achieve their project with the help of the public authorities.

Then we came to a case in Germany. Professor Seele gave us an account of a system that was widely different from all the others shown in the workshop. In the German system, the municipalities act as a kind of middleman between the different small owners of plots of land in order to make a reallotment, a redistribution of land, without resorting to extreme public interventions such as expropriation. He showed that the elaborate system of assessment of land pieces enables the German municipalities to calculate exactly how much each plot is worth at market price before development and make a comparison between that value and the value it would have at the same time if development or resubdivision had occurred. Thus each owner is assured that the share of land he gives to the subdivision will be compensated adequately in terms of money or of land (sometimes the land owned is the same, before and after) so that there would be no undue benefits and no undue loss, no windfall and no wipeout, in the process. The end product allows everybody to gain because the new subdivision has more value than the old one. His case showed the example of a capitalist country where the municipalities initiate and direct the development process.

Then we came to the case of Mexico. Mr. Gonzales is the head of MetroNet, a wholly owned subsidiary of the City of Mexico, which is in charge of a certain number of actions where it makes agreements with private landowners, private developers, in order to come to a kind of mixed economic cooperation. He gave a number of examples of how it works and how it allows the developer and the municipality to collaborate in order to take best advantage of existing land in order to create new urban development and new values.

Next was the presentation from England, which went very much along the same lines as the presentation from France. Mr. Smith indicated that codevelopment between municipalities and developers is usually a means by which the municipality helps put some land into a process by which new development can occur, new taxes can be generated, and development profits can be made. Most often the initiative comes from the developer, but on a few occasions the initiation of the process comes actually from the municipality. Mr. Smith used the example of Norwich, where the whole codevelopment was generated by the municipality in a spirit of urban rehabilitation.

Then, finally, I said a few words about a case in Belgium, where I have been personally involved. The Catholic University of Louvain was able to acquire two thousand acres and used that capital to develop a new university town. Therefore the university has played the development game in a way that is very close to private development but has used a certain number of specific techniques. For example, the land is not sold but leased on a ninety-nine-year basis. The rent is revised yearly according to the rate of inflation. The lease includes the right to the acquirer of the lease to sell it, with the guarantee that in that case the lease could start again from zero, which brings a solution to the problem of having all the leases finishing at the same time. Another technique consists of selling development rights for a specific amount of floor space, which avoids later discussion about increases of floor area ratio under pressure of the developer.

Public-private codevelopment seems to be an interesting technique, as long as the public authorities (or institutions of a similar nature) are fully schooled in the market-analysis technique and expertise. On the other hand, in assessing codevelopment one should never forget the balance between the three kinds of forces at play: the private sector, which wants to maximize its profits; the elected officials, who seek to increase their constituency before the next election and think in the short term; and the bureaucrats, who patiently build up their imperium, increase their budgets, and work in a long-term perspective. Codevelopment has to be assessed in that perspective.

Workshop 4: Property Taxation Measures

Joan Youngman: The workshop began with the most general issues concerning what rationale there is for a property tax at all, with some participants taking the view that it should be limited simply to a revenue-raising device and all attempts at further reform concentrated on improving its administration. In favor of this position, it was pointed out that the tax is uniformly imposed at low effective rates, even in a progressive system such as Jamaica's (merely being 1 to 4.5 percent of site value itself, just a fractional part of total capital value), that any attempt to raise the rates to the point of actually influencing taxpayer behavior, which one participant estimated would require 4 to 5 percent of the capital value annually, would be very dangerous in such a poorly administered tax, since undoubtedly there would be some taxpayers suffering under much higher effective rates and other ones enjoying much lower. Finally, the continuing uncertainty surrounding the incidence in the tax raised doubts about its effectiveness as an incentive to taxpayer behavior or as a tool for the redistribution of wealth. However, the great interest evoked by discussion of the French PLD (legal ceiling of density), a confiscatory tax upon development, on construction of buildings above a 1 to 1.5 floor area ratio, and discussion of the site-value tax indicated that there was no consensus that property tax should remain merely a revenue-raising device.

The same need to define the goals of the property tax surfaced again in the discussion of valorization charges and deferred special assessment, with controversy arising as to whether these charges should seek only to recover the costs of public improvements or should attempt to recapture a greater part or even the whole of the betterment enjoyed by the landowner.

The internal inconsistencies found within the property tax and also between the tax and other land-use measures figured in discussion of its appropriateness as a planning device. For example, the inconsistency between a progressive rate structure and special benefits for owner-occupied housing was criticized, as was the similar inconsistency between progressive structures and numerous exemptions, which have, in Jamaica, lost approximately half of the total tax base.

A discussion of the PLD pointed up numerous instances in which tax and zoning measures work at cross-purposes, as would, for example, the PLD itself, which seeks to penalize incentive developments of land, and site valuation which attempts to encourage it. These considerations simply reinforced the first point under discussion: the need to have clearly stated goals for the tax before any evaluation of its workings.

Discussion of the various forms of property taxation identified a number of elements that serve as limiting factors to its ideal operation. For example, taxpayer resistance to paying a cash levy upon real property with the attendant hardship upon widows and orphans and the need to break up family estates was apparently a factor in the recent retirement of all Australian estate and gift taxes. This highlights the problem of liquidity from the taxpayer's point of view and the need to consider new solutions, such as the proposal for deferred special assessment where assessment covering the cost of public improvements would be deferred, with interest accumulating at a floating market rate until sale of the property.

The Jamaican experience suggested another limiting factor in imposition of site-value taxation upon an economy already enjoying a certain level of development. Costly improvements were seen there to belong to high-income taxpayers and also to go untaxed, limiting public acceptance of the whole scheme. However, Jamaica's recent history also demonstrated the benefits attendant upon removing the most-common limiting factor: that of poor administration. Administrative problems concerning collection of the tax and accounting for inflation and interest, as well, appear to be the only factors limiting further success of the already successful system of valorization charges in Colombia.

A number of points in all of the discussions brought up the wisdom of occasionally settling for half a loaf rather than pursuing a tax scheme to its most theoretically satisfying resolution. The Australian estate and gift tax, which was recently repealed, for example, was vigorously progressive, even to the point of aggregating all real property owned by a single family throughout the entire country. The fate of this system might give pause to those commentators who criticized the Jamaican scheme, which refuses to aggregate any but contiguous parcels of property belonging to the same landowner. Even those measures that have been taken in Jamaica over the past six years, since introduction of site-value taxation to attempt to form a comprehensive rate base, have provoked such taxpayer protests as to require enormous exemptions and concessions from the government. Again, the success of the valorization charges in Colombia was attributed in part by some of the speakers to the willingness of the government simply to settle for recovering the costs of the project, and sometimes not even all of that, rather than to go for the entire unearned increment enjoyed by all of the landowners.

This discussion in the workshop identified a number of areas clearly of interest for further study. The participants were greatly interested in the Colombian experience and the special factors there that might have contributed to its success. Similarly the deferred special assessment was recognized as worthy of further inquiry to determine its general feasibility, especially in areas of low property turnover. Los Angeles was the example under discussion as a hypothetical setting that has very high turnover. Again, the problem for deferred special assessment of property under institutional ownership was pointed out, which might not change hands in a lifetime or even longer.

The presentation on site valuation in Jamaica pointed out the need for study to distinguish which effects have been due to the introduction of that tax and which have been due to the simultaneous economic upheaval over the past six years, stemming from the increase of oil prices. Questions arose, again, as to property-tax efficiency, discussions of its responsiveness to changes in income and price levels, and the effect of introducing accurate valuation in assessment. And finally, a very lively discussion of the PLD, which was in itself the topic of a presentation to the workshop, showed a great interest in examining what the manifold goals of this measure were, both for raising revenue and for regulating development; and evaluations of its success, which appear to be as varied as the goals.

Workshop 5: Women, Land Use, and Urbanization

Fran Hosken: We were very glad to have the opportunity to bring together several women from very different areas and from many different professional experiences to talk together about the basic problems that women face in the whole area of land and urban development and access to land. Our discussions were concerned primarily with the constraints that face women in gaining access to land use and property rights in both rural and urban areas and the effects of worldwide urbanization on women's lives as well as how women influence and contribute to urban development. To have a significant impact in these areas, women have to be there. Experience shows they are not. We are not participating actively anywhere in the land market or in the urban market as property owners, as active economic participants. Therefore the panel was concerned, first of all, with how women can participate more actively. It was also discussed that a large number of women are anxious, able, and willing to participate, but they have been ignored; they have been left out by legislation, very largely, in many countries. Therefore, our concern was to look at the constraints that women face in the legal systems all over the world that restrict their access to property.

I would like to present the summary, starting with the proposals for immediate action made by the group jointly, and then I will summarize the different contributions. It was difficult to come to a unified conclusion because we were people from very different experiences and very different professional areas. We therefore jointly pooled our experiences, our interests, and our professional capabilities to develop a proposal for immediate action, and since the Lincoln Institute urged that positive suggestions be made, we defined the development of an international advisory council on women and land policy, that such a council should be established. This advisory council will be available for advice and consultation in all areas of land policies and problems in order to achieve the overall objectives and effectiveness of the Institute and Centre: to suggest curricula changes, to recommend women participants as teaching faculty, to foster researchers, and to suggest research requirements and publication topics related to women. More and more women are becoming aware that access to land and property ownership is essential.

We also outlined a proposal, a world review of women's property rights and their relation to land policy, to make this study, a series of monographs. Since women are increasingly the sole source of economic support for themselves and their children, security of tenure is essential for the mobilization of capital. Persons who do not have security of tenure either through fee ownership, tenancy contracts, or land-use rights in collective schemes are unable to obtain credit. In rural developing economies, the inability to obtain credit for agricultural inputs results in less-productive farmland. In most parts of the world, women are engaged in food growing. Up to 80 percent, for instance, of the food grown in Africa, according to statistics of the Economic Commission of Africa, is grown by women. Unfortunately, they don't have access to modernization; they don't own the land that they till; and they aren't able to produce food in adequate amounts. Many of the food shortages, in Africa recently and in formerly self-sufficient countries, can be directly related to the failure of providing women access to modern technology.

It is known that laws exist that prevent women from obtaining security of tenure in property, but surveys of the literature in the fields of development and comparative law indicate that there is no coordinated information on women's property rights.

We suggested some specific areas to be studied. Women's property rights are frequently embodied in the following areas of the law: customary land tenure; marriage and family law, both customary and statutory; wills and intestate succession; and so on. A book, *Law and the Status of Women,* looks into the legal situation as far as women are concerned, in a very broad sense, in fifteen countries. We are suggesting that a similar monograph be developed with the assistance of the Lincoln Institute. It should start with a feasibility study on women and property rights, a completely neglected field. The sponsorship of the feasibility study by the Lincoln Institute of Land Policy in consultation with Women's International Network is sought. Sufficient funds for a feasibility study are requested to be used to hire a consultant to prepare a study of a detailed project proposal. The consultant shall develop the methodology and format of the individual studies and select the countries to be studied in terms of getting a diversity of experience. Such a study is long overdue.

The papers examined a wide range of experience—from rural to urban, from the developing world to the industrial world in the United States. Lisa Bennett discussed access to land and other income-producing property. Mangalam Srinivasan discussed rural employment and the relationship to world systems that eliminate women from active participation; as a result, land is less productive. Mary Racelis Hollnsteiner discussed the neighborhood developments, with examples particularly from the Philippines. The first two speakers used examples worldwide, though primarily from Asia. Hollnsteiner used examples from the Philippines to involve women in decision making on the community level and to mobilize women's participation in community development since women have the most experience in this area. Nellie Garcia Bellizzia talked about the experience in Mexico City, particularly of women immigrants in the urban areas whose experience in terms of learning modernization is far more valid than that of their male counterparts. Barbara Flint provided a historic overview of urbanization in the nineteenth century in the United States and the contributions that women made to this area. Tila Maria de Hancock talked about the present-day situation—the increasing number of women-headed households and how women are increasingly participating in the land market.

Although in the United States there are no longer formal barriers to women's acquisition of property and credit, numerous informal barriers and social conventions are still in place. The Department of Housing and Urban Development, despite the lack of any formal barriers, finds it necessary to start a country-wide campaign to eliminate the customary barriers, which are still very much in existence. The important issue is that women increasingly are heads of households in all societies. Certainly the statistics in the United States show that women heads of households have increased. And this trend, I think, is worldwide.

**Workshop 6: Physical Planning Measures to
Control the Land Market**

Darshan Johal: The workshop on physical planning measures had seventy-five participants; six case studies were presented. The workshop concluded that physical planning measures can contribute to increasing the supply of available land, help control excessive increases in land prices, recover to the public those portions of land values that may be said to be socially created, and increase accessibility to land as a means of production, provided that these measures are accompanied by other complementary measures and instruments.

Bearing in mind the recommendations of Habitat, the United Nations Conference on Human Settlements held in Vancouver in 1976, the following key issues were identified:

1. Development of a rational system of human settlements on a country-wide basis.
2. Integration of physical planning with other sectoral policies and plans.
3. Restructuring existing spatial and land-use patterns to meet present and future needs.
4. Development of procedures, practices, and standards that would contribute to human settlement development, particularly by making maximum use of local materials, human resources, and technologies.
5. Addressing the tragic situation of millions of people living in urban slum and squatter areas and in rural settlements.

The workshop emphasized the need for action and implementation, based on a realistic assessment of the needs, resources, and objectives of each country or region. It also stressed the need for international assistance to developing countries in the field of physical planning in relation to land policy, through technical assistance, research and development, training, and exchange of information.

Various physical planning measures were highlighted in the discussions. These are not necessarily the most important ones, but these are the ones that were discussed in the case studies. First is national physical planning. This was particularly highlighted in the presentation of the Netherlands experience. In the Netherlands, physical planning measures are applied at different spatial levels and in different degrees of detail. First, there is the national physical planning framework; at the second level, there are the regional development plans; the third level is municipal structural plans; fourth is the local allocation plan; and fifth, the site building plans as well as appropriate building regulations and physical planning procedures. In this case the need was also stated that physical planning should reflect community values and aspirations and allow for full public participation in the formulation and implementation of plans and measures.

The second instrument, which was discussed in the context of the experience in Delhi, is the master plan. The case study showed that it should address key social, economic, and environmental objectives. It should include safeguards against prolonged land-acquisition procedures and other abuses that are encountered in trying to implement the master plan. Land policy provisions of a master plan may be implemented by bringing under public ownership the entire land in the urban region, disposal of land on a leasehold basis, and sale of residential plots.

The next instrument that was mentioned is zoning laws, particularly in the case of São Paulo, Brazil. It was concluded that zoning should be based on performance rather than specification standards, and it should allow for full public participation.

The next instrument is land-use ordinances and fees. These were discussed in the context of the German Democratic Republic. Land-use ordinances and fees should be based not only on ideological but also on sound economic and social principles to be effective. They should be enforced fairly and provide adequate incentives or penalties to facilitate the desired pattern of land use.

The fifth case study discussed urban land ceiling as a physical planning measure. Here it was stated that it can be used to facilitate public land acquisition, regulate building construction, prevent concentration of urban land in the hands of a few persons, and bring about a more-equitable distribution of land in human settlements. It was concluded that the instrument of land ceiling is relatively simple, but it is difficult to implement due to the complexity of procedures, legislative loopholes, and susceptibility to evasion by ingenious persons.

Finally, the sixth case study, on Yugoslavia, mentioned the planned-development-districts approach. It was emphasized that this would require a multidisciplinary planning team; it should be used to improve adjacent areas, in addition to the district being planned; and it requires special attention to be paid to the integration of transportation networks with land use.

Workshop 7: Financial and Credit Interventions (Other than Taxation)

David Gouveneur: The first thing we did in workshop 7 was change the title to "Unconventional Methods for Land Development." The problem we came up with, which I think was common to the other workshops, was that we had fascinating presentations of different cases that had nothing to do one with another. But we tried to give them some common lines.

The general concern was to explore ingenious mechanisms to capture surplus value or to reduce the need for taxation or government finance in guiding high-quality land development; to address the issues of financial and credit interventions available to public institutions, which have the burden of solving the ever-growing problems with limited resources. We are dealing with municipalities and governments that are broke or have limited resources. Sometimes they gear to projects that have very little impact with a certain portion of the population, and many times the projects are not self-financing because there are no mechanisms for reinvesting.

Most of the policies discussed, which have been successfully implemented, were concerned with the process of incorporation of fringe land, rural land to urban development, and in one case, the development of a new city. Less work appears to have been done in policies concerning urban land. There is very little information as well on informal-sector financial and credit mechanisms.

The first case study was by Songman Lee from the Korea Land Development Corporation and showed situations where it's easier to use eminent domain to expropriate parcels to assemble larger parcels. They dedicate 30 percent of the parcel for public use, and 35 percent of it may be sold on the market, which is booming because of the high demand for housing by the public and private sectors. This quick cash obtained from the public sector is used to finance the other 35 percent for development of public housing. Thus it's a quick cost-subsidy mechanism.

The next case, presented by Professor Doebele, discussed a mechanism used in Korea, Japan, and Australia, called readjustment. The readjustment mechanism consists of the self-financing of urban development by making a public agency (such as the Korea Land Development Corporation) a codeveloper, taking a part of the land to be sold to pay costs of providing services. First, the fringe areas are selected, taking into account the availability of trunk infrastructure and the site potentials. The land is divided without charge by the original owners (farmers of paddy fields, for instance); then estimates are made of the percentage of land required for public facilities, like roads and schools. The expected value of the remaining serviced land is estimated, as well as the cost of providing the public services. Finally, the land is partially returned for public use, with a further deduction equivalent in value to the cost of providing the services. This amount, usually of returned land, is about two-thirds of the original parcels. So they give back less land, but now serviced land, to be used for urban development.

Another very interesting case was presented by Roque Gonzales on Cuautitlan Izcalli, a new city directed to ease pressures on the over-congested, ever-growing metropolitan Mexico City region. The city was designed for 1.6 million people; so far it has over 300,000. It began with a loan from the government of around $12 million. The idea was to buy a particular zone of the entire area (they could not buy the entire area) and then guide by physical organization, by physical design, the activities concentrated in such a way that the high commercial activities would locate exactly over the land that belonged to the government. By selling this land and creating plus value by the infrastructure, they were able to subsidize public housing, create centers for industrial development, and expand the scheme of acquiring further land. The interesting thing here was the physical planning, the physical organization mechanism as a base for the financial mechanism.

The case of Egypt, presented by Philippe Annez, contrasted the amount of housing built by the formal sector in Egypt, especially in the Cairo region, with the estimates that are provided officially by the government. It was a total disproportion; only a small percentage was actually reported to the government. As well, there was no awareness of the actual amount of credit available in the informal sector. He suggested that a lot of studies had to be made in this respect in order to guide financial mechanisms that would really help the bulk of the population. One of the issues that was brought up then was that if, without control or recognition by the government, this informal market was able to produce housing, which was far away from being inadequate, then why should there be intervention at all? On the other hand, Mr. Annez mentioned the idea of gradual legalization of the informal sector, which would reach a point of stability in which they could contribute to the city in taxation or other ways.

Finally, in a completely different environment, Adrian Walter spoke about Cuba where the government policy is to deurbanize cities and urbanize the countryside in order to discourage migration from rural areas to Havana, a difficult-climate, congested city. The interesting mechanism they use is the microbrigades, a group of people who work in industrial units or in agricultural units and take time off from their regular jobs to help in the construction of housing. Most of the land in Cuba is government owned, of course; it's all public housing. These workers who take off from their regular jobs keep receiving their regular wages, and their fellow workers just speed up to compensate for their loss. Thus housing is provided without a whole financial structure supporting it.

**Workshop 8: Institutional Factors: Problems of
Land-Use Legislation, Adequacy of Jurisdictional
Boundaries, Unrealistic Ceilings (Standards for
Housing and Subdivision), and so on**

Marsha Goldberg: Workshop 8, in which five papers were presented, was
initially titled, "Institutional Factors: Problems of Land-Use Legislation,
Jurisdictional Boundaries, Standards for Housing and Subdivisions, etc."
You can see it's a sort of a catch-all topic, and the papers presented were
very disparate, dealing with different parts of the world, different problems. There was no one technique or one approach with which we could
link everything together. Listening to the papers at the session, it became
clear that it might have been better to entitle the session "Institutional
Limiters to Land-Use Policies and Techniques" because the case studies
presented, sort of contrary to our hopes, did not give any glowing success
stories. Rather, they presented attempts at using different types of land-
development techniques and the constraints on their success.

The overall feeling from these papers was that although a technique
may be appropriate in one context, it must be translated very carefully in
other contexts. And many times, wholesale adaptation leads to disaster. A
corollary is that in developing policies or using techniques, flexibility is
essential. You have to be sensitive to what resources are available and what
constraints are apparent and adapt a policy. Professional or academic
niceties are really wasted on some of this; what works is the idea. That it's
not sophisticated or neat isn't the issue, and one shouldn't be concerned
with that.

This sort of concern with sensitivity to environment also applies to looking at standard analytical techniques or neoclassical economic models. You
have to be aware of the environment before you just go in and look at
standard market analysis. There were no truly positive case studies, but the
information gained underlined the need for sensitivity in developing policies
or techniques. The five case studies were primarily from Asia, but there was
a wide range of different types of techniques.

Professor Berry gave a brief discussion of four or five case studies of
public-works investments strategies in Indonesia, particularly focusing on
water-supply systems. He started by saying that after independence in
Indonesia, the administrative system was somewhat weak, and there was a
need for outside help in developing water-supply systems. Because of this
dependence on outside consultants and outside lending institutions, he
perceived that some problems arose in the types of systems that were
developed: the priorities of the helpers were not totally consistent with the
priorities of the country that invited them, and there seemed to be a favoring of large-scale projects that were technologically rather intense or

sophisticated and didn't totally serve the needs of the countries paying for them. Consequently, in setting standards for the development of systems in developing countries, there has to be a sensitivity to appropriate needs, the life-styles of the people involved, and the resources involved in order to have something that's compatible with the country in which the system is being located. This was the first warning to beware of wholesale adoption of systems. They don't work and they often cause problems.

This was somewhat reinforced by the paper by Professor Mandelker, who looked at land-use controls in Hawaii and the Soviet Union. There appear to be some similarities in the land-use-control systems in that both are very centralized with a powerful central government: the government in Hawaii and the national government in the Soviet Union. However, he said to beware of importing either capitalist or socialist systems because they may not work even within the context of their own environment. Both systems that were described have problems with conflicts between jurisdictions, and the conflicts cause some chaos in the allocation of land use or the implementation of rather complicated land-use-control systems.

In Hawaii, the state has developed a comprehensive land-use plan; there are several land-use regions and the state government has parceled out responsibilities over the state of Hawaii. However, local decisions made by counties often come in conflict with the state and are able to stop the state from controlling the development in the areas that they want. Frequently there have been deadlock situations where neither the state nor the county can do anything effective. Hence, a rather interesting system for land-use control has had problems in implementation due to jurisdictional problems.

In the Soviet Union it's somewhat similar. There are four levels of planning: the national, the public, the regional, and the local. The Soviet system is one of subordination, where the higher system takes precedence. There is one perturbation to this system in the sense that large industries, which are national-priority industries, can override local planning decisions and locate where they want. They also have the authority to build housing and provide infrastructure for their workers, which means that frequently in one city, if there are several large industries, there are several sets of houses, schools, and sewer systems provided by the industries, which are duplicative and often in conflict with the plans of the local system. So again you have jurisdictional problems here or administrative problems. Even though both systems are supposedly highly centralized, plans cannot be implemented without significant distortion.

Graciella Flores presented an interesting institutional problem. It is a historical study of Mérida, Venezuela, where land was controlled for over four hundred years by eight families. There were eight large haciendas, and through intermarriage they amassed large amounts of land, and various members of the families became prominent in national and local government.

There was a sort of synergistic effect that was possible to trace in some cases; infrastructure benefits were granted to various families because of their position in the national government. But the effect of this sort of procedure was to withhold land from general development. Various types of controls couldn't touch this land because of the close family connections, the connections of the families with the government, and the central hierarchy. Eventually, with the oil boom, much of the land was sold off so the money could be invested in other forms of capital, and pent-up demand could be determined by the speed with which the land was bought by other people. So apparently it was difficult to determine whether this successful withholding had an effect on price, but obviously it did. The families controlled how the land was used and the price.

Shlomo Angel talked about land tenure for the urban poor in several Asian countries. This is particularly interesting because of the growth of interest in land tenure for the poor, in the squatter settlements that have come up, and the increasing granting of land tenure to people in urban areas. He pointed out several lessons that could be learned from its application. He perceived a connection between housing improvement and security of tenure. People with tenure were more interested in upgrading their housing, which benefited the urban area. He did note that without security of tenure, even improvements in infrastructure had little effect on housing; that you could provide sewers and things of that sort, but without land-tenure security, people really still had no interest in upgrading. However, and this is where some of these cultural institutional factors come in, granting tenure alone is not sufficient to ensure housing improvement. There are issues of people being too poor to upgrade their homes, or there is a cultural indifference to doing this sort of thing. Even in different countries, different groups have different work ethics or home-improvement ethics, so it doesn't matter if they have money or own the land; they really don't want to spend their money on home improvement. So you can't just grant land tenure in a wholesale way and expect squatter settlements to be upgraded. There has to be a sensitivity to the cultural values, to the socioeconomic values of a country, before this sort of policy can work.

Finally, Max Falque presented some new techniques for land use and land control for agricultural preservation. Many times, in an effort to increase agricultural production, we end up destroying the land that we are trying to save. He has proposed two techniques that are linked with granting money to farmers to improve production. One is an environmental-impact-statement concept where people, when they apply for money, will also have to provide some sort of environmental assessment. In this way the state, in granting the money, can decide where it would like to take easements in exchange for better credit terms for the farmer. The second technique is irrigation, but frequently, by increasing irrigation you encourage urban development, which destroys the land that you are trying to save. In this situation, again, in exchange for free irrigation or low-cost irrigation, you will be given some sort of credit benefits and you provide an easement to the government, which will hold the land in agricultural use.

Workshop 9: Rural Workshop: Agricultural Land Policy; Legislation and Implementation Issues

Herman Felstehausen: We have been somewhat distressed, particularly in our discussions through the Land Tenure Center at the University of Wisconsin and other institutions, to find in the 1970s a decline in the sophistication of the argument. This opportunity provided by the Lincoln Institute draws refinement back into the discussion. The subject of rural land use and rural land policy is one that will not go away. We have repeated in our workshop a number of the standard items, and I think we have identified several new or additional ones and particularly have attempted to put refinement into the discussion. The first point is that there is a new shift of policy emphases for the 1980s, and those shifts have been in the direction of additional refinement:

1. From land reform to a disaggregation of land-reform policies to allow for a greater and richer set of comparisons.
2. From technology and technical assistance to land planning and analysis of land use.
3. From total production to productivity per unit.
4. From factors affecting the expansion or loss of available land to factors affecting the intensity of its use.
5. From a focus on laws and standards to one of implementation, strategy and practice.

For summary purposes, we have broken our discussion down into two subheadings: dimensions of rural land policy, going beyond the standard statements of land reform, and the dimensions of public action, the implementation of those policies. Let me illustrate. Ownership and access in terms of parcel size and holding size is a continuing question. We are still in need of rationalizing the use of landholdings, and we are still in need of giving a lot of attention to the question of parcel size. In land-use areas, that raises questions of consolidation, of course, and it continues to raise questions of the amount of idle land that still can be cultivated within the existing pattern of cultivation and the possibilities for capturing idle lands that rest essentially between parcels or on the edges of current consolidated areas.

Next we shifted to subjects of employment, conservation, and preservation, and to some of the dimensions of public action. We had a total of seven presentations representing seven different countries or regions of the world; and we had in our initial comments decided that production, employment questions, and equity should be kept foremost in our minds. It was pleasing to me to notice that we were able to go through the whole workshop in that session to talk about such subjects as displacement of labor and technology trade-offs without getting trapped with the words *green revolution* more than once or twice.

One of the new topics is the conservation and preservation of agricultural land, and I think it's one of the new issues that is increasingly coming into debate. The ecology of land use is important because of the tremendous pressure to use agricultural land more intensively; we are extending agriculture into fragile areas that are not able to sustain the kind of practices that are being carried out.

In the area of public action, a lot of debate is continuing around the question of pluralistic versus oligarchic control and the organization programs; and under the administrative options it gets related to the question of bureaucratic versus participatory kinds of programs. This I think, in our policy area, is a substantial addition and refinement to questions about how individual projects ought to be organized.

Finally, we turned to incentives and reviewed again the incentives of production, employment, equity, and customary systems of prestige and wealth. We also considered the obverse: the nontenurial policies. In this category we had a large number of social dimensions that still must be brought into our discussion. There were excellent reports about the customary and social form of land cultivation and land use as it is found in Africa, as it might be contrasted with what is found in the Philippines, in Thailand, in Taiwan, and in other parts of the world from which we had reports.

My final point will be to emphasize a point that has come up all week in this Congress: the conflicts between rural and urban land use. We are hearing increasingly everywhere in the world, developing world as well as in the advanced countries, that the taking of land for urban uses is taking a large amount of land out of agricultural use and that we are doing this in a context where the agricultural land availability is in some cases declining, and we are doing it in a context where the population is continuing to increase, with increasing demands for the opportunity to farm. This is one of the important policy questions, and it is increasingly addressed in the Third World as well as in the advanced countries.

20 Looking Ahead

Peter Oberlander

We all have our own views about land. In fact, perhaps there is no other word that engages our emotions, our concerns, our determination, and ultimately our pocketbooks than the word *land*. These views, which are very personal and to some degree collective, reflect our cultural heritage, and they certainly reflect ourselves as to how and where we were brought up. Land has a very curious grasp and grip on us—on our imagination, our experience, our values. If I were to summarize these infinite varieties of values and attitudes, I would come down on two words: land is food and land is space. Land, in fact, is the essence of life, and without it, life as we know it would never have started; it could never have continued throughout the ages; and there would be no future without it. It is the source of all food supply, and therefore it is a global concern—regardless of first world, second world, third world; regardless of political circumstances; regardless of social circumstances. There has been ample evidence that these concerns cut across deeply held political and social convictions.

In another sense, land is location; it is space and it is equally essential for our continuing existence. All of our activities need land—on which to live, on which to work, on which to be educated, on which to recreate, and above all a system of connections of transportation that makes life possible. Land is both source of living and the space on which to live. The conflict between those two functions emphasizes their interdependence and their complementarity.

Since time immemorial, food production and living space have competed for land, often the same land. From the Euphrates and Tigris Valley of biblical times to the Polders in Western Europe or the Niagara Peninsula in Ontario or my own Lower Fraser Valley in British Columbia—every one has specific examples of land-use conflict. Land as a precious and unique asset plays a unique role in human life, and since it is a scarce commodity, it has an ever-escalating price tag. Land is often referred to as real estate, as if it were the only real property, in a literal sense; and that concept has made it a commodity of trade, as distinct from being a natural resource of un- and irreplaceable value. Here is another source of conflict.

One further aspect of land compounds that dilemma. Because of its scarcity and because of its irreplaceable food-producing and space value, governments, acting on behalf of many constituencies, have entered the arena to decide how to use land, to arbitrate its social, economic, and spatial use, and above all to tax it.

349

Hence, those three sources of conflict over land have arisen: whether it should be used for food or to live on; whether it should be regarded as a commodity of trade or a unique resource; and whether it should be developed by private initiative, under free-market conditions of one sort or another, or whether the public, through its government, knows best and through its intervention, control, and its taxation should manage it. These conflicts are responsible for making land the source of argument throughout history to this very day, and presumably have brought us together around this very space. Indeed, time has sharpened the conflict as more and more people live on less and less land.

Urban settlements preempt many choices in terms of the use of land as a resource of finite quality and quantity. The current concern for urban land and its worldwide implications is the result of intensive international research and discussion, which was focused in Vancouver four years ago. That conference passed a series of interdependent resolutions. Seven of them dealt with land. Let me recall very briefly what these resolutions were about because I believe that if we are ever to look ahead, we have got to move on what we have done, and not try to reinvent or reargue or rediscuss things on which we all agree.

The first Habitat resolution dealt with land as a scarce resource that must be managed in the public interest for the common good. The second recommendation dealt with the control of use of land and that that change, above all, must be subject to public control and public policy. Number three dealt with that thorny of thorny issues. We invented a new word for it four years ago—*plus value*—a genteel construct that dealt with the unearned increment. And the United Nations at the time agreed that it is essential to recapture that plus value due to public investment, by the public. Resolution four dealt with public ownership and the importance of managing land. Number five dealt with the patterns of ownership and the rationalization of those in the interests of better use. Recommendation six dealt with the necessity to increase usable land as far as possible. And seven dealt with information needs.

It's critical to try to build on what we have done, particularly since, while Habitat succeeded, it also failed. It succeeded in raising public consciousness and the public's conscience about land and the essential value it represents. It succeeded, in some ways, in raising the discussion to debate and making it a central global issue. But it has failed in terms of following through. Progress since Habitat '76 has been exceedingly modest. There has been some progress, but most of it is only at the margin of the central issues, with little lasting consequences. Why has progress been so insignificant, so slow, and in some sense quite regressive? Therein lie some of the issues about looking ahead. Three points seem to be clear and deserve observation.

Policies for land and their related strategies and instruments of implementation are not technical matters. It is equally true, in my judgment, that they are not economic matters. And we have spent a great deal of time here going over the technical strategies and the economic consequences. We have been given a dazzling display of techniques, and we have discovered that we have plenty of them—tools to measure, tools to analyze, even tools to implement. The first observation in this context is that questions of land, in all its ramifications, are clearly political questions involving the essential collective political will of the community to govern itself and to allocate a unique but strategic resource for commonly agreed-upon purposes. We have learned that we know very well what to do; we also know how to do it. But we must ask ourselves why.

In most instances we have heard that the performance of those strategies and those tools has not achieved the expected goals because we have lacked the political will. And I suggest that political will, once again, cuts across all social political systems. The resolutions at Habitat recognized this by the following preamble: "Above all, governments [and they mean all governments, left, right, and center] must have the political will to evolve and implement innovative and adequate urban and rural land policy as a cornerstone of their effort to improve the quality of life in human settlements." I suggest *political* and *cornerstone* are essential to our looking ahead to what is in store. Raising consciousness is essential but meeting the expectations is far more critical. In looking ahead on the land question, one is clearly struck by its profound political implications and the required political will to act. I think Charlie Haar gave us a marvelous new phrase: "It is human to plan and divine to implement."

During the four years since Habitat '76, land in economic terms has demonstrated once again its extremely persuasive power. And thereby hangs the second reason for the lack of implementation of the recommendations. If the first was that we are dealing not with a technical and economic but a political issue, the second relates to land as real estate, which over the last four years more than any other item has demonstrated the age-old value it represents. It has demonstrated that it can withstand the ravages of inflation more than any other private or publicly owned good. We have witnessed once again that land is the only "real" estate, and everyone from the smallest to the most sophisticated owner of land has become acutely aware that land survives the most unexpected, the most savage losses of value through inflation. The experience affects the individual home owner just as much as the real estate developer or investor. Interestingly enough, land as an anchor against inflation and loss of value is now clearly understood. While the planned economies of Eastern Europe and other socially based economies claim that land belongs to the people, they all have recognized a continuing appreciation of land and its essential monetary value to state enterprises and to the collectivity. We had some excellent examples when Marsha Goldberg reported on the workshop on taxation, where the land "market" operates in the Soviet Union in roughly the same way as it does in the United States.

The finite nature of land and its unique productive capacity, together with increasing space needs for people, has combined to demonstrate the age-old lesson that land is value and more land is wealth. In this atmosphere of direct personal experience of increasing values in land, government is ever more reluctant to legislate, regulate, or indeed begin to recapture any publicly created values. That is the experience of the last three or four years. No wonder that more and more governments are less and less willing to act in the way that we all know they really ought to.

Let me give you one last example of how this erosion of the public will has not only affected national governments but even the U.N. agency. As a result of the 1976 conference, the U.N. Commission on Human Settlements was created for the explicit purpose of continuing the work in this field and to follow up on the resolutions. The commission met for a third time in Mexico City for the explicit purpose of reviewing progress on the resolutions in Vancouver and to urge new enterprises. The commission represented fifty-eight nations and dealt with a wide variety of issues. The most disturbing part is that it did not talk about land. It did not deal with land; it did not deal with any of the issues raised by the resolutions. And even more disturbing is that the new agenda for the meeting in Manila next year for the fourth commission once again does not have land on its agenda. Its first priority is the role and contribution of the construction industry. It is important, but is that a priority? And second is the provision of infrastructure in slums and squatter settlements in rural areas. That is also very important, but can you really separate the provision of infrastructure in slums and squatter settlements from the essential issue of land? One may have different views over it, but you must at least continue to discuss it. It appears that land associated with these issues is such a sensitive issue, so highly political in nature, that even the U.N. commission is not willing to deal with the issue or even discuss it.

What have we learned in this context of sensitive issues and the essential public will to act? First, we have certainly seen strategies and the tools concerned in implementation. But if you go back to the original title of the conference, it is the World Congress on Land Policy. This vast array of instruments, the dazzling array of tools and techniques, some simple and some highly sophisticated, seems to have outstripped our imagination as well as our political will to use them for some agreed-upon policy goal. A chosen policy can be implemented, but if there is no agreed policy, even the best tools in the world—of measurement, of analysis, of implementation—will accomplish nothing.

The second point is that there are some prevailing myths, some prevailing fallacies. And finally, the best collection of tools, the best programs, the best projects do not add up to a policy.

There is no question that we have a remarkable array of techniques that we ought to improve, that we ought to understand, but that we ought to apply for a social political purpose. Second, the prevailing myths tend to stand in the way. The first myth is that land problems can be solved through technical means and through economic measures. Bureaucratic solutions to nonbureaucratic problems simply do not work. Second is the myth that one solution is good for all problems. One solution is good for all jurisdictions; they are exportable and if you cannot export them, try to make them as attractive as possible and then everybody will copy them. One solution to all problems is a simplification that clearly we cannot share after this week's experience. And finally, perhaps, the socially desirable uses of land—this is one of the fallacies, I think—are incompatible with ownership. I don't think that's true because the question of who owns it is in a sense independent of the collective will to use it in a certain fashion. And there are many examples in this area.

Let me refocus on the notion that projects and programs do not make policies. The political will must be based on clearly articulated goals, clearly identified objectives, democratically arrived at; then you can begin to move toward implementation. The presentations here have made that clear. From the call to arms by Mr. Peñalosa to the carefully balanced and well-presented cases of Africa, Asia, Europe, Latin America, the Middle East, and North America, through the presentations by Dr. Lee and Bill Lim and Brian Berry, we have learned a great deal about specific issues; and you have already heard what remarkable work has been done in the workshops. We heard from Bill Doebele and Gregory Ingram and the two pioneers in that whole field of technology, the Brown and Roberts team. What they have said is indeed fascinating because they have given us a greater insight on the machinery, the process. But does it all really lead us to what I think the last four or five years have clearly established: the need to act? The need is to move that whole discussion from what is sometimes considered academic but moving in another direction where we can do perhaps two things.

The focus of almost all rules and regulations and techniques of measurement of analysis have focused on private land and the private ownership of that land. The presumption is that government does not need to be considered. I think this is a fallacy for the reason that the largest single owner of land, and therefore the largest single operative developer, is the government. I come from a country well known for its private market and its commitment to private enterprise. The government of Canada owns about half of all the land in Canada. The province of British Columbia owns something like 90 percent of our province. And you can go on. We heard here that in the United States, the federal government owns something like a third of all space. So if the government is the largest single landowner, surely there is another area of land process, development, and the public will to make sure that that space and that strategic use of land is used in as creative a way as possible.

Let me summarize my looking ahead under three ideas. First, land policy is public policy. It is the collective will to achieve an agreed-upon and clearly articulated goal. This, in my judgment, has not happened—certainly not sufficiently clearly and not sufficiently unique to the jurisdictions we are discussing. We must articulate our goals and objectives in terms of over-riding issues. Is land just a source of revenue, public or private? That is a very different goal from assuming that we are concerned with justice, equity, conservation, or even simple order. These are overriding value issues that could guide us to goals and objectives, which then can be achieved through the tools and techniques. I'm saying very little new, but I am trying to bring back our concern to policy and its future. The goals have to be clearly ar-ticulated and well understood after endless discussion in the body politic. If they are unclear, if they are conflicting, you will never be able to achieve whatever it is you want to achieve. You will obviously choose inappropriate tools, you will follow fads rather than facts, you will confuse goals with ob-jectives, and you will confuse strategies with goals and objectives. We know from a lot of experience that where the goals are clear, we can achieve them. In most countries income tax, which has a clearly articulated goal, works. And where that goal is not clearly articulated, it really doesn't work. I come from a province that established an agricultural freeze five years ago. You can argue whether it's good or bad, but the government of the day, reflec-ting the public will, said no more conversion of arable land to urban uses. And it happened, and it stuck, because there was an agreed goal and an agreed policy. Interestingly, the new government, which is far more conser-vative, supported this idea. And arable land today is literally frozen.

This brings me to the second point. Jurisdiction must be clear. Area and power must coincide. It makes no sense to try to describe goals for someone else's jurisdiction or to assume that some other jurisdiction will do whatever you want to achieve. If you have clear goals about land and its use, that must correlate to the power to act. Our reference to the U.N. resolutions is obviously frustrated by the fact that the United Nations is not a govern-ment; it has no jurisdiction. Its only value is discussion and increased recognition of issues. But the nation and all its subsets has that power, and in that sense jurisdiction and power, area and power, must coincide.

Finally, if we are committed to policy, as distinct from program and project, we must recognize that those three are clearly a continuum, a proc-ess. And a process, being continuing and continuous, demands monitoring, it demands auditing, and then it allows us the evaluation. So we can change the system. But without monitoring, without auditing, without evaluating, we can't change the system; and project and program remains isolated, in-sulated from the continuing process of policy.

21 Urban Land Policy for the 1980s

Arcot Ramachandran

It is indeed timely that we take stock of the progress made in human settlement development in the four years since the Habitat Conference in Vancouver. There are many advantages in reviewing the situation under separate detailed headings, such as land aspects of human settlements, rather than in attempting another comprehensive assessment, which may not get us much further forward. The subject of human settlements is so vast and intricate that any attempt to deal with the entire field runs the risk of merely repeating the same general statements and the same priorities that emerged from the Vancouver conference. These findings, which have been accepted in principle by every member government of the United Nations, represent the broadest statement of human settlement objectives that could be made in light of our current knowledge. Except for changes for the worse in human settlement conditions in most of the developing countries, there has been no breakthrough in the depth of human settlement knowledge over the past four years. Now we need to advance beyond global principles to specific actions aimed at implementing the objectives laid down by the Vancouver conference.

Land issues were classified as one of the six basic areas for human settlement action by the United Nations when the United Nations Centre for Human Settlements was established. The Centre has the responsibility, within the U.N. system, for carrying out research, training, and dissemination of information related to land issues, as well as for providing technical assistance to member governments of developing countries in solving land problems.

In progressing from the broad principles of the Vancouver conference to recommendations for action, we must focus our studies on more precisely defined elements of the whole human settlement picture. The matter of land policies is important because it is a subject on which the governments of developing countries need the most urgent guidance. In a sense I view land policies as an integral part of national development policies, which are in a greater state of flux throughout the world than they have been for the past thirty years.

There are two reasons for the upheaval in national development planning processes. The first and most important is that more and more governments are becoming disenchanted with the traditional processes of development planning, with their emphases on gross measures of economic growth and on aggregated econometric modeling simulations. Neat statistical projections of sectoral economic activity and similar measures did not take proper account of the locational and physical practicality of constructing the facilities needed to support planned economic changes. Also gross projections of increases in production failed to take account of the intolerable inequities in the distribution of benefits, which have robbed the vast majority of people of their rights to a fair share of national resources.

The second reason for the new scrutiny being given to national planning processes is that the world is facing a completely novel situation regarding fuel supplies, energy resources, food production, and other basic necessities. Until now, there has been a fundamental assumption in all planning that output in these fields could be expanded indefinitely and did not constitute a constraint on planning goals. Recent thinking on this matter has changed radically. Most countries are reexamining the foundations of their national planning policies to see how they can be adjusted to reflect new realities, and this factor has an important bearing in land use in settlement planning.

In this reappraisal of social and economic development policies and strategies, I see a great opportunity for the introduction of land and human settlement issues into the planning matrix, and, hence, you will appreciate my overriding concern that we be ready with practical, authoritative proposals for dealing with the planning and implementation problems involved in giving this new dimension to national programs.

I do not see how I could improve on the nine subheadings of this congress; they seem to cover every possible aspect of the question, insofar as they relate to mechanical and institutional needs. Therefore, I would like to pose a different question to the conference: Do we really understand what policies need to be implemented by all of these devices discussed here? I cannot avoid the fear that we are taking the actual policies too much for granted in our concern for identifying the most-efficient techniques for implementing them. Let us not fall into the same mistake for which macroeconomists are being criticized—of being so concerned with the tools of the trade that we lose sight of what we are trying to achieve by their use. Measures for implementing policies must relate to the policies to be implemented, and consequently, we should not miss the purposes and goals of the land and human settlements policy that we shall have to deal with in the 1980s. Therefore we might usefully concentrate on identifying the main concerns of national governments in connection with land and human settlements over the next ten years.

I am mainly concerned with the needs and problems of the developing countries, because the U.N. Centre for Human Settlements directs most of its efforts toward providing support and advice to Third World governments, which, naturally, have somewhat different concerns from those of Western European and North American countries. Even where basic goals are similar—say, efficiency in operation of human settlements or equity in the distribution of economic benefits—the policies for achieving these goals will be different in countries of different economic and technological status. I must ask you, accordingly, to bear with me if I concentrate my attention on the developing countries.

First, we have to resolve the question of what contribution human settlement activities can make to national economic development, in the sense of seeing that the balance of optimum efficiency is struck between economic and physical-development targets. Although one of the serious defects of conventional economic planning is that it failed to take into account physical planning constraints and although it is plausible to suppose that there is an optimum pattern of settlements and infrastructure networks that will maximize the return from economic inputs, we do not yet have the techniques to generate theoretically optimum patterns with precision and certainty. Consequently planned distributions of population and economic activity, where they exist today, are usually based on arbitrary assumptions and value judgments that may be incorrect, and measures for bringing about these land-distribution policies may be counterproductive to overall national development policies. I see, therefore, a need for considerable caution in introducing taxation and other fiscal incentives geared to particular land patterns until we are sure that the basic policies will achieve the desired goals. This is especially so because such measures, once introduced, are characteristically extremely difficult to change, and we could easily find ourselves in the role of Dr. Frankenstein—unable to control processes that we have set in motion and subsequently recognize as unwise.

Secondly, I would like us to know more about the settlement-building process itself as a contributor to the economy of developing countries. We know that the construction industry—particularly the informal sector of the construction industry—has great potential for absorbing semiskilled and unskilled labor and that most urban migrants have few skills to offer in the urban marketplace. Therefore governments might reasonably suppose that stimulating the informal, low-technology, labor-absorptive construction sector would meet a number of national development goals. However, the implications of such a decision in terms of land policy are rarely spelled out. It seems clear that it would call for a means of placing large quantities of low-cost urban land in the hands of entrepreneurs, builders, and householders, of devising financial mechanisms for property purchases by low-income households, of regulating property-tax scales to balance ability to pay with revenue requirements, and of monitoring land use in accordance with community needs. Have we really reconciled all of these needs in our proposed implementation measures, or are there not lacunae and conflicts that we still have to deal with to ensure that all our implementation measures have a consistent policy orientation?

Third, I wonder what urban land policies are consistent with goals of social equity in the distribution of benefits to disadvantaged groups. Too often tax measures, financial measures, and property-ownership measures are devised for an undifferentiated target population, with the result that benefits flow to better-off groups while those in the greatest need gain little, if they are not actually injured by the measures, as is not infrequently the case. In order to close the vast social and economic gaps that exist in the societies of developing countries, we shall need land policies that emphasize affirmative action rather than supposedly socially neutral measures based on statistical averages, because we know that untargeted actions almost invariably direct benefits away from the poor, the illiterate, and the politically powerless. Clearly this means that very few land policy measures can be recommended for universal application because implementation targets will have to be identified separately for the socioeconomic context of each developing country. Perhaps we could generate some general models to which we could insert factors for individual countries, to present an array of scenarios that would result from combinations of policy decisions. This would be an area for fruitful research.

Fourth, I would recommend your attention to the impact that we can expect from fuel and energy constraints on the development of human settlements. Here there will be a great contrast in the responses we can expect in developed and developing countries. In the developed countries, the normal situation is that we have a highly urbanized population, with a low rate of increase, living in well-developed cities reliant on a high level of technological services. In the developing countries, by contrast, we have high rates of population growth, high rates of urban migration, and cities that have barely the basic networks of infrastructure in place. Therefore we can expect that the cities in developed countries will not alter much in basic physical form over the next twenty or thirty years. Populations will not increase very much, and economic growth is likely to be slow, so that we do not anticipate extensive rebuilding. Radical rebuilding would, in any case, be discouraged by the elaborate infrastructure networks in place, which can only be changed gradually over a substantial time period. On the other hand, the cities in developing countries may expand to double or treble their size through new development over the next twenty years, and even much of an existing city may be rebuilt over this period, where it now consists of squatter settlements and other replaceable types of development. Since existing infrastructure networks will place little constraint on building and rebuilding patterns, we may see radically new forms emerging to respond to new energy-usage factors.

Will our land-development policies help or hinder this transformation process? If we are going to base our policies on existing conditions and on the assumption that past trends will continue more or less unaltered into the future, the probability is that the developing countries will miss the great opportunities open to them to respond to new energy conditions by building cities in harmony with the needs of the next century. Instead we must look to imaginative new land policies and implementation techniques that will enable the developing countries to break out of the straitjacket of conventional land-use practices and explore innovative patterns of urbanization. I refer here not only to layouts of individual cities but to networks and linkages of cities and to patterns of urban-rural relationships. All of these potential shifts in land use and in development will call for the rethinking of land policies and for the fashioning of new implementation tools to respond to the dynamic development demands.

While these technical questions raise many complex issues, the political implications of land policy are even more difficult to identify and deal with. Land is a subject that affects every individual citizen, a factor that cannot be ignored. It may be a problem of assessing the emotional attachment of an urban householder or a rural farmer to his family lot or it may be a matter of money, prestige, and power invested in large landholdings. In either case, governments are wary in introducing measures that alter land rights—for instance, by affecting profits from land transactions or by placing restrictions on land use.

If we do not appreciate the political subtleties in programs of land reform—and here I refer not only to questions of land distribution but also to forms of tenure, taxation, and control—then the best technical judgments may be ineffective in achieving the goals we are aiming for. Therefore, no matter how straightforward the solution to a land problem may seem to us as technocrats, we still have to consider whether the best solution can be introduced without antagonizing interests that can block implementation. A compromise plan that can be implemented is better than a theoretically superior scheme for which we cannot get acceptance. This is an aspect of land studies that will need increased attention if we hope to have an effective impact rather than merely an academic one.

By drawing on all the skills and disciplines that contribute to the human settlement sector, we can meet the challenge of devising new land and settlement policies for the 1980s and beyond. We have the ability, and we only have to marshal our resources and direct them in the most profitable way to come up with the solutions we require. We are on the threshold of a great breakthrough in human settlement activities and with proper policies and efficient implementation techniques, we can transform the lives of the bulk of the world's population over the next two decades.

**Part V
Papers Prepared for the
Congress But Not Presented**

22 Some Unexamined Aspects of Urban Land Markets: Proposals for Research

William A. Doebele

Land is a commodity that touches the life of every human being. It is, on the one hand, a consumption good. Indeed, our relations to land and the buildings upon it are among the most important of all consumption goods that constitute the quality of our lives. On the other hand, real estate is also an economic good. It is often the most valuable asset possessed by a family, and its purchase and sale, particularly among the poor, can easily be the most important single finanacial transaction in a lifetime. Given these rather obvious facts, it has always seemed peculiar to me that the literature about land and housing in both developed and developing countries has seemed to be almost exclusively oriented toward the consumption side of these issues, usually stated as: How can public policy give greater access to land and housing to more people?

Undeniably access is an important social question. Giving it exclusive attention, however, neglects an equally important question: What do the poor do with real property after access has been achieved? Undoubtedly many families do see it as a consumption good and use it simply as a shelter and a base for domestic life. The more enterprising may see access to real estate only partially as a home, perceiving that, properly used, it can be an important springboard to increased income and upward mobility. While systematic studies are rare, we do know from scattered observations that there may be a significant rate of informal sales of land and houses in squatter areas.[1] What do these sales mean? How do buyers assemble the capital to purchase? And more importantly, what use do sellers make of what might be the largest amount of capital ever to come into their hands? Do they buy more land and attempt to repeat the process? If so, what effect does this have on urban land markets? Do they resettle in inferior quarters and use the remaining capital to buy a taxi, start a small store, or establish a workshop? Do they waste the sudden wealth on extravagant luxuries, on elaborate weddings or funerals, or dissipate it in idleness until it is exhausted?

The fact of the matter is that we do not know. What we do know is that while all of the poor are not saints, the overwhelming majority are very rational when it comes to economic survival and no less calculating of financial advantage than those of other socioeconomic classes. We also know that employment in the so-called informal sector (that is, small businesses and service activities that are not part of the conventional economic system) may represent a third or even half of all urban employment in developing countries. Capital formation in this sector is therefore an issue of immense importance to governments. Yet the thousands of capital transactions occurring every day in the very economic sector in which capital is so critical have not been monitored, studied, or analyzed in any way. In short, the relation between sales of real property and the generation of capital for informal businesses is a field largely neglected by researchers.

Even if it is discovered that there is very little linkage between real estate transactions in the informal sector and the capitalization of new economic activities in that sector, the study of the real estate market would still be justified.

At what point and for what psychological motives does a poor family that has achieved recognizable rights in urban real property decide to sell out and move on? How are these decisions related to an overall strategy to achieve upward mobility? How often are they successful? What can government policy do to facilitate the process? All of these are significant, and largely unanswered, questions.

John Turner, as long ago as 1968, pointed out that in the psychology of urban migrants, the priority of land tenure shifts with time. In the earliest stages of urban life, access to employment is all important. In a later stage, landownership becomes critical. Still later, land per se becomes less important again.[2] Tomasz Sudra, in his pioneer work *Low-Income Housing Systems in Mexico City,* took the Turner thesis several steps further and provided one of the first comprehensive theoretical frameworks and empirical studies of housing in both its consumption and economic aspects. He demonstrates that while Turner's thesis reasonably described behavior in Mexico City through the 1950s, the situation in the last twenty-five years (roughly since the city passed the 4 million population mark) is vastly more complicated. His observations on the role of land and housing tenure in general, and in the lives of twenty-five families as recalled by them for several decades, are among the most suggestive studies in this field.[3]

Much more, however, remains to be done. My own suggestion would be to use a variation of the Brown-Roberts methodology to explore, through individual interviews, the significance of tenure and real property investment in the lives of the respondents, their reasons for buying and selling, and in particular the use made of the proceeds received from its sale.

A supplementary study would deal with low-income buyers of land and housing, both in the formal and informal sectors (that is, buying from other squatters or inhabitants of illegal subdivisions). How is capital assembled for the purchase? Does it represent a decapitalization of the rural sector (the selling of animals or farmland to purchase land or housing in the city)? How many sales are for cash, and how many on installments, in which the seller in effect takes back a formal or informal mortgage on his former property? (It is possible that there is a substantial credit market operating in this sector about which we have no information.) Do most buyers buy only for consumption (better housing for themselves) or for speculation (to make a profit at a later time), or some combination of both?

A related program of research might combine interviews with statistical analysis to ascertain the impacts of governmental programs and policies on the poor who attempt to use land and housing as economic as well as consumption goods. A priori, one is struck by the fact that most government programs (like most analytical studies) have been the victims of the consumption-oriented approach. Rent control in the central areas of Mexico City, for example, designed to protect the low-income consumers of housing, has in fact had a disastrous long-run effect on both the consumers and producers of one of the most essential types of housing supply.

To cite an even more direct example, it is the policy of almost all governments that when public-housing units, sites and services plots, or other forms of land or housing are awarded to selected needy families, such families are prohibited from selling their units to third persons. The only transactions permitted are sales back to the providing agency, usually under terms that will prevent the family from making any profit on the transaction. The stated purpose of this constraint is to ensure that projects designed to assist low-income families are not immediately transformed into middle-income projects as the low-income families sell out at large profits to higher-income persons who wish to speculate or who find the government projects more attractive than their own private-market possibilities. If this occurs, it is argued, the low-income beneficiaries will reenter the low-income market, and the project will not have improved the housing conditions of this class.

In these cases the government is furnishing a subsidy. This subsidy may be measured either in terms of the difference between what the government has invested and the price charged to the recipients, or it may be measured by the difference between the market value of the plot of land or housing unit and the price charged to the recipient. Because of the distorted supply-and-demand situation in most urban centers in developing countries, the second form of subsidy is generally much greater than the first; that is, the difference between what the recipient of a plot or a housing unit receives and its sales value on the market is a greater difference than the difference between what that plot or housing unit has cost the government and what it charges the recipient.

It is generally believed, however, that a beneficiary should not be permitted to convert either form of subsidy into cash. The selected family is able to use it only for housing. This represents a view that a plot in a sites and services project or a unit in a public-housing project is a consumption unit, which must be used by the recipient only for the consumption purposes intended by the government. It cannot be converted into an economic unit by means of a sale even though the beneficiary would prefer to have the cash rather than the improved housing opportunity. In other words, the public agency is saying that it is giving the selected family a subsidy in one particular form, even though the family has decided that its general position in life would be improved by a different subsidy than that which the government has given it.

Whether this is good policy depends on three types of information that are not now available to policymakers. First, to what degree does filtration in the housing market occur? In a system that filtered perfectly, the movement of a middle-class family into a sites and services plot or a public-housing unit would release that family's former unit into the market and produce an effect that would ultimately result in the availability of a unit at the bottom of the income scale. Whether this process works under conditions now prevailing in the major cities of developing countries is a large issue, and one that is beyond the scope of our present discussion.

A second issue is to what degree the insertion of middle-income families in a low-income area will create pressures for further conversions that will ultimately force out all lower-income families? There is some evidence that in low-income areas with very good locations with respect to job opportunities, this is a real fear, and such sales may be collectively resisted. This again is an issue beyond our present scope.

The third question, about which we know very little and which does touch directly on the main argument I am presenting is: What are the production consequences of a low-income family's turning a subsidy given to it in the form of a plot or housing unit into the form of cash-in-hand or capital? One consequence is that the government's investment subsidy (the difference between what it invested in the project and what it charges beneficiaries) is replaced by a larger sum: the difference between what the beneficiary has paid and the market value of the unit sold. A second and more important consequence, however, is that a low-income family now has in hand a considerable sum of capital. If, for example, research showed that most low-income families use windfalls of capital to start business enterprises that provide direct or indirect economic support for a half-dozen people, the government might achieve an important employment objective through a program that originally was intended to deal with the housing problem.

It is generally agreed that urban employment is a higher social priority than the provision of housing. It is also generally agreed that one of the important bottlenecks to expansion of employment in the so-called informal sector is the access of small entrepreneurs to capital. Thus, if the facts turned out to support the assumptions stated in the preceding paragraph, it would certainly be arguable that an initial government subsidy investment in a sites and services or housing project would have far more beneficial total social impact if the recipients of units were permitted to sell on the market than if they were prohibited from doing so, as is now typically the case. On the other hand, if studies showed that most low-income families who receive windfalls generally dissipate them in frivolous ways, the justification for current policies of forbidding sales would be reinforced.

I have used this example not to make a statement about the rightness or wrongness of current policies but to illustrate how useful it would be to know more about the role of real estate as an economic good (as opposed to a consumption good) in the lives of the urban poor. We must break out of the narrow view of access to land and housing as being ends in themselves and accept the larger concept of their being economic goods of high importance in the lives of all persons, particularly the poor. Let us not stop our studies when a family gets a plot of land or a house but move to the next step and discover how that plot or house is then used to achieve greater economic and social success. Let us begin to examine land and houses as unique instruments of production and capitalization and not simply as elements for shelter and consumption.

Notes

1. No studies dealing directly with the transfer of land and housing among persons in low-income areas and its economic consequences have been found. Some studies, however, deal peripherally with this issue.

For Caracas, see Kenneth L. Karst, Murray L. Schwartz, and Audrey J. Schwartz, *The Evolution of Law in the Barrios of Caracas* (Los Angeles: Latin American Center, University of California Press, 1973), esp. chaps. 2, 7.

For Bogotá, see Brian Blaesser, "The Private Market and the Process of Lower Income Urbanization in Colombia: The Pirate Housing Submarket of Medellin" (Master's thesis, Massachusetts Institute of Technology, 1979); Oscar Borrero and Sonia Sanchez, *Mercadeo de Tierras en Barrios Clandestinos de Bogotá* (Bogotá: Departamento Administrativo de Planeacion Distrital, April 1973); Alan Carroll, *Pirate Subdivisions and the Market for Residential Lots in Bogotá*, Urban and Regional Report No. 79-12, Urban and Regional Economics Division, Development Economics Department (Washington, D.C.: World Bank, April 1980); William A. Doebele, "The Private Market and Low-Income Urbanization in Developing Countries: The 'Pirate' Subdivisions of Bogotá," *American Journal of Comparative Law* 25 (1977):531-564; Timothy O. Gauhan, *Some Economic and Political Characteristics of Low-Income Housing Market in Bogotá, Colombia and Their Implications for Public Policy Alternatives* (Houston: Program of Development Studies, Rice University, Paper No. 64, Spring 1975); Rodrigo Losada Lora and Hernando Gomez Buendia, *La Tierra en el Mercado Pirata de Bogotá* (Bogotá; FEDESARROLLO, June 1976); Joan M. Nelson, *Public Housing, Illegal Settlements, and the Growth of Colombia's Cities* (Washington, D.C.: U.S. Agency for International Development, December 1973); Lisa R. Peattie, "A Case-Study of Las Colinas, Bogotá" (unpublished manuscript, 1980); and George Vernaz, *Pirate Settlements, Housing Construction by Incremental Development, and Low-Income Housing Policies in Bogotá, Colombia* (New York: New York City-Rand Institute, May 1973).

For Mexico, see Jan Bazant-S., *Rentabilidad de la Vivienda de Bajos Ingressos* (Mexico City: Editorial Diana, Noviembre 1979), and Tomasz L. Sudra, "The Low Income Housing System of Mexico City" (Ph.D. diss., Massachusetts Institute of Technology, 1974).

2. John C. Turner, "Housing Priorities, Settlement Patterns, and Urban Development in Modernizing Countries," *Journal of American Institute of Planners* (November 1968):354-363.

3. Sudra, "Low Income Housing System."

23 Land Taxation and Urban Finances in Less-Developed Countries

Alan R. Prest

Different Ways of Taxing Land

There are a number of standard ways in which different taxes can be appraised. The first is to take any individual tax and examine the resource allocation, equity, and administrative aspects of imposing it or of raising the rate at which it is applied. However, this approach is usually unsatisfactory because it is likely to be very difficult in practice to isolate the differences between the pretax and posttax positions that can be attributed to the tax change itself. Thus it is very common to adopt either of two alternative approaches, which are inherently preferable. We can either make explicit assumptions about a change in a tax being associated with a particular set of changes in expenditure and then analyze the joint results of tax and expenditure changes or we can assume a given pattern of expenditure and then analyze the relative effects of different methods of financing it. For the purposes of this paper, clearly the latter approach is more relevant in that we are postulating a situation where there are great and increasing calls on urban-authority expenditures and we are concerned with the most-effective or least-harmful ways of financing such demands. The comparison of different means of financing a given level of expenditure will be the dominant one in this discussion, but this does not preclude resort to the more-tax-and-more-expenditure alternative from time to time.

We shall look at the following taxes and parataxes in succession, examining resource allocation, equity, and administrative aspects in each case: property taxes, site-value rating, land-increment taxes, land-transaction taxes, vacant-land taxes, sales of development rights, and land-readjustment schemes (or land consolidation).

Property Taxes

Property taxes are the best known, most documented, and most frequent form of local taxation of land and buildings.[1] Given that this form of taxation has been so intensively discussed in so many places, I shall be extremely brief in my summary.[2]

The first point to make, and one that is frequently misunderstood, is that property taxation can take two different forms, which have different consequences. One version is a partial wealth tax. The gross capital value of the different interests in land and property, whether freehold or leasehold, is subject to an annual tax. A slight variant on this version is to levy a special tax on the annual income from such property; in principle, special taxes on investment income (including imputed income) and on capital are substitutes, though the practical applications can differ considerably. The alternative version is a tax on land or property usage, which can be approximated by levying a tax on rental income and on imputed owner-occupied income. This latter is essentially the basis of the system found in the United Kingdom, and although U.K. practice as such is of no special relevance to this paper, the same property-taxation practice was bequeathed to many Commonwealth and ex-Commonwealth countries. The crucial difference between the two systems is in respect of the tax base rather than the tax point. When the tax base is capital value, a short leasehold property of a given size, surroundings, and other characteristics will be valued at much less than a freehold property having similar physical characteristics, but this is not so if the base is current value to the user.[3] Similarly, the second system naturally points much more clearly to zero taxation of empty property than the first. On the other hand, the question of the tax point, owner or tenant, is not a fundamental one. On the whole, it will probably be more convenient to levy a capital-value tax on owners and a usage tax on tenants, but such arrangements are far from being preordained.

The consequences of levying a capital-value version of property taxation include the following.

1. The traditional view was that in the short run, this tax was absorbed by owners. In the long run, a distinction had to be drawn between land and building components; landowners continued to bear tax, but construction would be curtailed in the area where the tax had risen, thus leading to increases in rents. Hence some part of the tax was borne by tenants, with a general presumption of regressiveness insofar as domestic properties are concerned.

2. This traditional view has been challenged on two main grounds in recent years.[4] First, if one takes a measure of permanent rather than instantaneous income, the element of regressiveness is likely to be less pronounced in that the ratio of housing expenditure to permanent income is much more uniform than is such expenditure as a percentage of measured income. Second, if one assumes that the supply of capital is inelastic to the construction industry, it can be argued that even in the long run, the part of the tax ascribable to building will be borne by suppliers of capital rather than consumers of housing. The mechanism will differ depending on whether one is envisaging a locally differentiated or a country-wide uniform rise in the

property-tax rate, but the general result will be the same. Hence, it follows that as site-value tax falls on landowners and buildings tax on capital owners, then overall the tax may well be progressive rather than regressive with income.

3. Taxation of business premises, as distinct from domestic property, is likely to have widely diffused effects depending on such variables as the extent to which any one local area imports and exports goods and services from other areas, induced movements of factors between areas, and so on.

4. Whether one concentrates on ancient or modern views on this subject, one has to be careful about the exact nature of the question asked. Thus if one is inquiring into the distributional effects of both raising more property-tax revenue and spending it locally, site values and/or buildings might benefit in such a way as to leave property owners no worse off than before, even if one does accept the modern view.[5] And it goes without saying that the exact results will depend on assumptions about capital-supply elasticities, mobility of factors, and so on. One must also remember to set property taxation in the overall national tax context; efficiency effects (for example, less building) will be less serious if local taxes are superimposed on national taxes that exempt building from their coverage.

The idea of the usage basis for a local property tax evolved historically from the benefit principle. Owners of buildings received various local services, services were roughly proportional to the size of building, and so it was appropriate to levy a tax on occupation; in fact, if no such tax were levied, there would be an incentive to overbuild.[6] Correspondingly there was little, if any, case for taxing empty buildings or vacant land. According to this view, income distribution was unaffected by the tax in that benefits were deemed to be proportional to tax payments; so provided that those who paid the taxes also enjoyed the benefits, income distribution remained unaffected.

Few people today would accept such a simplified view when so much local-authority expenditure (education, for instance) is person related rather than buildings related. Nor was it ever possible to argue that taxation on business property fell within the simple theory. At the same time, the conclusions derived from the modern theory of property taxation do not fully apply in this usage tax context. A tax on annual value in current use would not necessarily have similar distributional consequences to a tax on capital value even if one were to assume that tenants bore no part of it.[7] The same point applies to sites as well as structures, in that capital values will reflect possible future usage, whereas current-usage value will be nil if a site is vacant.

As for resource allocation, one would expect a tax on usage value to have some deterrent effects on construction activity, both in respect of domestic and business property. One further point is that a tax on gross rental value is more of a stimulus than a tax on capital value to relatively long-lived and more solidly built property.[8] But any such effects depend on assumptions about the structure of national taxes, quite apart from the influence of countless other aspects of government activity such as rent controls.

Finally, I must say a word about property-tax administration. Although many people have argued that in built-up urban areas it is easier to determine values if one takes buildings and sites together (the normal state of affairs) than if one takes sites alone, the evidence is by no means clear-cut, as we shall see when we come to site-value taxation. No doubt if one already has a property tax and case law established on that basis, it will be a less-arduous matter to make valuations of property rather than sites. And as property taxation of one kind or another is much more common than site taxation, this point may be decisive.[9] Nevertheless, one must recognize the logical distinction between relative administration costs comparisons on the assumption of a clean slate and on the assumption that one of the taxes is already in being.

Site-Value Rating (SVR)

We assume initially, and somewhat contrary to our general method of reasoning, that we are imposing a local SVR but ignoring the effects of accompanying expenditure. We shall subsequently ask how the analysis changes if different and more-realistic assumptions are made.

It is important to recognize that in principle there are two possible forms of SVR. The first form is essentially a lump-sum tax. A view is taken when SVR is introduced about the highest and best value that a plot of land will ultimately command and that value is the basis for tax for all time, without any discounting for futurity or any amendments for changing expectations. Such a tax will be fully capitalized (subject to later qualifications) on existing landowners and will have no influence on decisions about land usage or land disposal if profits are already being maximized. One can cook up exceptions to the no-consequences view if one assumes that profits are not being maximized initially (for example, pretax an owner may keep idle a piece of land next to his house because he likes the view; post tax he cannot afford this luxury), but we can reasonably ignore such exceptions here. The fall in land values associated with full capitalization does not mean that annual land costs fall and so help to generate a building boom. The combined annual cost of interest charges and tax will be just as much as the old annual interest charges. It is an illusion to think that annual costs as a whole will fall.

The second form, and perhaps the more genuine one, of SVR is that the tax is levied each year on the current market value of land, as determined by the discounting of future rents computed afresh from year to year. There are grounds for arguing that this version of the tax is likely to have efficiency effects in that development may take place sooner than otherwise. Essentially one has to think of the tax as being equivalent to an increase in the rate of return sacrificed by holding land and, by analogy with standard examples of the effects of increases in interest rates on decisions about whether to leave wine to mature longer or to allow trees to grow more before felling, likely to lead to development sooner than would otherwise have happened. However, there are a number of both theoretical and empirical qualifications to the argument. For instance, doubts about the effects even in principle of an increase in interest rates on the timing of development and the likelihood that in practice the tax base may not be adjusted upward the nearer the proximity of the development make one hesitate about accepting earlier development as a certain, as distinct from a possible, outcome of SVR.[10]

How do these arguments change if we vary our assumptions? If SVR is accompanied by additional expenditure, the outcome depends on whether the form of the additional expenditure is such as to be noticed by the citizenry, thus cancelling out the income effects, which have to be taken into account when the SVR is considered in isolation. The more-relevant alternative for our purposes is to postulate that expenditure is the same, but we have the choice of financing it by SVR or a property tax. The exact outcome will depend on the version of each tax chosen, but the general result is that SVR will encourage building relative to the property tax. Exceptions can easily be thought of, but this result is the most likely one. However, another claim often made for SVR—that it would eliminate speculation in land—is incorrect as a general proposition. The tax rate has to be equal to 100 percent of net income accruing (including capital gains) for this to be true.[11] Finally, the assumption that the SVR will be fully capitalized does not hold under all circumstances. If this is not the case and land prices fall by less than the tax, there will be a consequential tendency to cut land inputs relatively to others in building operations.

If we look at the equity aspects of SVR, we can get almost any answer we like depending on the standard of reference. But suppose we postulate:

1. The alternatives are SVR in its genuine form and a property tax of the partial wealth tax genre.
2. There is full capitalization of SVR, and the modern theory of property-tax incidence applies.

There are then two main ways in which distributional effects may differ. Some local government areas will gain relatively to others; for example, the

SVR will benefit those with below-average site-building ratios. The consequences for interpersonal income distribution will depend on the correlation, if any, between income levels per head across local authority areas and site-building value ratios. Second, there will be redistribution effects within any given local government area, with those who use land extensively suffering relatively to intensive land users if SVR replaces property taxation. Distributional effects can be immensely variable depending on the exact scenario, but the main influences are likely to flow through one or both of these channels.[12]

Turning to administration, there has been argument for many years over the prerequisites and the mechanics of SVR. The subject, for instance, engaged the serious attention of a royal commission in the United Kingdom as long as eighty years ago.[13] One suspects that a summary of this ancient controversy should run on the following lines:

Bare sites are intrinsically easier to value than sites plus buildings.

It is more difficult in principle to value sites than sites plus buildings if one has to start with the latter and then extract the site component, but there are practical shortcuts to site valuation, which are a good enough approximation for most purposes.

People will always advocate the system to which they are accustomed.

Infrequent revaluation will play havoc with either tax base.

Selective evidence can be adduced by those people in favor of SVR and those against it. The former will point to the experiences of countries like New Zealand and Taiwan and the latter to that of Jamaica in recent years. The fair-minded comment would seem to be that administrative obstacles are not overwhelming either with property taxation or with SVR, but there is a presumption that from this standpoint most people would prefer the devil they know to the one they do not know.

Land-Increment Taxes

As with property taxes and SVR, one has to distinguish two varieties of land-increment taxation.[14] With the first, the tax is levied on all accruals (or, reluctantly, realizations) of land values without any regard to any system of land-use control in a country. With the second, the tax is related to gains associated with permission to use land for particular purposes and so does not apply to all land gains. We shall call the first type of land gains tax (LGT) and the second a development gains tax (DGT). In either case, it is likely that such a tax will be imposed at national or (if applicable) state level rather than local level, so as far as local governments are concerned, their main interest will be in some trickle-down result of some tax-sharing arrangement.

The strength of the argument for the LGT will depend on whether there is already a general tax on capital gains. We shall assume that this is so and direct our attention to whether there are then any good grounds for levying an extra tax on land gains. Several efficiency arguments can be put forward. The first is that because land cannot be created, site owners enjoy monopoly rents and no efficiency losses are likely to arise from taxing increments in market value due to increases in such rents. This is a sweeping proposition, which it would be inadvisable to accept without demur, as I have argued at length elsewhere.[15] And if nothing else, previous experience in various countries with excess-profit taxation (a close analogue to the proposal under discussion here) should warn that all sorts of resultant inefficiencies are likely. Even the wartime report of the famous Uttwatt Committee, which was not generally well-disposed to landowners, accepted that some part of the increases in site value was "due to private skill and initiative or to the fructification of past expenditure."[16]

Support is often claimed for extra-heavy land taxation on the basis of the long-established tradition of financing costs of public works by betterment levies (United Kingdom) or special assessments (United States).[17] The argument is not clear-cut. Taxation of increments in land values due to public works, public-utilities provision, and the like is not a perfect substitute for charging people on the basis of the marginal costs, properly defined, of supplying their needs. And if marginal-cost pricing is impossible or inapposite (for example, because of nonexcludability of consumers), it is also likely to be the case that land-increment taxation will be difficult to implement. There may be something in the proposition that if margin costs lie below average costs, a land-increment tax will be the least harmful way of covering the financial gap, but that judgment is clearly dependent on the range of relevant alternative sources of revenue.

Equity arguments for LGT are usually based on the principle that increments of this sort are unexpected windfalls, and so no one can possibly complain if he is debarred from receiving a large proportion of what he did not expect to receive. But several objections can be raised to this line of argument. Land gains may or may not be totally unexpected. Even if they are unexpected, it is hard to see why they should be singled out for special treatment. If the ordinary capital gains tax is good enough for other windfalls, why is the same not true for land? In fact, it is not difficult to construct an argument that land gains should be subject to lower-than-normal capital gains tax rates, given the degree of uncertainty involved in estimating land values. Nor does the idea of extra-heavy capital gains taxation on land make much sense from an administrative point of view. The injection of such a distinction is a guarantee that anomalies will be created in tax laws.

Rather different considerations arise if the special tax on land gains is confined to realizations rather than accruals. For instance, lock-in problems would be worse, but administration would be less formidable.

Turning to the DGT, the typical situation is that the barriers between uses arising from a land-use control system will make for larger price differentials between land in different uses than would come about in a freely functioning land market. Slowing down the pace of conversion from rural to urban usage is an obvious example. It may or may not be possible to justify these consequences by resorting to externality, merit-want arguments, and the like, but we are not so much concerned with that aspect as with whether the imposition of a DGT will lead to a net improvement or deterioration in efficiency. This subject has attracted a good deal of attention in recent years.[18] It would seem that some considerations (for example, when tax is payable at the time of development rather than at the time permission is granted) point toward earlier development as a result of the tax, whereas others (such as hopes and expectations that the tax may be removed) point to postponement of development. Thus there is no clear-cut efficiency argument for superimposing the tax on a system of land-use controls.

The equity arguments for a tax of this sort have also received a great deal of attention. Much of this argument has been at a superficial level, couched in such emotive terms as the community's being entitled to take back what it has given. A thorough analysis requires some understanding of the changes in income and wealth distribution brought about by the typical planning-permission system and the extent to which they might be modified by a tax associated with change of use. To illustrate, a land-use planning system that slows conversion from rural to urban use will increase urban and reduce rural land prices compared to those ruling in an unconstrained market. A tax on entrants to the urban club will catch one group of people, but that group only. If the tax itself affects the rate of transfer from one use to another, there will be further, though not easily predictable, effects on the distribution of income and wealth between factor owners. So the most one can say is that the tax will have a very partial corrective effect on redistribution occasioned by land-use planning.

Although there is no special focus on U.K. experience in this paper, there is a good case for discussing the administrative aspects of a DGT in the light of U.K. history. In the course of the last seventy years or so, the United Kingdom has made a number of efforts to levy a tax of this sort, and its administration has proved cumbersome in the extreme. Two particular problems arise: in defining the class of transaction (development, redevelopment, and so on) and the relevant date (the commencement of development or the realization of a gain, for example). But there are many other problems that can only be appreciated by detailed reference to U.K. experience. Of the many and varied tax experiments in that country during this century, development-gains taxation has proved to be the most complicated and formidable to administer.

Land-Transaction Taxes

Once again, there are two versions of this type of taxation.[19] The first is a special tax on all disposals of interests in land; stamp duties are a standard example. Two points need to be noted about such a tax. What is at stake here is a change of ownership rather than a change of use in that land can be sold while remaining in the same use (tax then being payable) and the use can be changed while remaining in the same ownership (tax then not being payable). Then one must be clear that it is the total proceeds of sale that are the occasions of tax and not in any sense the excess of such proceeds over the purchase price. This kind of tax bears no relation to those associated with use change or with capital gains.[20]

The great argument in favor of such taxes is that of administration, at least in any country where there is a reasonably well-defined set of titles to landownership. If disposals have to be recorded or registered with a public authority, it is relatively easy to impose a tax at that point. But on more purely economic grounds, such taxes do not score high marks. A tax payable on disposal, but not otherwise, is likely to have lock-in effects. And from an equity veiwpoint, such taxes would seem to be haphazard in their effects depending on whether those who sell land frequently happen to be in the higher wealth or income brackets.

An alternative type of proceeds tax is levied only if land is disposed of for development. Such a tax would not be difficult to assess and collect if disposals are publicly recorded, though perhaps it is less straightforward than a tax on all disposals. It clearly has advantages over a situation where imputed values enter into the tax base, as is the case with many forms of DGT. Nevertheless, there are some awkward problems. One question is why development should be singled out as the only occasion of tax and whether such singling out will not lead to lock-in effects, whether in the form of deferring developmnt or proceeding with development but on the basis of renting rather than outright disposal. Further complications also arise if land is sold for development, and the purchaser decides not to develop the land but to resell it to another developer. One then has to decide whether tax is payable twice or whether there is to be a system of crediting tax on the first sale against the second. The administrative consequences are obviously complex.

Vacant-Land Taxes

Vacant-land taxes are often referred to in LDCs and sometimes even enacted.[21] The main point of principle about such taxes is that whereas SVR amounts to a zero marginal tax rate if land is shifted from a nonuse to a use category, a vacant-land tax actually has a negative marginal tax rate, which is clearly a powerful incentive to bring land into some kind of use.[22] However, this extra stimulus applies only at the margin between use and nonuse; vacant-land taxes are irrelevant to choices between different uses.

While receiving high efficiency marks, at least in a limited context and on the assumption that speculative influences are not ovewhelmingly strong, advantages in respect of equity and administration are less clear-cut. Administration runs into the usual problems encountered by any tax authority attempting to extract tax revenues where there is no cash flow—a set of difficulties that applies in many other cases such as when taxing imputed rents of owner-occupied housing, capital gains accruals, and so on. Specific definitions of what is meant by vacant land are also needed.

Proposals are not unknown for a related kind of tax, one on land hoarding.[23] The general idea is that a tax is levied on land at a certain percentage of market value, the total amount payable being dependent on the length of time the land is held. The objective is to speed up the process of land transfer, and so the type of land subject to the tax might be that for which permission has been given for change of use but where no actual use change has taken place. It seems unlikely that such a tax would be very satisfactory even if there is a clearly defined and administratively satisfactory system of land-usage control. Anyone can easily avoid a tax of this kind by not applying for permission for change of use. The authorities would be likely to find themselves drawn into more and more detailed intervention in the land market to make any such proposal operative.

Sales of Development Rights

The idea of auctioning development rights has received attention on both sides of the Atlantic, the intention being to sell the rights of development to the highest bidder but perhaps giving some priority to the owner of existing use rights.[24] Similar ideas have often been advocated by economists whether in this context or in that of the sale of natural-resource rights, import and export licenses, and so on. The reason is easy to see; any such system readily fits in with general market-pricing principles.[25]

But popularity with economists is not the same thing as popularity with administrators, and one has to face the fact that administrators do not readily embrace such ideas. In the particular case of auctioning land-development rights, there are further issues to be faced. First is that development rights are vested in the state rather than individual landowners, not an easy proposition to accept in many countries. Second, it is highly unlikely that a system of this sort would be established except in circumstances where the state laid down the approximate timing of development, as well as disposing of the right to develop. One would have to accept that far-reaching controls over land usage would be likely to be associated with the auction system. This does not mean that an auction system is not a good way of implementing detailed land-use control but simply that one is unlikely to find the former without the latter (though the reverse, of course, does not hold).

Land Readjustment Schemes

Various types of land readjustment schemes, or land consolidation, have either operated or been proposed in different parts of the world. In principle, all land readjustment schemes involve the surrender of land by private owners to public authorities in exchange for some quid pro quo. Differences may arise in the following ways: the proposals may be instigated by the private or public sector; the purpose may be redevelopment of old urban land or servicing and development of new urban land; or the proportion of land permanently, as distinct from temporarily, surrendered to the public authority may vary considerably and so may the barter element involved.

Illustrations of the practical application of these general principles can be drawn from nineteenth-century England or twentieth-century Korea. In the former case, a system of recoupment (*excess condemnation* in American terminology) was used especially in the redevelopment of various areas of London.[26] If major reconstruction, such as a new road, was necessary, the local authority took powers to buy more land than was necessary for its reconstruction purposes. Subsequent to reconstruction, the surplus land was disposed of, the hope being that its disposal value would more than offset the cost of acquiring land surplus to permanent requirements. Therefore the success of these operations depended crucially on whether the surplus land could be bought at reasonable terms and on the extent to which the reconstruction enhanced the value of adjacent land. .

Attention has been drawn recently to a somewhat different type of land readjustment policy extensively practiced in South Korea but also known in Taiwan, Japan, and Australia.[27] The origins of these schemes owe much to the famous *Lex Adickes* adopted by Frankfurt-on-Main early in this century.[28] In this case, the public authority (maybe at the joint request of the landowners involved) takes over an area for servicing and development. Sufficient land is withheld by the authority to meet public needs (for streets and recreation areas, for example) and the cost of services provision. The rest is returned to private owners in proportion to their original inputs to the pool. Thus both city and owners gain; the former is able to finance development costs entirely from the landowners concerned, and the latter can expect that the value of the smaller area of serviced land returned to them will be higher than that of the larger area of unserviced land surrendered.

The principal differences between the two types of scheme are that private landowners play more of an initiating role in the Korea case. In the United Kingdom it was mainly a matter of redeveloping land that was already serviced rather than developing and servicing raw land; the proportion of land acquired that was retained permanently in public ownership perhaps tended to be greater in the United Kingdom;[29] and there was also less emphasis on returning land to the original owners in that type of scheme or, more generally, a greater emphasis on monetary transactions and less reliance on barter.

Such schemes were not at all successful from a financial point of view in nineteenth-century London, largely due to the compensation terms that the owners of land could demand at that time. Despite intensive discussion of their merits at or about the time the postwar land planning and taxation system was being formulated in the United Kingdom, they received no support worth mentioning.

Combinations of Taxes

Possible combinations of tax measures, taking account of national, state, and local tax jurisdiction, can also be considered. Of the various taxes reviewed, it would seem unlikely that local authorities anywhere would be given their heads other than in respect of property taxation and site-value rating, and even then they might have to operate within some fairly precisely defined limits. It is much less likely that they would be entrusted with, for instance, land-increment taxes (other than betterment levies) because these must be harmonized with national government capital gains taxes. Similarly, sales of development rights are likely to be an area in which higher-level governments would have a close interest. Land readjustment schemes might be a prerogative of local authorities, but it would seem unlikely that they would have powers to operate in this area without close reference to higher-level government land-use and land-development policy.

One particular comination of taxes is worth considering. It is sometimes argued that SVR is incompatible with land-increment taxation on the grounds that the base for SVR (at least in its more genuine format) rises as capital values appreciate, and so it is contended that to levy both would be double taxation. This proposition cannot be sustained. First, as Gaffney has shown, the base for land-increment taxation is not the same as for SVR, even though they are closely related.[30] Second, it would be just as valid to argue that net worth and capital gains taxation should not exist coterminously or that there is no case for a capital gains tax as share values rise on the grounds that increases in dividends paid out over time will mean increases in income-tax payments by recipients.

Nevertheless there are a large number of points at which local and national finances mesh. One is that substitution effects against construction activity resulting from a local property tax need to be seen in different lights depending on whether national taxes favor construction activity. Another is that the finances of a local authority may be affected rather crucially by the degree of applicability of local taxes to national installations in its area or by withdrawal or curtailment of central or state government grants if it improves its property-tax administration and collects more revenue thereby.

Land-Tax Alternatives in Urban Areas

Financial Position of LDCs

There have been a number of surveys of different aspects of this subject in recent years, and I make no pretense of mounting another one here. What I have to say is essentially a distillation of the information put together in these other surveys.[31]

On the expenditure side, the dominant theme of these studies is the constantly increasing pressure for local-government expenditure in such areas. There are several contributory causes. The first general point, frequently made with respect to governments at all levels in all countries, is that the price of services tends to increase over time relatively to the price of goods. Because public-sector expenditure tends to be more of the services than the goods variety (with obvious exceptions such as sophisticated weapons procurement), the result is that it is always a matter of running hard to stay still on the public-sector-expenditure front. Or in other words, even though public expenditure and GNP were both to increase at the same rate in terms of conventional constant-price series, there would be an increase in the ratio of public expenditure to GNP when both are expressed in current prices.

The second reason is increases in the indigenous population of cities, which has a variety of consequences for publicly provided goods and services. For instance, a rapidly growing population is likely to mean a disproportionate increase in the number of children, with consequential repercussions on the demand for education services. In fact, the population-growth situation in cities is aggravated by heavy net immigration from rural areas for a host of well-known and well-documented reasons. Extra population pressure adds to the general demand for public services in all forms—roads, water, sewerage, electricity, education, health, police, and so on—though the precise impact of population increases varies from service to service.[32] Thus for a pure public good, such as antimalaria spraying, extra population would not impose additional costs. In fact, average cost per head would fall as population increased. And insofar as immigrants tended to crowd into squatter settlements or shantytowns where it was felt that standards of service need not be as high as in the main part of a city, the public-expenditure repercussions would be less marked.[33] On the other hand, population increases may have marked effects on congestion, pollution, and the like if public expenditure is not increased drastically. These implications of population changes are fully documented elsewhere.[34]

A fourth reason for pressure on city finances is demands for increases in the standards of public provision over a broad range of services. Such demands arise in turn from both individual citizens and from commercial or industrial enterprises and for well-known reasons in both cases.

The exact impact of these combined demands on the public sector varies enormously among countries depending on such variables as the division of responsibility for the provision of particular services between the different levels of public authority. Thus Smith shows great variations in city expenditure between continents (for example, roads and transport are much more important in Africa than elsewhere), but it is also clear from his figures that there are very large variations within continents and countries.[35]

Rather than review such differences in detail, it may be helpful to single out one city to illustrate the forces at work. The experiences of Lusaka, Zambia, have been documented in various places.[36]

The following salient features should be noted:

Population grew at 13 percent per annum in the 1960s and at 9 percent per annum in the 1970s.

The informal sector absorbed a large proportion of the extra labor force.

The informal sector received substantial help from the public sector in the form of land-tenure legislation, assistance with housing, and low-cost infrastructure provision.

The additional costs of making such provisions were largely met by various charges levied on the people concerned rather than by resorting to subsidies from general revenue.[37]

Obviously experience in Lusaka must have differed very considerably from that of other cities, but it is instructive all the same to trace one set of changes in detail.

Turning to the revenue side, we again find enormous variations, as Lent, Smith, and Bahl chronicle in detail. These variations take two major forms. First, the ratio of land and property taxation to total revenue varies considerably depending on such factors as the importance of grants from higher-level governments and that of miscellaneous sources of local revenue.[38] Second, although a property tax on either a capital-value or an annual-value basis is the most common form of local tax, there are a number of riders to add. One is that property taxation can take many different forms, with multiple departures from uniformity being the rule rather than the exception.[39] Another is that examples are to be found of other types of land taxation in different countries, notably site-value taxation (Taiwan and Jamaica), betterment levies (Colombia and Philippines), vacant-land taxes (various Latin American countries), land-transactions taxes (many examples), and land readjustment schemes (Korea). This is quite apart from the curiosa that one habitually finds in the field, the usual explanation being that an arrangement lingers on long after any historical justification has disappeared; an example is the flood-control tax imposed on theater admissions in the Manila metropolitan area.

It would take too long to examine how far the very differing contributions of land and property taxation to local finances are explained by the usual concepts of tax effort and taxable capacity. Nor am I in a position to say much about the elasticity of the yield of property taxation with respect to income. Often it is extremely difficult to distinguish between revenue changes that result from tax rate and from income changes and also between real and nominal changes.[40] In principle one would expect land prices to rise at least in line with (and frequently more than in line with) nominal income, but failure to revalue the tax base is a common experience working in the opposite direction.

All in all, we should do well to remember R.S. Smith's conclusion: "In general, data limitations confronted in the study make for rather tenuous conclusions."[41]

Background to Policy

In light of these statistical findings, it is reasonable to argue that there is a strong case for improving the indigenous revenue base of many urban public authorities in many developing countries. There are a number of alternatives. One is to do nothing, which amounts to saying that one would retain nominal public responsibility for a variety of services but would not attempt to discharge it in any effective fashion. Another is to press for more grants from higher-level public authorities to facilitate execution of local responsibilities. Another is to withdraw from such responsibilities, whether in favor of the private sector or the higher echelons of the public sector. However, whatever one thinks of such alternative policies in the abstract, it seems reasonable to argue that even if all these lines are followed to some degree, the gap between revenues and expenditure demands is so great that one will still need more locally generated revenues. In fact, the scope for the alternatives is limited. Suppose we consider that of more grants from higher-level government. Quite apart from any difficulties in extracting such revenue from governments, which are likely to be financially hard pressed themselves, there is one extremely important argument of principle against it. It has often been argued that emigration from rural to urban areas in the LDCs in recent years has been in excess of that desirable on general economic and social-policy grounds. Insofar as urban services are made available to such people through the mechanism of higher-level government grants rather than locally raised revenues, immigration into cities is likely to be encouraged rather than discouraged. Obviously locally raised finance might not in practice fall on immigrants, but to rely on grants is to abandon all hope in that respect.

Given the case for raising more revenue at local level, this immediately points to land and/or property taxation, as many commentators have stressed. Thus Lady Hicks wrote, "Whatever means can be used to produce more revenue for urban authorities, a very great effort should be made somehow to include land values in the base."[42] Similarly Carl Shoup has written, "This great reservoir of finance for urban progress is, with few exceptions, being tapped at a rate far below what to most of the outside observers seems quite practicable and reasonable."[43]

Most commentators espousing the cause of raising more revenue from land taxation believe that this is by far the most likely source of increasing revenues to meet the general-expenditure purposes of urban authorities. It has not usually been a matter of arguing for land and property taxation to finance expenditure, which implicitly or explicitly is land and property related. Thus Lady Hicks explicitly argues against the earmarking principle.[44] I shall on the whole follow that line of argument here.

If it is accepted that there is a case for raising more revenue from land and property, it may be worthwhile inquiring whether there are any obvious dos and don'ts of a general nature before examining the details of individual tax possibilities. Perhaps the best way of starting is to list some of the positions taken by particular advocates of particular policies. One can very readily find support for the following propositions:

A particular form of land and property taxation has unquestionable advantages over all others.

Strict land-use planning is needed.

Land-tax policy should aim at stopping speculative purchases of land.

Any land-tax policy should include concessions to poor people.

Policies designed to tax imputed or accrued income are desirable.

One has only to list this series of propositions to see immediately how starry-eyed are some of their promoters. In judging the pleas of such advocates, it is as well to start by remembering that present land-tax systems vary considerably from country to country. Any idea that there should be a move toward a common pattern in all countries runs into some formidable difficulties. First of all, landownership rights in some countries, notably in Africa, are so diffused as to make delineation and valuation of individual property rights impossible.[45] Second, administrative limitations such as a scarcity of values or the inability or incapacity to make large-scale surveys rule out a number of possibilities.[46] Third, political constraints such as the untouchability of estates of high-ranking army officers may severely limit the scope of land and land-tax policy in many countries. Finally, quite apart from all these enduring problems, there are the transitional costs of switching from one system to another. These are not negligible, as recent experience in Jamaica has shown and the poorer the country, the heavier the relative burden.

Rather than engage in a wholesale recasting of land-tax policies as some advocate, it would seem more sensible to start on the basis that a prime requirement is to make existing systems work better. It is well known that yields of existing taxes are frequently well below the due level whether because of evasion by land and property owners, failure to revalue tax bases over time, or sheer inefficiency and corruption on the part of revenue officials.[47] Insofar as modifications to existing systems can be shown to be desirable, then one has to show flexibility in the light of local circumstances. For instance, the same expert was called upon in the 1950s to report on possible changes in Jamaica and Ghana. In the first case, the conclusion was to exclude land improvements from the tax base and in the second to confine property taxation to improvements. Another general principle must be to pay attention to the structure of national taxation when considering local tax reforms. Thus the case for a land-value increment tax is clearly stronger at the local level if there is no system or no effective system of taxing capital gains at the national level, as is indeed commonly so in LDCs.

Site-Value Rating

Site-value rating systems (SVR) frequently approximate a lump-sum tax in practice, even if not necessarily in strict principle. The exemption of improvements from the tax base means that it is likely to encourage development more than the usual type of property tax. Moreover, there is no general reason for thinking that any such resultant development will be much more likely to occur in suburbs than in city centers.[48] Distributional repercussions are less clear-cut (despite the usual assumption of tax capitalization) but are not such as to rule out SVR. From an administrative viewpoint, a good deal of evidence shows that SVR has advantages over property taxation despite the obvious problems of deciding on "highest and best" use and such well-known conundra as whether the tax base for a drained swamp should include the cost of drainage. The experience of countries where this tax has operated and general principles lead to the conclusion that valuation is easier, that it can be repeated more frequently, and that there are fewer problems of concealment than if improvements are included in the tax base.[49]

While acknowledging these advantages, many people have nevertheless felt reluctant to endorse SVR. The most general reason is that property tax is the sitting tenant, and it is reasonable to ask whether the long-term advantages of SVR are so great as to justify the costs of dispossession. The position here is something like that with national-level expenditure taxation proposals. If one were starting from scratch, one might wish to introduce a personal-expenditure tax rather than an income tax. But one is not starting from scratch, and so the decision can go the other way. Alternatively, one might say that the general principles of SVR have been known for a hundred years or so. If it were such a good tax, as is often claimed, would not many more countries have introduced it by now? A few countries have adopted it over the years, but in others, such as western Canada, the reverse has happened. Nor can the advocates of SVR point to those countries where the tax is in operation without some qualifications. Thus although improvements are excluded from the general tax on land in Taiwan, there is a separate tax on nonagricultural improvements; and some of the gilt comes off the gingerbread of the Johannesburg system when it is realized that payments for services are more important than land tax per se.[50]

Another argument frequently advanced against SVR is the sacrifice of the tax base involved in exempting improvements. Whatever the theoretical case for leaving out improvements, one clearly is likely to find it more difficult to charge at a higher tax rate on a low base than a low tax rate on a higher base. At the same time, one should not exaggerate. A number of studies have shown that the inclusion of potential site values in the tax base goes quite a long way toward compensating for the exclusion of improvements.[51] Nor should it be assumed unconditionally that the buoyancy of the tax base over time is less with SVR than with improvements. In principle, one would expect the opposite to hold.

Rather than spend more time on these general arguments and counterarguments, it may be more instructive to look at the history of one of the very few attempts at replacement of a property tax by SVR in the postwar period—in Jamaica.[52]

On the positive side, the transformation of the system was achieved, though not without a long passage of time from beginning to end. Undoubtedly there was a substantial increase in revenue collected under the new system compared to the previous one, though a fairer comparison would be with the (unknown) total, which might have been collected from the old system if the same administrative effort had been put into it. What in effect amounts to a progressive system of SVR has been introduced without any major redistributional effects, given the tendency in Jamaica for high-value improvements to take place on high-value land. It would also seem that land speculation has been less endemic than formerly, though other influences have also been at work here. Above all, public-administration costs of levying SVR have been far from formidable; for SVR they come out at 4 percent of tax yield, compared with an estimated 6.8 percent for a property tax on capital value.[53] So it can be claimed that the system has been made to work without any undue disasters.[54]

Nevertheless, there are a number of minuses. Although there is a nominal element of progression in the system, with an average tax rate of 0.84 percent for valuations of $2,000 (Jamaican dollars) and one of 5.5 percent at $50,000, much of this has in fact been lost by allowing objectors to valuations to self-assess themselves, with the result that owners of higher-valued properties objected to their valuations and then assessed themselves at much lower levels. Altogether there were some 45,000 objections to the 500,000 assessments, and the legal delays in dealing with them have been very protracted. Furthermore, in many cases people simply did not pay the due amount of tax, with the result that there were very considerable arrears of tax due by the late 1970s, some five years after the system was supposed to be fully operative. In addition, the lack of any system of aggregating different properties played havoc with the progressiveness of the system.

Nor was it only in the degree of progression that the tax departed in practice from what was intended in principle. Relief to agricultural land and hotels, for instance, meant that the lump-sum tax analogy no longer held. It is not surprising in these circumstances to find that there were no discernible improvements in land usage. And although valuation did not prove a problem as such, that did not mean that other aspects of administration were trouble free. Attempts to discover the ownership of vacant land seem to have caused some major problems, for instance.

The upshot is that the switch to SVR has not been a resounding success, and some observers are now suggesting that it would be better to plan in the longer term for reincorporation of improvements in the tax base. Nevertheless, there are some important lessons to be learned from the Jamaican experience. Some of the major ones follow:

1. Objections to valuations should not be a valid reason against tax payments on account. This is an old problem with income-tax administration in many countries. What has been learned in that area (liability to all payments of tax should not be delayed until an objection has been considered) applies equally in the land- and buildings- taxation field.

2. Transfers of property should not be registered before tax arrears have been cleared. This necessitates linkages between government departments responsible for tax collection and land registration.

3. Strong powers of recovery of tax arrears are necessary—for example, liens on property and the right to sell tax liens.

4. The local property-tax position of central government or statutory-authority properties often needs clarification. At best the position is frequently ambiguous, and at worst there is exemption against local taxes without compensation.

5. If particular activities need public encouragement and support, the appropriate method is open and outright public subsidy rather than (often-disguised) property-tax relief.

The last point leads directly to a suggestion that is often made in the local taxation field: if one has a property tax in being, why not give relief to improvements by specific exemption rather than incur all the costs of switching to SVR? In addition, it is claimed that such relief could, unlike SVR, be confined to new building only. Such an idea cannot be ruled out; indeed one finds it in a number of other countries already. At the same time, it is often a second-best expedient. First, there is a prima facie case for explicit subsidies rather than hidden ones of this kind. Second, if it is a matter of national policy to encourage new construction or some types of new construction, the costs should fall on the national rather than the local budget. There may be some particular local advantages justifying a policy of selective relief from local taxation, but one has to be sure of them before advocating such a policy.

Betterment Levies (Special Assessments)

This particular example of land-value-increment taxation is more unambiguously suitable as a local tax than are other alternatives. This technique is essentially an attempt to meet the capital costs of various types of local public works (roads provision, sewerage, water supply, and so on) by imposing special charges, related to increases in value, on land deemed to benefit from these works.[55] It is therefore an entirely different idea from another that is sometimes advanced: the desirability (or not) of tying in the level of expenditure on local public goods and services to the revenue that would be forthcoming if all land rents in an area were expropriated.

Advocates of betterment levies often point to its long history in the United Kingdom (where there are medieval origins of the technique) and the United States (where it can be traced back to 1691). And in the particular context of LDCs, Colombia is frequently pointed out as a leading example, although the same principles are also used in a number of other Latin American countries.[56] The application of this principle in Colombia has been the subject of intensive and detailed study, which I shall not recapitulate here.[57] Rather, I shall point out what one can reasonably aim at with this technique and also draw on historical experience about its efficacy.

The case for using this technique is usually based on two main arguments. The first is that it is equitable to levy charges on those who benefit from the particular public expenditure; it is simply an application of the benefit principle, often discussed in public-finance literature. Second, a tax on increments in value is deemed to have minimum resource-misallocation consequences. Thus R.M. Bird writes, "In view of the potential of special assessments for financing needed urbanization investments, their allocative merits and their general equity justification a more thorough investigation of this area seems long overdue."[58]

Additional arguments such as the possibilities of using finance from one betterment levy to meet the costs of the next public project are also sometimes put forward, though these are clearly not as straightforward in an age of inflation as when there is reasonable price stability.

Some important counterarguments must be fully understood. Let us start with a quotation from Sir Dennis Robertson:

> A particularly specious instance of the argument for earmarking rents for uses closely cognate to that in which they have arisen is that which is sometimes put forward in connection with the extension of costly transport undertakings, such as tube railways. Such extensions, it is argued, should be furnished partly out of the proceeds of "betterment" charges imposed on the owners of land whose rental value has been raised by the existence of the new facilities, such as residential building land in the vicinity of the new suburban tube stations. Otherwise, so the argument runs, this type of investment will not be carried as far as the public interest would dictate. So put, I do not think the argument is sound. There may be other reasons . . . for subsidising urban transport; and there may be general reasons . . . for taxing increments in rental values. But the case for linking the two together in any special manner seems to be illusory.[59]

arg against

The following propositions seem to be the relevant ones.

1. Betterment levies are not a perfect substitute for the usual marginal-cost-pricing principles. In the one or two investigations that have been made

into the effects of charging by one method rather than the other, considerable differences emerged.[60] This is what one might have expected a priori: charges related to areas under marginal benefit curves will differ from those related to areas under marginal cost curves.

2. Charging on a marginal-cost basis, however refined, may fail to cover average costs for well-known reasons such as economies of large-scale production or the impossibility of exclusion of some consumers.

3. The assumption that betterment levies are the most suitable means of bridging any such financial gap would have to rest on one of the following bases. First, there is a natural presumption that the balance of finance should be found from the people who benefit from the public expenditure. In effect, this is a strong application of the earmarking principle in that it is not just being said that specific expenditures must be accompanied by identifiable revenues but in addition that the revenues should be raised from beneficiaries. The appropriateness or nonappropriateness of earmarking can be debated, but if one does choose this justification, there is an important implication: by exactly parallel reasoning, compensation should be paid to those whose property values suffer from public works, often a much larger group than one might think at first sight. (This principle was recognized in the Middle Ages in England in that the four northernmost counties were given special reliefs to compensate them for the inability of the crown to defend them against the marauding Scots from across the border.) Alternatively, it can be argued that raising finance in this way (in the limit a system of perfect price discrimination) is preferable to any alternative means on the usual combination of allocation, distributional, and administrative criteria. This will depend on whether, for instance, landowners' rent increases are more in the nature of a surplus than other possible tax bases; whether landowners are richer than other possible taxpayers; or whether there is a national capital gains tax in existence, and so on. And even if it can be shown that in general betterment levies are at the top of this league table, it still has to be demonstrated that one could raise sufficient revenue from them to finance public improvements without a slip in their league position.

4. Assuming that one can surmount these theoretical hurdles, there are very real problems of administration; the determination of the boundaries of the area that is deemed to have benefited is one. Perhaps the most formidable is the difficulty of raising sufficient revenue by this means, given the likelihood that the value of land will start to appreciate long before the public works take place. A further difficulty concerns disentangling the effects of public works and other changes on land values. Difficulties may also occur with the extraction of contributions from landowners on the basis of accruals rather than realization of enhanced value. One way has been suggested of meeting this problem: wait until realization takes place

but charge interest on the time delay.[61] This solution, however, creates as many problems as it solves in that the public-sector cash-flow position receives no immediate help, administrative costs mount, and so on.

Some lessons on the difficulty of raising revenue from betterment levies can be drawn from both British and American experience. The London County Council applied the technique in a number of street and property improvements around the end of the nineteenth century but its experience was so unsatisfactory that it gave up the idea.[62] Similarly, a detailed investigation of New York City data in the period 1915-1934 also showed that relatively little revenue was received from special assessments in Flatbush, Brooklyn.[63] It is fair to add that there have been notable successes in this field such as the financing of Sydney Harbour Bridge and the Miami (Ohio) Flood Control Project, but they are not conspicuous by their frequency.

The overall conclusion must be that it would not be wise to put too much weight on betterment levies on either theoretical or practical grounds. Nor should one accept uncritically the claim that betterment levies have been highly effective in Colombia and elsewhere in Latin America. In the particular case of the valorization charges in Bogotá, it is quite clear when one examines the charging basis in detail that they amount to a method of recovering costs rather than of tapping benefits and that the basis of charge on any one property owner is an assessment of costs incurred in servicing that particular parcel of land (with concessions to lower-income groups) rather than of benefits conferred.[64] In effect, therefore, the system amounts to a component of marginal-cost pricing rather than of betterment appropriation in the traditional sense. This is in no sense a matter for disapprobation or for denigration of the careful advance preparations or of the political will needed to establish such a system but simply a call for understanding what is really happening.

As far as betterment levies in the strict sense are concerned, one should be very cautious about their endorsement. The most that one should be prepared to advocate is small-scale experiments to see if they are a valuable technique in a particular city. The warning of Macon and Mañon is highly relevant:

> Excessive enthusiasm should not initially be generated for the betterment levy as a major source of project financing; excessive expectations could become a source of disillusionment which could be a cause of failure for later projects.[65]

Other Radical Measures

Special land-increment taxes can take two main forms, betterment levies apart. The first is a tax on accruals of realizations of site values; the second is one associated with permitted changes of use under a system of land control. It is very difficult to visualize either of these taxes as being very effective at the local level. There have been plenty of attempts at one or other form of tax at national or state level, though the record is far from inspiring. But it is significant that the various recent surveys of practices in different countries do not list any examples of purely local taxes on these lines. The reasons are not far to seek. First, there is the obvious limitation of administrative resources. It is highly unlikely that local personnel will be of the necessary caliber for the purpose except in exceptional circumstances. Second, there are exceedingly awkward spillover problems. For example, city A permits a development on its boundary, which results in increases in land values in city B. Alternatively, city A may refuse to allow a development within its own area, and so the developer goes to city B instead. If such refusals are legitimate grounds for compensation of any kind, then city A's budget position is worsened while city B's is improved. (This is what tended to happen in the United Kingdom in the 1930s.) More generally, we do not find general capital gains taxes imposed at local level, and so why should anyone think that land might be an exception?

Ursula Hicks summarized the position in this way:

> There is however in many countries a strong feeling that it should be possible to tax betterment more specifically and a number of attempts have been made to do so. While everyone agrees that betterment exists it has proved a "will o' the wisp" exercise to identify, isolate and quantify it and then to determine to what extent it is due to public activity. LDC Metros would be well advised to reserve their scarce staff for more important investigations, relying on the change in market values to pick up most of the betterment.[66]

Land readjustment or consolidation schemes do not set out to be a way of capturing betterment in any systematic way as distinct from raising funds for land servicing or redevelopment. The history of such operations suggests that they are perhaps a much better way of providing a mechanism for ensuring land servicing than for helping local revenues. Nineteenth-century history in the United Kingdom is replete with schemes that were financial failures for the local authorities concerned.[67] Either compensation terms to landowners on taking over land were too generous or disposal values after redevelopment were too low, or both. Although the Doebele evidence about practices in South Korea and Japan gives a much more cheerful picture, other observers have been more cautious about these results.[68] Moreover, it would appear that in some cases, good results have come from particular cities in a country; if the technique was so advantageous, why did not all the other cities in a country adopt it? All in all one suspects that in just the same way as German practices in this area never caught on elsewhere in Western Europe, South Korea too may be an isolated example of the practicality and advisability of such a system in LDCs. Transplants of such schemes between countries may prove extremely difficult.

As further evidence, recent personal inquiries in Japan elicited the fact that special authorities have frequently been set up locally in the postwar period to acquire land suitable for development, service it, and then dispose of it to potential users. The usual objective seems to have been the provision of sites for industrial and other purposes rather than to make a net contribution to urban finances. One specific example was a joint scheme by the prefecture and city of Osaka in the 1960s to reclaim land in the port area for industrial purposes. Funds were borrowed from West Germany, the site was acquired, developed, and disposed of, and the loan paid off. The project was economically viable but did not contribute to the finances of the city or prefecture in any important way.

Finally, we can deal very quickly with direct price intervention. The idea that prices can be regulated easily by administrative fiat persists in the land case, as with many other goods and services. But there is no evidence to show that such devices, whether in the form of temporary freezing of land values or in the form of ordaining that land must change prices at, say, agricultural-use levels, can work in more than a limited context or for a limited time. Either land markets seize up, or the controls are eroded by various ruses, or both. Nor is it desirable that such policies should work if a major result would, as seems only too likely, be misallocation of land usage. Proposals of this sort should be strongly discouraged.[69]

Improvements in Existing Practices

If we want to make existing systems work better, pride of place must be given to examining the property tax, the most important tax found in LDC cities.[70]

The first rule is not to plunge into some new scheme without adequate study and preparation. There have been so many hundreds of experiments with property taxation in different countries at different times that it is highly unlikely that some seemingly new idea has not been tried elsewhere before. Possession of the ability or willingness to learn from other people's mistakes may be the cardinal virtue in this area. Nor can one assume that particular devices are necessarily worth trying even if they have no previous record of failure. Given the administrative limitations, there is a strong premium on not trying to be too clever and indulge in fancy ideas and whims.

As for the choice between capital- and rental-value bases, the initial presumption must be that costs of change are likely to be considerable, and so one should contemplate overall recasting of a property-tax system only if there are clearly demonstrable advantages, such as the impossibility of operating a rental base for domestic property if most of it is owner occupied. History shows that either rental- or capital-value systems can work, and there is certainly no presumption that one is always preferable to the other. Making an existing system work better has a far higher priority than recasting it. There are two obvious possibilities of improvement. One is that existing systems often fail to cover all the properties in an urban area, such as shantytowns and squatter settlements. Another is that revaluation is not carried out at regular intervals, with the consequential needs to raise tax rates above what they would otherwise have been and to make sharp adjustments in the tax basis at a later date.[71] Another important means of making an existing system go further is to fight against attempts to extend the area of exceptions or exemptions and, indeed, to reduce it if possible. This is particularly so with central-government and public-utility properties. Progressive tax rates are sometimes advocated for property taxation, but the case for subjecting business property to such a rate structure seems highly debatable.[72] And even with domestic property, one has to face the difficulties of aggregating property effectively when ownership is nominally divided among different members of the same family.

If it is believed that local property taxation is a serious impediment to land development, one could adopt the expedient of raising the tax rate for the land component more than for the buildings component, but there are some serious difficulties in this approach.

On the more purely administrative side, there are a number of well-known defects. A survey in the Philippines listed the absence of tax maps, the lack of cadastral surveys, the laxity of officials, and a tendency to rapid staff turnover as major handicaps.[73] In that country only half of the local property tax due is actually collected.[74] And as an example of other deficiencies, Jamaican legislation in respect of land-improvement taxation has been criticized as so badly drafted as to make it unworkable.[75]

One particular device, often suggested, is that of property self-assessment. Such a technique is clearly preferable to nonassessment but so clearly inferior to government assessment that I do not consider it further here. Perhaps the most relevant and revealing comment on assessment is to be found in a report on why local tax allocations in the Philippines in the mid-1970s were four times higher in nominal terms than in the mid-1960s.[76]

There is one last point to note about making property taxation more effective. Insofar as revaluations reflect rising land values, there is some element of betterment capture involved, even if not so effectively as when there is also a tax on increments in value.

Local taxation of vacant land is another common technique. But the first problem is to decide exactly what is meant by *vacant land*. Obviously it would be ridiculous to levy a special tax on a plot of land that has been vacant for a week between the clearing of an old building and the start of the construction of a new one. On the other hand, it would be inequitable to subject privately owned vacant land to a special tax but not publicly owned land.[77] Having defined what is vacant land, one has to trace the owner. It would not be unreasonable for local authorities to have powers to take over vacant land for which there is no identifiable owner, provided due legal processes are observed. Various questions arise in settling tax rates. In general, if speculative landholding promises quick and substantial gains, tax rates will have to be high to persuade owners to make use of the land. But the precise objective of the tax then comes into question: if it is to raise more revenue, one wants to see land kept vacant. There is obviously a trade-off here with land utilization objectives. Another point on tax rates is that vacant land is not all alike. A case could be made for taxing unserviced vacant land at a lower rate than serviced. Finally, objections are bound to be raised if vacant-land taxes impinge heavily on small landowners.

Further refinements can be introduced into such a tax, such as raising the rate of tax the longer land is not developed. But it would be wise to be careful here. Although the practice of levying vacant-land taxes in various countries makes it a serious device to contemplate, it does not seem so far to have made major contributions to local budgets, so it should be thought of as a subsidiary rather than a principal method and one that is unlikely to yield returns to efforts to make it very elaborate.

We now come to transactions taxes. To an economic theorist they are not an attractive tax, but they do exist in a wide range of countries and make some contributions to LDC city revenues. Clearly they can work only if there is an effective legal system of defining land-right titles and of registering changes in them. If this condition is fulfilled, one can then have either a national tax, the proceeds of which are readily attributable to local authorities, or, preferably, one under the jurisdiction of the local authorities themselves. Sometimes, as the data show, it will be easier to levy such charges on land and sometimes on land and buildings.[78] There can also be discrepancies between the treatment of domestic and business property and similarly between taxes levied on purchases and on sales. Finally, the tax-rate structure can be made progressive if it is desired. It seems extremely unwise to be dogmatic about which of these forms of tax should be applied in any particular local area. There is scope for a good deal of variation depending on local circumstances. At the same time, if one has a local rather than a national transactions tax, it is sensible to avoid large differences between tax design and tax rates in different cities in the same country. Land markets are hardly likely to function well if such differences are important.

One question likely to be raised is whether taxes of this kind can be levied regardless of other taxes imposed on land, whether at central or local level. The general answer would seem to be "yes." There is no reason in principle why transactions taxes should not coexist with local property taxes or national capital gains taxes, for instance. And if for any reason it is thought that the combined weight of such taxes is too great, the type of device encountered in Jamaica (people have the option on transferring property of either paying a 12½ percent tax on their capital gains or a 2½ percent tax on sales value) is available.

The next topic is that of charging for locally supplied services, whether of the traditional public-utility type or on a wider scale so as to include such items as garbage collection, local public bus services, and the like. In principle betterment levies are not to be regarded as a straightforward substitute for pricing policies for publicly provided services where pricing is feasible. We must now look at ways in which improvements can be made in these pricing policies as found in practice.

There is abundant evidence that failures to plan for appropriate types of services or to charge for them on an appropriate basis are a drain on local finances in many parts of the world. Sometimes sheer inefficiency enters into the picture. It has been reported, for example, that at one time, Lagos bus engines were kept running all night in case they would not restart the following morning.[79] But our main concern here is rather different. First, there is the danger of utilizing totally inappropriate technologies. This problem has been explored fully in a number of World Bank books and papers, especially those relating to the relative costs of alternative methods of provision of fresh water and of disposing of human waste.[80] Another illustration of the importance of choosing low-cost technology is to be found from the experience of Lusaka where an essential ingredient in coping with the additional sewerage costs imposed by heavy immigration was to install low-cost technology but to charge people sufficient to cover such costs.[81]

The design of the pricing system is of crucial importance. The general economic efficiency case for choosing a marginal cost basis is well known, but equally, there are severe constraints on the extent to which total costs may be allowed to exceed total revenues. It may well be that tariffs containing three elements could go a long way toward solving this dilemma.[82] Thus in the case of water one might have: a charge related to the marginal cost of providing the amount consumed, plus a lump-sum connection charge to the system, plus a distribution charge varying according to location of the consumer and the length of water mains needed.

Obviously the details must differ depending on the nature of the service and the capacity of the local administration, but the proposal is at the very least suggestive of the sorts of ways in which one should think about these problems.

Another issue frequently arises in this field: given that there is only limited scope for an excess of total cost over total revenue, is there nevertheless room for cross-subsidization within such a constraint? This brings us to the familiar lifeline type of proposal—that water and electricity consumers might be allowed to consume small quantities at especially low prices or that local authorities should juggle rents of publicly provided accommodation in pursuance of a similar objective. There are two main problems about such proposals. First, they may be a very inefficient way of redistributing income. The crucial question is how far people with low incomes are small-scale consumers of such services. It could quite easily be the case that rich people were small-scale consumers and poor people large-scale consumers of some public services. Hence a tariff involving higher prices for greater consumption would be perverse from an income-distribution standpoint. And even if the position of poor people were to improve as a result of cross-subsidization, it certainly does not necessarily follow that it is the richest elements as distinct from the middle strata who would be adversely affected. The second problem is the familiar asymmetry between the enormous difficulty of removing selective subsidies once they have become embedded in the system and the equally enormous difficulty of retaining the higher charges on others necessary to prevent recourse to general revenue financing.

Charging for local services is a vast subject, and there can be no question that it is one of the crucial aspects of the finance of many cities in many LDCs.

This catalog of the tools of the trade is meant to include the principal ones only rather than aim at comprehensive coverage. There are various other devices found in different cities in different countries. One obvious example is that of saving funds by purchasing land required for public purposes well in advance of requirements.[83] But many such devices involve administrative practices more than economic principles, and so I do not aim at describing them here.

Conclusions

First, there are no easy-to-come-by miracle solutions of universal validity. If there were, they would have been found already. It must be remembered that the problems I have been discussing are not new ones at all. In a number of major respects they closely resemble those found in the nineteenth century in other countries, so it is not as if no one had previously had any occasion to ponder on these matters.[84] In other words, there is a presumption that the rewards from attempting to be overclever and overadventurous in the search for solutions are unlikely to offset the risks involved. This applies most particularly to attempts at direct intervention in land markets by introducing price controls and cognate devices.

Furthermore there are a number of tight constraints on what urban authorities can possibly do. These may be of a political nature (untouchability of land rights of some powerful groups); they may be legal (no clear definition of land rights); or they may be administrative (lack of cadastral surveys, shortages of valuers, and so on). All such limitations circumscribe possible actions very tightly in the short run.

Generally it is more desirable to make existing systems work better rather than replace them completely. Whatever one thinks of the merits of SVR, betterment levies, and other land-increment taxes, land consolidation schemes, and so on, one has to be very careful about supplanting existing systems by such techniques. There is likely to be a heavy price to pay in terms of transitional costs, so unless it can be shown that there are very considerable long-run advantages—and usually that is not so—the case for wholesale change is very dubious. This is not to say that there are no opportunities for small-scale experimentation in levying additional taxes to those already in being, and still less that one should abandon SVR or land consolidation and other devices where any are already working. It is simply an argument in favor of retaining those taxes that are already well established unless a strong case can be made to the contrary.

The same proposition holds when looked at from another angle. Well-established tax procedures can be wrecked by intemperate land-tenure reforms as well as by ill-considered tax replacements. The history of Tanzania and Zambia shows how easily this can happen.[85]

When we consider how to make existing arrangements work better, there are a number of illustrations from recent case histories that have to be recalled. We might synthesize these various experiences in the following way:

Land and property titles need to be clearly defined in law, and an efficient machinery is needed for registering changes in such titles.

It takes time for any tax to bed down, but the process is helped if the legislation is studied in detail before being enacted.

Legislation, whether on property taxation or other forms of land taxation, needs to apply with as few exemptions and special reliefs as possible. Pleas for exemption of particular income groups, particular areas, and particular activities should be looked at with the greatest suspicion. Once such concessions are granted, they are extremely difficult to withdraw, and they are an invitation to other special-interest groups to ask for similar privileges.

On tax assessment, the most important point, especially in an age of inflation, is the need for regular revaluation.

On tax collection, there should be no question of allowing delays of payment while appeals are being considered. Nor should titles be reregistered until tax arrears have been settled. Legal powers of distraint in case of nonpayment need to be severe and enforced.

No amount of striving for higher levels of technical competence in tax administration will be worth much unless it has the backing of the politicians who matter. This is perhaps the most important point that can be made in this field.

Notes

1. Of the fifteen or so cities in various continents investigated by Bahl, all except Nairobi levied some form of tax on land plus buildings. See R.W. Bahl, ed., *The Taxation of Urban Property in Less Developed Countries* (Madison: University of Wisconsin Press, 1979), chap. 1.

2. See, for instance, D. Netzer, *The Economics of the Property Tax* (Washington, D.C.: Brookings Institution, 1966); and for discussion of the U.K. type of tax, see A.R. Prest, *The Taxation of Urban Land* (Manchester: Manchester University Press, 1981) and also *Intergovernmental Financial Relations in the UK*, Research Monograph No. 23 (Canberra: Centre for Research on Federal Financial Relations, Australian National University, 1978).

3. For the benefit of those who are not familiar with the distinction between leasehold and freehold interests in property commonly found in the United Kingdom (and to a lesser extent in some other countries with similar property laws), a rough nontechnical summary follows.

Interests in land and buildings can take a number of forms. A freehold interest exists when an individual has the right to use his land as he pleases in perpetuity, subject to other aspects of the law, such as those relating to nuisance. A leasehold interest in a particular piece of land is granted by a freeholder to a lessee in return for some form of payment (often an annual ground-rent) with various restrictions on the uses to which land can be put and with a limit to the period of time for which the lessee enjoys such rights. Leases may be granted in respect of land devoid of any structures or with buildings already erected, they may be for short or long periods of time, and they can be sold on the market (by assignment). In turn a lessee may assign rights to a sublessee and so on, always subject to the provisions of the headlease.

One feature of leasehold arrangements that is sometimes found puzzling is that a person may be granted a "building lease" on a piece of land for a certain period, often ninety-nine years. The lessee then erects a building on the land and pays a ground-rent for the use of the land during this period. At the end of ninety-nine years, all rights over the land and any building erected thereon revert to the freeholder. People are sometimes puzzled that the lessee should lose the rights over "his" building at the end of the period. They fail to realize that long leasehold interests of this sort are wasting assets in that it is part of the initial agreement that the value of the leaseholder's interest will drop to zero at the end of the stipulated period.

4. Standard references are P. Mieszkowski, "The Property Tax: An Excise Tax or a Profits Tax?" *Journal of Public Economics* 1 (1972), and H.J. Aaron, *Who Pays the Property Tax? A New View* (Washington, D.C.: Brookings Institution, 1975).

5. This argument was first developed at length by A. Marshall, *Principles of Economics* (London: Macmillan, 1920), appendix G.

6. Edwin Cannan was a well-known exponent of this view. See "The Proposed Relief of Buildings from Urban Rates," *Economic Journal* (1907) (and subsequent comments in 1908); also *The History of Local Rates in England*, 2d ed. (London: P.S. King, 1928), pp. 186ff.

7. It could easily differentiate against owners of low-value assets and in favor of owners of high-value assets—for example, if the same usage value, and hence the same tax, were deemed to be derived from a leasehold property with one year to run as from one with ninety-eight years to run.

8. Cf. C.S. Shoup in Bahl, *Taxation of Urban Property*, chap. 12.

9. Ibid., chap. 1.

10. Out of a large literature, see in particular D.C. Shoup, "Advance Land Acquisitions by Local Governments: A Cost/Benefit Analysis," *Yale Economic Essays* 9 (Fall 1969); R.S. Smith, "The Effects of Land Taxes on Development Timing and Rates of Change in Land Prices," in Bahl, *Taxation of Urban Property*; and A.A. Walters, "The Value of Urban Land," in *Urban Land Policy Issues and Opportunities*, World Bank Staff Working Paper No. 283, Vol. 1 (Washington, D.C.: World Bank, 1978). Using Shoup's notation we have

$$\frac{V'(T)}{V(T)} = r + a$$

where

$$\frac{V'(T)}{V(T)}$$

is the percentage rate of increase of the value $V(T)$ of a bare site at the time of development (T), r is the relevant interest rate, and a is the SVR tax rate.

11. Cf. J.R. Hicks, *Essays on World Economics* (Oxford: Oxford University Press, 1959), p. 242.

12. For one empirical investigation, see *The Incidence of Urban Property Taxation in Developing Countries: A Theoretical and Empirical Analysis Applied to Colombia*, World Bank Staff Working Paper No. 264 (Washington, D.C.: World Bank, 1977). It was concluded that as the ratio of land to buildings was inversely related to property values, a switch from property taxation to SVR would hurt low-income groups relatively more than others.

13. See *Final Report of Royal Commission on Local Taxation, England and Wales*, Cd. 638 (London: H.M. Stationery Office, 1901).

14. For a number of examples of such taxes in differing countries, see Smith, "Effects of Land Taxes," p. 141.

15. Prest, *Taxation*.

16. *Final Report of Expert Committee on Compensation and Betterment*, Cmd. 6386 (London: H.M. Stationery Office, 1942), p. 141.

17. As an example: "Indeed, if properly applied, there is as strong a case for financing urban expenditure through special assessments as one can find in support of using any fiscal instrument anywhere." R.M. Bird, *Charging for Public Services: A New Look at an Old Idea* (Toronto: Canadian Tax Foundation, 1976), p. 105.

18. See, for instance, a series of papers in *Urban Studies*: L.A. Rose (1973): 271-275; M. Neutze (1974): 91-92; C.D. Foster and S. Glaister (1975): 213-218; L.A. Rose (1976): 71-73.

19. See Smith, "Effects of Land Taxes," p. 145, for examples.

20. Despite statements sometimes made to the contrary. See U.K. Hicks, *The Large City: A World Problem* (London: Macmillan, 1974), p. 173.

21. See Smith, "Effects of Land Taxes," p. 140, for examples.

22. A mirror image of subsidies conditional on not growing any kind of crop on agricultural land.

23. It was announced in April 1973 that the United Kingdom would levy a charge on land not developed within a specific period after granting planning permission for such development. This would amount to 30 percent of market value if there was one year's delay and 60 percent if there was two years' delay. But in the end the proposal was not carried into law.

The idea has also been put forward in the Philippines of levying higher taxes the longer land is kept back from development. See A.Q. Yoingco, *Land Tax Policy in Developing Countries* (Manila: National Tax Research Center, 1976).

24. See F.G. Pennance, *Housing, Town Planning and the Land Commission*, Hobart Paper 40 (London: Institute of Economic Affairs, 1967), for a U.K. proposal, and D. Hagman and D. Misczynski, eds., *Windfalls for Wipeouts* (Chicago: American Society of Planning Officials, 1978), pp. 380-381, for an account of a proposal by M. Clawson.

25. For a particularly clear exposition of this point, see A.D. Scott, "Central Government Claims for Mineral Resources," Occasional Paper 8

(Canberra: Centre for Research in Federal Financial Problems, Australian National University, 1978).

26. See R. Turvey, *The Economics of Real Property* (London: Allen and Unwin, 1957), p. 103ff.

27. See, for instance, D.C. Shoup, "Land Taxation and Government Participation in Urban Land Markets," in *Urban Land Policy Issues and Opportunities*, World Bank Staff Working Paper No. 283 (Washington, D.C.: World Bank, 1980), 2:54-59; and W.A. Doebele, " 'Land Readjustment' as an Alternative to Taxation for the Recovery of Betterment: The Case of South Korea," in Bahl, *Taxation of Urban Property*; also O.F. Grimes, Jr., "Urban Land and Public Policy: Social Appropriation of Betterment," in P. Downing, ed., *Local Service Pricing and Urban Spatial Structure* (Vancouver: University of British Columbia Press, 1977).

28. For an account of this and related antecedents, see *Royal Commission on the Distribution of the Industrial Population: Final Report*, Cmd. 6153 (London: H.M. Stationery Office, 1940), p. 120.

29. Compare, for instance, the illustrative example by Doebele, "Land Readjustment," p. 165, with those cited by Turvey, *Economics*, p. 110, from nineteenth-century London experience.

30. M. Gaffney, "The Induced Slow Turnover of Capital," *American Journal of Economics and Sociology* (January, April, July, and October 1970; January 1971).

31. See, in particular, G.E. Lent, "The Urban Property Tax in Developing Countries," *Finanzarchiv* 33 (1974-1975); G.E. Lent, "Experience with Urban Land Value Tax in Developing Countries," *Bulletin for International Fiscal Documentation* (February 1978); R.S. Smith, "Financing Cities in Developing Countries," *International Monetary Fund Staff Papers* (July 1974); Yoingco, *Land Tax Policy*; R.W. Bahl, *Urban Property Taxation in Developing Countries* (Syracuse, N.Y.: Metropolitan Studies Program, Maxwell School, 1977); and Bahl, *Taxation of Urban Property*, chap. 1.

32. Effects of immigration and natural growth are not identical; for example, the former is less likely to involve a disproportionate growth in the number of children in the short run. Also the tendency for rich people to vacate city centers is less marked than in many advanced countries.

33. It is commonly said that such settlements are inhabited by 4 million people in Mexico City and by 2 million people in other cities such as Seoul and Calcutta.

34. See, for instance, J. Linn, *The Costs of Urbanization*, Urban and Regional Report No. 79-16 (Washington, D.C.: World Bank, March 1979).

35. Smith, "Financing Cities." Such figures necessarily relate to actual expenditures, which may or may not coincide with desired expenditures. See also R. Bahl, "Urban Government Financial Structure and Management in Developing Countries," mimeographed (January 1980), p. 35ff.

36. See, for example, J. Collins, I. Muller, and M. Safier, *Planned Urban Growth: The Lusaka Experience 1957-1973* (London: Development Planning Unit, University College, 1975); and Bahl, *Urban Property Taxation*.

37. The announcement in June 1975 that private rights in land, as distinct from improvements to land, were to be abrogated henceforth in Zambia fell outside the period of this study.

38. See, for example, Smith, "Financing Cities," p. 364, and Bahl, *Taxation of Urban Property*, p. 17.

39. See Yoingco, *Land Tax Policy*, for illustrations in respect of various Asian countries; and Lent, "Experience with Urban Land Value Tax," for the proposition that eleven of fifty-eight countries surveyed had differential taxes on land and improvements.

40. See Bahl, *Taxation of Urban Property*, p. 37.

41. Smith, "Financing Cities," p. 384.

42. Hicks, *Large City*, p. 217.

43. Shoup, in Bahl, *Taxation of Urban Property*, p. 272.

44. Hicks, *Large City*, p. 179.

45. See, for instance, R.H. Whittam, "Taxation of Urban Land and Buildings," in A. Adedeji and L. Rowland, eds., *Local Government Finance in Nigeria* (Ile-Ife, Nigeria: University of Ife Press, 1972), for an explanation of why land and property taxes apply only in Lagos and nowhere else in Nigeria.

46. For example, taxes on potential income, potential asset value, or potential sales have a poor record in many countries. For illustrations see S. Cnossen, *Excise Systems* (Baltimore: Johns Hopkins University Press, 1977), chap. 6.

47. See the comments on property taxation in Singapore by Grimes, "Urban Land."

48. A small experiment conducted in Nairobi points to this conclusion, even though it did suggest that SVR would bear relatively more heavily on nondomestic property. Cf. Bahl, *Urban Property Taxation*, pp. 43-46.

49. Cf. Lent, "Urban Property Tax," p. 66, for comparisons between valuation costs in New Zealand; costs were several-fold higher for property taxes than SVR.

50. McCulloch, in Bahl, *Taxation of Urban Property*, p. 265.

51. An SVR base for Jamaica of $1.869 million has to be compared with an improved value base of $2.5 million (in Jamaican dollars). See O. St. Clair Risden, *Property Taxation in Jamaica: An Analysis of Alternative Strategies for the Period 1977 to the Decade of the 1980s* (Kingston, Jamaica: Land Valuation Office, 1977). Potential values have their own problems of course.

52. Ibid., passim.

53. Ibid., table 2.

54. An essential ingredient in the changeover was a publicity campaign

to inform the public. See, for instance, the official leaflet, "One Country One System Fair and Square for All."

55. "The interception of a special and enhanced value," as the Uthwatt Committee phrased it. See *Final Report, Committee on Compensation and Betterment*, Cmnd. 6386 (London: H.M. Stationery Office, 1942).

56. See J. Macon and J.M. Mañon, *Financing Urban and Rural Development through Betterment Levies* (New York: Praeger, 1977), p. 37ff, for a review of the technique in eleven Latin American countries.

57. See, for instance, *Valorization Charges as a Method of Financing Urban Public Works*, World Bank Staff Working Paper No. 254 (Washington, D.C.: World Bank, March 1977).

58. Bird, *Charging for Public Services*, p. 113.

59. Sir Dennis Robertson, *Lectures on Economic Principles* (London: Staples Press, 1958), 2:48.

60. See, for instance, *The Costs and Benefits of Water Metering*, Report No. PUN 29A, Electricity, Water and Telecommunications Dept. (Washington, D.C.: World Bank, June 1977); see also *Economic Evaluation of Public Utilities Projects*, Report GAS 10, Electricity, Water and Telecommunications Dept. (Washington, D.C.: World Bank, 1974).

61. Cf. D.C. Shoup, "Land Taxation and Government Participation in Urban Land Markets," in *Urban Land Policy Issues and Opportunities*, World Bank Staff Working Paper No. 283 (Washington, D.C.: World Bank, May 1978), 2:49-50.

62. Thus the Kingsway-Aldwych development of 1912 cost £1.75 million, but betterment levy raised only £15,000. See R. Turvey, "The Rationale of Rising Property Values," *Lloyds Bank Review* (January 1962).

63. Cf. E.H. Spengler, "The Increment Tax v. Special Assessments," *Bulletin of National Tax Association* (June 1935, October 1935, March 1936, May 1936).

64. See, for example, *Valorization Charges*, pp. 21-22, 76-77.

65. Macon and Mañon, *Financing Urban and Rural Development*, p. 32.

66. Hicks, *Large City*, pp. 171-172.

67. See Turvey, *Economics of Real Property*, p. 108ff, for an account of the activities of the Metropolitan Board of Works in London. Only one such scheme (Northumberland Avenue) was financially successful.

68. See, for instance, Shoup, "Land Taxation," p. 54ff. See also Grimes, "Urban Land," for the comment that the South Korean experience has been gained in a climate of rapidly rising land prices and that it has been characterized by poor administration and tax evasion.

69. I give no space here to sales of development rights as a policy for LDC cities in that the prior conditions of clearly defined allocations of such rights and experience of operating such systems in more developed economies are lacking.

70. Evidence that the "new orthodoxy" on property-tax incidence is relevant to LDC conditions is far from plentiful, but the conclusions reached here do not depend on one's view about that argument.

71. This is sometimes true in countries with generally efficient local tax systems. See the comments on Taiwan site-value rating in Lent, "Experience with Urban Land Value Tax."

And for an account of the trouble experienced by Hong Kong in 1973 in trying to adjust crown rents on land to a more realistic basis, see Y.C. Yao, "Land Use Policy and Land Taxation in Hong Kong," in J. Wong, ed., *The Cities of Asia: A Study of Urban Solutions and Urban Finance* (Singapore: Singapore University Press, 1976).

72. See Shoup, in Bahl, *Taxation of Urban Property*, pp. 277-278, for further discussion.

73. *Local Finance Survey of 1967* (Manila: Joint Legislature—Executive Tax Committee, 1967).

74. R.W. Bahl, P. Brigg, and R.S. Smith, *Urban Public Finances in Developing Countries: A Case Study of Metropolitan Manila*, Urban and Regional Report No. 77-78 (Washington, D.C.: World Bank, April 1976).

75. F. Bougeon-Maassen and J.F. Linn, *Urban Public Finances in Developing Countries: A Case Study of Metropolitan Kingston, Jamaica*, Urban and Regional Report No. 77-7 (Washington, D.C.: World Bank, 1975), p. 97.

76. "The tremendous gain in the field of taxation with the onset of martial law in September 1972." "Trends in Property Tax Collection 1965-1975," *Tax Monthly* (Manila) (November 1977).

77. It has been suggested that if vacant land is owned by the local authority itself, it should be called on to pay tax to the national government at the same rate as it imposes on other vacant land.

78. Smith, in Bahl, *Taxation of Urban Property*, p. 145.

79. Hicks, *Large City*, p. 160.

80. See, for instance, R.J. Saunders and J.J. Warford, *Village Water Supply* (Baltimore: Johns Hopkins University Press, 1976). See also *Financing and Evaluation of Sewerage Projects*, Public Utility Report GAS 13, (Washington, D.C.: World Bank, 1977).

81. Collins, Muller, and Safier, *Planned Urban Growth*.

82. See Bird, *Charging for Public Services*, p. 40, for a reference to such a scheme. The principles behind the Bogotá valorization charge are not too dissimilar.

83. See Grimes, "Urban Land," for an appraisal of such policies in Singapore.

84. Cf. P. Hall, *Urban and Regional Planning* (Newton Abbot: David and Charles, 1975), p. 23, on nineteenth-century England: "The parallel with the cities of the developing world is in several ways only too exact. The

people . . . were overwhelmingly coming from the countryside. They tended to be drawn from the poorer section of the rural population . . . the social arrangements in the towns were quite incapable of meeting their needs for shelter, for elementary public services like water and waste disposal or for health treatment."

85. See Lent, "Experience," pp. 76-77.

24 Land-Tenure Systems and Land Reform in Botswana

B.K. Temane

The issue of land tenure is of great importance in most developing countries. Policymakers are often caught between conflicting arguments on the subject of land tenure and agricultural development. One position holds that traditional landholding systems are primary obstacles to increasing the economic and social performance of the rural sector. Others assert that the tenure system seldom creates serious obstacles to development, since once new and economically profitable opportunities appear, the participants will adapt the institutions.

Land-tenure systems define the formal and customary arrangements whereby individuals and groups secure access to the productive capabilities of the land. As a society begins to modernize, customary social and economic relationships are forced to change. The implications of these changes on development strategy must be addressed by government policymakers.

A variety of land-tenure institutions exist throughout the world:

1. Landlord-tenant system: While landownership may be concentrated among a few individuals, the managerial and labor functions are decentralized among a large number of tenants on small, often subdivided plots.
2. Dualistic structures: These systems may take the form of the latifundia-minifundia systems of Latin America where large estates (latifundia) formed by resident workers with plots and hired workers coexist alongside a large number of small, near-subsistence farms (minifundia). A second such system of tenure is that of plantation agriculture, devoted to export crops existing alongside small, individually farmed plots devoted to subsistence agriculture.
3. Family-farm system: Landownership predominates, though some tenancy arrangements may exist. This may take the form of the small, labor-intensive farms of eastern Asia or the larger capital-intensive farms of North America.
4. The traditional communal type of sub-Saharan Africa landownership (right of alienation) is vested in a collective body, while individual families have usufructory rights.

Botswana Land Tenure

Botswana is unique in the world in that there exist three distinct land-tenure systems within the country: freehold land comprising 6 percent of the land area, state land with 23 percent, and tribal land with 71 percent (see figures 24-1 and 24-2).

Freehold land encompasses four blocks of freehold farms—three on the eastern and southern borders of the country (the Molopo, Tuli block, and Tati farms) and one in the west (the Ghanzi farms). Title to these farms was secured by South African settlers from the tribal authorities during the colonial era. In the east these farms provided an effective buffer zone between Botswana tribesmen and the expansionist tribal pressures in southern Africa.

State land is land formerly declared crown land during the colonial administration. The land was secured from the tribal authorities for administrative purposes. Since independence large amounts of this state land have been tribalized (that is, reclassified tribal land).

Tribal land encompasses the vast majority of the total land of most of Botswana.

Historically, all land in Botswana was vested in the chiefs of various tribes, to be held in trust for members of that tribe. Land was allocated by the chiefs' representatives—the ward head and subward heads—upon application by tribesmen. Membership in a given tribe ensured an individual's right of access to tribal land for his use. (Some modification of this has taken place in the institution of freehold and state tenure blocks.)

Tribal land was divided into three classifications indicated by the use of the land: residence, arable lands, and communal grazing areas lands. These classifications can be visualized as a series of concentric circles. In the center was the village, where individuals obtained plots of land for construction of residences. Surrounding the village, land was allocated by the tribal authority upon request by individuals for arable production. As long as the land was used, security of tenure was assured. Farther from the village was land designated as communal grazing areas. Access to this land was open to everyone for the grazing purpose. Some individualization of tenure developed in the establishment of cattle posts surrounding privately developed water sources.

The Beginning of Reform

In 1968 the Botswana Parliament passed the Tribal Land Act, which provided for the establishment of tribal land boards (see figure 24-3). It vests tribal land in these boards and defines their powers and duties. With this

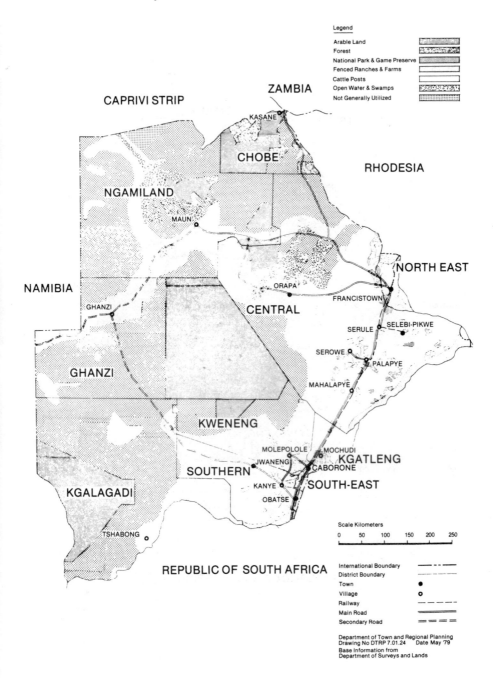

Figure 24-1. Present Land Use

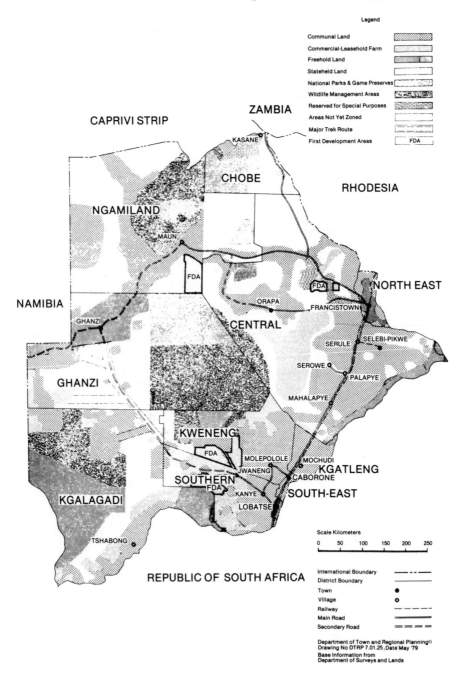

Figure 24-2. Proposed Land Use

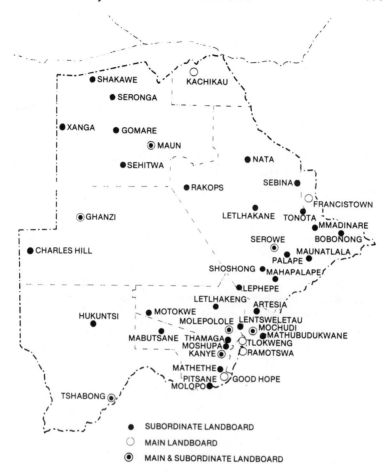

Figure 24-3. Main Land Boards and Subordinate Land Boards

legislation, the authority of the chiefs in relation to the land was transferred to the land boards, which now hold the land in trust for the members of the tribe. Tribal land was subsequently allocated according to either customary or common-law procedures as explained in the act. Nine tribal land boards were created in 1970. This proved to be inadequate in four cases, so twenty-seven subordinate land boards were established in 1973. With the creation of new tribal territories from state land in 1976, three additional main land boards were established. Land-board membership is generally comprised of one representative of the tribal authority, usually the chief; two members elected by the district council; and two members appointed by the minister of local government and lands.

Major difficulties have arisen in the evolution of land boards as arable land-allocation institutions, principally in delineating their relationship to the district councils and to the chiefs. These issues were discussed in the report of the Interministerial Commission on Land Board Operations (February, 1978). The commission's recommendations have not been implemented, however, because the government is waiting for recommendations to be presented by a subsequent local government structure review commission. This report is due shortly.

The land board-chief interrelationship presents a number of difficult administrative issues. Traditionally land allocations were part of the chief's activities, administered fairly simply by his subordinates. With the institutionalization of the land board, this allocation procedure has been administratively complicated by the necessity of applying for land through the land board rather than directly to an individual. Thus in areas where access to land boards is difficult, the potential of reverting to the old allocation system or self-allocation is evident. Second, a question arises in the settlement of land disputes. Traditionally such disputes were settled in the customary courts; however, with the advent of the land board, a functioning, understood system has been replaced by one that initially lacks the administrative capacity to deal with the questions it faces.

The land board-district council interrelationship presents similar administrative problems. District councils are elected bodies charged with providing and maintaining services to the districts, as well as formulating and implementing development policy. Two members of the council sit on the land board, and the council secretary is often the land-board secretary. The council can issue policy directives to the land board, although the land boards make the final decisions on land allocation. These types of issues logically present themselves as a new institution is created. The government has been criticized for replacing an old institution (the tribal authority) with a new institution that is not as effective. This is being addressed by the development of training programs for land-board members and staff, recruitment of a cadre of technical officers for land boards, and the improvement of channels of information flows from the districts to the central government.

The difficulty of this situation, however, lies not only in the development of a new, viable, effective institution but also in that other government needs must be addressed at the same time. Thus, government programs having significant tenure implication have gone ahead while the institutions charged with the responsibility are still trying to understand their role.

Tribal Grazing Lands Policy

In 1975 the government issued a white paper, Tribal Grazing Lands Policy (TGLP). This program is unique in Africa and perhaps the world in the extent of consultation involved in the development and implementation of the program. The policy presented a number of issues. Tenure modifications were occurring on communal grazing land through the perverse applications of traditionally accepted water-use rights. Under traditional land-use patterns, surface water is treated as communal property. However, if an individual develops his own water point, he has exclusive right over it. By limiting the access of others to that water point, an individual effectively establishes control over the surrounding grazing land. In the last decade, improved range management and favorable beef prices have led to increasing numbers of cattle. This larger herd has led to increasing range degradation, soil erosion, and bush encroachment, particularly at surface water points and boreholes where cattle are concentrated. Given the existing water rights, wealthier members of the population could ensure grazing and water for their herds by drilling private boreholes. Individuals unable to do so were forced to keep their herds on the deteriorating land surrounding existing water sources.

The objectives of TGLP were threefold: to stop overgrazing and degradation of the veld, to promote greater equality of incomes in the rural areas by safeguarding the interest of those who own few cattle or none at all, and to allow for growth and commercialization of the livestock industry.

To ensure the success of this program, a major land-use planning exercise was mounted in the tribal areas. Initially four major land areas were zoned:

1. Commercial areas to be demarcated into ranches for allocation to groups or individuals who will be given exclusive rights to definable areas of land.
2. Communal areas that generally follow traditional land-use patterns with consideration for the future in terms of arable agriculture, water rights, and so on.
3. Wildlife areas to be zoned for the development of wildlife-management programs.
4. Reserved areas set aside for the future, to be utilized by expanding human population. As the zoning process progressed, reserved areas were combined with communal areas for land-use planning exercises.

Each district was charged with the responsibility of drawing up a land-use plan for the district, which designated priorities for the development of the commercial ranching sector as first- and second-development areas. Once the land boards and district councils had agreed upon the land-use plans, the plans were submitted to the Lands Development Committee for final approval by the central government before implementation.

A second and more important program was carried out at the same time. The objective was a publicity campaign mounted by the government to explain TGLP to the people. The campaign consisted of a series of radio programs, *Kgotla* (village) meetings addressed by senior government officials, and the formulation of discussion groups to solicit ideas from the people for the implementation of the program.

Once the land-use plans had been approved and technical capacity permitted, ranches were demarcated in each district requesting ranches. After ranches are demarcated, a careful allocation procedure takes place. During or shortly after demarcation, a detailed population survey of the ranch area is carried out to determine who is living in the ranch area, has land rights, or is utilizing the land for hunting and gathering purposes. Such claims are registered and, if they are substantial, ranches may be redemarcated or dezoned. Following the population survey, the land board then advertises the availability of commercial ranches in the area, inviting people to apply for them.

This advertising campaign consists of radio, newspaper, and poster advertisement, as well as conducting informational *Kgotla* meetings near or in the ranch area itself, again informing the people of the area of the communalization of the land and inviting the registration of claims over that land. Review of these claims may again result in dezoning some ranching areas. During the advertising campaign, applications for individual ranches are submitted to the land board. The final step in the procedure is that of the allocation hearing at which time applicants and individuals registering claims to land come before the land board. If no claims are presented on the ranches, applications are approved and the ranches are allocated. If claims exist, compensation for these claims is negotiated between both parties if they are willing to arbitrate an agreeable solution. If such an agreement is not reached, the ranch is dezoned.

Once the allocation is complete, leases are signed by the applicant and the land board. Exclusive rights to the land are given to the leaseholder. The initial period of the lease is fifty years and is renewable. The leaseholder is also subject to a rent on the land payable to the land board, subject to review every five years.

Recognizing the difficulties faced by the land boards in implementing this program, the government has provided assistance to the boards during the early stages of each district's program. This assistance includes a series of guidelines that explain TGLP and provide the legal background of the program, a step-by-step discussion of the allocation procedure, and a discussion of some of the policy implications of the program. Additionally, central-government staff organized training programs for land-board members and staff to review the procedure and policies associated with the program.

A number of difficulties have been encountered by the land boards and the central government in the implementation of this program, which are under review by the government at this time. First, the rate of demarcation and allocation of ranches has been hampered by technical and administrative breakdowns. The initial demarcation procedures went slower than expected as technical and logistical problems were overcome. As these were solved, administrative delays related to implementation needed to be faced. The process of consultation and explanation of government policies has taken longer than anticipated. Second, an early assumption that sizable amounts of land were unused has had to be revised. Increased detailed investigations of ranching areas have shown a greater human population than originally anticipated in terms of hunters and gatherers, necessitating the consideration of development programs for these people to secure their livelihood. And somewhat related but including other aspects as well is the issue of compensation. If an area is commercialized and an individual has made some capital improvements on the land, how is that individual to be compensated for those improvements? This would include situations where the land board secures the land as well as where a third party is granted use of the land.

Table 24-1 summarizes the status of TGLP to date, including the number of ranches demarcated, advertised, and allocated in each district.

While the implementation of TGLP moves ahead, the government is continually being forced to address issues related to that program. That the policy is moving slowly is indicative not only of the government's concern for the people's acceptance of the program but also of its continued conviction that it is a viable program.

While TGLP has concentrated government efforts on the communal grazing lands, a second rural-development program is moving ahead in the communal arable lands: the Arable Lands Development Program (ALDEP). The general framework of the ALDEP program is to provide input subsidies to arable activities.

A major project included in the ALDEP program is that of a fencing

Table 24-1
TGLP Ranches

District	Ranches Demarcated	Ranches Advertised	Ranches Allocated
Central	12	12	7
Kgalagadi	43	10	9
Kweneng	65	11	1
Ngamiland	72	72	39
Ngwaketse	37	37	12
Total	229	142	68

subsidy, which tentatively will function on a sliding scale of subsidy levels to individuals and groups. Subsidies to individuals will be fairly high but will be limited to a maximum amount of hectarage. Group subsidies, while lower, will be designed to encourage the separation of communal grazing areas and arable land areas.

The implications related to land tenure are obvious. As increased amounts of capital investments are made on arable lands, an increased sense of security of tenure is likely. The limitation of the fencing subsidy to a maximum hectarage will limit a certain speculative aspect potentially associated with such a scheme. However, the likelihood of land boards' reallocating fenced but unused plots may be significant.

A second component of the ALDEP program is the determination of minimal arable holdings to provide adequate incomes for people involved in arable agricultural production. Individual land boards determine their policy for allocation of arable plots, but a comparison of actual plot size allocated to that necessary for subsistence production has never been carried out. The result of this study may result in the necessity of reviewing land-board allocation policies and may have significant implications for districts that have a land shortage and are allocating below-subsistence-size plots.

The original ALDEP proposals concentrated on providing assistance to small-farmer agriculture. Recent proposals are now considering the inclusion of subsidies for larger commercial farmers. Given that some areas of the country may have substantial underutilized land capacity, the commercialization of the arable-lands sector in these districts may necessitate a consultation program similar to that of TGLP. Further considerations must be addressed in the implications of a commercialization orientation of the arable agricultural sector in relation to the subsistence producer.

A fourth major component of the ALDEP program is a draft-power subsidy scheme. Early studies have indicated that major constraints to increasing arable production are associated with timely access to draft power. The subsidization of this sector in all likelihood will increase the number of animals near the lands. This presents a basic problem having two components. Given that there currently exists a conflict between arable lands and communal grazing land, an increase in the numbers of livestock in the area will exacerbate the problem. Not only will increased numbers of livestock necessitate increased demands for pasturage, but similarly with increasing inputs into arable production, in all likelihood pressure for expansion of arable lands will occur, reducing the availability of grazing lands.

The tenure implications of increased inputs into the arable agricultural sector necessitate close monitoring of such programs. The government is aware of these implications and is trying to incorporate these considerations into the programs designed to respond to the needs of arable agricultural producers.

A third program, not yet formulated as a government program as TGLP and ALDEP have been but being dealt with more on administrative terms, is that of a land-inventory and registration program. With increasing numbers of people requesting plots of land for arable production, areas of heavy population concentration are anticipating, if not already faced with, a land shortage. Currently individual land boards set their policy for allocation of plots. These policies include such considerations as sizes of plots, numbers of plots available to an individual, and reallocation policies. As indicated in table 24-2, these vary considerably among districts.

As a land shortage approaches, three options will be open to land boards for the temporary solution to the problem: restriction of the size and numbers of plots an individual has access to; identification of unused plots of land; and the reallocation of unused plots. All of these solutions are associated with the need for a basic land inventory of existing land allocation. The development of detailed maps of existing areas of arable population concentration is necessary before proceeding with an inventory program. Initially this program is anticipated to take the form of pilot projects utilizing aerial photographs transferred to maps of given areas. With such maps delineating fields, a simple land inventory can be carried out, identifying basic land uses as well as registering the names of people having plots.

Three districts in the country are now undertaking pilot inventory projects, concentrating on small areas in these districts. Given the existing landboard work load and administrative and technical capacities, any greater effort would probably result in an inadequately thought through and implemented project.

Two preparatory programs are being implemented to alleviate this problem. First, emphasis is being placed on enhancing the effectiveness of land boards through administrative training programs for land-board members and staff, as well as increasing the technical staff and technical capabilities of land-board members.

Major emphasis of the training programs will include increasing administrative capacities (such as filing systems and record keeping), as well as improving staff and members' technical skills associated with basic land allocations (for example, drawing sketch plans and simple linear measurements). These skills are needed not only for future inventory programs but also to bring up to date records associated with earlier allocations. Second, a major consideration of the small pilot project being implemented is the close monitoring of these projects. A series of detailed reports concerning each exercise will discuss all aspects of the project: planning, consultation, and implementation. The extent of detail of these reports will permit better planning and implementation of future projects.

With the creation of a land inventory, land boards will know not only who has land but the size and number of plots allocated to that individual.

Table 24-2
Arable Allocation Policy of Land Boards so Far Received

	Size of Plot	Number of Plots	Areas of Allocations	Fencing	Reallocations
Central	40 hectares by SLB Larger areas by LB only considered if are groups	1 plot per person	Communal	Individual OK, groups encouraged	TLA is the policy
Tati	20 acres	1 plot per person	Outside village	Encourage	
Tawana	No policy but feels should be one	No limit; people tend to have 2-3	No specific areas	No defined policy	TLA with preference to person reapplying
Mathete/Tlokweng	140 m × 140 m	1 per person		No objection	TLA is the policy
Rolong	250 acres in unit of 25 areas	No limit up to maximum area of 250 acres	Designated ploughing areas		
Kweneng	400 m × 480 m		Fossil beds and in south and east of district	No objection	Only if person surrenders the plot
Kgalagadi	275 paces × 275 paces	1 per person	Only in Matsheng where zoning	No policy	
Kgatleng	No limit; 400 m × 400 m	No policy	Some areas are reserved	Encouraged	As per TLA
Chobe	500 m × 250 m	Further allocation if present one utilized	No specific areas	Encouraged	As per TLA
Ghanzi	No policy	No policy	No policy	No policy	As per TLA

Note: TLA: Tribal Land Act; LB: Land boards.

Second, as plots are identified as having been allocated to individuals, unallocated land can also be identified and subsequently allocated. More significantly and because land boards are empowered to reallocate plots that have remained unused for five years or more, additional land may become available.

As land-board administrative and technical capacities are built up and experience is gained through these small pilot projects, larger projects will be designed and implemented. Efforts are currently underway to design a uniform recording and indexing system so that all district pilot projects can be incorporated into one comprehensive system. Additionally, this system must be designed for the possible eventuality of a sophisticated land-registration program at some time in the future.

Urban Development and Land Policy

It is important to appreciate the true nature of so-called urban areas in Botswana. They are those areas where settlements have been developed on state land. Although they have other characteristics that differentiate them from the village, the fundamental difference is of land tenure. All settlements developed on tribal land are known as villages, even though some of them may have larger populations than the towns and cover more land.

National Settlement Policy

A spatial analysis of achievements in national development revealed an unsatisfactory distribution of benefits, which was not entirely consistent with national goals and objectives. The imbalance in favor of urban areas was quite pronounced and most noticeable in favor of Gaborone, the capital. This appeared likely to be continued in the next National Development Plan 1979-85 (NDP V) when analysis of draft proposals revealed 52 percent of development expenditure would exclusively benefit residents of the five urban areas (containing 15 percent population) and 57 percent of capital expenditure would be made there. Fully one-third of all capital investment in the draft plan would be made in Gaborone alone. This urban bias reflects to some extent the comparative ease of investment and development on state land compared to tribal land.

In an effort to redress this bias, the NDP V now contains the outline of a national settlement policy, which is to be developed during the plan period and will provide a framework for investment. As a first step, three levels of settlement have been identified, with the primary level including the four main towns and the six main villages together. The secondary level includes two smaller towns and the remaining major village centers. By adopting a consistent development strategy at each level, it is intended to remove the urban-rural dichotomy.

Land Tenure

The difference in land tenure has been identified as a significant factor in the differing rate of development between towns and villages. The most notable aspect of this has been the reluctance of financial institutions to make credit facilities available. Although the tenure under the Tribal Land Act is secure enough to the individual, the right of the land board as trustees of the people to determine transfers of rights in the landownership of the structures on the land, means that in the event of default, the financial institution has no guarantee of obtaining the property in lieu of payment.

In the tribal land-tenure system, land has no marketable value because it remains the property of the tribe. Thus speculation in land is avoided, and even the poorest member of the tribe is not landless. This socially admirable situation is in danger of being lost in the towns because of the use of other forms of tenure, which are apparently necessary for urban development.

So far, the government view has prevailed; there is no overall profit to be made from urban development, so that land that has the benefit of planning permission for urban development, but no services, has no greater value than for agricultural use. It is only by investing in the provision of engineering services that the land acquires an additional value. However, the very existence of freehold, fixed-term grant, and leasehold titles means that dealing in land for money can take place and a market value for serviced and unserviced land can be generated. This is especially so where urban growth is rapid and demand exceeds supply.

Urban Land Policy

Current policies of the Botswana government in relation to development of urban land, including sources of finance, agencies for development, development standards, plot sizes, control of growth, maintenance, and land-tenure policies, are contained in a report, *Urban Development and Land Policy*, by the Ministry of Local Government and Lands (April 1978). Under this policy statement, there are forms of tenure in existence in the urban areas: freehold, fixed-term grant, leasehold, and certificate of rights. The last is not strictly a tenure but a guarantee of rights to construct a dwelling and reside in it. It is used in the site and service areas so that low-income families have security of tenure without the costs of formal title to land. It is closest to the tribal land system and capable of inheritance. However, although it is intended to be sufficient for mortgage or loan-guarantee purposes, financial institutions have some reluctance to use it as security, although their reticence may be due mainly to the low income of the occupier.

Freehold tenure exists in towns as a relic of the colonial past. It is now considered inappropriate to grant freehold title because this deprives the state of any future voice in the ownership of the land unless it is acquired compulsorily. As an alternative to this, in a situation where people had become used to the strength and security of freehold title, it was decided to issue fixed-term grants. These are normally for fifty or seventy years and commonly have been used for residential and industrial plots. The 1978 report states that fixed-period grant should not be converted to freehold and that all future allocations of land for residential use should be under fixed-price grant. This was in response to pressure for change because some grants, with the passage of time, had relatively short periods left. In the latter part of the fixed-grant period, investment in the property declines, negotiability is reduced, and the asset depreciates.

Leasehold tenure of state land has been used from anything as brief as two or three years up to thirty years, which is the highest so far. These are more common for commercial premises and seem to be generally not favored because of the freehold tradition. The availability of so many forms of tenure appears to increase the uncertainty and feeling of unreliability in anything less than freehold. The evidence from other countries appears to bear this out; that is, if there is only one form of tenure available, then that is accepted as sufficiently reliable and trustworthy. When various tenures become associated with different economic groups, then the financial institutions find it easier to blame the form of tenure rather than the economic circumstances of the applicant when they refuse a loan.

A Way Forward

The most significant requirement to ease tenure limitations on development in towns and villages in Botswana is to reeducate the financial institutions so that they will accept the adopted tenures as adequately secure. This will need complementary revisions (modest ones) of the tenure system and specific support to make adequate guarantees in the event of default. Illogical doubts on the part of financial institutions must be removed, but this needs to be coupled with the ability to get their money back in practice should the need arise.

In the urban areas the way forward would be to make more use of long leases so that the basic requirement for the state to retain ultimate control is kept, but sufficient security is given for financial investment. Renewal options in leases avoid the fixed-term grant problem.

In the major villages on tribal land, the requirement is to provide security, perhaps in the form of government financial backing, to the land board as the trustee for the land. The financial institutions' redress could then be to the land board.

Government, tribe, or state ownership of the land in the ultimate, ensures that land values are increased if at all for the community's benefit and that community investment does not unevenly favor some individuals simply because they happen to own some land.

Conclusion

Botswana is keenly aware of the significance of land tenure and its relationship to development. A number of programs have been and are being designed to ensure continued access of individuals to the productive activities on the land. The likelihood of success rests on the government's commitment to these programs and its continuing desire to involve district and local institutions in the evolution of land-tenure-related programs.

Appendixes

Appendixes

Appendix A: Program

Monday, June 23

Opening Remarks *Matthew Cullen*, chairman of conference; *Arlo Woolery*, moderator of the day; *Nathaniel Lichfield*

Land in Historical Perspective: How Different Civilizations and Cultures Have Regarded Land *Lewis Mumford*

Current Land Policy Issues in a Changing World *Enrique Peñalosa*

Panel of Commentators on Peñalosa, Making Special References to Urban Land Issues in Their Respective Regions
Africa (sub-Sahara) *Isaac Ofori*
Asia *William Lim*
Western Europe *Pierre Laconte*
Latin America *Guillermo Geisse*
Middle East and North Africa *Mona Serageldin*
North America (United States and Canada) *Charles Haar*

Land Policy as a Tool for Social and Economic Development *Robert C.T. Lee*

Major Differences between Developed and Developing Countries in Application of Land Policy Instruments *William Lim*

Urbanization and Counterurbanization: The Future of World Metropolitan Areas in the 1980s *Brian Berry*

Introduction to the Workshops

Each chairperson will describe the content of the workshops so that participants may select the workshop(s) that most interest(s) them.

Each workshop will focus upon a specific instrument of implementation and will address four basic issues:

1. How well can this instrument increase the supply of available land?
2. How well can it control excessive increases in land prices?
3. How effective is it in recovering to the public those portions of land values that may be said to be socially created—plus values?
4. How well can it increase accessibility to land as a means of production?

Wherever possible, specific, practical cases of the instrument in operation will be examined.

Description of workshops by the chairperson:

1. Achieving Effective Systems of Land Cadastres, Evaluation, and Title Registration
2. Public-Land Ownership
3. Public-Private Codevelopment
4. Property Taxation Measures
5. Women, Land Use, and Urbanization
6. Physical Planning Measures to Control the Land Market
7. Financial and Credit Interventions (Other than Taxation)
8. Institutional Factors: Problems of Land-Use Legislation, Adequacy of Jurisdictional Boundaries, Unrealistic Ceilings (Standards for Housing and Subdivision), and so on
9. Rural Workshop: Agricultural Land Policy; Legislation and Implementation Issues

Tuesday, June 24
Introduction to Day's Discussion: Urban Land Markets and Methodologies for Their Analysis *William Doebele,* moderator of the day

Land in Perspective: Its Role in the Structure of Cities *Gregory Ingram*

New Methodologies for Understanding Urban Land Markets *H. James Brown* and *Neal Roberts*

Urban Land-Market Studies in Latin America: Methodologies and Issues *Guillermo Geisse*

Urban Land Markets in the Yugoslavian System *Miodrag Janic*

Report on Urban Land-Market Research in Tokyo *Tokunosuke Hasegawa* and *Yuzuru Hanayama*

Report on Urban Land-Market Research in São Paulo, Brazil *Emilio Haddad*

Report on Urban Land-Market Research in Bogotá *Rakesh Mohan*

Transportation Investment and Urban Land Values: Emerging Empirical Evidence *Marcial Echenique*

Monitoring Land Prices in the United States *Jim Hoben*

Some Unexamined Aspects of Urban Land Markets: Proposals for Research *William Doebele*

Preliminary Meetings of Workshops

Workshop 1: Achieving Effective Systems of Land Cadastres, Evaluation, and Title Registration

Chairperson: *Ramon Casanova*, director, Bureau of Lands, Philippines

Case Studies: Tegucigalpa, Honduras, and Manila, Philippines: *John Marcilla*, Louis Berger International, Inc., New Jersey

United States and Canada: *Martin Miller*, appraiser and property tax consultant, Chicago

Stockholm: *Eric Carlegrim*, Royal Institute of Technology, Stockholm

Multipurpose cadastre concept: *John McLaughlin*, University of New Brunswick, Canada

Workshop 2: Public-Land Ownership

Chairperson: *Neal Roberts*, professor, Faculty of Law, York University, Toronto

Case Studies: Belgrade: *Miodrag Janic*, director, Institute of Urbanism and Housing

Philippines: *José Leido, Jr.*, minister of natural resources, Philippines

Stockholm: *Peter Heimbüger* managing director, Planning Department, National Board of Physical Planning and Building, Stockholm

United States: *Joan Towles*, Advisory Commission on Intergovernmental Relations, Washington, D.C.

France: *Emilio Tempia*, professor, Lille Institute of Technology, Lille, France

Workshop 3: Public-Private Codevelopment

Chairperson: *Pierre Laconte*, Louvain

Case Studies: France: *Jacques de Lanversin*, professor, University Aix-en-Provence

Germany: *Walter Seele*, professor, University of Bonn

London: *Geoffrey Smith*, International Centre for Land Policy Studies

Mexico: *Roque Gonzales*, director general, Servicios Metropolitanos, Mexico City

Workshop 4:	Property Taxation Measures
Chairperson:	*Oliver Oldman,* Learned Hand Professor of Law, Harvard University
Cochairperson:	*Daniel Holland*, professor, Sloan School of Management, Massachusetts Institute of Technology
Case Studies:	General property tax in Colombia, Korea, Philippines, United States: *Roy Bahl*, professor, Maxwell School, Syracuse University, New York
	Site-value taxation in Jamaica: *St. Clair Risden*, commissioner of valuation, Kingston, Jamaica
	Valorization in Colombia: *Johannes Linn*, the World Bank
	Deferred special assessment: *Donald Shoup*, professor, University of California, Los Angeles
	Death and inheritance taxes: *Willard Pedrick*, dean, School of Law, Arizona State University, Tempe (Paper to be presented by Arlo Woolery)
Workshop 5:	Women, Land Use, and Urbanization
Chairperson:	*Fran P. Hosken*, editor, *Women's International News*

Case Studies: *Lisa Bennett*, consultant, United Nations Center on Transnational Corporations

Mangalam Srinivasan, consultant to the U.N. Research Associate at New York University

Mary Racelis Hollnsteiner, senior adviser, Family/Child Welfare and Community Organization, UNICEF, New York

Barbara J. Flint, professor, Department of History and Political Science, Rensselaer Polytechnic Institute, Troy, New York

Tila Maria de Hancock, assistant to the secretary for international affairs, Office of International Affairs, Department of Housing and Urban Development, Washington, D.C.

Nellie Garcia Bellizzia, professor, National School of Architects, National University of Mexico

Workshop 6:   Physical Planning Measures to Control the Land Market

Chairperson: *Darshan Johal*, U.N. Centre for Human Settlements, Nairobi, Kenya

Case Studies: Brazil: *Emilio Haddad*, Technological Research Institute, São Paulo

Netherlands: *Jacques Kwak*, city planner, Amsterdam

East Germany: *Professor Dr. Helmut W. Jenkis*

India: *Sayed S. Shafi*, chief planner, New Delhi, India

Belgrade: *Ljiljana Zlatić,* architect

India: *Nirmal Brito Mutunayagam*, Virginia Polytechnic and State University

Workshop 7:	Financial and Credit Interventions (Other than Taxation)
Chairperson:	*Harold Dunkerley*, The World Bank
Case Studies:	Korea: *Songman Lee*, director, Appraisal Division, Korea Land Development Corporation

Egypt: *Philippe Annez*, Urban Studies and Planning Department, Massachusetts Institute of Technology

Mexico, New City of Cuautitlan Izcalli: *Roque Gonzales*, director general, Servicios Metropolitanos, Mexico City

Korea: *William Doebele*, Harvard University

Cuba: *Adrian Walter*, Urban Planning Department, MIT

Workshop 8:	Institutional Factors: Problems of Land-Use Legislation, Adequacy of Jurisdictional Boundaries, Unrealistic Ceilings (Standards for Housing and Subdivision), and so on

Chairperson:	*Ann Louise Strong*, chairman, City Planning Department, University of Pennsylvania, Philadelphia
Case Studies:	Australia, Hawaii, Soviet Union: *Daniel Mandelker*, professor, Washington University Law School, St. Louis, Missouri
	Pakistan: *Milton Kaplan*, professor, School of Law, State University of New York at Buffalo
	Indonesia: *Brian Berry*, professor, Graduate School of Design, Harvard University
	Asia: *Dr. Shlomo Angel*, chairman, Division of Human Settlements, Asian Institute of Technology, Thailand
	Venezuela: *Graciella Flores*
	France: *Max Falque*, Aix-en-Provence
Workshop 9:	Rural Workshop: Agricultural Land Policy; Legislation and Implementation Issues
Chairperson:	*John D. Montgomery*, professor, Kennedy School of Government, Harvard University
Case Studies:	Taiwan: *Dr. Robert C.T. Lee*, chairman, Council for Agricultural Planning and Development, Taiwan, Republic of China
	Thailand and Philippines: *Sein Lin*, director, International Programs, Lincoln Institute

India: *S. Ramakrishnan*, joint secretary, Government of India, Kennedy School of Government, Harvard University

Africa (Ghana): *Isaac Ofori*

Bangladesh: *Wasim Zaman*

Latin America: *Antonio Gayoso*, U.S. AID

Wednesday, June 25	**Introduction to Day's Discussion and Activities** *Charles Haar*, moderator of the day

Cities Fit to Live In   *Alfred Wood*

Questions and Comments from the Floor

New York City as a Case Study in the Problems and Opportunities of Improving Urban Environments   *William H. Whyte*

Questions and Comments from the Floor

Guided Tour of Quincy Market and Waterfront Area: A Study in Successful Urban Renewal *Marc L. Older*

Boat Tour of Boston Harbor with Commentary on Land Policy Decisions Affecting Harborside Cities *Marc L. Older*

Thursday, June 26   **Opening Remarks**   *Harold Dunkerley*, moderator of the day

Workshops

Friday, June 27   **Introduction and Opening Remarks**   *C. Lowell Harriss*, moderator of the day

Reports of Rapporteurs of Each Workshop and General Summation   *Matthew Cullen*

Appendix B:
List of Participants

Australia
John de Monchaux

Belgium
Bernard Delaval
Pierre Laconte
Claude Van de Maele

Bermuda
Erwin Percy Adderley
Dr. the Hon. John Stubbs

Botswana
Miss B. Mathuba
Bahiti Ketaraka Temane

Brazil
Emilio Haddad

Canada
Daniel Arbour
Prof. Ronald W.G. Bryant
John Carson
Marius Diament
Maurice Egan
Octavio Gonzales
Prof. Ann G. Haggart
Jonathan Kauffman
Dr. John McLaughlin
Donald L. Newman
Peter Oberlander
Murray Pound
Prof. Mohammad A. Qadeer
Gerard Raymond
Prof. Neal Roberts
Garfield Wright

Chile
Guillermo Geisse
Francisco Sabatini

Colombia
Guillermo Anzola Lizarazu
Dr. Antonio Losada
Enrique Peñalosa
Julian Velasco
Rodrigo Villamizar

Dominican Republic
Carlos Aguilo Estrada
Roberto Luis Berges
Cristobal Valdez Gomez

Egypt
Dipl. Ing. Nagwa Rabie

El Salvador
Carlos Benjamin Luna
Arq. Ramon Melhado Guillen
Orlando Nolasco
Mario Ronald Soundy

England
Marcial Echenique
Fred Harrison
David Hughes-Evans
Nathaniel Lichfield
B.J. Pearce
Geoffrey Smith
Alfred Wood

Fiji
Mr. Josevata N. Kamikamica

France
Mr. Bousquet
Max Falque
Francois Garraud
Jean Jacques Granelle
Georges Harter

France *(cont.)*
  Jacques de Lanversin
  Arne Renberg
  Vincent Renard
  Prof. Emilio Tempia
  Mr. Trapitzine

West Germany
  Prof. Dr. Helmut W. Jenkis
  Rainer Müller
  Prof. Dr.-Ing. Walter Seele

Ghana
  Isaac Ofori

Greece
  Yannis Pyriotis

Guatemala
  Carlos Escobar A.

Guyana
  Charles Roland King

Honduras
  Edgardo R. Derbes

India
  Sayed Shafi

Indonesia
  Boedi Harsono
  Radinal Moochtar
  Ali Muhamad
  Prapto Prajitno
  Yusuf Sofyan
  Sutardja Sudradjat
  Endang Teruna Sukardi
  Tedjo Suminto
  Oskar Surgaatnadja
  Soelistijo Tjitrohamidjojo
  Sulisto Widodo

Ireland
  Luke Boyle
  Joseph Connolly
  K. Crotty
  M. Cullen
  Joseph Cummins
  R. Dowling
  Donald Dunne
  John Farrelly
  Tom Feighery
  R.M. Fenlon
  J. Fennelly
  James Flanagan
  Brian Fleming
  Michael McDonagh Fleming
  Chris Flood
  Michael Guckian
  Thomas Noel Hand
  James Harty
  Seamus Hayes
  Sean Healy
  Michael Henebry
  J. Hickey
  P. Hyland
  Richard Jones
  Thomas Keenan
  C.A. Kelly
  James Kelly
  John Loughlin
  Sean M. MacBride
  William McDonnell
  Farrell McElgunn
  Richard McGrath
  M. McGuinness
  Frank McLoughlin
  Sean McNelis
  W. McWey
  Ciaran Murphy
  Sean Nyhan
  Sean O'Donnell
  John O'Neill
  S. Pattison
  Eamonn Rafter

Ireland *(cont.)*
Tom P. Rice
Stephen Rogers
Sib Rooney
Myles Tierny

Israel
Jacob Aknin
Sapir Avishai
Harold Baker
Shlomo Belkind
Dan Darin
Moshe Gat
Meira S. Gluskinos
Mr. Hashimshony
Zion Urieli

Italy
Francesco Bandarin

Japan
Prof. Yuzuru Hanayama
Tokunosuke Hasegawa

Kenya
Raphael Mwangi Muigai
Reuben G.M. Mutiso

Korea
Mr. Chong-Jik Ahn
Mr. Gil-Soung Hong
Mr. Eui-Won Kim
Mr. Sang-ku Lee
Mr. Songman Lee
Gun Young Lee
Gen. Kun-chang Ryu
Dr. Yong Ju Whang
Jei Wha Woo

Kuwait
Ali A. Al-Fouzan

Liberia
Hilary A. Dennis
John Payne Hammond
Amos J. Smith

Malawi
Austin T.B. Mbalanje

Mexico
Rafael Arias
Nellie Garcia Bellizzia
Carlos Camacho Gaos
Lic. Joaquin Contreras Cantu
Francisco Covarrubias Gaytan
Charles Du Tilly
Arq. Jorge Octavio Falcon Vega
Arq. Judith Garza Fassio
Roque Gonzales
Pedro González
Daniel A. Hiernaux N.
Carlos Morales Schechinger
Juan Felipe Ordonez
Javier Septien
Carlos Tejeda

Netherlands
Paul Baross
B. De Graaf
L.A. De Klerk
J.L.G. Henssen
P. Hofstee
A. Jense
Jacques Kwak
M.J. Rodell
Jan Willem Vader

New Hebrides
Peter Larmour

Nigeria
Olalekan Adeola Dosunmu
Dr. Ajato Gandonu
Kasimu Idris
Clarence Rosyi Abayomi Mann

Norway
Erik Knudser

Panama
Arq. Humberto Augusto
Appleton
James M. Chavers

Philippines
Alfred Xerez Burgos
Ramon Casanova
Orlando M. Danao
Manuel Lagunilla
José Leido
Salvador Pejo
Alma D. Recio
Christine Reyes
Lino Sanchez
Manuel Serapio

Republic of China
James C.C. Chan
Tsu-chuen Chang
Wei-I Chang
David C. Chen
Bai-ping Fu
Ta-chou Huang
Dr. Robert C.T. Lee
Dr. Yu-kang Mao
Yu-liang Yeh

Singapore
William Lim

South Africa
Philip R. Nel
Andrea Walt
Ethel Walt

Spain
José Carlos Trullops Gil-Delgado
Salvador Martinez-Moya Ros
Amaro Tagarro Tagarro

Swaziland
H.S. Dlamini
M. Dlamini
A.H. Flatt
P.H. Mtetwa
Don B. Nkambule
N. Nkambule

Sweden
Prof. Eric Carlegrim
Göte Güstavsson
Peter Heimbürger
Arne Källsbo
Nils Yngvesson

Switzerland
Ben F. Reiner

Thailand
Dr. Shlomo Angel
Prajiad Buasri
Mrs. Apornpun Chansawang
Nid H. Shiranen
Boonterb Tantrakul

United States
Prof. Charles E. Aguar
Timothy Alexander
Victor Allan
Philippe Annez
Prof. Roy Bahl
Edward D. Baker
Carol Banks
MacDonald Barr
John O. Behrens
Ms. Lisa Bennett
Michael M. Bernard
Prof. Brian Berry
Donald W. Bradley
Roger Winston Bray
Prof. H. James Brown
Kingsbury Browne
Thomas A. Brunton

United States *(cont.)*
Jay Chatterjee
David C. Clark
Dr. Gerald L. Cole
Charles C. Cook
M.A. Corzo
John M. Courtney
Matthew Cullen
Jonathan R. Cunningham
S.S. Cutler
John DeGrove
Prof. William Doebele
Maurice Dorton
John M. Dugan
Harold Dunkerley
Patricia J. Dusenbury
Earl Epstein
Rosemary Farley
James A. Fawcett
Prof. Herman Felstehausen
Ms. Mary Fiksel
Philip Finkelstein
Prof. Malcolm FitzPatrick
Prof. Barbara J. Flint
Ms. Graciella Flores
Paul W. Fox
Hays B. Gamble
Wilson Garces
Harry Garnett
Antonio Gayoso
Prof. Charles C. Geisler
Marsha Goldberg
Michael Goldberg
Charles J. Gonzales
David Gouveneur
Oscar Graver
Diana Guthrie
Prof. Charles Haar
Dr. Courtney A. Haff
Jerry Hagstrom
Natalie D. Hahn
Ms. Tila Maria de Hancock
Covington Hardee

Dr. C. Lowell Harriss
Edgar Hayes
James Hoben
Prof. Daniel Holland
Ms. Mary Racelis Hollnsteiner
Annelies Fulscher-Homuth
Ms. Fran Hosken
Jonathan B. Howes
Bryan Hutchinson
Bruce Hyland
Gregory Ingram
Harvey M. Jacobs
Fernando Jimenez
Darshan Johal
Prof. Milton Kaplan
Peter M. Kimm
Dr. Eugene C. Kirchherr
Will Knedlik
Elisabeth Ladd
George Lefcoe
Aaron Levine
Sein Lin
Johannes Linn
Mathew MacIver
Prof. Daniel Mandelker
Uriel Manheim
John Marcilla
Frederic S. Marquardt
Clyde McQueen
Martin D. Miller
Rakesh Mohan
Prof. John D. Montgomery
Vincent J. Moore
John E. Mulford, Jr.
N. Brito Mutunayagam
Mary O'Brien
Marc L. Older
Prof. Oliver Oldman
Kermit C. Parsons
Prof. Thomas G. Pelham
Richard F. Perkins
Viviann G. Petersson
Steven D. Plofker

United States *(cont.)*
S. Ramakrishnan
H. Clyde Reeves
George Reigeluth
Alan Richman
W. Victor Rouse
Sally Rue
Frank Schnidman
Prof. Milton R. Schroeder
Warkentin Schroeter
Ms. Mona Serageldin
John Sevy
Ms. Sharon Shea
Mitsuo Shimizu
Prof. Donald Shoup
James R. Sitzman
Ms. Mangalam Srinivasan
Joel Stern
Ms. Ann Louise Strong
Edward J. Sullivan
Paul T. Tajima
Ms. Kit Teo
Ms. Joan E. Towles
William A. Utic
Ms. Mary Jo Waits
Maxine T. Wallace
Ms. Adrian Walter
Herb Werlin

William H. Whyte
William T. Wildman
Jack Williams
Margaret D. Woodring
A.M. Woodruff
Arlo Woolery
Sharon Woolery
Chang-Ho Yim
Ms. Joan Youngman
Wasim Zaman

Venezuela
Luis Gonzalez Cardenas
Graciella Flores
Arq. Victor M. Fosssi
Oscar Gomez-Navas

West Indies
Fr. Gerard Leo McLaughlin
Lascelles Patterson
St. Clair Risden
Miss Margaret Rodgers
Calford Scott

Yugoslavia
Miodrag Janic
M. Ljiljana Zlatić

About the Contributors

Brian J.L. Berry is an international consultant on urban and regional planning. He was Williams Professor of City and Regional Planning at Harvard University and is dean of the School of Urban and Public Affairs at Carnegie-Mellon University, Pittsburgh.

H. James Brown is a professor of city and regional planning in the Graduate School of Design at Harvard University.

Ramon Casanova is director of the Bureau of Lands in the Philippines.

William Doebele is a member of the Faculty Advisory Committee of the Lincoln Institute of Land Policy, and a professor of advanced environmental studies and the curator of the Loeb fellowship program at the Graduate School of Design at Harvard University. He is also a member of the Harvard Institute for International Affairs. He holds degrees from Princeton University, the Harvard Law School, and the University of California at Berkeley.

Harold Dunkerley is senior advisor for the Urban Projects Department of the World Bank in Washington, D.C.

Marcial Echenique is a professor and a reader at Cambridge University, England.

Herman Felstehausen is a professor of natural resources at the Land Tenure Center of the University of Wisconsin.

Adrian Flatt is a land-valuation officer in the Ministry of Agriculture and Co-Ops in Mbabane, Swaziland.

Guillermo Geisse is a professor at the Catholic University in Santiago and the coordinator of the Latin American Urban Land Research Project in Santiago.

Marsha Goldberg, a specialist on the impact of U.S. energy policies on land use, is with the U.S. Department of Energy.

David Gouveneur of Caracas attends the Graduate School of Design at Harvard University.

441

Charles Haar is Brandeis Professor of Law at the Harvard Law School, chairman of the Lincoln Institute Land Policy Roundtable, and a member of the Lincoln Institute Faculty Advisory Committee. He was assistant secretary of the Department of Housing and Urban Development, and chairman of the Joint Center for Urban Studies at Massachusetts Institute of Technology and Harvard University.

Emilio Haddad is advisor for urban and regional development affairs at the Technological Research Institute in São Paulo.

Yuzuru Hanayama is a professor at the Tokyo Institute of Technology.

C. Lowell Harriss is executive director of the Academy of Political Science. A long-time associate of the Lincoln Institute, he is also a member of its regular faculty. He has been a professor of economics at Columbia University.

Tokunosuke Hasegawa is with the Japan Housing Corporation in Tokyo.

James E. Hoben is program manager of Land Use Research, U.S. Department of Housing and Urban Development in Washington, D.C.

Fran Hosken is the editor of *Women's International News*. She is also a practicing architect-planner and has worked extensively on urbanization, including consulting for the World Bank on sites and service projects.

Gregory K. Ingram is a senior economist in the Urban and Regional Economics Division of the Development Economics Department of the World Bank, and is a lecturer in the Department of City and Regional Planning at Harvard University.

Miodrag Janic is the director of the Yugoslav Institute for Urbanism and Housing in Belgrade, and is a professor of urban economics at Belgrade University.

Darshan Johal is chief of program policy and planning for the U.N. Centre for Human Settlements (HABITAT) in Nairobi.

Pierre Laconte is director of expansion for the Catholic University at Louvain-la-Neuve, president of the World Environment and Resources Council, and director of education and training at the International Centre for Land Policy Studies.

Robert C.T. Lee received the Ph.D. in agriculture from Cornell University. He has been the chairman of the Council of Agricultural Planning and Development and is also chairman of the board of directors of the Land Reform Training Institute in Taoyuan, Taiwan. He is currently the president of the National Chung Hsing University.

Nathaniel Lichfield is director of research at the International Centre for Land Policy Studies, professor emeritus of the economics of environmental planning at the University of London, and a partner in Nathaniel Lichfield and Partners, planning, development, and economic consultants.

William S.W. Lim is an architect and urban planner who was with DP Architects Pte. and DP Consultant Service Pte. Ltd. in Singapore. He is currently engaged in research and publication on land for housing for low-income families.

Rakesh Mohan is a member of the Development Policy Staff of the Department of Development Economics at the World Bank, Washington, D.C., as well as a member of the World Bank City Study Project on Bogotá and Cali.

John Montgomery is a professor of public policy and the chairman of the Government Department at the Kennedy School of Government of Harvard University.

Lewis Mumford, author and social critic, is a member of both the American Philosophical Society and the National Institute of Arts and Letters, as well as a Fellow of the American Academy of Arts and Sciences. His latest book is *My Works and Days, A Personal Chronicle.*

Peter Oberlander is a professor of regional planning at the University of British Columbia and director of the Centre for Human Settlements, created as a result of the Habitat Conference in Vancouver in 1976. On leave as deputy minister of urban affairs from the Dominion of Canada, he was active in the planning and organization of the Habitat Conference.

Isaac Ofori was managing director of the Volta Regional Development Commission. He is currently the secretary to the Environmental Protection Council of Ghana and a member of the International Centre for Land Policy Studies Executive Committee.

Oliver Oldman is Learned Hand Professor of Law and director of the International Tax Program at the Harvard Law School.

Dr. Enrique Peñalosa is an architect with offices in Bogotá. He was secretary general for Habitat '76 in Vancouver and is the president of the International Centre for Land Policy Studies.

Robyn Swaim Phillips, coauthor with Professors Brown and Roberts, is a research fellow at the Graduate School of Design at Harvard University.

Alan R. Prest is a professor of economics at the London School of Economics and Political Science. He is a graduate of Christ's College, Cambridge, England.

Arcot Ramachandran is under secretary general of the United Nations and executive director of the U.N. Centre for Human Settlements (HABITAT) in Nairobi.

Neal A. Roberts was a professor of law at Osgoode Hall Law School, York University, Toronto. He is now a practicing attorney with Wyman, Bautzer, Rothman, Kuchel & Silbert in Los Angeles.

Francisco Sabatini, coauthor with Mr. Geisse, is a junior professor of the Catholic University in Santiago.

Mona Serageldin is a specialist in Middle East housing and planning and a senior associate with Nash-Vigier, Inc., planning consultants in Cambridge, Massachusetts.

Ann Louise Strong is chairman of the City Planning Department at the University of Pennsylvania.

B.K. Temane is permanent secretary for the Ministry of Local Government and Lands in Gaborone, Botswana.

Rodrigo Villamizar, coauthor with Mr. Moran, is a researcher for the Corporacion Centro Regional de Poblacion, Bogotá.

William H. Whyte is director of the Street Life Project in New York City. He is the author of several books including *The Organization Man.* Vice-chairman of the board of trustees of The Conservation Foundation, he has also served on the Hudson River Commission, the New York State Environmental Board, and the President's Task Force on Natural Beauty.

Alfred A. Wood, architect and town planner, is county planner to the West Midlands Metropolitan County Council, Birmingham, England. He is also a visiting professor at the Centre for the Conservation of Historic Towns and Buildings at the College of Europe in Bruges.

Arlo Woolery is executive director of the Lincoln Institute of Land Policy. He has held this post since 1975, when the Lincoln Institute of Land Policy was created by action of the directors of the Lincoln Foundation. Prior to joining the Lincoln Institute, he was director of the Arizona State Department of Property Valuation.

Joan Youngman is research associate for the International Tax Program at the Harvard Law School.

About the Editors

Matthew Cullen, an independent consultant in planning and management, assisted the Lincoln Foundation in establishing the Lincoln Institute of Land Policy. He continues to serve the institute as director of regional programs. A graduate of Harvard University and the George Washington University Law School, he was program associate at The Ford Foundation and vice-chancellor of the State University of New York. He is executive director of the International Centre for Land Policy Studies.

Sharon Woolery is the editorial assistant and conference reporter for the Lincoln Institute of Land Policy, and assistant to the executive director of the International Centre for Land Policy Studies.